Inspiring Leaders

Edited by

Ronald J. Burke and
Cary L. Cooper

Routledge
Taylor & Francis Group

LONDON AND NEW YORK

First published 2006
by Routledge
2 Park Square, Milton Park, Abingdon, Oxon OX14 4RN

Simultaneously published in the USA and Canada
by Routledge
270 Madison Ave, New York, NY 10016

Routledge is an imprint of the Taylor & Francis Group, an informa business

Typeset in Perpetua and Bell Gothic by
Florence Production Ltd, Stoodleigh, Devon
Printed and bound in Great Britain by
MPG Books Ltd, Bodmin, Cornwall

British Library Cataloguing in Publication Data
A catalogue record for this book is available from the British Library

Library of Congress Cataloging in Publication Data
Inspiring leaders / edited by Ronald J. Burke and Cary L. Cooper.
    p. cm.
Includes bibliographical references and index.
1. Leadership.   2. Management.   I. Burke, Ronald J.
II. Cooper, Cary L.
HD57.7I575 2006
658.4′092—dc22   2005030132

ISBN10: 0–415–36302–0 (hbk)
ISBN10: 0–415–36303–9 (pbk)
ISBN10: 0–203–01319–0 (ebk)

ISBN13: 978–0–415–36302–0 (hbk)
ISBN13: 978–0–415–36303–7 (pbk)
ISBN13: 978–0–203–01319–9 (ebk)

Inspiring Leaders

Thousands of articles and books have been written on leadership and billions of dollars are spent annually on developing leaders. Yet despite these efforts most organizations report a shortage of leaders – a leadership gap.

Inspiring Leaders realistically addresses the leadership gap issue. The text is divided into five distinct parts:

- Part I reviews emerging models of leadership including full-range, authentic and transformational concepts.
- Part II highlights leadership qualities such as competencies, emotional intelligence, values and ethical principles, and character.
- Part III explores the role of leadership in building effective work teams and creating peak performing workplace cultures.
- Part IV considers flaws that commonly contribute to leadership failure and derailment, personality characteristics, perfectionism and workaholism among them.
- Part V focuses on developing leaders and leadership, emphasizing a balance of skills, the critical role of feedback in learning and development, and innovative thoughts on developing women leaders.

This international collection provides readers with an innovative approach to understanding and learning the skills required to be a leader. It will be invaluable reading to all those engaged with studying leadership or undertaking the difficult task of leading within organizations.

Ronald J. Burke is Professor of Organizational Behavior at the Schulich School of Business, York University in Toronto, Canada. He serves as a consultant on organizational effectiveness issues to both private and public sector organizations.

Cary L. Cooper, CBE, is Pro Vice Chancellor (External Relations) of Lancaster University and Professor of Organizational Psychology and Health at the Lancaster Management School, in the UK. He is the author of over 100 books on occupational stress, women at work, and the link between human resource management practices and organizational performance.

Contents

CONTENTS

Figures

Tables

Contributors

Richard E. Boyatzis, Weatherhead School of Management, Case Western Reserve University, USA

Ronald J. Burke, Schulich School of Business, York University, Canada

Cary Cherniss, Rutgers University, USA

James G. Clawson, Darden School of Business Administration, University of Virginia, USA

Cary L. Cooper, CBE, Lancaster School of Management, Lancaster University, UK

Margaret Cording, Jesse H. Jones Graduate School of Management, Rice University, USA

Gordon L. Flett, Department of Psychology, York University, Canada

R. Edward Freeman, Darden School of Business Administration, University of Virginia, USA

Joanne H. Gavin, College of Business Administration, University of Texas at Arlington, USA

Terry R. Halfhill, Division of Business and Economics, Pennsylvania State University-Fayette, USA

Paul L. Hewitt, Department of Psychology, University of British Columbia, Canada

Larry Hughes, Department of Management, Gallup Leadership Institute, University of Nebraska-Lincoln, USA

Robert Kaplan, Kaplan DeVries, Greensboro North Carolina, USA

Fred Luthans, Department of Management Gallup Leadership Institute, University of Nebraska-Lincoln, USA

Kirsten Martin, Darden School of Business Administration, University of Virginia, USA

Tjai M. Nielsen, School of Business, George Washington University, USA

Ioannis Nikolaou, Athens University of Economics and Business, Athens, Greece

Steve Norman, Department of Management Gallup Leadership Institute, University of Nebraska-Lincoln, USA

Bidhan Parmar, Darden School of Business Administration, University of Virginia, USA.

Jonathan D. Quick, Management Sciences of Health, Washington, DC, USA

James Campbell Quick, Goolsby Leadership Academy, University of Texas at Arlington, USA

Robert E. Quinn, Ross School of Business, University of Michigan, USA

Ivan T. Robertson, Robertson Cooper Ltd, Manchester, UK

Marian N. Ruderman, Center for Creative Leadership, Greensboro, North Carolina, USA

Marc J. Schabracq, Department of Work and Organizational Psychology, University of Amsterdam, The Netherlands.

John J. Sosik, Department of Management, Great Valley School of Graduate Professional Studies, Pennsylvania State University, USA

Gretchen M. Spreitzer, Ross School of Business, University of Michigan, USA

Maria Vakola, Athens University of Economics and Business, Athens, Greece

Patricia H. Werhane, Darden School of Business Administration, University of Virginia, USA

Foreword

The phenomenon of leadership parallels the development of civilization. Early Egyptian hieroglyphics for leadership (*seshemet*), leader (*seshemu*), and follower (*shemu*) from over 5,000 years ago testify to the durability of these concepts. The desire to understand what leadership is and what actions of distinction or uniqueness that leaders make has been a part of applied Social Science since its inception. Some have attempted to measure leaders' actions and their impact on individuals who followed them and on the groups and larger collectivities they led.

Biographers and other observers write of their insights about the nature of leaders and what they do to contribute to some definition of success. Some who have occupied influential positions within a hierarchy write their own recollections of the events of their tenure and deduce principles from these 'self-studies-of-one'. Still others look for insights by the study of unsuccessful institutions, businesses, and governmental organizations, or of social movements that fail. All search for behaviour that distinguishes successful from unsuccessful leadership. For it is clear that all who are in positions of influence ought not be emulated.

Leaders' behaviours have been correlated with individual differences, as well as group and organizational phenomena, in search of insights into how leader behaviour may be related to varying outcomes, however assessed. From this confluence of facts, hunches, and insights come our ideas about what effective leaders do and what effective leadership is. Yet three major areas seem to beg for further study. These are the role of culture, the impact of change on the role of the leader, and the necessity for maintaining and renewing relationships. These three are of enormous importance in understanding long-term effective leadership.

Culture. The nature of the milieu that surrounds the actions of leaders will determine the criteria used in assessing a person's leader behaviour. The demand characteristics for successful leadership are a function of the nature of those being led and the nature of the situation (e.g. governmental, highly competitive business, not-for-profit, military). That is not to suggest that there are no elements in common among those called successful leaders in each situation. It is to say that attention to the unique characteristics within each situation that surrounds individual actions will be highly important in an accurate portrayal of what makes a person successful as leader.

This is easily seen when there are obvious differences. In business one can think of the difference in demands between a start-up situation such as a biotech company and an ongoing business such as a large multinational like General Electric that must continually adapt to changing environmental conditions. Similarly, in politics, one can think of what will be required of a leader like the British Prime Minister as compared to the leader of an emerging nation like South Africa.

But cultural impact is less obvious when the nuances are found to be related to the individual differences of those being led. Leadership, as a dyadic concept, is highly related to the willingness of those led to follow. The unspoken but generally accepted expectations found in each situation are highly important in understanding how one leads others successfully. While we recognize the importance of cultural differences, there do not seem to be useful guidelines on how a leader should accommodate to culture and change it to remain successful.

Impact of change on the desire to have what others have. It is a truism that humans learn by imitating others. We learn what we want by seeing what others want. Those in leadership positions model the ideal and those who follow tend to emulate them. The culture determines what is desirable, what others wish for, and what outcomes are considered of importance. The successful leader helps those who follow to progress to some goal. Often this means a change in follower behaviour. This can be accomplished with the greatest success by working within the existing cultural values.

In this day and time, the *speed of change* occurring almost everywhere makes decisions about changing even more perilous, especially for groups and organizations. By their design, groups and organizations make the behaviour of their members predictable to one another through norms of behaviour. Any disruption of routines and expectations for what others are to do makes changing very difficult. Those who lead have to model stability to those experiencing change. When the established behaviour patterns of a situation are disrupted, it is difficult to anticipate just what the future will bring. The only reasonable guides for this behaviour are found in the values of the culture. All of these things are recognized about change but our models for how a leader is to successfully navigate these problems needs a great deal of work.

Maintaining and renewing relationships. Most of the literature on leadership emphasizes the trust component that must exist between the leader and those led. Trust is earned and can be lost. In the process of changing, it is possible for followers to question how much trust to place in the leader. Even the questioning of the relationship tends to strain the degree of trust one gives to another in that relationship. If the relationship breaks, it is difficult to re-establish trust. Usually one or all in the relationship feel the others have failed in some way to deliver what was expected. The feelings of betrayal, of anger, of shock, and all of the other negative reactions that accompany broken trust require some attention or the relationship will remain broken. Even when there is only the perception of a broken trust, this still requires a process of renewal to begin to rebuild trust again. Leaders who find themselves no longer trusted are usually required to relinquish their positions of leadership.

In politics, in democratic societies, a leader will likely lose a bid to retain his or her position. In business, the leader is often removed. Occasionally, there is an attempt to rehabilitate a person who at one time has lost the trust of his or her constituency. Yet we really have no models for how to re-establish relationships. The maxim is, 'It is easier to give birth to a new relationship, than it is to raise one from the dead.'

After decades of research and thousands of studies, a generally accepted, comprehensive theory of leadership eludes researchers and students of the leadership phenomenon. This lack of a comprehensive theory testifies to the complexity of the issues involved in the study of leader behaviour. But the pervasiveness of the recognition of the importance of having a greater understanding of leader–follower behaviour in all of dyadic and group experiences has led to continued study of what effective leaders do, and think, and feel and believe. Those unwilling to await a comprehensive theory still continue to develop measures of generally accepted leader behaviour and compile anecdotes to help guide the practice of leadership. It is in this vein that the collection, *Inspiring Leaders*, addresses the many facets of the characteristics often attributed to successful leaders.

William F. Weitzel
Emeritus Professor of Management
College of Business Administration
University of Oklahoma,
Independent Consultant and co-author of
Leadership: Magic, myth or method (1992)
New York: AMACOM

Acknowledgements

Although I have been teaching organizational behaviour for almost 40 years, I have only recently appreciated how very important leadership is in the functioning of organizations and society as a whole. I have seen too many leaders that have fallen short. And although there is a voluminous literature on leaders and leadership, there is a glaring shortage of capable leaders and the most commonly used methods for developing leaders have had a relatively limited impact on closing this gap. I hope this collection sheds new light on what makes leaders successful, why they fail, and the steps we need to take to foster leadership at all levels. Leaders matter.

I would also like to acknowledge my appreciation for the work of my colleagues who continue to add to our understanding of behaviour in organizations through their research even though they may receive little support from their universities. It is certainly easier to carry out research and write about it when your institution provides high levels of financial, secretarial, research assistant, and reduced teaching load support. Yet many colleagues continue to advance our understanding without these resources. I applaud their efforts.

I thank our international contributors for sharing their latest thinking with us. Preparation of this collection was supported in part by the Schulich School of Business at York University.

Finally, to my partner, Susan, whose love motivates and sustains me as I struggle with the right balance in life.

Ronald J. Burke

I would like to dedicate this book to one of my ex-students, Sir Terry Leahy of Tesco PLC, who has made me proud of his achievements and inspirational leadership style.

Cary L. Cooper, CBE

Abbreviations

ALD	authentic leadership development
ASA	attraction–selection–attrition
ASSET	a shortened stress evaluation tool
BEI	Behavioural Event Interview
BHAG	big, hairy, audacious goal
CCL	Center for Creative Leadership
CEO	chief executive officer
CFO	chief finance officer
CFI	Colorado Fuel and Iron
CLS	Center for Leadership Studies
CR	contingent reward
DCP	Development Challenge Profile
EA	Enthusiastic Addicts
ECI	Emotional Competence Inventory
EDS	Electronic Data Systems Corporation
EI	emotional intelligence
EIQ	emotional intelligence questionnaire
EQ-i	emotional questionnaire-intelligence
FDIC	Federal Deposit Insurance Corporation
FRL	full range leadership
FSL	Fundamental State of Leadership
GMAT	Graduate Management Aptitude Test
GLI	Gallup Leadership Institute
HP	Hewlett Packard
HR	human resources
HRM	human resource management
IC	individualized consideration
II-A	attributions of idealized influence

II-B	idealized influence
IM	inspirational motivation
IS	intellectual stimulation
LF	laissez-faire
KSA	knowledge, skills, and abilities
MBA	Master of Business Administration
MBE-A	management by exception – active
MBE-P	management by exception – passive
MLQ	Multifactor Leadership Questionnaire
MMPI	Minnesota multi-phasic personality inventory
MPS	Multidimensional Perfectionism Scale
MSCEIT	Mayer–Salovey–Caruso Emotional Intelligence Test
OB	organizational behaviour
OCB	organizational citizenship behaviour
ODQ	Organizational Description Questionnaire
POB	positive organizational behaviour
PSPS	Perfectionistic Self-Presentation Scale
RW	Relaxed Workers
SAT	Scholastic Aptitude Test
SIT	store inventory team
TAB	Texas American Bancshares
TCB	team citizenship behaviour
TCB	Texas Capital Bank
UW	Unengaged Workers
VABE	values, assumptions, beliefs, and expectations
WABA	Within and Between Analysis
WART	Work Addiction Risk Test
WE	Work Enthusiast

Chapter 1

Inspiring leaders

An introduction*

Ronald J. Burke

The practice of leadership has existed for thousands of years and research efforts have been undertaken to better understand leadership in organizations for well over 50 years (Bass, 1990). Leaders and leadership matter. Effective leaders are associated with successful work teams, high morale, and peak levels of performance; ineffective leaders are associated with dissatisfaction, low commitment, and failing performance (Avolio and Bass, 2002; Bass, 1998, 1999; Collins, 2001a, 2001b; Day, Zaccaro and Halpin, 2004).

There have been thousands of published articles and books dealing with leadership in organizations over the past 40 years. Winum (2003) reports that a recent literature search on google.com using the key word leadership yielded 9,450,000 references; leadership development produced 2,876,000 references. Amazon.com lists 12,538 books on the topic of leadership. ABInform and PsychLit list over 5,200 published articles on leadership since 1968. Yet, Bennis and Nanus (1997) write that 'leadership is the most studied and least understood concept of any in the social sciences' (p. 4) and that 'never have so many labored so long to say so little' (p. 20).

Fulmer (1997) notes that management training and education is now a huge business with corporations spending $45 billion per year. About $12 billion is spent on executive education. The average company spends $2 million annually with over 1,000 executives at each firm receiving training. And leadership development is costly. Fulmer estimates the cost to develop such programmes runs from $100,000 to $250,000 and from $50,000 to $150,000 per session to deliver them. The leadership industry is big business.

* Preparation of this chapter was supported in part by the Schulich School of Business, York University. Lisa Fiksenbaum participated in the search of the literature. Louise Coutu prepared the manuscript.

Despite the considerable investment of both time and effort by researchers and practitioners most organizations appear to be badly led. Ulrich, Zenger, and Smallwood (1999), based on other published work, note that only 54 per cent of companies surveyed believed they had the leadership they needed to respond to change and only 8 per cent of executives rated their firm's leadership as excellent. Another survey of 312 respondents rated the most important people issue facing their companies; leadership was most important with over 70 per cent rating it as 'extremely important'. Companies with more leadership and depth were also found to be more profitable in a study reported by McKinsey. The gap between required and available leadership has widened, due in part to restructuring, downsizing, and mergers that may have reduced the number of leadership opportunities available.

This introductory chapter sets the stage for the rest of the collection. It first indicates why there is increased interest in leadership today. In plain and simple terms, leaders are critical to the success of organizations and societies in general, and there is currently a shortage of qualified and effective leaders. Second, the chapter provides a brief review of leaderships concepts and models that are currently commanding research interest and attention. Third, it summarizes initiatives shown to be useful in developing leaders and leadership, if well implemented.

Several factors have come together to increase interest and urgency in better understanding and development of leadership. These include the following:

- greater competitive pressures facing organizations today calling for greater leadership skills at all levels (Palus and Horth, 2003);
- business has become more complex; leaders need more skills to deal with increasingly challenging problems (Mumford et al., 2000);
- the increasing globalization and internationalization of business increases the demands for leaders to be able to work across distances, cultures, and countries (Dalton et al., 2002; Gregersen, Morrison, and Black, 1998; Kets de Vries and Florent-Treacy, 1999; Leslie et al., 2002);
- there is a need for new leadership approaches for both traditional and new industries. Most current views on leadership are more appropriate to the Industrial Age than the twenty-first century knowledge era (Nevins and Stumpf, 1999);
- there will be a shortage of leaders as those approaching retirement leave and fewer leadership entrants are available to replace those that leave;
- there will also be a leadership shortage if business activity grows only moderately over the next ten years;
- a large number of leaders are failing; more leaders are now being terminated for failing to achieve objectives (Hogan, 1999);
- there is increasing accountability being placed on leaders and the performance bar has been raised leading to both voluntary and involuntary departures;

- leaders are now more likely to change organizations given the decline in loyalty;
- recruiters are more aggressively encouraging leaders to change jobs;
- though billions of dollars are spent annually in leadership development programmes, there is still a shortage of effective leaders (Conger, 1992);
- organizations are doing a poor job of developing leaders internally (Csoka, 1997);
- most organizations have little leadership bench strength (Fulmer and Conger, 2004);
- leaders hired from outside an organization have a high rate of failure;
- few firms are prepared for the war for executive talent (Michaels, Handfield-Jones, and Axelrod, 2001);
- the rate of change will continue unabated;
- traditional approaches to leadership development such as MBA programmes, management training courses in universities, and public seminars have failed to deliver (Bennis and O'Toole, 2005; Mintzberg, 2004).

The Center for Creative Leadership and *CEO Magazine* collaborated on a study to explore what CEOs thought about leadership (Center for Creative Leadership, 2002). Seven hundred and fifty-six CEOs responded to a 20-question survey. They report that 79 per cent of CEOs saw leadership development as either 'the most' important or 'one of the top five' factors in achieving competitive advantage; 90 per cent were actively involved with leadership development practices in their organizations with 54 per cent indicating that they were primarily responsible for leadership development. CEOs saw people management skills (inspiring others, communicating expectations) and personal characteristics (adaptability, flexibility) as central to leadership success. A majority (61 per cent) identified leadership succession as their top concern. They also found a gap between the goals and wants CEOs indicated for leadership development and their current practices.

We have also come to know more about the development of leaders (Conger and Benjamin, 1999; Day, 2001; McCauley and VanVelsor, 2004). There is an emerging consensus that leadership cannot be effectively taught in MBA programmes, the main source of managerial talent, or in a one week training session (Conger, 1992; Schriesheim, 2003). As Mintzberg writes 'The MBA is a 1908 degree based on a 1950s strategy' (Mintzberg, 2004, p. 2). Leaders are best developed within organizations by organizations, and some organizations are doing this very well (see Tichy, 1997, 2002 for examples).

Although there are tens of thousands of articles and books on leadership, less than 5 per cent of this work focuses on executive leadership (Zaccaro, 2001). There has also been a primary focus on the interpersonal aspects of leadership, the ways that leaders can influence their followers. Sadly, there only little attention has been given to applied problems or policy issues.

3

Hernez-Broome and Hughes (2004) note three emerging themes in leadership development. First, leadership development is increasingly being undertaken in ongoing managerial and business work incorporating training, mentoring, coaching, action learning and developmental job assignments, real-world action and knowledge being the goal. They see this as providing opportunities for individuals to learn from their work rather than taking them away from their work to learn (Hernez-Broome and Hughes, 2004, p. 27). Best practice leadership development organizations are adopting a systemic rather than simple programme or event approach linking leadership development with HRM initiatives and business strategy (Aldridge *et al.*, 2003). Second, more emphasis is being placed on the identification of leadership competencies in the development of leaders (Barrett and Beeson, 2002; Fulmer and Conger, 2004). It is important to note that these competencies must fit the organization's strategy and business model. Third, increasing attention is being paid to the psychological and physical well-being of leaders with a particular emphasis being given to the integration of work and personal life. Organizational leaders work long hours (Brett and Stroh, 2003) and face multiple and often conflicting demands.

Hernez-Broome and Hughes (2004) suggest several other trends likely to play a significant role in the practice of and development of leadership in the future. These include: the belief that leadership competencies will still be relevant but will change in response to changes in the global competitive market, a greater emphasis on the development of global/international leaders, changes brought about by the technological revolution in access to information and modes of communication, increasing interest in the character and integrity of leaders (Bass and Steidlmeier, 1999; Collins, 2001a; Sankar, 2003), a need to demonstrate that leadership development impacts the bottom line, and incorporating new perspectives on leadership and leadership development (Day, 2001; McCauley and Van Velsor, 2004; Vicere, 2002).

We believe that there will be a shortage of effective leaders in the next 20 years, that many people now in leadership roles are not faring well with estimates that at least half of these individuals are falling short, that traditional OB and management texts devoting one or two chapters to the topic are not particularly helpful, but that the field has developed considerable understanding of leadership development events and processes in organizations (Antonakis, Cianciolo, and Sternberg, 2004; Charan, Drotter, and Noel, 2001; George, 2003; Lipman-Blumen, 1996; Rosen and Brown, 1996; Useem, 2001; Zacarro, 2001).

We believe that four conclusions are warranted based on this huge volume of work. First, we know a lot about effective leadership (Chemers, 1997; Conger and Kanungo, 1998; Drath, 2001; House and Aditya, 1997; Kouzes and Posner, 2002; Vicere and Fulmer, 1998; Zaccaro, 2001; Zaccaro and Klimoski, 2001). Second, leadership, as traditionally defined and measured, typically accounts for only moderate to low criterion variance in leadership outcomes suggesting a need for fresh thinking. Third, there is a large gap between leadership research findings and practice (Zaccaro and Horn, 2003). Fourth, there is evidence that a considerable number of leaders are falling short, estimated at between 50 and 75 per cent (Hogan and Hogan, 2002), and most organizations have little leadership bench strength.

WHAT IS LEADERSHIP?

Locke (1991) defines leadership 'as the process of inducing others to take action toward a common goal' (p. 2). Leadership is *relational* (i.e. involves followers), is a *process* (leader does something), and *induces others to act*.

Conger (1992) defines leaders as 'individuals who establish direction for a working group of individuals, who gain commitment from these groups members to this direction, and who then motivate these members to achieve the direction's outcomes' (p. 18).

According to Avolio (1999) leadership does not and should not directly impact performance directly but rather indirectly. That is, leadership affects the processes that directly or indirectly lead to performance. Most leadership influence in organizations is indirect; many of these effects are two-way or system-wide, when one considers executive leadership.

How do leaders impact the performance of their organizations? They do so through their immediate subordinates, whose influence spreads throughout the firm. The personality of the manager affects employee satisfaction, which in turn affects firm performance (Harter, Schmidt, and Hayes, 2002). The literature on top management teams suggests that the leader's personality affects the culture and processes of the top team and this influences firm performance (Hambrick, 1994). Similarly, Peterson *et al.* (2003), based on data from CEOs of 17 very large companies, found that CEO personality was correlated with top team functioning, which in turn was correlated with several quantitative indicators of firm success.

Leadership makes a difference to firm success (Barrick *et al.*, 1991; Day and Lord, 1988; Joyce, Nohria, and Roberson, 2003, Nohria, Joyce, and Roberson, 2003; Thomas, 1988; Waldman *et al.*, 2001). Barrick *et al.* (1991) report that high-performing executives, compared to average-performing executives, add an additional $25 million in value to their organizations during their tenure. Joyce, Nohria and Roberson (2003) indicate that CEOs account for about 14 per cent of the variance in the financial performance of their firms. Kincaid and Gardick (2003) also review studies showing the financial gains resulting from investments in leadership development.

A BASIC MODEL OF LEADERSHIP

Locke (1991) developed a leadership model having four elements:

1　Motives and traits
   - *Motives*
   - drive (achievement, ambition, energy, tenacity, initiative)
   - leadership motivation, must want to lead, want to use power to achieve goals
   - *Traits*
   - honesty, integrity – can be trusted and trusts others
   - self-confidence, emotional stability
   - creative, original
   - flexible, adaptable
   - sometimes charismatic

2　*Knowledge, skills, and abilities*
   - knowledge – technology, industry and organizational – gained from experience
   - skills – people-communication, conflict resolutions, relationship building
   - managing – planning, goal setting, decision-making, problem-solving abilities – intelligence

3　*Vision*
   - develop a vision
   - articulate the vision
   - identify how the vision will be achieved
   - enlist commitment from followers

4　*Implementation of the vision*
   - developing an agenda
   - selecting staff
   - motivating staff
   - managing information
   - building top management teams
   - bringing about change.

Traits (energy, honesty, motivation to lead) are a precondition for leadership. But these traits are not enough by themselves. To be effective, leaders must use their traits to acquire skills, develop a vision, and implement this vision within their organizations.

Locke presents 'the leadership core – the essentials of the leadership process. If there are contingencies, they more likely involve the weight or degree of importance that should be accorded the various parts or subparts of the model rather than the core components themselves'. Leaders differ dramatically in style. But effective leaders do not differ in substance – who they are and what they do (Bennis, 1994).

Leadership qualities or traits such as character, knowledge, style and values are important, but these must be connected to the achievement of results (Ulrich, Zenger, and Smallwood, 1999). These results are provided to employees, customers, the organization itself, and shareholders. Such results are measurable and connected with the organization's strategy and culture. Leadership effectiveness should consider the fate of organizations – the performance of organizations and the teams that comprise them. The job of a leader is to build, maintain, and guide a team that can outperform its competitors (Hogan, Curphy, and Hogan, 1994). Effective leadership, while influenced by personal qualities, is only effective if it produces results.

LEADING VERSUS MANAGING

Locke (1991) believes that the distinction between leadership and management is valid and simple. The leader establishes vision (purpose, mission, overarching goals, an agenda), as well as the means and the strategy for reaching the goals/purpose. The manager implements the vision; the manager controls the means to reaching the goals set by the leader.

Kotter (1990) makes a similar distinction. He writes that leadership and management are two distinct and complementary systems and both are needed. Management is about coping with complexity; leadership is about coping with change. Managing consists of planning, budgeting, organization, staffing, controlling, and problem solving. Leading consists of setting a direction for change, aligning people, motivating people, and creating a culture of leadership. Kotter feels however that most organizations are over managed and under led.

WHAT DO LEADERS DO?

Kotter (1999) has written extensively on what leaders do. He undertook a landmark study which included interviews with 150 managers from 40 companies, questionnaire surveys from 900 top-level executives, intensive case studies of 15 companies with a reputation for good management practices and a study of five companies trying to improve their capacity to attract, develop, and retain talent.

7

What do leaders do? Leaders had two main activities: Create an agenda for change (vision and strategy) and build a strong implementation network (a strongly motivated core group). The leaders he observed spent lots of time with people, had lots of relationships at various levels both within and without the organization, discussed a wide range of topics, collected information in these discussions, rarely gave orders, rarely made big decisions, and worked long hours (60 hours per week on average).

ARE LEADERS BORN OR MADE?

A flip answer to this question would be that one has never seen a leader that wasn't born! On the other hand, most writers believe that all people have untapped leadership potential. Everyone, regardless of organizational level, can make improvements in their leadership (Bennis, 1994; Conger, 1992; Doh, 2003).

Three forces appear to operate in the development of leaders: genetics, childhood dynamics within families and other early life experiences, and work experiences. Genetics plays a role in that both intelligence and physical energy are important in leadership; and aspects of temperament may also be relevant. Other aspects of intelligence (e.g. emotional, creativity) may also have a genetic component.

Childhood and life experiences may also play a role in later leadership development as well (Keller, 1999; 2003). Families may foster intellectual interests, talents, confidence, and interpersonal skills. Families also set expectations for performance, achievements, and success. Family and early life experiences in school and sports likely influence one's motivation to lead. Family support for individuality and risk taking may also encourage future leadership efforts.

Work experiences likely play the most important role in leadership development. Kotter (1999) has written that it takes 10 to 20 years of work experience to develop a general manager. Work experiences found to be important in the development of leaders include the job itself, hardships, mentors, and supervisors. Thus, the shortage of leaders in organizations is likely a reflection of neglected and underutilized skills and abilities rather than a shortage of talent.

Bennis and Thomas (2004) examined the qualities and experiences that help good managers become great leaders. They interviewed successful leaders from two eras: geeks were women and men between the ages of 25 and 35, geezers were women and men over 65 years of age. They were interested in similarities and differences between geeks and geezers in their leadership competencies and behaviours (the effects of era) and events or experiences that fostered effective leadership.

Bennis and Thomas identified a common experience that they labelled a *crucible* to be significant in predicting who would become and remain a successful leader.

The crucible refers to one or more intense transformational experiences from which individuals can emerge broken and defeated or strongly committed to lead. They suggest that to become a successful leader one may have to suffer, though many who suffer will fail as leaders. The difference is how the individual develops meaning out of these difficult events and challenges – the crucibles – and uses the experience to better themselves. It is important to add that transformational experiences may be either positive (e.g. having a mentor) or negative (e.g. losing a child, getting terminated).

CAN LEADERSHIP BE LEARNED?

Conger (1992) took part in five of the most popular leadership training programmes to gain insight in to the role training plays in leadership development. These included four approaches to leadership development: personal growth, conceptual analysis, feedback, and skill development. Companies spend millions of dollars for leadership training. Yet there remains a pressing shortage of leaders. Can managers be trained to become leaders?

Conger examined actual training programmes and the results they produced. He participated in these programmes, keeping a detailed record of events and his reactions to them. In addition, he interviewed other participants both during and following the training sessions.

Conger concluded that each approach could be helpful and no one approach was best. To be effective, leadership training must incorporate elements of all four approaches (see above). The main benefit of training is awareness building. There is too little time for one to master actual leadership skills. How can a one-week programme build lasting skills? In the end, it rests on the individual's own motivation and talent and the organization's willingness to support and coach such skills. In addition, not every person can turn learning experiences into awareness, or awareness into action. Some will be unable or unwilling to change their attitudes and behaviours.

Conger suggests no behavioural change and limited awareness for 10 to 20 per cent of participants; greater conceptual awareness of leadership for another 30 to 40 per cent; some behavioural changes coupled with greater awareness for another 20 to 30 per cent; and significant behavioural change for 10 per cent. Conger concludes, based on these expectations, that leadership programmes are worth the time and money invested in them.

Yet Conger believes these programmes will not meet the leadership challenges facing organizations. Awareness training is not enough. A one-week programme is not enough. Many organizations do not want leaders; instead they prefer managers. In addition, the value of a leadership programme is almost impossible to determine.

There are some ways to improve the value of leadership training. One way is to emphasize specific and teachable skills. A second is to design training over several sessions (course–break–course) using one's current leadership situation as a source of reflection and action. A third is to provide a coach to work with the leader following the course. A fourth is the use of change-partners, teams that work together during and following the course. Finally, ensuring greater company involvement in the design and use of the training has been shown to have value (Tichy, 1997).

Raelin (2004), though citing a $50 billion annual investment in leadership training, also finds this kind of leadership training has limited value. Individuals receiving training all too often go back to the same unchanged workplaces. Instead he advocates work-based learning, a form of action learning, to improve collective leadership (Raelin, 2003). Work-based learning uses action projects, learning teams, and interpersonal experiences such as mentors, which foster learning dialogues throughout the organization. He uses the term 'leaderful' to refer to shared leadership or collective leadership.

It is also useful to make a distinction between leader development and leadership development. Leader development is the process of developing individual leaders. Leadership development is the whole process for creating direction, alignment, and commitment. Both are needed though we currently emphasize leader not leadership development (Raelin, 2003, 2004).

EMERGING LEADERSHIP CONCEPTS AND MODELS

Leadership and intelligence

The role of intelligence in leadership has been considered since the 1920s. The early research showed that leaders were more intelligent than their followers and leaders were thought to be more intelligent than were followers (see Bass 1990, for a review). This research focused on the traditional IQ-based concept of intelligence. It is only in the past decade that broader notions of intelligence have surfaced in leadership writing (Gardner, 1995). These include concepts such as social maturity, social competence, tact, savvy, and social intelligence and emotional maturity (Mayer and Salovey, 1993, 1997).

Goleman's work (1995, 1998) on emotional intelligence provided a renewed emphasis on intelligence in leadership. Goleman's work places a high priority of the emotions, on emotional skills, and on learning to manage our emotions; emotional intelligence is a distinct type of intelligence.

Salovey and Mayer (1990) suggest five abilities in their definition of emotional intelligence: knowing one's emotions, managing emotions, marshalling emotions, recognizing emotions in others, and handling relationships.

Goleman (1998) later proposed five dimensions of emotional intelligence, along with 25 emotional competencies. The five dimensions were similar to those put forward by Salovey and Mayer (1990); self-awareness, self-regulation, motivation, empathy, and social skills. The competencies (Goleman, 1998, pp. 26–7) would seem to offer a solid basis for successful leadership, realizing that no one is strong on all of them.

Others have broadened even further the notion that multiple types of intelligence exist and likely play a role in leadership effectiveness. Sternberg (1997, 2002, 2003) identifies practical and creative intelligence as two aspects of successful intelligence. Zaccaro (2002) considers the relationship of social intelligence and organizational leadership. Hogan and Hogan (2002) identify socio-political intelligence, a generalized role-taking ability, as the core leadership skill. Aditya and House (2002) consider interpersonal acumen, the ability to read others behaviour, to be a core competence of leadership.

Sternberg (2003) presents a model of leadership that includes and synthesizes wisdom, intelligence, and creativity. Intelligence has both academic and practical aspects. Leaders need these three components working together to be effective. In addition, these components can be developed as individuals interact with their environment. Successful intelligence is the ability to succeed in life. Academic intelligence refers to possessing and using information to make decisions and evaluate various courses of action. Practical intelligence is the ability to solve everyday problems using knowledge gained from prior experience. Creativity involves generating ideas and products that are novel, of high quality and relevant to the task at hand. Wisdom involves the use of successful intelligence to reach a common good balancing values, own and others' interests, and both short and long run concerns (Aditya and House, 2002).

Leadership and emotions

Goleman, Boyatzis, and McKee (2001, 2002) believe that emotions are the key to effective leadership. The main task of a leader 'is to prime good feelings in those they lead' (2002, p. ix). Such leaders create resonance – a reservoir of positive feelings that brings out the best in people. The primal (prime) job of leadership is emotional. As a result, emotional intelligence –being intelligent about emotions – is so vital.

Leaders' moods and actions have a powerful impact on those they lead (George, 2000). Toxic leadership poisons the emotional climate of the workplace. Employees turn to leaders for emotional guidance, particularly in times of crisis. Leaders manage meaning for the organization. The success of a leader depends on how they do things – how they drive emotions in the right direction.

They distinguish between Resonant Leadership and Dissonant Leadership. In resonant leadership the leader is tuned into people's feelings and moves the group in a positive direction. The followers get in sync with the leader's enthusiastic energy. Emotional intelligence is vital here. Dissonant leadership is associated with toxic emotions (anger, fear, apathy, sullen silence). Dissonant leadership likely produces burnout and higher turnover.

They describe six leadership styles showing how each creates resonance and is linked to outcomes. Visionary leaders create resonance through moving people toward shared dreams. Consulting leaders build resonance by connecting individual needs with organizational goals. Affiliative leaders build resonance by connecting people with each other. Democratic leaders build resonance by getting commitment through participation. Commanding leaders build resonance by providing direction and calming fears. The first four styles usually have positive effects, whereas the last two frequently have negative effects.

Task? People? Or both?

Kaplan and Kaiser (2003a, 2003b) address the classic distinction in much of previous leadership writing between task-oriented and people-oriented leadership, which they term forceful and enabling. Rather than seeing these as opposites or contradictory, they envision them as complementary virtues. Forceful leadership is primarily based on asserting one's own power; enabling leadership fosters leadership and contributions from others.

Kaplan and Kaiser then link these approaches to leadership performance. Leaders fell short when they used too much or too little of a particular behaviour (e.g. too forceful or not forceful enough). They believe that most leaders are lopsided, i.e. too enabling and not forceful enough or too forceful and not enabling enough.

They developed a novel measure that addressed the distinction between too little, too much, and the right amount of a given behaviour. They found, in a sample of executives, a large negative correlation between forceful and enabling leadership in assessments provided by superiors, peers, subordinates, and the executives themselves; executives were indeed lopsided.

Managers exhibiting the right amount of both forcefulness and enabling, termed versatile by Kaplan and Kaiser (2003a), were also rated more effective by each rating source except executive self-ratings. Thus leaders showing a balance of forcefulness and enabling were seen as more effective. Interestingly, and perhaps not surprisingly, the most lopsided executives saw themselves as not very lopsided; they failed to see or acknowledge what was clear to others – that their lopsidedness hurt their effectiveness.

They draw several practical implications for leadership consulting based on both assessments of forcefulness and enabling behaviours from others besides the executives themselves and from feedback processes. There is also power in the use of simple and broad labels such as forcefulness, enabling, and versatility. The latter concept, in fact, has received much attention of late in the use of such terms as social intelligence, behavioural flexibility, and behavioural complexity. Based on their executive coaching work, Kaplan and Kaiser (2003b) report that lopsided executives often have distorted beliefs that diminish the value of the neglected side. Thus, development must also take place at an inner level, not just at the behavioural level. This places leadership development in the realm of personal development where executives come to grips with their attitudes, prejudices, and fears.

Why are executives unbalanced? The root causes of imbalance likely include uneven skill development (overdeveloping one skill while neglecting to develop others), distorted assumptions, beliefs and attitudes, overemphasizing what is thought to be important and underemphasizing what is thought to be unimportant, fear of being incompetent, and the inherent human tendency to see things in either/or terms.

The good news is that leaders can improve themselves. The first step is to acknowledge that one is in imbalance. Unfortunately, self-ratings have been shown to be highly inaccurate; ratings of others including peers, superiors, and subordinates are critical here. Then leaders need to strengthen the weak side and moderate the overused side. Both of these efforts require intellectual, emotional, and behavioural changes and this turns out to be a tall order for many.

Transactional and transformational leaders

Transactional and transformational leadership emerged as the dominant leadership framework in the 1990s (Bass, 1990, 1992). Transactional leadership has two components: the transactional leader exchanges rewards contingent upon the exhibition of desired behaviours and results, and intervenes when performance falls short. Transformational leadership consists of three components (Avolio and Yammarino, 2002). One, charisma, instils faith, pride, and respect for the leader. The second, individualized consideration, involves treating all staff as respected individuals with unique needs. The third, intellectual stimulation, encourages staff to think in new ways.

Transactional leaders work within the existing culture of the organization, take few risks, focus on deadlines and efficiency, emphasize process over substance and a means of control. Transactional leaders function best in stable predictable environments. Transformational leaders, on the other hand, search for new ways of working, are willing to change the way things are usually done (the status quo) use symbolism and imagery to heighten staff effort and look for creative courses of action in the fact of uncertainty and risk. These styles however are complementary – not polar opposite styles. Both styles may be associated with the achievement of desired performance objectives. A given leader can be both transformational and transactional; transformational leadership augments transactional leadership to achieve even higher levels of job performance.

13

Followers of transformational and charismatic leaders identify with the leaders (individual identification) and with the organization and its mission (social identification). Transformational leaders have a motivation to lead, believe they will be successful as leaders (leadership self-efficacy), are motivated and able to relate well to others, hold optimistic views about themselves and their environment, and are open to new ideas and experiences. Avolio (1999) used the term 'vital force' to describe the emotional aspects of the leader–follower relationship most likely to be realized by transformational and charismatic leaders.

The work on transformational leadership (Bass, 1999; Bass and Steidlmeier, 1999) placed a spotlight on the nature and strength of a leader's emotional impact on others. This was followed by work on the leader's authenticity, trustworthiness, credibility, and genuineness (Collins, 2001b; Goleman, Boyatzis, and McKee, 2002; Quinn, 2004).

Servant leadership

Hunter (2004) advocates servant leadership. Servant leadership is relationship-oriented; servant leaders are more concerned with the needs of their people than with their own needs (Block, 1996; Conger, 1994). As a result, they exhibit patience, honesty, good listening skills, and appreciation of their employees. Hunter believes, as do others such as Bennis (1994), Quinn (1997; 2004), and Clawson (1999), that leadership development and character development are one and the same. Character can be developed leading to habits and behaviours that result in servant leadership. Servant leaders are humble and selfless (Badarocco, 2002; Badarocco and Ellsworth, 1993). Servant leaders make a commitment to be the best they can be. They treat people with respect and dignity in ways that convey a love for them. Servant leaders gain their influence over others through their authority not their power. Servant leaders love their employees; they have a deep passion for their people.

Shared leadership

It has become increasingly difficult for one individual to accomplish the work of leadership. The challenges facing organizations are large, difficult, complicated, and unpredictable. What is needed is a more inclusive and shared leadership (Drath, 2003; Gronn, 2005). Pearce (2004) argues that since knowledge work is becoming more common and no one person can know everything, knowledge work is becoming increasingly team-based. As a consequence, vertical leadership needs to be augmented with shared leadership in many circumstances. Team-based leadership needs to be both vertical (one person in charge) and shared (rotating to the person with knowledge, skills, and abilities relevant to specific problems – that is shared by leaders and team members. He cites evidence indicating that poorly

14

performing teams were dominated by the team leader while highly performing teams had more shared leadership. The role of the vertical leader is still critical in the success of shared leadership however.

Shared leadership is more complicated and time consuming than is vertical leadership. Thus shared leadership is best used only in certain circumstances. Shared leadership is best used when the tasks are highly interdependent, require creativity, and are highly complex.

The traditional leader has an obvious role in the implementation of shared leadership. Specific leadership activities include designing the team, indicating the mission, providing necessary resources, selecting team members, helping determine the group process, and dealing with external constituencies.

During the team meetings, vertical leaders should provide information that only they possess, which is relevant to the task at hand, offering perspectives and ideas on an ongoing basis to facilitate takes performance. It is also important for the vertical leader continuously to reinforce the use and value of shared leadership.

A number of vertical and shared leadership behaviours are likely to lead to team success. These include task-focused directions, the provision of psychological and tangible rewards based on team progress, support of the team vision, and inspiring members to contribute.

The organization can also take steps to foster the development and use of team leadership (Pearce and Conger, 2003). Training and development initiatives can equip both leaders and team members with skills and attitudes necessary in the use of shared leadership. Rewards can be provided to support and recognize effective us of shared leadership. Finally, top management can both endorse and practise the use of shared leadership as part of their culture (Day, Gronn, and Salas, 2004).

Authentic leadership

Avolio *et al.* (2004) review the literature on the processes by which authentic leaders impact follower attitudes and behaviours. The core of authenticity is 'to know, accept, and remain true to ones self' (Avolio *et al.*, 2004, p. 402). Authentic leaders are:

> those individuals who are deeply aware of how they think and behave and are perceived by others as being aware of their own and others values/ moral perspective, knowledge, and strengths; aware of the context in which they operate; and who are confident, hopeful, optimistic, resilient, and high on moral character.
>
> (Avolio *et al.*, 2004, pp. 403–4)

Authentic leaders increase the motivation, commitment, and satisfaction of followers culminating in increased job performance (Luthans and Avolio, 2003).

Authentic leaders, through processes of personal and social identification, enhance positive emotions of followers (hope, trust, optimism), which impact followers' work attitudes (commitment, engagement) resulting in follower behaviours that increase performance (more effort, fewer withdrawal behaviours).

Avolio and his colleagues believe that authentic leadership incorporates transformational and ethical leadership. Authentic leaders can exhibit various behavioural styles (participative, directive, authoritarian). Authentic leaders behave consistently with deeply held personal values; this builds credibility in the eyes of followers, gaining their trust and respect (Gardner and Schermerhorn, 2004; May et al., 2003).

Leadership starts with you and me

Quinn (2004) developed a new model of leadership, which he termed the 'fundamental state of leadership'. This state rests on eight practices that develop the theme of ever-increasing integrity: reflective action, authentic engagement, appreciative inquiry, founded vision, adaptive confidence, detached interdependence, responsible freedom, and tough love. Quinn (2004) believes that most people spend most of their time in the normal life state (comfort centred, self-focused, externally driven, internally closed). Yet each can enter the extraordinary state which he calls the fundamental state of leadership (results centred, internally directed, other focused, externally open). When individuals act this way, they become a catalyst for change by others and their organizations. The fundamental state of leadership is the movement towards ever-increasing levels of personal and collective integrity.

This process begins with personal transformation, which in turn changes others (Quinn, 1997). The foundation of leadership is who we are (who one is). Thus the search for behaviours, tools, techniques, and practices that distinguish effective leaders is misguided. Effective leadership does not begin with imitation – it begins with origination – by the person him or herself.

Bushe (2001) makes the case for the importance of leader self-awareness, curiosity, and telling it like it is, in eliminating 'interpersonal mush' (i.e. people's understanding of each other is based on fantasies and stories they have made up about each other) and bring about 'interpersonal clarity'. When interpersonal clarity exists, people can work effectively and competently with one another and produce both knowledge (organizational learning) and positive organizational change.

DEVELOPING LEADERS IN CONTEXT

We need to place more emphasis on the context of leadership practice if we are to advance our understanding of leadership in the real world (Zaccaro and

Klimoski, 2001). The following sections review some of the most important initiatives for leader and leadership development.

Leadership coaching

Lyons (2002), in a study of senior executives who took part in an intensive executive development process involving 360-degree feedback, found they benefited personally and professionally from the experience. In fact, London and Beatty (1993) believe that 360-degree feedback could become a significant competitive advantage. Key features of the process for it to be effective were: the feedback data, the design of meetings to discuss the data and plan development, the contribution of the consultants, and the opportunity for ongoing consultation. The process was emotionally intense. Participants reported that their leadership changed as a result of the experience; they valued and expressed more often the 'softer side' of their leadership, they were more authentic and assertive, they were both more forceful and more openly intimate with their feelings, and they were calmer and more confident as leaders. Caproni (2001), Hunt and Weintraub (2002), and Hudson (1999) offer practical suggestions for developing effective coaching programmes.

Peterson (1996) describes the executive coaching programme developed by Personnel Decisions International (PDI). PDI defines coaching as 'the process of equipping people with the tools, knowledge and opportunities they need to develop themselves and become more effective' (Peterson, 1996, p. 78). Coaching at PDI involves the participant, a sponsor (usually the boss or a HR representative), and a PDI coach. Individuals and their organization are encouraged to share responsibility for development. Five coaching strategies are commonly used: forging a partnership, inspiring commitments, developing skills, encouraging and supporting persistence, and creating organizational support to reward learning and reduce barriers to development.

Kets de Vries (2005) highlights both the process and benefits of leadership coaching in a group setting. Group coaching builds one-on-one coaching and the use of 360-degree feedback. In the group coaching context, changes in leadership behaviours are more likely to occur he contends. Leadership group coaching increases trust, helps with conflict resolution, increases team performance and commitments, and makes people accountable to each other.

Developing on the job

How do managers become leaders? Most development takes place on the job not in classrooms, seminars, and MBA programmes (McCall, 2004). McCall, Lombardo, and Morrison (1988) asked successful senior executives about the experiences that had the greatest impact on their careers and the lessons they took from those experiences. They collected data from 191 successful executives from six major corporations. The experiences that were helpful were jobs (specific assignments on jobs), supervisors (other people who had an impact), and hardships (setbacks and tough times). The lessons these executives learned fell into five themes: setting and implementing agendas, handling relationships, basic values, executive temperament, and personal awareness. Mentoring, career planning programmes, and job rotation were found to have limited value.

Two actions are vital in developing leaders. First, it is important to select the best people one can. Second, it is critical that these employees gain the skills and experiences necessary to lead the company. It is therefore important to understand the developmental value of already existing jobs in the organization. It is also possible to create developmental jobs however. The following job assignments were found to have developmental value: the first supervisor job, project and task force jobs requiring leading by persuading others, line to staff switches, starting an operation from scratch, fix-its or turn-it-around jobs, and an increase in job scope.

The majority of learning comes from job assignments, with job challenge being critical; the second most important source of learning come from bosses – good bosses, bad bosses, a boss that was some of both (McCall, 1998).

McCauley *et al.* (1998) show the validity of the Developmental Challenge Profile (DCP), a measure of the developmental components of managerial jobs and on-the-job learning, job transitions, objective features of jobs and psychological status of job incumbents. The DCP contains 15 scales under three categories: Job transitions (unfamiliar responsibilities, proving yourself), Task-related characteristics (developing new directions, inherited problems, reduction decisions, problems with employees, high stakes, managing business diversity, job overload, handling external pressure, influencing without authority), Obstacles (adverse business conditions, lack of top management support, lack of personal support, difficult boss).

Job experiences are developmental because they give managers an opportunity to try out skills and behaviours in real life situations that matter (McCauley, Eastman, and Ohlott, 1995). There is research evidence that on-the-job experiences contribute more to development than do classroom training programmes. On-the-job learning occurs when individuals face challenging job situations. These situations provide both the opportunity and the motivation to learn.

McCall, Lombardo, and Morrison (1988) conclude that on-the-job learning comprises basic management skills and ways of thinking. In their study, they found 33 lessons that were learned by executives, which they grouped into five categories: setting and implementing agendas, handling relationships, basic values, executive temperament, and personal insights. It is also possible for a manager to experience too much challenge (i.e. be overwhelmed) in a particular job assignment, minimizing their learning.

Succession planning

Charan (2005) believes that something is seriously wrong in the development and hiring of CEOs. He states that about half of large companies with revenues greater that $500 million have no meaningful CEO succession plan and cites evidence from a survey of HR executives from 276 large organizations indicating that only 20 per cent were satisfied with their management succession process. The global average of CEO tenure continues to shrink and two out of every five CEOs fail in the first 18 months.

Most organizations do a reasonable job developing middle managers but do less well in developing CEOs. Very few effective middle managers will be qualified to be the CEO as well. Companies also want leaders to hold the job for ten years or more, taking the job when they are about 50 years of age. Thus, in order to be ready to undertake the CEO job at 50, their development should start when they are about 30.

Companies need to do three things to develop long-serving leaders according to Charan. First, they need to create a large pool of internal candidates through a leadership development process. Second, they need to create, update, and refine a succession plan and a process for making solid decisions about candidates. Third, if outside candidates are being considered, the company should direct recruiters in the executive search process rather than having the search professionals direct it.

Fulmer and Conger (2004) studied succession management in six global companies. Succession planning has traditionally been used to identify replacements for senior executives who would eventually depart the organization through death or retirement. All too often it has been a mechanical process involving the filling out of forms (Karaveli and Hall, 2003). Fulmer and Conger suggest two purposes of succession management: to serve the organization by providing a continuous and deep supply of talent, and to serve employees. The latter keeps high performers challenged and motivated to remain with the firm and reduce staff turnover.

Succession planning has historically focused on executive replacement. Now the emphasis is on both replacement and development as well as on retention of talented people. In addition, succession planning was focused on the top levels of the organization. When a vacancy appeared, the organization selected someone on the short list. The process was formal and bureaucratic. Today the emphasis is on development of talent. Education and training have been found to have limited value. As already mentioned, studies carried out by the Center for Creative Leadership have shown that challenging jobs and people are critical for development. There is also more emphasis today on future performance instead of present job performance.

The approach has become more fluid and less rigid. The emphasis has shifted to looking for talent pools instead of developing short lists. There is also a trend towards more widespread ownership of the succession management processes. The top team is more involved in the process with less involvement of HR staff. The process has also become more open and less secretive. They suggest that a good succession management system is: simple and easy to use, developmentally oriented not replacement oriented, one that involves the senior executive gleam, good at identifying gaps in talent and jobs that are critical to the continued success of the organization, and is one that monitors the succession process so that the right people are in the right jobs.

People are usually given little information, explanation, preparation, and support to make these transitions. People are typically promoted based on past performance rather than on potential to succeed in the new job. Deficiencies at lower levels may not be important there but become more important as one rises in the hierarchy. In addition, strengths at lower levels may also become weaknesses at higher organizational levels. There is too much 'sink or swim' (Downs, March, and Berkman, 2001; Freedman, 1998) in leader development.

Fulmer and Conger spell out a number of benefits to organizations using competency models as a key part of their succession management process: greater clarity of roles and performance expectations, more uniform data, development linked to organizational goals, providing specific guidelines for leadership development, and quantifying performance management.

Fulmer and Conger found that their best-practice organizations pursued similar developmental activities: they invested most time and resources on executive-level talent; they used mentoring, coaching, and informal or formal feedback; they used action learning and special job assignments; and they moved high potentials across the organization.

Leadership engines

Tichy (1997) describes how organizations build a continuous stream of leaders at every level. These are 'organizations with a leadership engine – where leaders exist at all levels and leaders actively develop future generations of leaders'. Interestingly these winning organizations are teaching organizations: they have good leaders who work at developing other leaders.

Leaders in these organizations took direct responsibility for developing other leaders. These leaders articulated and taught others how to make the organization successful. They frequently told stories that conveyed the essence of their lessons and spent time developing leaders through coaching and teaching techniques.

These leaders personalized their vision and ideas by telling stories that reached people's emotions (Tichy, 2002). They managed through times of change – determining the direction in which the organization would move; where it was now and where it needed to be. Such leaders made things happen, they shaped culture, and used management tools. These leaders were revolutionaries. They faced reality and identified courses of action to solve problems and encouraged others to do the same. Great leaders were great teachers; they taught others to be leaders and made teaching a priority. Great leaders had clear ideas and values based on knowledge and experience that they shared with others (Dotlich and Noel, 1998).

Organizational practice

Fulmer and Conger (2004) observed that best-practice leader development organizations used more, and more intense, leadership interventions than did firms doing less well in developing leaders. Their best-practice firms also measured the success of their efforts and the development processes themselves.

We know a lot about developing leaders, but the application of this knowledge is where organizations fall short. These factors include weak selection and development processes, competing organization needs, changing priorities, poorly designed and poorly used systems, and outdated views on how leaders develop (Wilcox and Rush, 2004).

The *Academy of Management Executive*, in their Executive Ask section, Kerr (2004) took on the question 'How can organizations best prepare people to lead and manage others?' This collection included five articles by professors from schools of business and management along with an introduction provided by a professor-turned-practitioner.

Kerr (2004) describes efforts by Goldman Sachs to develop leaders. This programme, in its first offering, provided 83 vice-presidents with stretch assignments outside their regular responsibilities for one year, the assignment of executive coaches to provide feedback and facilitate reflective learning, contact with each other for advice, for a sounding board, and specific training customized around the emerging needs of the group. Goldman Sachs considered the programme a success and launched it again for a second group of vice-presidents and a group of managing directors.

Although many people highlight job assignments as a critical contribution to leadership development, not everyone learns from experience. You can learn nothing, the wrong things, or only some of what might have been learned. In addition, learning from experience is often a lonely and solitary activity. Tying these experiences to developmental relationships with bosses and peers added considerably to the value of the work experiences as a source of learning and growth.

Kerr draws three conclusions for the Goldman Sachs efforts:

1   It is better to start development early but this is rarely done in organizations since it is too costly, those being developed may leave and take their learning with them, there is still little data available on their performance needs, and it is not clear which ones are the high potentials.

2   The stretch assignment must be 'real work', and these assignments are typically given to the strongest (not the weakest) people.

3   The more important and riskier the stretch assignment, the less willing managers are to use it for their development.

The Center for Creative Leadership has created short case studies of their leadership development efforts at several organizations, including Bayer, Catholic Healthcare Partners, the Federal Reserve Bank of Richmond, and the Methanex Corporation, which are available on their web-site. Tichy and DeRose (1996) describe efforts by the Pepsi organization to build a leader-driven organization. These case studies are informative to other organizations attempting to develop both leaders and leadership.

Ulrich and his colleagues (Intagliatta, Ulrich, and Smallwood, 2000; Ulrich, Smallwood, and Zenger, 2000) use the term 'leadership brand' as one way for an organization to differentiate their leadership competencies and strategy from those of their competitors. A leadership brand includes the firm's leadership theory, its leadership strategy, and its investments in leadership development. The development of a leadership brand would also provide a source of competitive advantage.

THIS COLLECTION

This collection focuses on what we know about inspiring leaders. It has four sections. The first section reviews some broad leadership concepts and viewpoints (e.g. authentic leadership, values and ethical performance, adaptability, balance and well-being). The second section explores issues in effective leadership (e.g. the role of charisma, transformational and transactional leadership, team leadership, and developing women leaders). The third section examines the dark side of leadership (e.g. fatal flaws and derailment factors, perfectionism, workaholism). The last section considers organizational initiatives and HRM practices that have been found to be successful in developing leaders (e.g. 360-degree feedback, executive coaching, mentoring and social networks, developmental jobs, succession planning).

The title of this collection has an intended double meaning. On the one hand, we need to inspire leaders to take informed and principled action that produces results; on the other hand, these leaders need to inspire and excite their teams and support them in achieving peak performance.

The chapters that follow will pick up the themes of this introduction and more fully develop them. All are based on the premise that leaders matter. Effective leaders are associated with committed followers and high performing units; ineffective leaders are associated with low morale, sub-par contributions, and failing performance. The largest source of employee dissatisfaction results from the quality of their leaders (Hogan, 1999). Thus we need to address a major organizational problem.

This collection will hopefully bring concern about ineffective leadership and potential solutions together in one volume. Leadership and leader development has been shown to be a time consuming and potentially painful process (Quinn, 1997, 2004). Each of us, whether leader or followers, has a role to play in improving leadership. It starts with you and me.

REFERENCES

Aditya, R. N. and House, R. J. (2002) Interpersonal acumen and leadership across cultures: Pointers from the GLOBE study. In R. E. Riggio, S. E. Murphy, and J. P. Pirozzolo (eds) *Multiple intelligences and leadership*. Mahwah, NJ: Lawrence Erlbaum, pp. 215–40.

Aldridge, M., Johnson, C., Stolzfus, J., and Vicere, A. A. (2003) Leadership development at 3M: New processes, new technologies, new growth. *Human Resource Planning*, 24: 45–55.

Antonakis, J., Cianciolo, A., and Sternberg, R. J. (2004) *The nature of leadership*. Thousand Oaks, CA: Sage.

Avolio, B. J. (1999) *Full leadership development: Building the vital force in organizations*. Thousand Oaks, CA: Sage.

Avolio, B. J. and Bass, B. M. (2002) *Development potential across a full range of leadership*. Mahwah, NJ: Lawrence Erlbaum.

Avolio, B. J. and Yammarino, F. J. (2002) *Transformational and charismatic leadership: The road ahead*. New York: Elsevier Science.

Avolio, B. J., Gardner, W. L., Walumba, F. O., Luthans, F. T., and May, D. R. (2004) Unlocking the mask: A look at the process by which authentic leaders impact follower attitudes and behaviors. *Leadership Quarterly*, 15: 801–23.

Badaracco, J. L. (2002) *Leading quietly: An unorthodox guide to doing the right thing*. Boston, MA: Harvard Business School Press.

Badaracco, J. L. and Ellsworth, R. R. (1993) *Leadership and the quest for integrity*. Boston, MA: Harvard Business School Press.

Barrett, A. and Beeson, J. (2002) *Developing business leaders for 2010*. New York: The Conference Board.

Barrick, M. R., Day, D. V., Lord, R. G., and Alexander, R. A. (1991) Assessing the utility of executive leadership. *Leadership Quarterly*, 2: 9–22.

Bass, B. M. (1990) *Bass and Stogdill's handbook of leadership*. New York: The Free Press.

Bass, B. M. (1992) Does the transactional–transformational leadership paradigm transcend organizational and national boundaries? *American Psychologist*, 52: 130–9.

Bass, B. M. (1998) *Transformational leadership: Industrial, military and educational impact*. Mahwah, NJ: Lawrence Erlbaum.

Bass, B. M. (1999) Two decades of research and development in transformational leadership. *European Journal of Work and Organizational Psychology*, 12: 47–59.

Bass, B. M. and Steidlmeier, P. (1999) Ethics, character, and authentic transformational leadership behavior. *Leadership Quarterly*, 10: 181–217.

Bennis, W. (1994) *On becoming a leader*. Reading, MA: Addison-Wesley.

Bennis, W. and Nanus, B. (1997) *Leaders: The strategies for taking charge*. New York: Harper Business

Bennis, W. and Thomas, R. (2004) *Geeks and geezers: How era, values and defining moments shape leaders*. Boston, MA: Harvard Business School Press.

Bennis, W. G. and O'Toole, J. (2005) How business schools lost their way. *Harvard Business Review*, 83: 96–104.

Block, P. (1996) *Stewardship: Choosing service over self-interest*. San Francisco, CA: Berrett-Koehler.

Brett, J. M. and Stroh, L. K. (2003) Working 61 plus hours a week: Why do managers do it? *Journal of Applied Psychology*, 88: 67–78.

Bushe, G. R. (2001) *Clear leadership: How outstanding leaders make themselves understood, cut through the mush, and help everyone get real at work*. Palo Alto, CA: Davies-Black Publishing.

Caproni, P. J. (2001) *The practical coach: Management skills for everyday life*. Upper Saddle River, NJ: Prentice-Hall.

Center for Creative Leadership (2002) *What CEOs think: A leadership survey*. Greensboro, NC: Center for Creative Leadership.

Charan, R. (2005) Ending the CEO succession crisis. *Harvard Business Review*, February, 72–81

Charan, R., Drotter, S., and Noel, J. (2001) *The leadership pipeline*. San Francisco, CA: Jossey-Bass.

Chemers, M. M. (1997) *An integrative theory of leadership*. Mahwah, NJ: Lawrence Erlbaum Associates.

Clawson, J. G. (1999) *Level three leadership*. Englewood Cliffs, NJ: Prentice Hall.

Collins, J. I. (2001a) Level 5 leadership: The triumph of humility and fierce resolve. *Harvard Business Review*, January, 66–76.

Collins, J. I. (2001b) *Good to great*. New York: Harper Business.

Conger, J. A. (1992) *Learning to lead: The art of transforming managers into leaders*. San Francisco, CA: Jossey-Bass.

Conger, J. A. (1994) *Spiritual work: Discovering the spirituality in leadership*. San Francisco, CA: Jossey-Bass.

Conger, J. A. and Benjamin, B. (1999) *Building leaders: How successful companies develop the next generation*. San Francisco, CA: Jossey-Bass.

Conger, J. A. and Kanungo, R. N. (1998) *Charismatic leadership in organizations*. Thousand Oaks, CA: Sage.

Csoka, L. S. (1997) *Bridging the leadership gap*. New York: The Conference Board.

Dalton, M., Ernst, C. F., Deal, J., and Leslie, J. (2002) *Success for the new global manager: How to work across distances, countries and cultures*. San Francisco, CA: Jossey-Bass.

Day, D. V. (2001) Leadership development: A review in context. *Leadership Quarterly*, 11: 581–613.

Day, D. V. and Lord, R. G. (1988) Executive leadership and organizational performance. *Journal of Management*, 14: 453–64.

Day, D. V., Gronn, P., and Salas, E. (2004) Leadership capacity in teams. *Leadership Quarterly*, 15: 857–80.

Day, D. V., Zaccaro, S. J., and Halpin, S. M. (2004) *Leadership development for transforming organizations. Growing leaders for tomorrow*. Mahwah, NJ: Lawrence Erlbaum.

Doh, J. P. (2003) Can leadership be taught? Perspectives from management educators. *Academy of Management Learning and Education*, 2: 54–67.

Dotlich, D. L. and Noel, J. L. (1998) *Action learning: How the world's top companies are re-creating their leaders and themselves*. San Francisco, CA: Jossey-Bass.

Downs, D., March, T., and Berkman, T. (2001) *Assimilating new leaders. The key to executive retention*. New York: AMACOM.

Drath, W. H. (2001) *The deep blue sea: Rethinking the source of leadership*. San Francisco, CA: Jossey-Bass.

Drath, W. H. (2003) Leading together: Complex challenges require a new approach. *Leadership in Action*, 23: 3–7.

Freedman, A. (1998) Pathways and crossroads to institutional leadership. *Consulting Psychology Quarterly*, 54: 131–51.

Fulmer, R. M. (1997) The evolving paradigm of leadership development. *Organizational Dynamics*, 26: 59–72.

Fulmer, R. M. and Conger, J. A. (2004) *Growing your company's leaders*. New York: AMACOM.

Gardner, H. (1995) *Leading minds: An anatomy of leadership*. New York: Basic Books.

Gardner, W. L. and Schermerhorn, J. R. (2004) Unleashing individual potential: Performance gains through positive organizational behavior and authentic leadership. *Organizational Dynamics*, 33: 34–41.

George, B. (2003) *Authentic leadership: Rediscovering the secrets to creating lasting value*. San Francisco, CA: Jossey-Bass.

George, J. M. (2000) Emotions and leadership. The role of emotional intelligence. *Human Relations*, 53: 1027–55.

Goleman, D. (1995) *Emotional intelligence: Why it can matter more than IQ*. New York: Bantam.

Goleman, D. (1998) *Working with emotional intelligence*. New York: Bantam.

Goleman, D., Boyatzis, R., and McKee, A. (2001) Primal leadership: The hidden driver of great performance. *Harvard Business Review*, 79: 42–51.

Goleman, D., Boyatzis, R., and McKee, A. (2002) *Primal leadership: Learning to lead with emotional intelligence*. Boston, MA: Harvard Business School Press

Gregersen, H. B., Morrison, A. J., and Black, J. S. (1998) Developing leaders for the global frontier. *Sloan Management Review*, 40: 21–32.

Gronn, P. (2005) *Distributed organizational leadership*. Greenwich, CA: Information Age Publishing.

Hambrick, D. C. (1994) Top management groups. *Research in Organizational Behavior*, 16: 171–213.

Harter, J. K., Schmidt, F. L., and Hayes, T. L. (2002) Business-unit-level relationship between employee satisfaction, employee engagement, and business outcomes: A meta-analysis. *Journal of Applied Psychology*, 87: 268–79.

Hernez-Broome, G. and Hughes, R. L. (2004) Leadership development: Past, present and future. *Human Resource Planning*, 25: 24–32.

Hogan, J. and Hogan, R. (2002) Leadership and sociopolitical intelligence. In R. E. Riggio, S. E. Murphy, and J. P. Pirozzolo (eds) *Multiple intelligences and leadership*. Mahwah, NJ: Lawrence Erlbaum, pp. 75–88.

Hogan, R. (1999) Trouble at the top: Causes and consequences of managerial incompetence. *Consulting Psychology Journal*, 46: 1061–87.

Hogan, R., Curphy, G. J., and Hogan, J. (1994) What we know about leadership: Effectiveness and personality. *American Psychologist*, 49: 493–504.

House, R. J. and Aditya, R. N. (1997) The social scientific study of leadership: Quo vadis? *Journal of Management*, 23: 409–73.

Hudson, F. M. (1999) *The handbook of coaching: A comprehensive resource guide for managers, executives, consultants and human resource professionals*. San Francisco, CA: Jossey-Bass.

Hunt, J. G. and Weintraub, J. R. (2002) *The coaching manager: Developing top talent in business*. Thousand Oaks, CA: Sage.

Hunter, J. C. (2004) *The world's most powerful leadership principle: How to become a servant leader*. New York: Crown Business.

Intagliatta, J., Ulrich, D., and Smallwood, N. (2000) Leveraging leadership competencies to produce leadership brand: Creating distinctiveness by focusing on strategy and results. *Human Resource Planning*, 23: 12–23.

Joyce, W. F., Nohria, N., and Roberson, B. (2003) *What really works: The 4 + 2 formula for sustained business success*. New York: Harper Business.

Kaplan, R. E. and Kaiser, R. B. (2003a) Developing versatile leadership. *MIT Sloan Management Review*, 44: 19–26.

Kaplan, R. E. and Kaiser, R. B. (2003b) Rethinking a classic distinction in leadership: Implications for the assessment and development of executives. *Consulting Psychology Journal: Practice and Research*, 55: 15–25.

Karaveli, A. and Hall, D. T. (2003) Growing leaders for turbulent times: Is succession planning up to the challenge? *Organizational Dynamics*, 32: 62–79.

Keller, T. (1999) Images of the familiar: Individual differences and implicit leadership theories. *Leadership Quarterly*, 10: 589–607.

Keller, T. (2003) Parental images as a guide to leadership sensemaking: An attachment perspective on implicit leadership theories. *Leadership Quarterly,* 14: 141–60.

Kerr, S. (2004) Introduction: Preparing people to lead. *Academy of Management Executive,* 18: 118–20.

Kets de Vries, M. F. R. (2005) Leadership group coaching in action: The Zen of creating high performance teams. *Academy of Management Executive,* 19: 61–76.

Kets de Vries, M. F. R. and Florent-Treacy, E. (1999) *The new global leaders: Richard Branson, Percy Barnevik, and David Simon.* San Francisco, CA: Jossey-Bass.

Kincaid, S. B. and Gardick, D. (2003) The return on investment of leadership development: Differentiating our discipline. *Consulting Psychology Journal: Practice and Research,* 55: 47–57.

Kotter, J. P. (1990) *A force for change: How leadership differs from management.* New York: Free Press.

Kotter, J. P. (1999) *What leaders really do.* Boston, MA: Harvard Business School Press.

Kouzes, J. M. and Posner, B. Z. (2002) *Leadership challenge* (3rd edn). San Francisco, CA: Jossey-Bass.

Leslie, J. B., Dalton, M., Ernst, C., and Deal, J. (2002) *Managerial effectiveness in a global context.* Greensboro, NC: Center for Creative Leadership.

Lipman-Blumen, J. (1996) *The connective edge: Leading in an interdependent world.* San Francisco, CA: Jossey-Bass.

Locke, E. A. (1991) *The essence of leadership.* New York: Lexington Books.

London, M. and Beatty, R. W. (1993) 360-degree feedback as a competitive advantage. *Human Resource Management,* 32: 353–72.

Luthans, F. and Avolio, B. J. (2003) Authentic leadership: A positive development approach. In K. S. Cameron, J. E. Dutton, and R. E. Quinn (eds) *Positive organizational scholarship.* San Francisco, CA: Jossey-Bass, pp. 241–58.

Lyons, D. (2002) Freer to be me: The development of executives at mid-life. *Consulting Psychology Journal: Practice and Research,* 54: 15–27.

McCall, M. W. (1998) *High flyers: Developing the next generation of leaders.* Boston, MA: Harvard Business School Press.

McCall, M. W. (2004) Leadership development through experience. *Academy of Management Executive,* 18: 127–30.

McCall, M. W., Lombardo, M. W., and Morrison, A. M. (1988) *The lessons of experience: How successful executives develop on the job.* New York: Lexington Books.

McCauley, C. D. and Van Velsor, E. (2004) *The Center for Creative Leadership handbook of leadership development* (2nd edn) San Francisco, CA: Jossey-Bass.

McCauley, C. D., Eastman, L. J., and Ohlott, P. J. (1995) Linking management selection and development through stretch assignments. *Human Resource Management,* 34: 93–115.

McCauley, C. D., Ruderman, M. N., Ohlott, P. J., and Morrow, J. E. (1998) Assessing the developmental components of managerial jobs. *Journal of Applied Psychology,* 79: 544–60.

May, D. R., Chan, A., Hodges, T., and Avolio, B. J. (2003) Developing the moral component of authentic leadership. *Organizational Dynamics*, 32: 247–60.

Mayer, J. D. and Salovey, P. (1993) The intelligence of emotional intelligence. *Intelligence*, 17, 433–42.

Mayer, J. D. and Salovey, P. (1997) What is emotional intelligence? In P. Salovey and D. Sluyter (eds) *Emotional development and emotional intelligence: Implications for educators*. New York: Basic Books, pp. 3–31.

Michaels, E., Handfield-Jones, H., and Axelrod, B. (2001) *The war for talent*. Boston, MA: Harvard Business School Press.

Mintzberg, H. (2004) *Managers not MBAs*. San Francisco, CA: Berrett-Koehler.

Mumford, M. D., Zaccaro, S. J., Harding, F. D., Jacobs, T. O., and Fleishman, E. A. (2000) Leadership skills for a changing world. *Leadership Quarterly*, 11: 11–35.

Nevins, M. and Stumpf, S. (1999) 21st century leadership: Redefining management education. *Strategy, Management, Competition*, 3rd quarter, 41–51.

Nohria, N., Joyce, W., and Roberson, B. (2003) What really works. *Harvard Business Review*, 81: 43–52.

Palus, C. and Horth, D. (2003) *The leader's edge: Six creative competencies for navigating complex challenges*. San Francisco, CA: Jossey-Bass.

Pearce, C. L. (2004) The future of leadership: Combining vertical and shared leadership to transform knowledge work. *The Academy of Management Executive*, 18: 47–57.

Pearce, C. L. and Conger, J. A. (2003) *Shared leadership: Reframing the hows and whys of leadership*. Thousand Oaks, CA: Sage.

Peterson, D. B. (1996) Executive coaching at work: The art of one-on-one change. *Consulting Psychology Journal: Practice and Research*, 48: 78–86.

Peterson R. S., Smith, D. B., Martorona, P. V., and Owens, P. D. (2003) The impact of chief executive officer personality on top management team dynamics. *Journal of Applied Psychology*, 88: 795–808.

Quinn, R. E. (1997) *Deep change*. San Francisco, CA: Jossey-Bass.

Quinn, R. E. (2004) *Building the bridge as you walk on it*. San Francisco, CA: Jossey-Bass.

Raelin, J. A. (2003) *Creating leaderful organizations: How to bring out leadership in everyone*. San Francisco, CA: Berrett-Koehler.

Raelin, J. A. (2004) Don't bother putting leadership into people. *Academy of Management Executive*, 18: 131–6.

Rosen, R. and Brown, P. (1996) *Leading people: Transforming business from the inside out*. New York: Viking.

Salovey, P. and Mayer, J. D. (1990) Emotional intelligence. *Imagination, Cognition and Personality*, 9: 185–211.

Sankar, Y. (2003) Character, not charisma, is the critical measure of leadership excellence. *Journal of Leadership and Organizational Studies*, 9: 45–55.

Schriesheim, C. A. (2003) Why leadership research is generally irrelevant for leadership development. In S. E. Murphy and R. E. Riggio (eds) *The future of leadership development*. Mahwah, NJ: Lawrence Erlbaum, pp. 181–97.

Sternberg, R. J. (1997) Managerial intelligence: Why IQ isn't enough. *Journal of Management*, 23: 475–93.

Sternberg, R. J. (2002) Successful intelligence: A new approach to leadership. In R. E. Riggio, S. E. Murphy, and F. J. Pirozzolo (eds) *Multiple intelligences and leadership*. Mahwah, NJ: Lawrence Erlbaum, pp. 9–28.

Sternberg, R. J. (2003) WICS: A model of leadership in organizations. *Academy of Management Learning and Education*, 2: 386–401.

Thomas, A. (1988) Does leadership make a difference to organizational performance? *Administrative Science Quarterly*, 33: 388–400.

Tichy, N. M. (1997) *The leadership engine: How winning companies build leaders at every level*. New York: HarperCollins.

Tichy, N. M. (2002) *The cycle of leadership: How great leaders teach their companies to win*. New York: HarperCollins.

Tichy, N. M. and DeRose, C. (1996) The Pepsi challenge: Building a leader-driven organization. *Training and Development*, 50: 58–66.

Ulrich, D., Smallwood, N., and Zenger, J. (2000) Building a leadership brand. *Leader to Leader*, 15: 40–6.

Ulrich, D., Zenger, J., and Smallwood, N. (1999) *Results-based leadership*. Boston, MA: Harvard Business School Press.

Useem, M. (2001) *Leadership: How to lead your boss so you both win*. New York: Crown Business.

Vicere, A. A. (2002) Leadership and the networked economy. *Human Resource Planning*, 25: 26–33.

Vicere, A. A. and Fulmer, R. M. (1998) *Leadership by design:* Boston, MA. Harvard Business School Press.

Waldman, D. A., Ramirez, G. G., House, R. J., and Puranam, P. (2001) Does leadership matter? CEO leadership attributes and profitability under conditions of perceived environmental uncertainty. *Academy of Management Journal*, 44: 134–43.

Wilcox, M. and Rush, S. (2004) *The CCL guide to leadership in action: How managers and organizations can improve the practice of leadership*. San Francisco, CA: Wiley.

Winum, P. C. (2003) Developing leadership: What is distinctive about what psychologists can offer? *Consulting Psychology Journal: Practice and Research,* 55: 41–6.

Zaccaro, S. J. (2001) *The nature of executive leadership: A conceptual and empirical analysis of success*. Washington, DC: American Psychological Association.

Zaccaro, S. J. (2002) Organizational leadership and social intelligence. In R. E. Riggio, S. E. Murphy, and F. J. Pirozollo (eds) *Multiple intelligences and leadership*. Mahwah, NJ: Lawrence Erlbaum, pp. 29–54.

Zaccaro, S. J. and Horn, Z. N. J. (2003) Leadership theory and practice: Fostering an effective symbiosis. *Leadership Quarterly*, 147: 799–806.

Zaccaro, S. J. and Klimoski, R. J. (2001) *The nature of organizational leadership*. San Francisco, CA: Jossey-Bass.

Part I

Emerging models of leadership

Chapter 2

Full range leadership

Model, research, extensions, and training

John J. Sosik

Transforming change flows not from the work of the great man who single-handedly makes history but from the collective achievement of a great people.

(James MacGregor Burns, 2003)

Adaptation has become a fact of life for most organizations. Increasingly, organizations are turning to their leadership to promote positive changes in employee work engagement and collaboration, creativity and innovation, mentoring of associates, workforce diversity, product and process quality, technology adoption, and strategy execution (Fulmer and Goldsmith, 2001). Consequently, organizational researchers and managers are confronted with a number of challenging questions about leadership behaviour that is able to inspire collective success in such initiatives. What repertoire of trainable leader behaviours is appropriate for attaining collective excellence and achievement? What effects do these behaviours have on individual, group, and organizational outcomes? How do they influence followers to meet or exceed performance expectations? What contextual factors constrain the effectiveness of these leader behaviours?

The purpose of this chapter is to answer these questions from the perspective of Bass and Avolio's (1994) Full Range Leadership (FRL) model, which highlights transformational leadership as a particularly effective means of promoting adaptive and effective collective action. The transformational leadership construct is grounded upon seminal work by Burns (1978) and Bass (1985). The FRL model represents a refinement of Bass (1985) and is the foundation of extensive training of individuals from industry, education, military, religious, and non-profit sectors and organizations around the world. My purpose here is to provide a comprehensive overview of the FRL model and a framework for extending and expanding the model in future research and training programmes on transformational leadership.

This chapter first describes the historical background leading to the development of the FRL model. I then delve into the components of the FRL model and its factor structure. Based upon a review of the extant literature, I then describe who transformational leaders are and what they do. Next, I present a conceptual framework for elaboration and extension of the FRL model to understand better the processes and outcomes associated with its component behaviours. I conclude with some practical strategies for implementing effective FRL training programmes in organizations.

THE FULL RANGE LEADERSHIP MODEL

The FRL model was developed in response to calls from both researchers and practitioners to move the leadership field ahead in meaningful and practical ways. The model is grounded in the behavioural tradition of leadership research and implicit theories of exemplary leadership of industrial and military leaders as validated in their real-world life experiences. An appreciation of the importance and content of the FRL model requires an understanding of its historical background and components.

Background

At its inception, the FRL model was 'an idea whose time had come' given the negative attitudes toward the leadership field shared by several scholars in the late 1970s, who viewed the extant research as fragmentary, dull, redundant, and uninformative. During this period of 'doom and gloom' regarding the field of leadership (Hunt, 1999), a sense of excitement was ignited in the mind of Bernard Bass, when his former student John Miller suggested that he read political scientist James McGregor Burns's (1978) new book on transformational leadership. Burn's book inspired Bass to examine transformational leadership from an industrial/organizational psychology perspective, building upon Robert House's (1977) work on charismatic leadership. Bass collaborated with colleagues including Bruce Avolio and others in the Center for Leadership Studies (CLS) at the State University of New York at Binghamton. They collected and analysed data on the initial FRL model first presented in Bass's (1985) seminal book, *Leadership and Performance Beyond Expectations.*

During the late 1980s and early 1990s, a flurry of activity emanated from the CLS. Bass and Avolio, who co-directed the CLS, teamed up to develop and revise the Multifactor Leadership Questionnaire (MLQ) as a measure of the leadership behaviours in the FRL model and outcomes of leader effectiveness and followers' extra effort and satisfaction. Since its inception, the MLQ has become the world's most widely used measure of transformational leadership in research and training settings. The revised MLQ-5X has been translated into German, Italian, Swedish, Spanish, Turkish, Portuguese, French, Norwegian, Hebrew, Arabic, Chinese, Thai, and Korean.

An emerging literature on transformational and transactional leadership measured with the MLQ (see p. 39) also began to appear during that period. A number of grants, including a Kellogg Foundation Grant for developing and evaluating transformational leadership training, were obtained and managed through the CLS. Avolio also developed and launched a new PhD programme at SUNY Binghamton, which provided training for a new generation of FRL scholars including the author. All of these activities formed the bedrock for examining the FRL model and its outcomes.

Model components

Associates of the CLS and others have studied and validated the FRL model for the last 20 years with leaders from military, industry, and non-profit sectors from all continents except Antarctica (Bass, 1998). According to the FRL model, leaders have a repertoire of leadership behaviours that they can display as shown in Figure 2.1. Leaders display these behaviours in various *frequencies* depending on their mental model of leadership, personality, and the situation. They can avoid leadership and be passive. They can use leadership to correct things as required. They can actively exchange rewards for followers' performance. They also can actively promote changes in people, processes, groups, and organizations (Bass and Avolio, 1994).

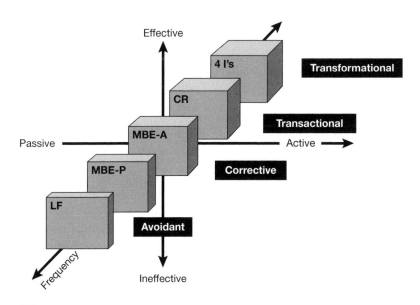

Figure 2.1 *Full range leadership model (Bass and Avolio, 1994).*

Meta-analytic studies of the FRL model (see, for example, Lowe, Kroeck, and Sivasubramaniam, 1996) indicate that leadership that is passive is generally ineffective, and leadership that is active is generally effective. The most effective leaders display the active forms of leadership behaviour more frequently than they display the passive forms of leadership behaviour. Descriptions of the nine specific leadership behavioural factors in the FRL model appear in Table 2.1.

Laissez-faire

The most passive and ineffective leadership behaviour is *laissez-faire* (LF) leadership, where the leader avoids getting involved, making decisions, and dealing in chronic problems. The leader is absent when needed, delays and fails to follow up on tasks. This leader behaviour generally results in very low levels of follower performance, motivation, and satisfaction. Followers may become disengaged in their work, or disillusioned with the leader who is perceived to be 'missing in action.' If followers are self-motivated professionals, they may substitute for the lack of their superior's leadership by usurping the leader's role. Former CEOs William Agee of Morrison Knudson, James Robinson of American Express, and John Sculley of Apple Computer exhibited LF behaviour that resulted in either their being forced out, seeing their company taken over, and/or seeing their company go astray (Charan and Colvin, 1999).

Transactional management-by-exception

A somewhat more effective behaviour is *passive management-by-exception* (MBE-P) leadership. With MBE-P, the leader intervenes only if standards are not met, waits for things to go wrong before taking action, and believes 'if it ain't broke, don't fix it.' MBE-P behaviour is passive in the sense that it focuses on mistakes *after* they occur and relies on patching problems instead of preventing them. Followers typically respond by maintaining the status quo. For example, information technology systems managers may rely on MBE-P leadership in their systems maintenance or implementation tasks where keeping systems in steady state is imperative.

A more active and effective behaviour is *active management-by-exception* (MBE-A) leadership, where the leader closely monitors work performance for errors, focuses attention on mistakes, complaints, failures, deviations, infractions, and arranges to know if and when things go wrong. The problem with MBE behaviours is that they may promote fear and mistrust in followers, and a focus on maintaining the status quo rather than innovation. In a sense, followers are treated as children who need to be monitored because they are assumed to be at a lower stage of development than the leader. For example, the micro-managing executive who delves into the minutiae of the daily tasks of followers, searching for what's done wrong, not what's done right, displays MBE-A behaviour. Albeit, this leader behaviour may be

Table 2.1 Behaviours in the full range leadership model (Bass and Avolio, 1990)

Behaviour	Definition	Sample MLQ-5X item	Proposed followers' reactions
Transformational leadership			
Inspirational motivation	Articulating a compelling and evocative vision.	Talks optimistically about the future.	Followers are willing to exert extra effort.
Idealized influence (behaviour)	Role modelling high ethical and performance standards.	Considers the moral and ethical consequences of decisions.	Followers desire to achieve to show support for the leader.
Idealized influence (attribute)	Follower's reflecting trust and respect to leader.	Instils pride in you for being associated with him/her.	Followers are willing to trust and emulate the leader.
Intellectual stimulation	Questioning the status quo and continuously innovating.	Re-examines critical assumptions to questions whether they are appropriate.	Followers are willing to think. Followers work toward creativity and innovation.
Individualized consideration	Energizing people to develop and achieve their full potential/performance.	Spends time teaching and coaching.	Followers are willing to develop and appreciate diversity.
Transactional leadership			
Contingent reward (active)	Developing well-defined roles and expectations to achieve desired performance outcomes.	Provides assistance in exchange for your efforts.	Followers achieve expected performance. Followers focus on extrinsic rewards (instead of processes).
Management-by-exception	Searching for what's done wrong, not what's done right.	Focuses attention on irregularities, mistakes, exceptions, and deviations from standards.	Followers avoid risk taking and initiation. Followers' creativity is inhibited.
Management-by-exception (passive)	Focusing on mistakes after they occur and patching problems.	Shows that he/she is a firm believer in 'If it ain't broke, don't fix it.'	Followers maintain the status quo.
Non-leadership			
Laissez-faire	Avoidance of leadership; abdication of responsibility.	Avoids making decisions.	Followers may become disengaged in their work or usurp leader's role.

appropriate for some situations that require command and control approaches to leadership, such as auditing or nuclear power safety regulation.

Transactional contingent reward

An effective and active leadership behaviour is *transactional contingent reward* (CR) leadership where the leader uses goal setting and contingent rewards to influence followers. CR leader behaviour clarifies followers' expectations, discusses specifically expected outcomes and performance targets, and uses rewards to reinforce the positive performance of followers. As a result followers perform to levels specified by the leader. However, such extrinsic motivation can make followers feel manipulated and does little to develop their knowledge, skills and abilities or leadership potential. Former US presidents Lyndon Johnson and Dwight D. Eisenhower have been described as transactional leaders who excelled at cutting deals with their colleagues to move their political agendas forward (Neustadt, 1990).

4Is of transformational leadership

Transformational leadership does not replace transactional leadership. Rather, transformational leadership augments the effectiveness of transactional leadership (e.g. Bass, 1985; Seltzer and Bass, 1990). The most effective leaders add the 4Is of transformational leadership to transactional leadership in order to get their followers to perform *beyond* expectations. Transformational leaders use *inspirational motivation* (IM) to energize their followers to do more than is expected. IM involves speaking optimistically and enthusiastically, articulating an inspiring or evocate vision, expressing confidence, and championing teamwork and high standards of performance. For example, Steve Jobs inspired his people to attain high levels of success, empowered them to feel stronger, more confident and competent, and more in control of their destinies after his return to Apple Computer as CEO in the late 1990s.

Transformational leaders also display *idealized influence* (II-B) or pro-social charismatic behaviours to role model organizational values such as high levels of ethical and performance standards. Such behaviour elicits *attributions of idealized influence* (II-A) or charisma from followers who perceive the leader as trustworthy and worthy of respect and emulation. As a result, followers are willing to show support for the leader's vision. For example, the Virgin Group's CEO Richard Branson exemplifies an idealized leader who holds high expectations of performance and ethical behaviour for his associates.

Transformational leaders use *intellectual stimulation* (IS) to get followers and constituents to re-examine assumptions, seek different perspectives, look at problems in new ways, and encourage non-traditional thinking and re-thinking to break through inappropriate or outdated business models. Such leader behaviour encourages followers to be willing to think for themselves, re-engineer work processes, and be more creative. For example, Hewlett Packard CEO Carly Fiorina is known for her work with technology and former corporate makeovers. By articulating her vision to 'Invent', Fiorina has transformed Hewlett Packard from a slow-moving engineering company to an information technology champion.

Transformational leaders also use *individualized consideration* (IC) with their followers and customers to recognize their unique potential to develop into leaders themselves. They spend time listening, teaching, and coaching followers. They treat others as individuals with different needs, abilities and aspirations, and get them to appreciate the benefits of diversity. They also help others to develop their knowledge, skills, and abilities. As a result, followers begin to value personal learning and development and may appreciate the breadth of knowledge, skills, and abilities associated with collaborating within a diverse team. For example, Unisys CEO Larry Weinbach has promoted employee development with former mentoring programmes and Unisys University, which offers a wide variety of technical, leadership, team building, and development courses for Unisys employees.

To summarize, research on the FRL model indicates that leaders who spend more time displaying the more active transformational and transactional CR behaviours and less time displaying the more passive leadership behaviours are associated with the highest levels of individual, group and organizational effectiveness and satisfaction.

MLQ factor structure

A large amount of research attention has been given to the factor structure representing the leadership behaviours in the FRL model as measured by the MLQ. Previous versions of the MLQ have been criticized for their failure to generate empirically the factor structure (eight behaviours and one attribute) proposed by Bass and Avolio (1997) to underlie transformational leadership (Tejeda, Scandura, and Pillai, 2001; Yukl, 2002). However, transactional and recent research (e.g. Antonakis, Avolio, and Sivasubramaniam, 2003; Garman, Davis-Lenane, and Corrigan, 2003) has shown the revised MLQ-5X to be a psychometrically sound instrument in terms of measuring the constructs constituting what Bass and Avolio refer to as a full range of leadership behaviours.

Bycio, Hackett, and Allen (1995) found support for a two-factor structure comprised of active (IM, II, IC, IS, CR) versus passive (MBE-P) leadership in a sample of 1,376 registered nurses. Bycio and his colleagues used an old version of the MLQ and failed to consider MBE-A and LF items in their analysis. Using a sample of 1,389 MLQ-5X ratings of 695 international banking branch managers, Carless (1998a) found that transformational leadership represented a single higher order construct comprised of II-A, IC, and IS. Carless did not include ratings of IM and II-B in her study.

In response to these studies, Avolio, Bass, and Jung (1999) analysed a total of 3,786 respondents from 14 independent samples and found support for a six-factor structure: (1) a charismatic leadership factor comprised of IM, II-A and II-B; (2) IS; (3) IC; (4) CR; (5) MBE-A; and (6) MBE-P and LF. Vandeberghe, Stordeur, and D'hoore's (2002) study using a sample of Belgium nurses (N = 1,059) also found support for this six-factor solution. However, because of high interscale correlations and a lack of discriminant validity with criterion variables, Vandeberghe, Stordeur, and D'hoore suggested that the 4Is of transformational leadership and CR leadership could be combined into a higher-order Active Leadership factor.

Yammarino, Spangler, and Bass (1993) found support for a five-factor model in a sample of 186 US Naval officers using an older version of the MLQ. The factors were (1) II and IM; (2) contingent promises, contingent rewards, and IC; (3) MBE-A; (4) MBE-P; and (5) LF. The first factor represents charismatic/transformational leadership while the second represents transactional leadership. IS was not included in the study.

Tejeda, Scandura, and Pillai (2001) used four independent US business firm samples to test the factor structure of an initial version of the MLQ-5X. The data failed to support the hypothesized structure of the MLQ-5X. The authors reduced the number of items in the MLQ-5X to 27 and found support for the nine-factor model proposed by Bass and Avolio (1997). However, there were several problematic aspects of the data analysis performed by Tejeda, Scandura, and Pillai (see Antonakis, Avolio, and Sivasubramaniam, 2003, p. 262 for details of this criticism).

In the most comprehensive analysis of the MLQ's factor structure, Antonakis, Avolio, and Sivasubramaniam (2003) assessed the factor structure of the MLQ-5X using a sample of 6,525 raters of 18 independently gathered samples controlling for contextual factors of environmental risk, leader–follower gender and leader hierarchical level. Results supported the nine-factor FRL model proposed by Bass and Avolio (1997). Garman, Davis-Lenane, and Corrigan's (2003) study of 236 leaders from 54 mental health teams using the MLQ-8Y found support for an eight-factor model as originally proposed by Bass (1985).

Despite many challenges to the validity of its factor structure, the FRL model appears to be holding its own. Overall, the preponderance of valid evidence to date suggests that the factor structure underlying the FRL model as measured by the MLQ-5X is empirically supportable. As suggested by Antonakis, Avolio, and Sivasubramaniam (2003), the conflicting results reported in prior research on the FRL model may be a function of mixing organizational types and environmental conditions, gender composition of the leader–follower dyad, and hierarchical level. Therefore, these contextual variables need to be modelled into theoretical frameworks for FRL and controlled for in empirical studies. The factor structure also may be more complex than originally proposed given the findings of several studies indicating that some of the original transformational factors may be

40

embedded within higher-order factors. Accordingly, more research is needed before any firm conclusions may be drawn.

RESEARCH ON FULL RANGE LEADERSHIP

The 4Is of transformational leadership represent the most effective behaviours in the FRL model for promoting individual, group, and organizational development. Consequently, most research to date has focused on the antecedents and consequences of transformational leadership and provides us with a good base of knowledge regarding who transformational leaders are and what they do.

Who are transformational leaders?

To understand which leaders are most likely to be perceived as transformational requires an assessment of the leader's traits, life experiences, and gender. *Traits*, such as personality, physique, or cognitive style, represent relatively enduring characteristics that describe the way an individual reacts and interacts with others. *Life experiences* such as parents' behaviour, schooling, personal activities, or critical events also may shape a leader's behaviour. *Gender differences* represent personal attributes that differentiate men from women (Avolio, 1999).

Traits

Bass's (1998) review of relevant empirical studies linked the following traits to transformational leaders: intelligence, ascendancy, optimism, humour, need for change, behavioural coping, nurturance, internal locus of control, self-acceptance, extraversion, hardiness, and physical fitness. Judge and Bono (2000) reported similar results indicating that leader extraversion, agreeableness, and openness to experience were positively associated with the transformational leadership of community leaders. Ross and Offerman (1997) found that high scores on transformational leadership of US Air Force officers were associated with higher levels of pragmatism, nurturance, and feminine attributes and lower levels of criticalness and aggression. Taken together, these results suggest that positive, adaptive, developmental, and people-oriented traits form a distinct personality pattern that supports transformational leadership's social influence process.

Based on his review of relevant empirical research, Bass (2002) proposed that social, emotional, and cognitive intelligences present personal traits that contribute to the display of transformational leadership. *Social intelligence* represents the ability to adapt to social situations. Preliminary evidence of the link between social intelligence and transformational leadership is provided by Sosik, Potosky, and Jung (2002) who reported a positive predictive relationship between

41

leader self-monitoring and follower ratings of transformational leadership in a sample of 64 information technology managers. Aspects of social intelligence may provide transformational leaders with the ability to engage in impression management and image building required to influence followers to perform beyond the call of duty (Bass, 1985).

Emotional intelligence

Emotional intelligence represents the awareness and ability to control one's emotions as well as understanding the emotions of others (Goleman, 1995). In support of Bass's (2002) proposition, Sosik and Megerian (1999) reported significant positive relationships between followers' ratings of transformational leadership and leaders' interpersonal control, and leaders' self-ratings of transformational leadership and leaders' purpose-in-life, personal efficacy, interpersonal control and, social self-confidence (aspects of emotional intelligence identified by Goleman, 1995) in an information technology setting. Mandell and Pherwani (2003) reported a positive predictive relationship between emotional intelligence as measured by the EQ-i (Bar-On, 1996) and transformational leadership. Social and emotional intelligence appear to be important to a transformational leader's ability to inspire and build developmental relationships with followers.

Transformational leaders also possess a cognitive intelligence style based on more sensing, less thinking than feeling, and less superstitious thinking than transactional leaders. Psychological types theory suggests that individuals who process information via feelings are more skilled at interpersonal relations (Bass, 1998; Roush and Atwater, 1992). Building relationships is a core activity of transformational leaders (Avolio, 1999; Sosik, et al., 2004).

In a study of the 2000 US presidential vote, perceptions of candidate proactivity, empathy, and need for achievement were shown to be related to transformational leadership (Pillai, Williams, Lowe, et al., 2003). With political or non-political leaders, the role of a leader's values, ethics, and character has been proposed to be important for shaping transformational leadership behaviour (Bass and Steidlmeier, 1999; Burns, 2003). In a scenario-based study of the role of ethical preferences of Indian managers, Banerji and Krishnan (2000) found ratings of IM to be negatively related to a manager's preference for bribery and favouritism, and ratings of IS to be negatively related to a manager's preference for bribery. These initial results can guide future work that may link additional FRL behaviours to leaders' ethical preferences and values.

Unfortunately, many leaders are neither appropriately centred in their ethical preferences nor entirely transparent in their behaviour. In a study of 218 managers from high-tech companies, Sosik (2005) found the relationship between self-enhancement values and ratings of IM, II-A, and II-B to be significantly more positive for high performing managers than low performing managers. Aided by 'dog-eat-dog' cultures and strong self-monitoring and impression management skills, some leaders appear to display transformational behaviours, but in reality are *pseudo-transformational* or *inauthentic* transformational leaders. Leaders such as Jeff Skilling of Enron or Bernie Ebbers of Worldcom cater to their own self-interests. These leaders are proposed to be self-centred, self-aggrandizing, exploitative, and power-oriented. They may believe in distorted utilitarian or warped moral principles and engage in deception, sophistry, and pretence. In contrast, authentic transformational leaders are proposed to make decisions at a higher stage of moral development and to be guided by transcendence, agency, trust, striving for congruence in values with followers, and cooperative action (Bass and Steidlmeier, 1999; Kuhnert and Lewis, 1987).

Life experiences

The proverbial question during FRL training classes is '*Are leaders born or made?*' The answer to this question is that whereas traits and genetics play some part in predetermining one's leadership potential, much of leadership is shaped by life experiences, self-determination, and the choices we make in establishing the next chapter in our lives. Leadership can and should be viewed as a lifespan developmental process, reflected in continuous personal improvement (Avolio, 1999).

Lifespan perspectives to understanding FRL development are grounded in the psychodynamic (Zaleznik, 1977) and developmental perspectives of leadership (Avolio and Gibbons, 1988; Kuhnert and Lewis, 1987). Zaleznik (1977) argued that certain leaders move to higher stages of personal awareness and ability by overcoming life crises or events or by solving inner conflicts stemming from critical events. They are the *twice-born leaders* whose life stream of events is relatively turbulent, but who project their 'victory over the self' to the outside world to draw others to them. Their internal sense of guidance is highlighted by Kuhnert and Lewis (1987) who proposed that transformational leaders are at higher stages of moral development than other leaders. Rather than basing their decisions on avoiding punishments or seeking rewards, or conformity to peer pressure, they are guided by their values, beliefs, and internal standards, which are refined over the lifespan.

One lifespan approach to understanding the development of transformational leaders is provided by Avolio and Gibbons (1988). These authors argue that leader development is a function of the reciprocal relationships between innate individual differences and personal characteristics (e.g. emotional intelligence), experiences, events and the meaning drawn from them (e.g. implicit theories of leadership), developmental outcomes (e.g. learning), and transformational leadership behaviour. This system of interrelations is embedded within the critical positive and negative incidents of an individual's life, which are embedded within a historical context (e.g. the Great Depression, the 1960s, September 11, 2001).

According to Avolio and Gibbons (1988), transformational leaders are likely to come from families with parents predisposed to transformational leadership, who hold high expectations and high standards of performance, and hold them responsible for their actions. They are likely to be 'twice-born,' experiencing difficult, but not overwhelming, personal challenges. They are likely to face and deal well with conflict and disappointment. Their previous leadership experiences are likely to be many and varied and serve to develop an evolving sense of personal efficacy toward their leadership. Transformational leaders also are likely to have been mentored by many influential people on a personalized basis. They also are likely to have attended leadership workshops and events and persisted in personal development activities. Bass (2004) argued that transformational leaders receive strong nurturing from their mothers who substitute for fathers who are often absent. For example, Bill Clinton's close relationship with his mother, his substitution for his absent father in caring for his siblings, and his childhood meeting with John F. Kennedy represent key development elements in his leadership development (Clinton, 2004).

An initial empirical test of propositions set forth above regarding life events associated with transformational is provided by Avolio (1994), who reported several interesting results. Transformational leaders described themselves as more satisfied with life, better performers in high school and college, enjoyed school more and received recognition for their achievements, and viewed their prior work experiences as more positive. Leaders rated by followers as transformational had parents who showed interest in their development, displayed high moral standards of behaviour, and provided strong, supportive homes.

Bass (1998) reported the results of an intuitive-empirical analysis of MLQ and biodata of 167 community leaders. Leaders rated above the median on charisma (IM and II) experienced distinct parental upbringing, school-age experiences, and early adult life events. Specifically, they had 'good' mothers *and* fathers, strict, but fair upbringing, and a stable homestead. They were almost always the leader of the 'gang' or clique. They were usually picked near first for team games, were popular and active in high school, and liked teachers who were hard graders. They also were bothered by people's lack of initiative, were active in clubs and communities, accomplished high goals in their work, and engaged in religious activity a few hours a week. Taken together, these results may provide important practical implications for parental counselling given that parenting may be the most important transformational leadership role an individual assumes over the lifespan.

Gender differences

When it comes to displaying the more active and effective behaviours in the FRL model, women may have an advantage over men. While some empirical research indicates few gender differences in leader and manager behaviour (e.g. Powell

1990), other research, including two meta-analyses (Eagly and Crowley, 1986; Eagly, Johanneson-Schmidt, and van Engen, 2003) and several individual studies (e.g. Bass, Avolio, and Atwater, 1996; Carless, 1998b; Gibson, 1995) indicate that women are perceived as more participative, socially interactive, and development-oriented than men.

Eagly and her colleagues' (2003) meta-analysis revealed that female leaders were more transformational than male leaders and also engaged in more transactional CR behaviour. Male leaders were more likely to display MBE-A, MBE-P, and LF behaviour. Along the same lines, Carless (1998b) found that superiors and managers from a large Australian bank rated female managers as more transformational than male managers. In their study of 76 top executives of American and Israeli high-tech organizations, Sosik *et al.* (2004) found male executives to be rated higher on MBE-P and LF behaviour than female executives.

What theoretical explanations account for these findings? To answer this question, Eagly, Johanneson-Schmidt, and van Engen (2003) cited the *social role theory* approach to leadership, which proposes that 'leaders occupy roles defined by their specific position in a hierarchy and simultaneously function under the constraints of their gender roles' (p. 572). Reviews of the gender-role literature (e.g. Eagly and Crowley, 1986) indicate that on average *men* are characterized as generally being task-oriented, results-driven, competitive, rational, strategic, and unemotional. Men have been stereotypically associated with *agentic* behaviour aimed at being independent, masterful, assertive, and instrumentally competent. In contrast, *women* are characterized as generally being relationship-oriented, nurturing, cooperative, intuitive/rational, empathic, and emotionally expressive. Women have been stereotypically associated with *communal* behaviour aimed at being friendly, unselfish, concerned with others, and expressive. Mandell and Pherwani (2003) reported that female managers were associated with higher emotional intelligence scores than male managers. Gibson (1995) studied 209 managers in Norway, Sweden, Australia, and the US and found female managers to exhibit more socially interactive behaviour than male managers across all countries.

The advantages of women over men in displaying a more effective repertoire of FRL behaviour may be based on three reasons identified by Eagly, Johanneson-Schmidt, and van Engen (2003). First, the combination of transformational and CR behaviour allows women to resolve some of the incongruities between leadership roles and the female gender role. Display of transformational leadership may allow women to avoid overly masculine impressions that can be produced by using traditional command and control or agentic approaches to leadership. Second, the female gender role influences leadership behaviour via spillover and internalization of gender-specific norms. Conceptual overlaps between stereotypical female roles (e.g. nurturance, networking, team building) and transformational leadership (e.g. IC, IM) may make transformational behaviour 'more natural' for women than for men. Third, the glass ceiling and its resultant double standard produces more highly motivated and effective female than male leaders. It may be that women have to work harder to gain acceptance in traditionally male-dominated organizations. Such extra effort on the part of female leaders may result in higher ratings of transformational leadership, despite a reluctance to give women power over others at work.

Future research may provide empirical support for these and other explanations of gender differences in the display of behaviours in the FRL model. Whatever reasons emerge, it appears that women have the ability to perform very well in contemporary organizations given that their success depends on teaming, professional and strategic networking, and providing excellent products, services, and experiences (Sosik *et al.*, 2004). It is also important to note that the behavioural differences between male and female leaders in Eagly, Johanneson-Schmidt, and van Engen's (2003) meta-analysis were small. Moreover, gender is only one of many individual differences that influence leader behaviour. Accordingly, researchers and trainers should take into account the wide variety of personal attributes that may explain FRL behaviour. We need to pay attention not only to who transformational leaders are, but also to what they do to elevate their followers' motivation and performance.

What do transformational leaders do?

Transformational leaders promote higher-order changes in people, work groups, organizations, and entire social and political systems. Burns highlighted the meaning and significance of the type of change transformational leaders initiate and support:

> But to transform something cuts much more profoundly. It is to cause a metamorphosis in form or structure, a change in the very condition or nature of a thing, a change into another substance, a radical change on outward form or inner character, as when a frog is changed into a prince or a carriage maker into an auto factory. It is change of this breadth and depth that is fostered by transforming leadership.
>
> (Burns, 2003, p. 24)

For people, transformation represents alterations of attitudes, beliefs, values, and needs. Such changes may result in higher levels of personal, professional, and moral development. For work groups, transformation means significant shifts in levels of cohesion, trust, efficacy beliefs, productivity, and creativity. For organizations, transformation means profound changes in work processes, organizational structures and culture, strategic initiatives, and relationships with customers, suppliers, and business partners. For broader social and political systems, transformation means revolutions that replace one power structure with another.

Changing people

Transformational leaders produce changes in followers by influencing their beliefs, values, and attitudes and arousing their motives. Followers enter into dyadic relationships with leaders with pre-established 'world-views' based on their personal attributes and life experiences. By displaying IS, transformational leaders get followers to view concepts and ideas from different perspectives that they may have not previously considered. By displaying IM, transformational leaders get followers to put the interests of the group or organization ahead of their personal agendas. Such sacrifices are re-framed as being in the best interest of the collective and raise the follower's level of moral development to consider the systemic implications of their actions. Empirical evidence for such changes in followers' behaviour is provided by links between transformational leadership and followers' extra effort and performance (e.g. Lowe, Kroeck, and Sivasubramaniam, 1996) and organizational citizenship behaviour (OCB; Pillai, Schriesheim, and Williams, 1999; Podsakoff, MacKenzie, and Bommer, 1990).

One particularly important follower belief that has been theoretically and empirically linked to transformational leadership is *self-efficacy,* the conviction that one can successfully perform a task. Social cognitive theory (Bandura, 1986) proposes that self-efficacy beliefs can be elevated through the influence of significant others (e.g. leaders). Elevating followers' self-efficacy levels is an important leader role because high levels of self-efficacy promote high levels of individual performance. In support of this idea, positive correlations between transformational leadership ratings and followers' level of self-efficacy have been demonstrated in several studies (e.g. Kark, Shamir, and Chen, 2003; Schyns, 2001). The associations between transformational leadership and self-efficacy appear to be particularly positive and strong when the task demands are challenging and complex. With these tasks, transformational leadership appears to provide meaning and importance to tasks and may motivate persistence and performance beyond expectations in public administration contexts (Felfe and Schyns, 2001).

Changing the way followers view their work may be an important means of promoting higher levels of follower engagement and satisfaction. In a study of 736 multi-level marketing organizational members, Sparks and Schenk (2001) demonstrated that transformational leadership changes followers by encouraging them to see higher purposes in their work. Results of this study suggest that belief in the high purpose in one's work is a mechanism through which transformational leadership achieves its positive outcomes on cohesion, satisfaction, effort, and performance. These results are also consistent with results reported by Sosik and Dworakivsky (1998) indicating that technology managers' strong purpose-in-life predicted ratings of IM, II-A, and II-B. Transformational leadership behaviour, particularly IM, also can promote intrinsically motivated follower creativity (Shin and Zhou, 2003; Sosik, Kahai, and Avolio, 1999).

Changing followers' attitudes, values, and ideas about justice represents an additional influence that transformational leaders have on followers in motivating them to perform beyond expectations. Pillai, Schriesheim, and Williams's (1999) results of a two-sample study supported the indirect effect of transformational leadership on followers' OCB through procedural justice and trust. In a study of 194 students working on a brainstorming task, Jung and Avolio (2000) found transformational leadership to have both direct and indirect effects on performance mediated through followers' trust in the leader and value congruence. By getting followers to trust others, transformational leaders appear to shape more positive attitudes in followers and may raise their level of moral development.

Changing work groups

Work groups and teams have become the basic building blocks for organizational leaders to structure the way work is completed. The advent of virtual teams, where members are separated from each other and their leader by physical distance, time zones, and culture, provides additional challenges for leaders (Avolio, Kahai, and Dodge, 2001). Getting group members to engage in positive rather than dysfunctional group dynamics is an important task for contemporary leaders. Evidence suggests that transformational leadership may be effective in attaining these goals.

The capacity of transformational leadership to build empowered and effective work groups has been demonstrated in several studies. In a series of studies of computer-mediated work groups, transformational leadership has been linked with higher levels of group potency (Sosik, Avolio, and Kahai, 1997), more questioning and supportive comments (Sosik, 1997), and more creative outcomes in terms of elaboration and originality (Sosik, Kahai, and Avolio, 1998) versus transactional leadership. Transformational leadership is particularly effective in fostering supportive comments among group members, group potency, and satisfaction with the task in anonymous brainstorming conditions (Kahai, Sosik, and Avolio, 2003). Anonymous computer-based interactions make group members feel less self-conscious and less differentiated from other group members. These deindividuating effects appear to provide a favourable social condition that is consistent with transformational leadership's emphasis on collective action.

Similar effects are found in studies of traditional face-to-face groups. For example, in study of 47 Korean work groups, Jung and Sosik (2002) found transformational leadership to predict group cohesiveness and empowerment, which predicted subsequent collective efficacy (i.e. group members' shared perceptions about how capable they are in completing a task; Bandura, 1986) and performance. These results provide empirical support for previous theoretical arguments highlighting the role of transformational leadership in promoting positive group processes and outcomes (e.g. Bass, 1985; Burns, 2003).

How does transformational leadership influence group processes and outcomes? A theoretical consideration of the 4Is provides one possible explanation. Although transformational leaders may be directive in dealing with their followers, they often seek followers' participation in group work by displaying the 4Is (Bass, 1998). Transformational leaders get followers to appreciate and learn from the broad skill sets and experiences of diverse groups (IC). They highlight the importance of cooperation in performing collective tasks (IM). They role model and talk about the importance of making sacrifices for the good of the group (II-B). They also get group members to view problems from different perspectives, taking into consideration a broader array of constituents (IS). Such behaviours create a group environment where followers feel confident in their groups, become empowered, and work to achieve high levels of performance (Sosik, Avolio, and Kahai, 1997).

An interesting alternative explanation of what happens to group members influenced by transformational leadership is provided by Avolio (1999). His perspective suggests that value congruence and trust shared among team members elevates the entire leadership system from the individual level to the group or team level of analysis. In other words, members of a cohesive and trusting group who identify with the vision and values of a transformational leader begin to share leadership over time. Here we see a shift from 'leadership of the team' (by the formal leader) to 'leadership by the team' (shared leadership responsibilities and roles among team members who become empowered to lead). *Shared leadership* means that the team, as a whole, shares and participates fully in the leadership tasks of the team. If empowered team members have the authority, self-efficacy, and knowledge of the leadership tasks, they can accomplish much of the leadership formerly delegated to the formal leader.

Avolio's (1999) notion of shared leadership is interesting in the sense that it harkens back to Burns's (1978) original idea of leaders using collective action to transform followers into higher moral stage leaders themselves. The emergence and maintenance of shared leadership warrants future longitudinal work to test this idea using Within and Between Analysis (WABA; Dansereau, Alutto, and Yammarino, 1984) or alternative multi-level data analytic tools.

Changing organizations

Executives of many of the world's top corporations are often hired to bring about positive change in cultures, strategies, work structures, and financial performance. Likewise, coaches of college and professional sports teams are held to similar expectations by fans and team owners. When profound changes are needed in these organizations, transformational leadership appears to be most appropriate.

Empirical research indicates that transformational leadership is effective in promoting positive organizational changes in terms of total quality management programme implementation (Sosik and Dionne, 1997), safety-conscious climates

49

(Barling, Loughlin, and Kelloway, 2002), long-term financial performance of German banks (Geyer and Steyrer, 1998), unit performance of Canadian banks (Avolio, Howell, and Sosik, 1999; Howell and Avolio, 1993), Army unit perform-ance (Bass et al., 2003; Kane and Tremble, 2000), and financial accounting indices in a business simulation (Avolio, Waldman, and Einstein, 1988).

Perhaps the most essential change at the organizational level is a shift in organ-izational culture, where entire groups of organizational members begin to realign their shared values, beliefs, and practices. Research on cultural changes in organ-izations is particularly burdensome given the logistical and voluminous longitu-dinal data collection requirements. For that reason, little research has examined the role of FRL behaviours in shaping or changing organizational cultures. However, measures of organizational culture linked to the FRL model are avail-able and some preliminary assessment of this topic has been undertaken.

Bass and Avolio (1993) developed and validated a survey called the *Organ-izational Description Questionnaire* (ODQ). This 28-item survey instrument measures different types of organizational cultures. The ODQ generates nine cultural profiles of an organization based on how much it is transformational or transactional: (1) Predominantly 4Is; (2) Moderated 4Is; (3) High-Contrast; (4) Loosely Guided; (5) Coasting; (6) Predominately Bureaucratic; (7) Moderated Bureaucratic; (8) Pedestrian; and (9) Garbage Can. A detailed description on each of these ODQ cultural types can be found in Bass and Avolio (1990).

Sosik et al. (2004) used the ODQ to survey three direct reports of the execu-tives in their sample. Three different direct reports rated the executive's leader-ship using the MLQ-5X. Sosik and his colleagues compared the mean frequencies of leadership behaviours displayed by these executives across the ODQ cultural profiles that emerged from their sample. Executives in organizations with Predominately Bureaucratic cultures displayed less IM than executives in organ-izations with Moderated Bureaucratic, Coasting, Pedestrian, Predominately 4Is, and Moderated 4Is cultures. Executives in organizations with Coasting cultures displayed less IM than executives in organizations with Moderated 4Is cultures. Similar patterns or results were observed for II-A, II-B, IS, and IC. Taken together, these preliminary results suggest that the Moderated 4Is culture may represent an effective context for dealing with the turbulence that characterizes high-technology environments requiring continuous and accelerated change.

Changing political and social systems

History is replete with examples of leaders who have introduced radical change to political and social systems. Political leaders, such as George Washington and the framers of the US constitution, Franklin Delano Roosevelt, Vladimir Lenin, Adolf Hitler, Nelson Mandela, and Mikhail Gorbachev, have introduced new political paradigms and structures to their nations. Social and religious leaders, such as Abraham, Moses, Jesus, Muhammad, Buddha, Krishna, Martin Luther King Jr, and Susan B. Anthony, have shaped the values of people through the establishment of new thoughts and movements. These examples represent case studies that are primarily the domain of political and sociological discourses and analyses (e.g. Burns, 1977, 2003; Weber, 1947). However, they afford rich opportunities for leadership researchers to use methods such as psycho-historical assessment to examine the lives of the great leaders of history (see Gardner and Cleavenger, 1998, for details).

FULL RANGE LEADERSHIP: A CONCEPTUAL FRAMEWORK

To assist further understanding of and research on the FRL model, I present a conceptual model that allows researchers to develop and test hypotheses regarding the antecedents, processes, and outcomes of transactional and transformational leadership. The model, shown in Figure 2.2, is based on research reviewed above and other relevant work described below. It proposes that leader and follower personal attributes influence the composition of the leader/follower dyad, each of which influence the leadership behaviour displayed (perceived) by the leader (follower). These antecedents also moderate the associations between leadership behaviour, follower influence processes and outcomes. Leadership behaviours are proposed to impact follower influence processes that affect individual, group, and organizational outcomes. Finally, the linkages between antecedents, leadership behaviour, follower influence processes and outcomes are moderated by organizational context variables.

Leader/follower antecedents

According to FRL theory, leaders take into consideration the developmental stage of followers and their unique personal attributes to determine the appropriate leadership behaviour to display (Avolio, 1999). As noted above, the leader's own personal attributes also influence his/her behaviour.

Leader personal attributes

Besides personality traits, life experiences and gender, a leader's age, self-actualization, hierarchical level, motives, psychological state and needs may influence the dynamics of the leader/follower dyad and the leader's display of behaviour in the FRL model (Bass, 1998). For example, self-actualized managers were rated higher on IM and II-B (Jung and Sosik, in press). Kane and Tremble (2000) found

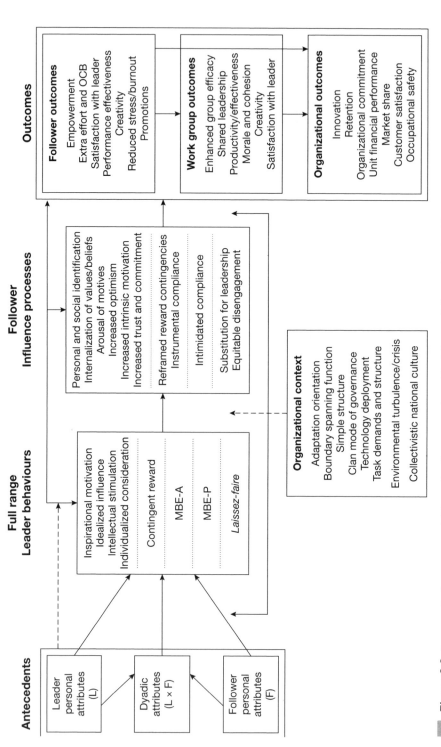

Figure 2.2 *A conceptual process model for extending research and training on full range leadership.*

that higher ranking US Army officers were perceived as more transformational and less passive than lower ranking officers.

Follower personal attributes

Most of the empirical research on FRL has been leader-centric, ignoring the characteristics of followers. Because followers represent an important part of the leader–follower relationship, the same set of characteristics associated with leaders should be considered for followers and should influence dyadic attributes and leader behaviour. In one of the few follower-centric studies of transformational leadership, Dvir and Shamir (2003) reported that followers' initial developmental level (self-actualization needs, internalization of organization's moral values, collectivistic orientation, critical-independent approach, active engagement in tasks, and self-efficacy) positively predicted transformational leadership among indirect followers. These relationships were negative for direct followers. Thus, social distance between leaders and followers appears to be a key moderating aspect of the leader/follower dyad.

Leader/follower dyad attributes

The 'chemistry' or degree of bonding between members of the leader/follower dyad may influence the type and degree of leadership behaviour displayed. Whereas some research suggests that leader behaviours are a function of individual differences (e.g. Yammarino and Dubinsky, 1994), other research suggests that dyadic bonding occurs based upon the degree of perceived similarity or mutual attraction between members in the dyad. Sosik, Godshalk, and Yammarino (2004) reported that mentors and protégés who shared similarly high levels of learning goal orientation both provided high ratings of the mentor's transformational leadership behaviour. The relationships between learning goal orientation, transformational leadership, and expected career balance were based upon differences between dyads. Yammarino *et al.* (1997) found that female managers formed unique dyadic relationships with each subordinate that was independent of their group membership. These results suggest that researchers and trainers should pay greater attention to the composition of the leader/follower dyad (e.g. gender, congruence of personal attributes and values) and its influence on leadership behaviour, processes, and outcomes.

Leader behaviours

Do the behaviours shown in Figure 2.2 represent *all* of the active and passive behaviours used by transformational and transactional leaders? What behaviour is missing or needs to be consolidated into a more parsimonious collection? Such questions of the completeness of the leadership behaviours in the FRL model have been raised (Cox, Pearce, and Sims, 2003; Yukl, 2002). Noting contemporary requirements for shared leadership in team-based work contexts, Cox, Pearce, and Sims (2003) argued that the behavioural focus of leadership development should be expanded to include directive and empowering leadership. Bass (1998) presented examples of how transformational leaders can be both directive and empowering (i.e. participative). While displaying IC, for example, a leader might inquire of followers what they can do to support the development of each other (participative), or personally promise to provide developmental support (directive).

Determining whether the FRL model needs to be expanded to include more behaviours is a fertile area for future research. The manifestation of shared leadership through empowering leadership proposed by Cox, Pearce, and Sims (2003) actually may represent Avolio's (1999) idea of a group-level shared leadership construct. Determining whether the FRL model is actually 'full' or simply one possible manifestation as suggested by Avolio (1999) should be assessed using multi-level data analytic techniques and the alignment of theory and data.

Follower influence processes

Once a leader displays a particular FRL behaviour, followers react in a way that either motivates or demotivates them. What happens to them internally from a motivational standpoint has been the subject of a few conceptual arguments and empirical studies. Transformational leadership appears to influence followers through arousal of motives (Burns, 1978; Wofford, Whittington, and Goodwin, 2001), increased optimism (Peterson and Seligman, 2004), increased intrinsic motivation (Shin and Zhou, 2003; Sosik, Kahai, and Avolio, 1999) and increased trust and commitment (Jung and Avolio, 2000).

Bass (1998) and Avolio (1999) have suggested that transformational leaders influence followers through processes of personal identification and internalization. *Personal identification* is evident when a follower's belief about a leader becomes self-referential and self-defining (e.g. follower relates to leader's vision based on common life experiences or opinions). *Internalization* is evident when the ideas, values, and beliefs of a leader become deeply held guideposts of behaviour for the follower.

Expanding on this theoretical background, Kark, Shamir, and Chen (2003) proposed that transformational leaders raise a follower's levels of confidence and esteem through *social identification*, evident when a follower's belief about a group is self-referential or self-defining. The phrase 'once a Marine, always a Marine' illustrates social identification where an individual's self-concept and self-esteem is based partly on being a Marine. Kark, Shamir, and Chen found support for personal and social identification's role in transformational leadership processes. Specifically, these forms of influence mediated relationships between transformational leadership and follower dependence, self- and collective-efficacy, and organization-based self-esteem.

In a law enforcement setting, Deluga and Souza (1991) found transformational leadership to be more closely related with follower *rational* influencing behaviour than transactional leadership. These surprising results may be due to the male-dominated organizational setting and police officer personalities in their sample, and/or the high correlations between transformational and CR behaviours in this and most MLQ-based studies. Nevertheless, CR behaviour is likely to influence followers through processes of reframed reward contingencies and instrumental compliance. Rewards linked to the successful attainment of goals increase followers' persistence and effort. Goals provide direction for followers who are likely to comply with the leader's directive to attain the promised extrinsic rewards (Bass, 1985).

The influence of MBE-A and MBE-P behaviour may also be based upon instrumental compliance focused on not deviating from standards. However, it is also likely that these leader behaviours may influence followers through *intimidated compliance* because MBE behaviour is often viewed by followers as controlling, vindictive and finger-pointing micro-management that focuses on negative aspects of performance (Sosik *et al.*, 2004).

The influence of LF behaviour may be based upon the disengagement of followers. Equity theory (Adams, 1965) suggests that when a leader is 'missing in action', followers may reciprocate in an equitable fashion by disengaging in their own work, with resultant decreases in performance and satisfaction. Alternatively, highly professional followers may become self-motivated to substitute for the lack of leadership by picking up the slack or usurping the leader's role (Bass, 1998). Future research should examine the empirical connections between FRL behaviours and follower influence processes listed in Figure 2.2 and other influence tactics described in Yukl (2002).

Leadership outcomes

Resulting from the leadership processes shown in Figure 2.2 are sets of individual, group, and organizational level outcomes. Because individuals are embedded within groups, and groups within organizations, social influence processes are likely to create associations between the outcomes. For example, if followers within groups hold similar ideas about their level of empowerment, shared leadership may emerge at the group level (Avolio, 1999). If creativity is shared and fostered within and between work groups, the organization may experience high level of innovation and retention as at the SAS Institute (Sosik *et al.*, 2004). Multi-level research is needed to validate these ideas.

Individual follower outcomes

Reviews of the FRL literature indicate that transformational and contingent reward leadership have the potential to reap a variety of follower outcomes including empowerment (Cox, Pearce, and Sims, 2003), extra effort, effectiveness and satisfaction with the leader (Lowe, Kroeck, and Sivasubramaniam, 1996), OCB (Pillai, Schriesheim, and Williams, 1999), creativity (Shin and Zhou, 2003; Sosik, Kahai, and Avolio, 1999), reduced stress and burnout (Seltzer, Numeroff and Bass, 1989; Sosik and Godshalk, 2000) and promotions (Yammarino and Bass, 1990). This wide range of outcomes suggests that transformational leadership offers organizational members both professional and psychological benefits.

Work group/team outcomes

The model shown in Figure 2.2 also portrays outcomes at the work group or team level. As a result of effective collective action, transformational leadership augmenting CR leadership can yield enhanced group efficacy, morale, cohesion, and productivity, effectiveness and creativity (Jung and Sosik, 2002; Sosik, Avolio, and Kahai, 1997), shared leadership (Avolio, 1999), and satisfaction with the leader and task (Sosik, 1997; Sosik, Kahai, and Avolio, 1999). These outcomes are highly desirable in contemporary organizations that depend on work groups to complete work assignments and execute strategic initiatives.

Organizational outcomes

Organizational outcomes are expected to be generated as a result of leadership processes and from the individual and group-level outcomes through social influence processes (Dansereau, Alutto, and Yammarino, 1984). These outcomes may be as diverse as innovation (Jung, Chow, and Wu, 2003), retention (Sosik *et al.*, 2004), organizational commitment (Bass, 1998; Podsakoff, MacKenzie, and Bommer, 1990), business unit goal attainment (Avolio, Howell, and Sosik, 1999), unit financial performance (Howell and Avolio, 1993), market share and customer satisfaction (Geyer and Steyrer, 1998), and occupational safety (Barling, Loughlin, and Kelloway, 2002). Given the breadth of outcomes associated with transformational leadership, organizations appear to have much to gain from fostering transformational leadership.

Organizational context as a moderator

A criticism of the FRL model is that its processes and outcomes are proposed to be essentially the same in all situations (Yukl, 2002). Bass (1997) argued that transformational leadership and its outcomes are 'universal' and presented empirical evidence indicating that it transcends organizational and national boundaries.

However, several writers (Jung, Bass, and Sosik, 1995; Pawar and Eastman, 1997) have argued that situational variables may moderate the relationships between FRL behaviours and their antecedents and consequences shown in Figure 2.2.

A high receptivity to transformational leadership is likely in organizations that are adaptive, use boundary spanning functions and clan governance/culture to reach strategic goals, and are adhocracies or simple structures, not multi-levelled hierarchies (Pawar and Eastman, 1997). Transformational leadership is appropriate in organizations that deploy technology to assist in attaining strategic goals (Sosik et al., 2004) or in unstructured tasks or organizational structures (Felfe and Schyns, 2002). Several writers have pointed out that transformational leadership is most appropriate during times of crisis or in periods of environmental turbulence (Bass, 1985; Burns, 2003). All of these contextual variables may help researchers and trainers to more fully understand transformational leadership as an organizational process.

The national culture that embeds the organization may also moderate the influence of transformational and transactional leadership on followers. Jung and Avolio (1999) found that collectivists working in groups led by a transformational leader generated more ideas, but individualists generated more ideas with a transactional leadership. Jung and Avolio's findings provide support for Jung, Bass, and Sosik's (1995) contention that transformational leadership may be particularly effective in collectivistic cultures. Future research should now examine core FRL behaviours and their antecedents and consequences in cultures using theoretical and methodological frameworks established by House and his colleagues' (2004) GLOBE project.

Implications for research

The conceptual framework shown in Figure 2.2 suggests several implications for future research. First, we need to learn much more about the non-transformational behaviours in the model. Goal setting and contingent rewarding appear to be quite effective in sales (Dubinsky et al., 1995) and strategic planning (Sosik et al., 2004) contexts. Other contexts where MBE-A behaviours may have positive influences should be identified in future work. Second, further assessments of the MLQ's factor structure across a wider variety of contexts and controlling for contextual variables should be pursued (Antonakis, Avolio, and Sivasubramaniam, 2003). Third, levels-of-analysis theorizing and testing (Dansereau, Alutto, and Yammarino, 1984) shows great promise for topics of shared leadership and organizational cultures influenced by FRL behaviours.

Fourth, considerations of introducing more behaviours into the FRL model should be theoretically and empirically explored so that the model reflects contemporary requirements of leadership in face-to-face and virtual (Avolio, Kahai, and Dodge, 2000), and close and distant (Dvir and Shamir, 2003) leader/follower relationships. Greater attention also needs to be paid to the conceptual overlaps between authentic transformational leadership and the emerging field of positive psychology (Peterson and Seligman, 2004). A promising area of research concerns the character strengths and virtues underlying the emergence of informal leaders and their display of FRL behaviours during crises. Moreover, longitudinally assessing real changes in followers and their roles in the FRL process will go a long way in clarifying the appropriate 'fit' for display of FRL behaviours. Other areas for future research include examining the influence processes underlying the more passive behaviours in the model, organizational context moderators, and empirically testing specific links between components of the model shown in Figure 2.2.

TRAINING FULL RANGE LEADERSHIP

The FRL model has been used in training programmes around the world to introduce the transformational-transactional leadership paradigm to professionals in industry, military, and education (see Bass, 1998 for details of prototypical workshops). FRL training programmes are grounded in research and have been shown by several research-based evaluations to promote positive changes in leaders and followers.

Barling, Weber, and Kelloway (1996) completed a field experiment with 20 managers trained in FRL and compared them to control groups. They found positive training effects, especially on the managers' IS. Followers' commitment and financial performance also increased as consequences of their managers' training to display higher levels of transformational leadership behaviour. Evaluation of FRL training by Avolio and Bass (1998) found that for 115 community leaders who had been rated by their followers prior to training, there were significant increases in IM and IS and a significant decrease in MBE behaviour immediately following training. The organizational culture of the trainees was assessed by the followers before and after training. Significant increases in both positive aspects of the transformational and transactional organization's culture were revealed.

Dvir *et al.* (2002) conducted a field experiment reporting that according to their company leaders' and followers' MLQ ratings of Israeli Defense Force infantry platoon commanders, the platoon commanders who had undergone the training were more transformational, less passive, and less likely to manage by exception. The comparison group did not demonstrate the same effects on either ratings of leadership or performance. In contrast, the platoons led by the leaders trained in transformational leadership had higher senses of self-efficacy and belonging, and were higher in four of six measures of objective performance six months following training.

Results of these studies and others suggest that behaviours in the FRL model can be taught and learned. While these programmes appear to be effective, four improvements in training based on the conceptual framework presented in Figure 2.2 are recommended. First, more attention should be paid to the characteristics of the follower (Dvir and Shamir, 2003). Follower-centric approaches to training could include overviews of follower needs and motives, motivational mechanisms, and techniques for leveraging diversity. Second, given the importance of life history and biodata to the development of transformational leadership (Avolio and Gibbons, 1988), a psychodynamic evaluation of the leader's self-concept and critical life events may elucidate the leader's purpose-in-life, thereby helping to enhance their display of IM and II-B (Sosik and Dworakivsky, 1998).

Third, modules on developing followers' trust and commitment need to be developed and used in FRL training. Trust and commitment are key motivational mechanisms in FRL processes (Jung and Avolio, 2000). These topics are especially important given the increasing number of leadership and ethical meltdowns in corporations like Enron and Worldcom. Training leaders in the ethical decision-making frameworks and their connections to FRL behaviours can go a long way in building follower's trust and commitment (Bass and Steidlmeier, 1999).

Fourth, the 'one-size fits all' approach to promoting transformational leadership as being most effective needs to be reevaluated. Studies indicate that CR leadership appears to be more efficient and effective than transformational leadership in sales management (Dubinsky *et al.*, 1995) and electronic brainstorming (Kahai, Sosik, and Avolio, 2003) contexts. Consideration of the leader's industry, organizational structure, hierarchical level, job type, and culture may be useful to leaders when they meet with trainers to review their MLQ results.

CONCLUSION

Abraham Zaleznik was correct when he predicted that Bass's (1985) seminal book on FRL would 'recast leadership research for the next decade or more.' Since then, a tremendous volume of research has advanced our understanding of the processes and many outcomes associated with transformational leadership. True to Burns's (2003) idea of transforming leadership, Bass and Avolio's (1994) FRL model has helped breathe new life into the study and practice of leadership and its development. Scholars have delved further into related and important branches of research including charismatic leadership, authentic leadership, follower motivation, personality profiles of leaders, gender and racial differences in leaders, and e-leadership.

While much has been accomplished since 1985, researchers' attention to the theoretical and methodological issues described above when evaluating and refining the FRL model will foster its full potential for theoretical completeness and empirical validity. I hope that this chapter and the conceptual framework provided within are useful in directing future research and training on FRL.

Studying and training the FRL model will help realize Burns's (2003) overarching vision of creating and expanding the empowerment of people pursuing satisfaction in life through the development of self and others.

REFERENCES

Adams, J. S. (1965) Inequity in social exchanges. In L. Berkowitz (ed.) *Advances in experimental social psychology*. New York: Academic Press, pp. 267–300.

Antonakis, J., Avolio, B. J., and Sivasubramaniam, N. (2003) Context and leadership: An examination of the nine-factor full-range leadership theory using the Multifactor Leadership Questionnaire. *Leadership Quarterly,* 14: 261–95.

Avolio, B. J. (1994) The 'natural': Some antecedents to transformational leadership. *International Journal of Public Administration,* 17: 1559–81.

Avolio, B. J. (1999) *Full leadership development: Building the vital forces in organizations.* Thousand Oaks, CA: Sage.

Avolio, B. J. and Bass, B. M. (1998) You can drag a horse to water, but you can't make it drink except when it's thirsty. *Journal of Leadership Studies,* 5: 1–17.

Avolio, B. J. and Gibbons, T. C. (1988) Developing transformational leaders: A life span approach. In J. A. Conger and R. N. Kanungo (eds) *Charismatic leadership: The elusive factor in organizational effectiveness.* San Francisco, CA: Jossey-Bass, pp. 276–308.

Avolio, B. J., Bass, B. M., and Jung, D. I. (1999) Reexamining the components of transformational and transactional leadership using the Multifactor Leadership Questionnaire. *Journal of Occupational and Organizational Psychology,* 72: 441–62.

Avolio, B. J., Howell, J. M., and Sosik, J. J. (1999) A funny thing happened on the way to the bottom line: Humour as a moderator of leadership style effects. *Academy of Management Journal,* 42: 219–27.

Avolio, B. J., Kahai, S., and Dodge, G. (2000) E-leadership and its implications for theory, research and practice. *Leadership Quarterly,* 11: 615–70.

Avolio, B. J., Waldman, D. A., and Einstein, W. O. (1988) Transformational leadership in a management game simulation: Impacting the bottom line. *Group and Organization Studies,* 13: 59–80.

Bandura, A. (1986) *Social foundations of thought and action: A social cognitive theory.* Englewood Cliffs, NJ: Prentice-Hall.

Banerji, P. and Krishnan, V. R. (2000) Ethical preferences of transformational leaders: An empirical investigation. *Leadership and Organizational Development Journal,* 21: 405–13.

Barling, J., Loughlin, C., and Kelloway, E. K. (2002) Development and test of a model linking safety-specific transformational leadership and occupational safety. *Journal of Applied Psychology,* 87: 488–96.

Barling, J., Weber, T., and Kelloway, K. E. (1996) Effects of transformational leadership training on attitudinal and financial outcomes: A field experiment. *Journal of Applied Psychology,* 81: 827–32.

Bar-On, R. (1996) *The Emotional Quotient Inventory: A measure of emotional intelligence.* Toronto, ON: Multi Health Systems.

Bass, B. M. (1985) *Leadership and performance beyond expectations.* New York: Free Press.

Bass, B. M. (1997) Does the transactional/transformational leadership paradigm transcend organizational and national boundaries? *American Psychologist,* 52: 130–9.

Bass, B. M. (1998) *Transformational leadership: Industry, military, and educational impact.* Mahwah, NJ: Lawrence Erlbaum Associates.

Bass, B. M. (2002) Cognitive, social and emotional intelligence of transformational leaders. In R. E. Riggio, S. E. Murphy, and F. J. Pirozzolo (eds) *Multiple intelligences and leadership.* Mahwah, NJ: Erlbaum, pp. 105–18.

Bass, B. M. (2004, August) Reflections on life as a leadership scholar. In F. Lohrke (Chair) *Management history social in honor of Bernie Bass' retirement.* Symposium conducted at the national meeting of the Academy of Management, New Orleans, LA.

Bass, B. M. and Avolio, B. J. (1990) *Full range leadership development basic workshop manual.* Binghamton, NY: Center for Leadership Studies, SUNY- Binghamton.

Bass, B. M. and Avolio, B. J. (1993) Transformational leadership and organizational culture. *International Journal of Public Administration,* 17(1): 112–21.

Bass, B. M. and Avolio, B. J. (1994) *Improving organizational effectiveness through transformational leadership.* Thousand Oaks, CA: Sage.

Bass, B. M. and Avolio, B. J. (1997) *Full range leadership development: Manual for the Multifactor Leadership Questionnaire.* Palo Alto, CA: Mind Garden.

Bass, B. M. and Steidlmeier, P. (1999) Ethics, character, and authentic transformational leadership behavior. *Leadership Quarterly,* 10: 181–217.

Bass, B. M., Avolio, B. J., and Atwater, L. (1996) The transformational and transactional leadership of men and women. *Applied Psychology: An International Review,* 45: 5–34.

Bass, B. M., Avolio, B. J., Jung, D. I., and Berson, Y. (2003) Predicting unit performance by assessing transformational and transactional leadership. *Journal of Applied Psychology,* 88: 207–18.

Burns, J. M. (1978) *Leadership.* New York: Harper & Row.

Burns, J. M. (2003) *Transforming leadership: A new pursuit of happiness.* New York: Atlantic Monthly.

Bycio, P., Hackett, R. D., and Allen, J. S. (1995) Further assessments of Bass's (1985) conceptualization of transactional and transformational leadership. *Journal of Applied Psychology,* 80: 468–78.

61

Carless, S. A. (1998a) Assessing the discriminant validity of transformational leader behavior as measured by the MLQ. *Journal of Occupational and Organizational Psychology,* 71: 353–8.

Carless, S. A. (1998b) Gender differences in transformational leadership: An examination of superior, leader and subordinate perspectives. *Sex Roles,* 39: 887–902.

Charan, R. and Colvin, G. (1999, June 21) Why CEOs fail. *Fortune,* 139(12): 69–78.

Clinton, B. (2004) *My life.* New York: Knopf.

Cox, J. F., Pearce, C. L., and Sims, H. P. (2003) Toward a broader leadership agenda: Extending the traditional transactional-transformational duality by developing directive, empowering and shared leadership skills. In R. E. Riggio and S. E. Murphy (eds) *The future of leadership development.* Mahwah, NJ: Lawrence Erlbaum, pp. 161–79.

Dansereau, F., Alutto, J. A., and Yammarino, F. J. (1984) *Theory testing in organizational behavior: The variant approach.* Englewood Cliffs, NJ: Prentice-Hall.

Deluga, R. J. and Souza, J. (1991) The effects of transformational and transactional leadership styles on the influencing behavior of subordinate police officers. *Journal of Occupational Psychology,* 64: 49–55.

Dubinsky, A. J., Yammarino, F. J., Jolson, M. A., and Spangler, W. D. (1995) Transformational leadership: An initial investigation in sales management. *Journal of Personal Selling and Sales Management,* 15: 17–31.

Dvir, T. and Shamir, B. (2003) Follower developmental characteristics as predicting transformational leadership: A longitudinal field study. *Leadership Quarterly,* 14: 327–44.

Dvir, T., Eden, D., Avolio, B. J., and Shamir, B. (2002) Impact of transformational leadership on follower development and performance: A field experiment. *Academy of Management Journal,* 45: 735–44.

Eagly, A. H. and Crowley, M. (1986) Sex and helping behavior: A meta-analytic review of the social psychological literature. *Psychological Bulletin,* 100: 283–308.

Eagly, A. H., Johannesen-Schmidt, M. C., and van Engen, M. L. (2003) Transformational, transactional, and laissez-faire leadership styles: A meta-analysis comparing men and women. *Psychological Bulletin,* 129: 569–91.

Felfe, J. and Schyns, B. (2002) The relationship between employees' occupational self-efficacy and perceived transformational leadership: Replication and extension of recent results. *Current Research in Social Psychology,* 7: 137–62.

Fulmer, R. M. and Goldsmith, M. (2001) *The leadership investment: How the world's best organizations gain strategic advantage through leadership development.* New York: American Management Association.

Gardner, W. L. and Cleavenger, D. (1998) Impression management behaviors of transformational leaders at the world-class level: A psycho-historical assessment. *Management Communication Quarterly,* 12: 3–41.

Garman, A. N., Davis-Lenane, D., and Corrigan, P. W. (2003) Factor structure of the transformational leadership model in human service teams. *Journal of Organizational Behavior,* 24: 803–12.

Geyer, A. L. J. and Steyrer, J. M. (1998) Transformational leadership and objective performance in banks. *Applied Psychology,* 47: 397–420.

Gibson, C. B. (1995) An investigation of gender differences in leadership across four countries. *Journal of International Business Studies,* 26: 255–79.

Goleman, D. (1995) *Emotional intelligence.* New York: Bantam.

House, R. J. (1977) A 1976 theory of charismatic leadership. In J. G. Hunt and L. L. Larson (eds) *Leadership: The cutting edge.* Carbondale, IL: Southern Illinois University Press, pp. 189–207.

House, R. J., Hauges, P. J., and Javidan, M. (2004) *Culture, leadership and organizations: The GLOBE study of 62 societies.* Thousand Oaks, CA: Sage.

Howell, J. M. and Avolio, B. J. (1993) Transformational leadership, transactional leadership, locus of control, and support for innovation: Key predictors of consolidated business-unit performance. *Journal of Applied Psychology,* 78: 891–902.

Hunt, J. G. (1999) Transformational/charismatic leadership's transformation of the field: An historical essay. *Leadership Quarterly,* 10: 129–44.

Judge, T. A. and Bono, J. E. (2000) Five-factor model of personality and transformational leadership. *Journal of Applied Psychology,* 85: 751–65.

Jung, D. I. and Avolio, B. J. (1999) Effects of leadership style and followers' cultural orientation on performance in group and individual task conditions. *Academy of Management Journal,* 42: 208–18.

Jung, D. I. and Avolio, B. J. (2000) Opening the black box: An experimental investigation of the mediating effects of trust and value congruence on transformational and transactional leadership. *Journal of Organizational Behavior,* 21: 949–64.

Jung, D. I. and Sosik, J. J. (2002) Transformational leadership in work groups: The role of empowerment, cohesiveness, and collective-efficacy on perceived group performance. *Small Group Research,* 33: 313–36.

Jung, D. I. and Sosik, J. J. (in press) Who are the spellbinders? Identifying personal attributes of charismatic leaders. *Journal of Leadership and Organizational Studies.*

Jung, D. I., Bass, B. M., and Sosik, J. J. (1995) Bridging leadership and culture: A theoretical consideration of transformational leadership and collectivistic cultures. *Journal of Leadership Studies,* 2: 3–18.

Jung, D. I., Chow, C., and Wu, A. (2003) The role of transformational leadership in enhancing organizational innovation: Hypotheses and some preliminary findings. *Leadership Quarterly,* 14: 525–44.

Kahai, S. S., Sosik, J. J., and Avolio, B. J. (2003) Effects of anonymity, rewards, and leadership style in an electronic meeting system context. *Leadership Quarterly,* 14(4–5): 499–524.

Kane, T. D. and Tremble, T. R. (2000) Transformational leadership effects at different levels of the Army. *Military Psychology,* 12: 137–60.

Kark, R., Shamir, B., and Chen, G. (2003) The two faces of transformational leadership: Empowerment and dependency. *Journal of Applied Psychology,* 88: 246–55.

Kuhnert, K. W. and Lewis, P. (1987) Transactional and transformational leadership: A constructive developmental analysis. *Academy of Management Review,* 12: 648–57.

Lowe, K. B., Kroeck, K. G., and Sivasubramaniam, N. (1996) Effectiveness correlates of transformational and transactional leadership: A meta-analytic review. *Leadership Quarterly,* 7: 385–425.

Mandell, B. and Pherwani, S. (2003) Relationship between emotional intelligence and transformational leadership style: A gender comparison. *Journal of Business and Psychology,* 17: 387–404.

Neustadt, R. E. (1990) *Presidential power and the modern presidents: The politics of leadership from Roosevelt to Reagan* (3rd edn) New York: Free Press.

Pawar, B. S. and Eastman, K. K. (1997) The nature and implications of contextual influences on transformational leadership: A conceptual examination. *Academy of Management Review,* 22: 80–109.

Peterson, C. and Seligman, M. E. P. (2004) *Character strengths and virtues: A handbook and classification.* New York: Oxford/American Psychological Association.

Pillai, R., Schriesheim, C. A., and Williams, E. S. (1999) Fairness perceptions and trust as mediators for transformational and transactional leadership. *Journal of Management,* 25: 897–933.

Pillai, R., Williams, E. A., Lowe, K. B., and Jung, D. I. (2003) Personality, transformational leadership, trust and the 2000 US presidential vote. *Leadership Quarterly,* 14: 161–92.

Podsakoff, P. M., MacKenzie, S. B., and Bommer, W. H. (1990) Transformational leader behaviors and substitutes for leadership as determinants of employee satisfaction, commitment, trust, and organizational citizenship behaviors. *Journal of Management,* 22: 259–98.

Powell, G. N. (1990) One more time: Do female and male managers differ? *Academy of Management Executive,* 4: 68–75.

Ross, S. M. and Offerman, L. R. (1997) Transformational leaders: Measurement of personality attributes and work group performance. *Personality and Social Psychology Bulletin,* 23: 1078–86.

Roush, P. E. and Atwater, L. E. (1992) Using the MBTI to understand transformational leadership and self-perception accuracy. *Military Psychology,* 4: 17–34.

Schyns, B. (2001) The relationship between employee self-monitoring and occupational self-efficacy and perceived transformational leadership. *Current Research in Social Psychology,* 7: 30–42.

Seltzer, J. and Bass, B. M. (1990) Transformational leadership: Beyond initiation and consideration. *Journal of Management,* 16(4): 693–703.

Seltzer, J., Numeroff, J., and Bass, B. M. (1989) Transformational leadership: Is it a source of more or less burnout or stress? *Journal of Health and Human Resource Administration,* 12: 174–85.

Shin, S. J. and Zhou, J. (2003) Transformational leadership, conservation, and creativity: Evidence from Korea. *Academy of Management Journal,* 46: 703–14.

Sosik, J. J. (1997) Effects of transformational leadership and anonymity on idea generation in computer-mediated groups. *Group and Organization Management,* 22: 460–87.

Sosik, J. J. (2005) The role of personal values in the charismatic leadership of corporate managers: A model and preliminary field study. *The Leadership Quarterly,* 16: 221–44.

Sosik, J. J. and Dionne, S. D. (1997) Leadership styles and Deming's behavior factors. *Journal of Business and Psychology,* 11: 447–62.

Sosik, J. J. and Dworakivsky, A. C. (1998) Self-concept based aspects of the charismatic leader: More than meets the eye. *The Leadership Quarterly,* 9: 503–26.

Sosik, J. J. and Godshalk, V. M. (2000) Leadership styles, mentoring functions received, and job-related stress: A conceptual model and preliminary study. *Journal of Organizational Behavior,* 21: 365–90.

Sosik, J. J. and Megerian, L. E. (1999) Understanding leader emotional intelligence and performance: The role of self-other agreement on transformational leadership perceptions. *Group and Organization Management,* 25: 291–317.

Sosik, J. J., Avolio, B. J., and Kahai, S. S. (1997) Effects of leadership style and anonymity on group potency and effectiveness in a group decision support system environment. *Journal of Applied Psychology,* 82: 89–103.

Sosik, J. J., Godshalk, V. M., and Yammarino, F. J. (2004) Transformational leadership, learning goal orientation, and expectations for career success in mentor-protégé relationships: A multiple levels of analysis perspective. *Leadership Quarterly,* 15: 241–61.

Sosik, J. J., Kahai, S. S., and Avolio, B. J. (1998) Transformational leadership and dimensions of group creativity: Motivating idea generation in computer-mediated groups. *Creativity Research Journal,* 11: 111–21.

Sosik, J. J., Kahai, S. S., and Avolio, B. J. (1999) Leadership style, anonymity, and creativity in group decision support systems: The mediating role of optimal flow. *Journal of Creative Behavior,* 33: 1–30.

Sosik, J. J., Potosky, D., and Jung, D. I. (2002) Adaptive self-regulation: Meeting others' expectations for leadership and performance. *Journal of Social Psychology,* 142: 211–32.

Sosik, J. J., Jung, D. I., Berson, Y., Dionne, S. D. and Jaussi, K. S. (2004) *The dream weavers: Strategy-focused leadership in technology-driven organizations.* Greenwich, CT: Information Age.

Sparks, J. R. and Schenk, J. A. (2001) Explaining the effects of transformational leadership: An investigation of the effects of higher-order motives in multilevel marketing organizations. *Journal of Organizational Behavior,* 22: 849–69.

Tejeda, M. J., Scandura, T. A., and Pillai, R. (2001) The MLQ revisited: Psychometric properties and recommendations. *Leadership Quarterly,* 12: 31–52.

Vandenberghe, C., Stordeur, S., and D'hoore, W. (2002) Transactional and transformational leadership in nursing: Structural validity and substantive relationships. *European Journal of Psychological Assessment,* 18: 16–29.

Weber, M. (1947) *The theory of social and economic organizations*. New York: Wiley.

Wofford, J. C., Whittington, J. L., and Goodwin, V. L. (2001) Follower motive patterns as situational moderators of transformational leadership effectiveness. *Journal of Management Issues,* 13: 196–211.

Yammarino, F. J. and Bass, B. M. (1990) Long-term forecasting of transformational leadership and its effects among Naval officers: Some preliminary findings: In K. E. Clark and M. R. Clark (eds) *Measures of leadership*. Greensboro, NC: Center for Creative Leadership. West Orange, NJ: Leadership Library of America, pp. 151–69.

Yammarino, F. J. and Dubinsky, A. J. (1994) Transformational leadership theory: Using levels of analysis to determine boundary conditions. *Personnel Psychology,* 47: 787–811.

Yammarino, F. J., Spangler, W. D., and Bass, B. M. (1993) Transformational leadership and performance: A longitudinal investigation. *Leadership Quarterly,* 4: 81–102.

Yammarino, F. J., Dubinsky, A. J., Comer, L. B., and Jolson, M. A. (1997) Women and transformational and contingent reward leadership theory: A multiple-levels-of-analysis perspective. *Academy of Management Journal,* 40: 205–22.

Yukl, G. (2002) *Leadership in organizations* (5th edn). Englewood Cliffs, NJ: Prentice Hall.

Zaleznik, A. (1977) Managers and leaders: Are they different? *Harvard Business Review,* 55: 67–80.

Chapter 3

Entering the fundamental state of leadership

A framework for the positive transformation of self and others

Robert E. Quinn and Gretchen M. Spreitzer

> Although learning about how the environment influences actors is important, learning more about how actors influence the environment is the first step not only to understanding the world, but changing it.
>
> (Ganz, 2005, p. 231)

In the extensive literature on leadership there are hundreds of definitions and new ones keep coming. There is, however, a theme that runs across most of the definitions. Leadership is about influencing people (Yukl, 1998). Much of the literature assumes self-interested social exchange and focuses on the influence wielded by people in positions of hierarchical authority. A smaller segment of the literature focuses on transformational leadership. Here the emphasis is on getting people to transcend their self-interests and embrace the common good (Shamir, House, and Arthur, 1993). This chapter will focus on positive transformational influence. More specifically, we will provide a framework that anyone might use to elevate themselves into a higher state of transformational influence.

We follow Hackman (2005) who calls for theories that bridge the two worlds of scholarship and practice. He notes that while scholars tend to be concerned with causes, practitioners tend to be concerned with outcomes. Nevertheless, it is possible, he argues, to generate frameworks that are both conceptually sound and able to guide constructive action. We seek to do this by generating ideas that lend themselves to empirical examination as well as practice. We present a theoretical framework that is designed to be of value to both scholars and practitioners.

We present a framework derived from the analysis of people facing extreme challenges (Quinn, 2004). The people were forced by their extreme challenges to extend themselves in ways that they would never have predicted. In the process, they experienced some form of personal transformation. After facing the challenges, they reported, among other things, having an altered self-concept, an increased awareness of external resources, and the tendency to engage in new patterns of behaviour. They report having an increased capacity to lift other people to higher levels of performance. From the analysis of such cases, Quinn specifies a concept called the fundamental state of leadership (Quinn, 2004, 2005). He indicates that people are often driven by naturally occurring challenges or trigger events (Luthans and Avolio, 2003) to higher levels of integrity and greater capacity to exert transformational influence.

From such events, he argues, it is possible to derive an applied framework – called the Fundamental State of Leadership (FSL) – that anyone can choose to employ. Here we elaborate the FSL framework. Table 3.1 highlights the four core dimensions that make up the fundamental state of leadership: intention, integrity, subordination, and adaptability. In the sections below, we provide an overview of the framework by elaborating on its key elements and tying them to relevant academic literature. This link to the literature makes evident the central mechanisms and how they might relate to each other.

THE FUNDAMENTAL STATE OF LEADERSHIP FRAMEWORK

The normal state

As human beings, we seek to reduce uncertainty and create conditions of equilibrium (Heifetz and Linsky, 2002; Langer, 2002). Under conditions of increased certainty and equilibrium, we tend to know how to do what we need to do. Any learning that is required tends to be incremental in nature, and we feel a relative sense of comfort and control. Under such normal conditions, relationships tend to be organized around assumptions of instrumental exchange (Blau, 1971). Under these conditions we develop conscious theories of status, role, and identity and tend to employ self-interested strategies of resource acquisition. When we get feedback suggesting we need to make a significant change, we tend to resist making such a change to our existing concepts and theories (Langer, 2002). As the first line of Table 3.1 indicates, in this normal state we tend to become increasingly comfort-centred, externally directed, self-focused, and internally closed.

Comfort-centred

To be comfort-centred means we organize our lives to stay on the path of least resistance, to stay in our zone of comfort, to do that which we already know how to do (Fritz, 1989). We seek to avoid or reduce uncertainty to preserve our current mind-set. Yet the world keeps changing, and this rigidity results in losing the very control we seek to preserve (Langer, 2002). We end up in a reactive orientation.

Table 3.1 Moving from the normal state to the fundamental state of leadership

	Intention	Integrity	Subordination	Adaptability
It is normal to be:	Comfort, centred	Externally, directed	Self-focused	Internally, closed
Which may lead to disintegration of:	Potential and contribution	Values and behaviour	Self and others	Knowledge and learning
Which may lead to feelings of:	Futility and meaninglessness	Insecurity and fear	Isolation and loneliness	Defensiveness and stagnation
Transformational question:	What result do I want to create?	Am I internally directed?	Am I other-focused?	Am I externally open?
The question may lead to:	Visualizing future possibility	Clarifying personal values	Recognizing interdependence	Recognizing the need to adapt
It may shift our focus from:	Reactive to proactive	External to internal	Self-focus to collective good	Certainty to exploration
Which may trigger positive feelings:	Commitment, purpose and meaning	Integrity, courage and authenticity	Attachment, empathy and self-sacrifice	Vulnerability, alertness and insight
Which may lead the actor to:	Pursuing a challenge	Modelling confidence	Building trust	Sharing strategic insight
And increase the frequency of transformational leadership behaviours:	Inspirational motivation: provide vision, enrich meaning of the work, increase challenge and urgency	Idealized influence: modelling unconventional behaviours, engaging reality, surfacing conflict	Individualized consideration: providing support, encouragement, coaching, raising confidence to meet the challenge	Intellectual stimulation: expand consciousness, create new perspective, develop new values
Creating in others a sense of:	Hopeful aspiration	Honest communication	Personal empowerment	Transcendent understanding
And establishing a group with:	Shared sense of purpose and increased motivation	Shared sense of reality and increased accuracy	Shared sense of identity and increased cohesion	Shared sense of efficacy and increased resilience

The emphasis is on problem solving or the preservation of what is. It is not on the creation of new outcomes or contributions.

This pattern occurs naturally. To be comfort-centred is to be grounded in a hedonic perspective on life where individuals seek out comfortable and pleasurable experiences (Waterman, 1993). The hedonic perspective is common. It is a normal part of human nature for us to spend much of our time being comfort-centred and living reactive lives, while we claim to be pursuing the proactive creation of new outcomes. This is a normal self-deception. It is an erosion of personal integrity not only because it is deceptive but because it a disintegration, or separation, of our potential from our contribution. We are not giving what we are capable of giving. And the inability to pursue a significant purpose may increase feelings such as futility and meaninglessness.

Externally driven

Under normal conditions, relationships are organized around assumptions of scarce resources, norms of exchange, and the exercise of hierarchical authority. Consequently, it is natural to pay great attention to those people who have more power and influence (Fiske, 1993; Kramer and Gavrieli, 2005). We imagine their assessments of our contributions and act upon those imagined assessments. This self-monitoring behaviour is necessary to social life (Snyder, 1987). Yet, over time we may become increasingly concerned about the assessments of others. As we do, we become more externally directed and cease to live by our own core values. We take on an increasingly external locus of control (Rotter, 1966). As we do, we may live in fear of enacting our core values and simply behave in ways that we assume the world expects. We thus present an acceptable, common self and fail to enact our more authentic, unique, or best self (Roberts et al., 2005).

This process is also normal. We tend to spend much of our time living as we imagine we are expected to live. We comply by espousing a particular perspective or engaging in certain behaviours while exhibiting limited commitment to the perspective or the behaviours (Argyris, 1993). In engaging this kind of normal behaviour we experience the disintegration of our values and behaviour, and we may experience feelings of insecurity and fear, causing us to become still more externally focused.

Self-focused

In order to survive, nature requires that we be self-focused (Kegan, 1994). In a world of limited resources, we must pursue self-interested strategies. In social relationships, we must also engage in patterns of exchange that allow us to acquire needed resources. As we become focused on the acquisition of resources and the execution of self-interested exchange, we may also tend to exercise various forms of egocentric control. In doing so, we may tend to objectify others, see them as instruments to be manipulated for our ends. As a result, we are likely to lose the capacity to understand and honour their perspectives (Galinsky, Gruenfeld, and Magee, 2002). In exercising control without concern, we may gain short-term compliance but build long-term resentment (Quinn, Spreitzer, and Brown, 2000).

This process is normal. We spend large amounts of time being self-interested and attempting to negotiate and control. Yet the need to be in control may destroy trust and the willingness of others to engage in spontaneous contribution (Quinn and Spreitzer, 1997). Even as others comply, they send us tacit messages that they are withdrawing their emotional support. As we gain intuitive or conscious awareness of their withdrawal, the awareness may lead us to further increase our efforts at control (Mayer, Davis, and Schoorman, 1995) and this may initiate a vicious cycle. This self-defeating pattern represents the disintegration of relationships (Dutton, 2003), and it may give rise to negative feelings such as isolation and loneliness.

Internally closed

In a world that is constantly changing there is pressure to adapt. While we may be comfortable with incremental or controlled adaptation, we tend to resist the process of deep change, which requires the surrender of control and the risk of real-time learning (Quinn, 1996). When we receive feedback that suggests we need to make deep change, we tend to engage in various forms of denial (Heifetz and Linsky, 2002). We distort the messages we receive, insisting that the world is still best represented in the images and categories derived from our past experience (Langer, 2002).

This process is also normal. External feedback that suggests we need to change is often met with the deployment of defensive routines (Argyris, 1993). As we protect our existing images and categories, we experience the disintegration or separation of knowledge and learning. We adhere to what we know and resist adapting to the changing world. As we do this we tend to experience feelings of defensiveness and stagnation.

In summary, the normal state is a condition of equilibrium in which natural, entropic forces tend to operate. In the normal state, we tend to become comfort-centred, externally directed, self-focused, and internally closed. We tend to become increasingly disintegrated and self-deceptive and therefore hypocritical. Paradoxically, as we describe below, this seemingly negative sentence, is actually an identification of an enormous source of potential for transformational influence.

Entering the fundamental state of leadership

To enter the fundamental state of leadership is to increase personal influence. The approach taken here does not begin with trait-like leadership characteristics that are more stable (Bass, 1990), but on the state-like characteristics that are more amenable to change (Luthans and Avolio, 2003). It focuses in on our own current state of being. More specifically it focuses on a topic we prefer to avoid, our own current lack of integrity and virtue.

The capacity to learn in anxiety is a distinguishing feature of effective leaders (Hackman, 2005). Weick (2003) indicates that positive organizing 'occurs concurrent with wading into circumstances and dealing with whatever unexpected events occur using tools that themselves were unexpected recombinations of existing repertoires' (p. 68). To lead is to be adaptive, to make personal change and to help others change (Heifetz and Linsky, 2002). Schein (1996) suggests that personal change happens when we unfreeze our defences and look internally to determine what is ultimately important to us. Torbert (1987) suggests that the confidence to learn in the face of uncertainty is a function of integrity. He goes on to suggest that we build our integrity through the constant self-monitoring or increasing awareness of our lack of integrity.

The literature lends support to such assertions. In terms of awareness, research on self-change shows that people who effectively transform follow a pattern in which commitment to change is preceded by increased consciousness, increased awareness of alternatives, emotional arousal, and self-reevaluation (Prochaska, Norcross, and DiClemente, 1994). In terms of integrity and confidence, the literature suggests that integrity is associated with increased self-esteem, self-regard, productive interpersonal relationships, teamwork, and a positive climate (Cameron, 2003).

Following this line of thought, we assert that we can increase our integrity and virtue, by becoming more conscious of both our hypocrisy and our potential. Csikszentmihalyi (1991) suggests that how we develop is determined by how we allocate our attention. Here we identify four questions that can redirect our attention and elevate our current psychological state

It is important that the elements are posed in the form of questions. The process of asking ourselves questions has several important effects that stimulate a person to action. First, asking questions enhances mindfulness. Mindfulness is the ability to pay attention to an experience from moment to moment – without drifting into thoughts of the past or concerns about the future, or getting caught up in opinions about what's going on (Langer, 1990). Langer suggests that if we want to change things in our lives, we need to change the way we think about ourselves. These questions can help us change our self-perspective. And second, by asking ourselves questions, we move from a passive state to a more active state. We could just tell people about the fundamental state of leadership, but the process of asking people a series of questions moves them to think about what the fundamental state of leadership means for them. The asking process puts people into an enquiry mode that enhances thinking and action (Torbert, 2004).

What result do I want to create?

To be comfort-centred is to move on the path of least resistance (Fritz, 1984). Fritz argues that this is the normal life stance and that it is inherently reactive. In a hedonic perspective, we are continually solving problems and fighting fires, trying to preserve equilibrium to increase our happiness and stay within our zone of comfort. In problem solving, we are trying to make something negative go away (Fritz, 1984). In contrast, the question 'What result do I want to create?' is grounded in a eudaimonic perspective on psychological functioning and development (Fritz, 1984; Waterman, 1993). In simple terms, the eudaimonic perspective emphasizes that we seek to realize our full potential as human beings. Living in accordance with the daimon or 'true self', this approach gives meaning and direction to our life. In answering the question 'What result to I want to create?' we are challenged to think outside our comfort zone. Asking and answering this question moves us to a more eudaimonic state where we seek to make a contribution and make a different to the world. To ask the question 'What result do I want to create?' is to put an emphasis on envisioning future achievements and triggering a shift in attention form actuality to possibility.

To ask and answer the question 'What result do I want to create?' is to identify something positive that we want to bring into existence. It creates a self-determined, positive discrepancy that may trigger transcendent behaviours (Phillips, Hollenbeck, and Ilgen, 1996). It is a shift from a reactive to a proactive orientation and is likely to result in an increase of positive feelings including sense of commitment, purpose, and meaning. These may be associated with other positive characteristics such as intrinsic motivation and a tendency to persist in what we are doing (Bateman and Porath, 2003; Csikszenmihalyi, 1991; Myers and Diener, 1995). These in turn can take on characteristics of the self-fulfilling prophecy or virtuous cycle (Eden, 2003; Fredrickson, 2003).

With an elevated sense of purpose, we are more likely to engage in some of the behaviours associated with what Bass (1997) calls inspirational motivation. Because we are pursuing a creative purpose, we are more likely to be able to articulate a compelling vision, to challenge people, increase their sense of urgency, and help them find greater meaning in their work. Such behaviours are likely to surface hopeful aspirations and entice others to engage challenge. Doing so is likely to make their work more intrinsically rewarding (Ryan and Deci, 2001). In a group, such dynamics are likely to result in a sense of shared purpose. People may begin to develop a compelling personal vision of their own future (Bennis, 1989). Having a personal vision may also help people to find their tasks more interesting, challenging, and important; they may also set higher goals and have higher trust in the leader (Kirkpatrick and Locke, 1996). These kinds of changes may infuse the group with hope (Snyder, 1994) and optimism (Seligman, 1998). Such feelings may result in greater dedication and persistence. It may also inspire awe in others increasing the possibility that one person's transformational influence may inspire others to change (Fredrickson, 2003; Keltner and Haidt, 2003).

Am I internally driven?

To be in the normal state is to attend to the expectations of others. As we do, we tend to drift towards an external locus of control and are likely to experience disintegration between our values and behaviour, resulting in feelings of insecurity and fear (Quinn and Spreitzer, 1997). Such feelings tend to increase our need to impress and control others, and we may attempt to present ourselves as we imagine we are expected to act (Snyder, 1987). When we do this, others may sense a lack of authenticity and tend to distance themselves (Luthans and Avolio, 2003). The distancing may then further stimulate our insecurities, and we may accelerate the vicious cycle.

Here the question 'am I internally driven' directs our attention to our fears and the need to clarify our values. To ask this question is to shift attention to the ways we are externally controlled and specify the need to take a more internal locus of control (Rotter, 1966). The shift requires value clarification (Quinn, Spreitzer, and Brown, 2000). Value clarification leads to a sense of personal growth and awareness that we are becoming the kind of person we want to be (Prochaska, DiClemente, and Norcross, 1992). We thus increase our sense of meaning (Ganz, 2005). In the process of value clarification and change, we reorganize our self-concept and become more self-aware and better able to regulate our feelings, thoughts, and behaviours. We are more naturally able to present an integrated or authentic self (Luthans and Avolio, 2003). We are likely to feel an increased sense of integrity, courage, and authenticity. These and other positive emotions associated with moral progress and growth are likely to increase our awareness of previously unnoticed resources and thus increase our sense of confidence or efficacy (Fredrickson, 2003). Increased self-efficacy is associated with increased willingness to accept a challenge, to invest effort and to persist in the face of obstacles (Bandura, 1997). Notice that the positive outcomes derived from asking this second question begin to overlap with the positive outcomes derived from asking the first question.

As we courageously act from our core values, we may infect others with feelings of strength and courage (Worline and Quinn, 2003). In this way, we stimulate increased collective awareness and realism (Goleman, Boyatzis, and McKee, 2002). We are also more likely to engage in those behaviours associated with what Bass (1997) calls idealized influence. Free of external expectations and full of confidence, we are more likely to be spontaneous and model unconventional behaviours. As we more confidently pursue an intrinsically motivating purpose, we may insist on dealing with the reality hidden by political dynamics and thus engage others in the positive confrontation of ideas. This surfacing of conflict may offend some but inspire others. Increasingly honest and authentic communication may give rise to a shared sense of reality and increased accuracy in the work of the group or organization (Weick, 2003).

Am I other-focused?

It is normal to be self-focused. Yet self-focused behaviour and 'sham altruism' is readily recognized by others and leads others to withdraw their commitment and support (Messick, 2005). We then tend to experience the disintegration of the self–other relationship, and we tend to live with feelings of isolation and loneliness. To ask the question 'am I other-focused' is to increase our awareness of our isolating self-interest and our need to operate from the good of the relationship, group, organization, or society. To do so is to recognize our interdependence and the fact we live in a social ecology. That which we put into the ecology tends to return to us. If we objectify others we are likely to be objectified.

The question thus challenges us to recognize our interdependence and shift from a self-focus to a more communal orientation (Spreitzer, Quinn, and Fletcher, 1995). This means seeking to build a community in which everyone identifies with the group and puts the common good first (Hogg, 2005). Fletcher (1998) and Kegan (1994) emphasize the critical role that relationships and community play in moving people to higher levels of moral development and action. People in the fundamental state of leadership touch others' hearts by building deep, engaging relationships that go beyond the basic notions of exchange and self-interest (Goleman, Boyatzis, and McKee, 2002; Parker and Axtell, 2001).

In such a group we transcend norms of exchange and operate by norms of generalized reciprocity (Putnam, 2001). As we turn to such a communal and perhaps synergistic orientation we are more likely to experience the positive emotions of empathy and concern and increase the likelihood of feeling attachment, expressing love, and engaging in sacrifice for others (Dutton, et al., 2005). Such behaviours tend to build deep levels of trust and engagement (Greenleaf and Spear, 2002; Weick, 2003).

When we put the common good first we are more likely to engage in behaviours having to do with individualized consideration (Bass, 1997). These include providing support, encouragement, and coaching so as to raise the confidence of others and entice them to engage in challenges that help them empower themselves (Spreitzer and Quinn, 1996). To be more other-focused is to thus attract others to live beyond assumptions of self-interest (Goleman, Boyatzis, and McKee, 2002). The group gains a shared sense of identity and the members of the group are more likely to engage in self-sacrificing and caring behaviours that attract still others to a collective focus, increasing harmony, and stimulating extra effort for the benefit of others (Bagozzi, 2003; Fredrickson, 2003). Hogg (2005) notes that when we develop such strong, empathic bonds and a common in-group identity, it becomes nearly impossible for us to coerce or harm group members because doing so is nearly equivalent to coercing or harming ourselves.

Am I externally open?

To be internally closed is to experience the disintegration of knowledge and learning. We may become so attached to what we know that we avoid the risk of learning that which might disconfirm what we know (Langer, 2002; Weick, 2003). This suggests the need for a high level of adaptive capacity (Heifetz and Linsky, 2002). To ask the question 'Am I externally open?' is to increase awareness of our closed state and the fact we are not moving forward into the anxiety associated with real time learning (Hackman, 2005). The question may thus increase our awareness of the need for constant adaptation in a world of continuous change. If we commit to move forward into uncertainty, we are usually forced to shift from an orientation of knowing, to an orientation of exploration; this shift may result in feelings of increased vulnerability, interest, alertness, and insight (Weick, 2003). We may gain the motivation to seek out the challenges that will extend our capacities for learning (Ryan and Deci, 2001). In exploration, we are also likely to recognize the necessity for interdependence and realize that our success is dependent upon giving and receiving accurate feedback (Avolio, 1999). By responding to feedback, we tend to increase trust (Ashford and Cummings, 1983). With increased trust, we are more likely to experience the emergence of the group mind and the increased capacity to improvise, strategize, and co-create (Ganz, 2005; Weick, 2003). Again, notice how asking this question produces outcomes that overlap with outcomes stimulated by previous questions.

As we move through uncertainty, our learning is likely to generate new strategic insights and draw us to behave in new ways and to share our insights with others. We are more likely to engage in the behaviours associated with intellectual stimulation (Bass, 1997). Operating from an expanded consciousness, we are more likely to help others to discover new perspectives and develop new values and attitudes that then give rise to extra role behaviours (Tyler, 2005). Such shifts in values may alter our cognitive structures and put us in a condition in which we are better able to 'imaginatively recontextualize' the environment and thus identify new resources and opportunities (Ganz, 2005). In doing so, we are more likely to gain a shared sense of efficacy and increase collective resilience (Sutcliffe and Vogus, 2003).

DISCUSSION

This chapter argues that in social life there is a natural inclination towards comfort, external control, self-interest, and stagnation. In the normal state, the self is becoming increasingly less integrated and energized. It is dying. The fundamental state of leadership is a psychologically elevated state in which we experience an increase in creative intention, integrity, subordination, and adaptation. This means we are striving to create something new, we have the courage to enact our truest feelings, we do so within the needs of the larger context and we do it with the humility to learn and grow. As we move towards this higher level of functioning, we experience a sense of self-repair, self-renewal, rebirth, reintegration, or being made whole. It is a state of optimum balance in which normal polarities are transcended.

The fundamental state of leadership is a state of optimal balance in which we are more likely to challenge others to envision possibility, engage reality, build community, and move forward in learning. The framework thus opens a connection between the literature on leadership and other areas such as peak performance, emotions and spirituality. The framework was originally derived from the analysis of people facing challenges that greatly exceeded their ability (Quinn, 2004; Spreitzer, Quinn, and Fletcher, 1995). The fundamental state of leadership is therefore a concept of episodic, peak performance. Like the concept of flow, which was derived from the analysis of 'just manageable' challenges (Csikszentmihalyi, 1991), it emphasizes such things as engagement of a challenge, purposive focus, intrinsic motivation, reduced self-consciousness, attention to feedback, adaptive confidence, and increasing awareness. Yet the concept differs from flow in three ways. First, flow is an individualistic concept. There is no requirement of human relationship. The fundamental state of leadership is focused on self-alteration or the repair or reintegration of self while operating in relationships. It is about transformational influence. Second, the state of flow is amoral. The flow experience may derive from an ethical or unethical act. The fundamental state of leadership is more ethically demanding. It requires increasing integrity on four dimensions including the integration of purpose and potential, values and behaviour, self and others, knowledge and learning. Finally, the fundamental state of leadership integrates the state and the method for getting into the state. It is formulated around the four basic questions for transcending our normal hypocrisy and becoming a leader of transformational influence. It is, in this sense, simple and immediately applicable in any setting.

In our clinical work with executives, they often note that the four questions and the overall concept have spiritual undertones. In reflecting on this observation, we turned to the literature on spirituality and found clear support for our framework. In a review of the empirical literature on creativity in the emotional domain, for example, Averill (2002) discusses spirituality and the mysticism of everyday life. His discussion includes four elements that are very closely linked to our four questions. One is the integration of emotions with core beliefs and values. These are identified as true emotions as opposed to more spurious emotions. He notes that emotional truths that are realized in one situation are not necessarily stable and may lose their validity as the context changes. People are thus in need of constant self-repair. Consistent with our work, he indicates that true emotions are typically discovered during times of challenge and transition when values and beliefs must be modified. Confusion, depression, and anxiety provide the context from which the true emotions emerge. Averill (2002) further suggests that true emotions are intensely felt and 'reflect a state of clarification and resolve, an affirmation of values and self-worth' (our second question). Empirically associated with this condition of increased integrity and spirituality are three characteristics: vitality, meaning, and connectedness. Vitality is a creative attitude in which a person is more adventurous and open to new experience (our fourth question). Meaning derives from a deeply felt experience that gives rise to new interpretations and direction (our first question). Connectedness reflects an increased sense of union and harmony and may be associated with feelings of self-transcendence, being identified with something larger than the self (our third question). These are in essence the same four dimensions that occur in our framework. They suggest that our four questions may be avenues to emotional self-repair and the elevation of interpersonal influence.

A next important step will be for researchers to test the framework empirically. A warning, however, is in order. In transcendent systems, normally differentiated positive categories tend to collapse (Munch, 1981, 1982). Normally polar, positive characteristics may become mutually reinforcing (Fredrickson, 2003; Quinn, Kahn, and Mandl, 1994; Weick 2003). As noted above, some of the outcomes called forward by one of the four questions may begin to overlap some of the outcomes called forward by the other questions. While the questions are different, they themselves are mutually reinforcing. In the study of transcendent people and groups, observers are likely to identify the presence of a particular positive characteristic and fail to notice the presence of a highly differentiated or paradoxical, positive characteristic (Bass, 1997, p. 16; Quinn, 2004, p. 89; Quinn, Spreitzer, and Hart, 1992; Schriesheim, House, and Kerr, 1976). Researchers are also likely to have difficulty with issues of discriminate validity because elements combine in a synergistic way. Therefore, more sophisticated methods that can model the complex interpenetrations may be necessary.

The framework is designed to assist people in elevating themselves and others to higher states of influence. This may be done by our asking ourselves the four questions or assisting others in asking themselves the four questions. Tools for facilitating this process can be found in Quinn (2005). Here, however, a warning is also appropriate. In our clinical work with executives, we find that it is not easy for them to ask and answer these questions. People think, for example, that in a given situation, they know what result they want to create. Their answers, however, tend to be superficial. Once they give their answer, we often ask them to ask 'why' five times. In the process they eventually get to a greater state of clarity. When they do, their perspective begins to change. A similar dynamic holds for the other three questions. We suggest approaching the four questions mindfully and regularly. Practice with the questions greatly increases their utility.

In spite of these warnings, we believe that the fundamental state of leadership framework offers deep insight into how we can each better tap our transformational potential. The framework challenges each of us to see our own possibilities for greatness. Many leadership theories look across people for attributes of greatness. This framework directs us to look for greatness within. The questions are designed to transform how we see ourselves and our context. They lead us to more positive emotions, insights, behaviours, and relationships. They increase the likelihood that we can influence our environment because in the fundamental state of leadership we better understand the nature of world and how we can change it by changing ourselves.

REFERENCES

Argyris, C. (1993) *Knowledge for action.* San Francisco, CA: Jossey-Bass.

Ashford, S. J. and Cummings, L. L. (1983) Feedback as an individual resource: Personal strategies for creating information. *Organization Behavior and Human Performance,* 32: 370–98.

Averill, J. R. (2002) Emotional creativity: toward 'spiritualizing the passions.' In C. R. Snyder and S. J. Lopez (eds) *Handbook of positive psychology.* New York: Oxford University Press, pp. 172–88.

Bagozzi, R. P. (2003) Positive and negative emotions in organizations. In K. S. Cameron, J. E. Dutton, and R. E. Quinn (eds) *Positive organizational scholarship: Foundations of a new discipline.* San Francisco, CA: Barrett-Koehler, pp. 176–93.

Bandura, A. (1997) *Self-efficacy: The exercise of control.* New York: Worth Publishers.

Bass, B. (1990) *Bass and Stogdill's handbook of leadership.* New York: Free Press.

Bass, B. (1997) *Transformational leadership: Industrial, military, and educational impact.* Mahwah, NJ: Lawrence Erlbaum.

Bateman, T. S. and C. Porath (2003) Transcendent behavior. In K. S. Cameron, J. E. Dutton, and R. E. Quinn (eds) *Positive organizational scholarship: Foundations of a new discipline.* San Francisco, CA: Barrett-Koehler, pp. 48–65.

Bennis, W. (1989) *On becoming a leader.* Reading, MA: Addison-Wesley.

Blau, P. (1971) *The structure of organizations.* New York: Basic books.

Cameron, K. S. (2003) Organizational virtuousness and performance. In K. S. Cameron, J. E. Dutton, and R. E. Quinn (eds) *Positive organizational scholarship: Foundations of a new discipline.* San Francisco, CA: Barrett-Koehler, pp. 48–65.

Csikszentmihahlyi, M. (1991) *Flow: The psychology of optimal experience.* New York: Perennial.

Dutton, J. (2003) *Energize your workplace.* San Francisco, CA: Jossey-Bass.

Dutton, J. E., Worline, M., Frost, P., and Lilius, J. (2005) Explaining compassion organizing competence. Ross School of Business, University of Michigan working paper.

Eden, D. (2003) Self-fulfilling prophecies in organizations. In J. Greenberg (ed.) *Organizational behavior: The state of the science* (2nd edn). Mahwah, NJ: Lawrence Erlbaum, pp. 91–122.

Fiske, S. T. (1993) Controlling other people: The impact of power on stereotyping. *American Psychologist*, 48: 621–8.

Fletcher, J. K. (1998) Relational practice: A feminist reconstruction of work. *Journal of Management Inquiry*, 7: 163–86.

Franks, F. M. (1996) Battle command: A commander's perspective. *Military Review*, May–June.

Fredrickson, B. J. (2003) Positive emotions and upward spirals in organizations. In K. S. Cameron, J. E. Dutton, and R. E. Quinn (eds) *Positive organizational scholarship: Foundations of a new discipline*. San Francisco, CA: Barrett-Koehler, pp. 163–75.

Fritz, R. (1984) *The path of least resistance: Learning to become the creative force in your own life*. New York: Fawcett.

Galinsky, A., Gruenfeld, D., and Magee, J. C. (2002) Power to action. *Journal of Personality and Social Psychology*, 83: 453–562.

Ganz, M. (2005) Why Davis sometimes wins: Strategic capacity in social movements. In D. M. Messick and R. M. Kramer (eds) *The psychology of leadership: New perspectives and research*. Mahwah, NJ: Lawrence Erlbaum Associates, pp. 209–40.

Goleman, D., Boyatzis, R., and McKee, A. (2002) *Primal leadership: Realizing the power of emotional intelligence*. Cambridge, MA: Harvard Business School Press.

Greenleaf, R. K. and Spears, L. C. (2002) *Servant leadership: A journey into the nature of legitimate power and greatness*. Mahwah, NJ: Paulist Press.

Hackman, R. J. (2005) Rethinking team leadership or team leaders are not music directors. In D. M. Messick and R. M. Kramer (eds) *The psychology of leadership: New perspectives and research*. Mahwah, NJ: Lawrence Erlbaum Associates, pp. 115–42.

Heifetz, R. and Linsky, M. (2002) *Leadership on the line: Staying alive through the dangers of leadership*. Cambridge, MA: Harvard Business School Press.

Hogg, M. A. (2005) Social identity and leadership. In D. M. Messick and R. M. Kramer (eds) *The psychology of leadership: New perspectives and research*. Mahwah, NJ: Lawrence Erlbaum Associates, pp. 53–80.

Kegan, R. (1994) *In over our heads: The demands of modern life*. Cambridge, MA: Harvard University Press.

Keltner, D. and Haidt, J. (2003) Approaching awe, a moral, spiritual, and aesthetic emotion. *Cognition and Emotion,* 17: 297–314.

Kirkpatrick, S. A. and Locke, E. (1996) Direct and indirect effects of three core charismatic leadership characteristics on performance and attitudes. *Journal of Applied Psychology*, 81: 36–51.

Kramer, R. M. and Gavrieli, D. (2005) The perception of conspiracy: Leader paranoia as adaptive cognition. In D. M. Messick and R. M. Kramer (eds) *The psychology of leadership: New perspectives and research*. Mahwah, NJ: Lawrence Erlbaum Associates, pp. 241–74.

Langer, E. (1990) *Mindfulness*. New York: Addison-Wesley.

Langer, E. (2002) Well being: mindfulness versus positive evaluation. In C. R. Snyder and S. J. Lopez (eds) *Handbook of positive psychology*. New York: Oxford University Press, pp. 214–43.

Luthans, F. and Avolio, B. (2003) Authentic leadership development. In K. S. Cameron, J. E. Dutton, and R. E. Quinn (eds) *Positive organizational scholarship: Foundations of a new discipline*. San Francisco, CA: Barrett-Koehler, pp. 241–58.

Mayer, R. C., Davis, J. H. and Schoorman, F. D. (1995) An integrative model of organizational trust. *Academy of Management Review,* 20: 709–34.

Messick, D. M. (2005) On the psychological exchange between leaders and followers. In D. M. Messick and R. M. Kramer (eds) *The psychology of leadership: New perspectives and research*. Mahwah, NJ: Lawrence Erlbaum Associates, pp. 81–96.

Munch, R. (1981) Talcott Parsons and the theory of action. I: The structure of the Kantian core. *American Journal of Sociology*, 87: 709–39.

Munch, R. (1982) Talcott Parsons and the theory of action. II: The continuity of action. *American Journal of Sociology*, 88: 771–826.

Myers, D. G and Diener, E. (1995) Who is happy? *Psychological Science*: 6, 10–19.

Parker, S. K. and Axtell, C. (2001) Seeing another viewpoint: Antecedents and outcomes of employee perspective taking. *Academy of Management Journal*, 44(6): 1085–2001.

Phillips, G. M., Hollenbeck, J. R., and Ilgen, D. (1996) Prevalence and prediction of positive discrepancy creation: Examining a discrepancy between two self-regulation theories. *Journal of Applied Psychology*, 89(5): 498–518.

Prochaska, J. O, DiClemente, C. C., and Norcorss, J. C. (1992) In search of the structure of change. In Y. Klar, A. Nadler, J. D. Fisher, and J. M. Chinsky (eds) *Self change: Social psychological and clinical perspectives*. New York: Springer-Verlag.

Putnam, R. (2001) *Bowling alone: The collapse and revival of American community*. New York: Simon & Schuster.

Quinn, R. E. (1996) *Deep change: Discovering the leader within*. San Francisco, CA: Jossey-Bass.

Quinn, R. E. (2004) *Building the bridge as you walk on it: A guide for leading change*. San Francisco, CA: Jossey-Bass.

Quinn, R. E. (2005) Moments of greatness: Entering the fundamental state of leadership. *Harvard Business Review*, 83(7): 74–83.

Quinn, R. E. and Spreitzer, G. M. (1997) The road to empowerment: Seven questions every leader should consider. *Organizational Dynamics*, 26(2): 37–51.

Quinn, R. E., Kahn, J., and Mandl, M. J. (1994) Perspectives on organizational change: Exploring movement at the interface. In J. Greenberg (ed.) *Organizational behavior: The state of the science*. Hillsdale, NJ: Lawrence Erlbaum, pp. 109–34.

Quinn, R. E., Spreitzer, G. M., and Hart, S. (1992) Challenging the assumptions of bipolarity: Interpenetration and effectiveness. In S. Srivastva and R. Fry (eds) *Executive Continuity*. San Francisco, CA: Jossey-Bass.

Quinn, R. E., Spreitzer, G., and Brown, M. (2000) Changing others through changing ourselves: The transformation of human systems. *Journal of Management Inquiry*, 9(2): 147–64.

Roberts, L. M., Dutton, J., Spreitzer, G., Heaphy, E., and Quinn, R. (2005) Composing the reflected best self: Building pathways for becoming extraordinary in work organizations. *Academy of Management Review*, 30(4): 712–36.

Rotter, J. B. (1966) Generalized expectancies for internal versus external control of reinforcement. *Psychological Monographs*, 80.

Ryan, R. M. and Deci, E. L. (2001) On happiness and human potentials: A review of research on hedonic and eudaimonic well-being. *Annual Review of Psychology*, 52: 141–66.

Schein, E. H. (1996) Kurt Lewin's change theory in the field: Notes toward a model of managed learning. *Systematic Practice*, 9: 27–47.

Schriesheim, C. A., House, R. J., and Kerr, S. (1976) Leader initiating structure: A reconciliation of discrepant research results and some empirical tests. *Organizational Behavior and Human Performance*, 16: 297–321.

Seligman, M. (1998) *Learned optimism: How to change your life and mind*. New York: Free Press.

Shamir, B., House, R. J., and Arthur, M. B. (1993) The motivational effects of charismatic leadership: A self-concept based theory. *Organization Science*, 4: 1–17.

Snyder, C. R. (1994) *The psychology of hope: You can get there from here*. New York: The Free Press.

Snyder, M. (1987) *Public appearances/private realities: The psychology of self-monitoring*. New York: W. H. Freeman.

Spreitzer, G. M. and Quinn, R. E. (1996) Empowering middle managers to be transformational leaders. *Journal of Applied Behavioral Science*, 32(3): 237–61.

Spreitzer, G. M., Quinn, R. E., and Fletcher, J. (1995) Excavating the paths of meaning, renewal, and empowerment: A typology of managerial high performance. *Journal of Management Inquiry*, 4: 16–39.

Sutcliffe, K. M. and T. J. Vogus (2003) Organizing for resilience. In K. S. Cameron, J. E. Dutton, and R. E. Quinn (eds) *Positive organizational scholarship: Foundations of a new discipline*. San Francisco, CA: Barrett-Koehler, pp. 94–110.

Torbert, W. (1987) *Managing the corporate dream*. Homewood, IL: Dow Jones-Irwin.

Torbert, W. (2004) *Action inquiry: The secret of timely and and transforming leadership*. San Francisco, CA: Berrett-Koehler.

Tyler, T. R. (2005) Process-based leadership: How do leaders lead? In D. M. Messick and R. M. Kramer (eds) *The psychology of leadership: New perspectives and research*. Mahwah, NJ: Lawrence Erlbaum Associates, pp. 163–90.

Waterman, A. S. (1993) Two conceptions of happiness: Contrasts of personal expressiveness (eudaimonia) and hedonic enjoyment. *Journal of Personality and Social Psychology,* 64: 678–91.

Weick, K. E. (2003) Positive organizing and organizational tragedy. In K. S. Cameron, J. E. Dutton and R. E. Quinn (eds) *Positive organizational scholarship: Foundations of a new discipline*. San Francisco, CA: Barrett-Koehler, pp. 66–80.

Worline, M. C. and R. E. Quinn (2003) Courageous principled action. In K. S. Cameron, J. E. Dutton, and R. E. Quinn (eds) *Positive organizational scholarship: Foundations of a new discipline*. San Francisco, CA: Barrett-Koehler, pp. 122–37.

Yukl, G. A. (1998) *Leadership in organizations* (4th edn). Upper Saddle River, NJ: Prentice-Hall.

Chapter 4

Authentic leadership

A new approach for a new time

Fred Luthans, Steve Norman, and Larry Hughes

When the bubble burst following the 1990s boom economy, its effects spread across the corporate seascape like oil from the ruptured hull of a tanker ship. It seemed like everything in the path of the effluents became tainted: not only auditors, accounting practices, and securities violations, but also organizational leaders. We are still suffering from the aftershocks of the ethical meltdown of Enron, WorldCom, Anderson, and Adelphia. Unfortunately, these widely publicized scandals have proven to be just the tip of the iceberg. The need for new thinking on organizational leadership seems unprecedented.

In this chapter we briefly present such possible new thinking with what we call authentic leadership. We are members of the Gallup Leadership Institute (GLI) at the University of Nebraska. Our mission under the founding Director Bruce Avolio is to build the theory, research, and practice of authentic leadership development or simply ALD. The working definition of ALD is 'the process that draws upon leaders' life course, psychological capital, moral perspective, and a highly developed supporting organizational climate to produce greater self-awareness and self-regulated positive behaviors, which in turn foster continuous, positive self-development resulting in veritable, sustained performance' (Avolio and Luthans, 2006, p. 2).

Other papers on this proposed authentic leadership from our group have recently been published (Avolio *et al.*, 2004; Gardner *et al.*, 2005; Luthans and Avolio, 2003; May *et al.*, 2003), but in this chapter after first giving some of the theoretical foundation of authentic leadership and its development, we also give attention to the role that positive organizational behaviour (POB) (Luthans, 2002a, 2002b) and psychological capital or PsyCap (Luthans, Luthans, and Luthans, 2004; Luthans and Youssef, 2004; Luthans, Youssef, and Avolio, 2007) plays in ALD and the development of authentic followership in a highly developed, strength-based organizational context.

THE THEORETICAL DIMENSIONS OF AUTHENTIC LEADERSHIP

Rooted in ancient Greek lore and philosophy, the modern concept of authenticity has evolved during the past 80 years (Erickson, 1995). In the positive psychology literature, authenticity is defined as owning one's personal experiences (e.g. thoughts, emotions, needs, wants, preferences, or beliefs) (Harter, 2002). In addition to owning one's personal experiences, authenticity also involves acting in accordance with the true self (expressing true thoughts and beliefs and acting accordingly) (Harter, 2002). Erickson (1995) asserts that people are neither completely authentic nor inauthentic, but are best described as existing on a continuum from more to less authentic. Therefore, we concentrate on how to develop leaders' and followers' levels of authenticity, which will result in both organizational and personal growth.

We treat authentic leadership as a root construct and foundation that serves as a point of departure for other forms of leadership (e.g. transactional or transformational leadership). In other words, a transactional or transformational leader can be more or less authentic, but the authentic leader is not defined as being a particular style of leader per se (Avolio and Gardner, 2005; Gardner et al., in press; Luthans and Avolio, 2003).

As part of a larger theory of 'optimal' self-esteem, Kernis (2003) defines authenticity as 'the unobstructed operation of one's true, or core, self in one's daily enterprise'. He identifies four key components of authenticity: self-awareness, unbiased processing, authentic action, and relational transparency. We will examine these components suggested by Kernis and will integrate them with current operationalizations as proposed by our GLI group (Avolio and Luthans, 2005; Avolio et al., 2004; Gardner et al., 2005; Luthans and Avolio, 2003).

Self-awareness components

Increased self-awareness is a critical developmental factor for the authentic leader (Avolio and Luthans, 2005; Gardner et al., 2005; Luthans and Avolio, 2003). Through reflection, authentic leaders can attain a degree of clarity with regard to their core values, identity, emotions, and motives/goals. By clearly knowing oneself, authentic leaders have a strong sense of self that guides them in their decisions and subsequent behaviour.

Marcus and Wurf's (1987) notion of the working self-concept, which includes self-views, provides a supporting theoretical framework for authentic leaders' self-awareness. Self-views are those in which an 'individual's perceptions of his or her standing on the attributes made salient by a given context' (Lord, Brown, and Freiberg, 1999, p. 177). This supports Kernis's (2003) assertion that self-awareness

– including self-knowledge – is an important determinant of psychological well-being.

Kernis (2003, p. 13) describes self-awareness, within authenticity, as 'having awareness of, and trust in, one's motives, feelings, desires, and self-relevant cognitions.' Self-awareness implies an awareness of one's strengths, and weaknesses, as well as one's multifaceted self-nature. Self-awareness is a process during which, as mentioned above, individuals reflect upon their unique values, identity, emotions, and motives/goals. A closer examination of each of these four components leads to a better understanding of the role that self-awareness plays in authentic leadership.

Values

Within the context of authenticity, if one is true to oneself, then one is true to one's core values (Erickson, 1995). Authentic leaders resist social or situational demands to compromise their internalized values. These values can be defined as 'conceptions of the desirable that guide the way social actors (e.g. organizational leaders, policy-makers, individual persons) select actions, evaluate people and events, and explain their actions and evaluations' (Schwartz, 1999, pp. 24–5). As trans-situational, normative standards for behaviour and evaluation, values provide the basis for actions conforming to the needs of the leader's community in general and organizational unit in particular. Values are learned through socialization processes. However, once internalized, they become integral to one's self-system. When internalized, authentic leaders are unwilling to compromise their values in the course of influencing their followers.

Identity

Identity is 'a theory (schema) of an individual that describes, interrelates, and explains his or her relevant features, characteristics, and experiences' (Schlenker, 1985: p. 68). Two types of identities have been discussed in the context of authentic leadership (Gardner et al., 2005): personal and social identities. Personal identities are self-categorizations based on one's unique characteristics, including traits and attributes, that specify differences between an actor and other people (Bananji and Prentice, 1994). Social identities, on the other hand, are those based upon the extent to which an individual classifies oneself as being a member of certain social groups, as well as an assessment of the emotional and value significance of the membership (Hogg, 2001). Personal and social identities are related in that they form, over time, as a consequence of the actors' reflections on their selves and their interaction with other people (Erickson, 1995). Authentic leaders clearly understand and are aware of their personal and social identities.

Emotions

In addition to self-awareness of values and identity, authentic leaders are also emotionally self-aware. Drawing from the emotional intelligence construct (see Goleman, 1995), George (2000) has found that those with higher levels of emotional intelligence are more aware of their emotions and understand the influence of such emotions on their cognitive processes and decision-making capabilities. It follows that self-awareness of one's emotions may be a key predictor of effective leadership (Avolio, 2004; Caruso and Mayer, 2001; George, 2000). For example, Ashkanasy and colleagues (Ashkanasy and Daus, 2002; Ashkanasy and Tse, 2000) propose that transformational leaders possess high levels of emotional intelligence that heighten their self- and other- emotional awareness, thus enhancing their abilities to display individualized consideration to their followers. We would argue that such emotional self-awareness is also a key component of authentic leadership.

Motives/goals

Authentic leaders are future-oriented and continually develop themselves and their followers (Avolio and Luthans, 2006; Luthans and Avolio, 2003). As such, we would expect authentic leaders to be driven by self-verification motives. They seek out accurate feedback from key stakeholders (e.g. followers, peers, mentors, customers) not only to confirm current self-views, but also to identify discrepancies from self-relevant standards as well (Avolio, 2004). In their quest for self-improvement, authentic leaders provide genuine self-presentations of their strengths and weaknesses to secure accurate reflected appraisals from others.

Closely related to the role that motives play in authentic leaders' self-awareness are self-set goals. Drawing from the previous discussion of the working self-concept, authentic leaders' goals can be defined as 'contextualized schema that direct current information processing' (Lord, Brown, and Freiberg, 1999, p. 180). Authentic leaders' goals may range from an overarching or strategic goal that is expressed as a vision to specific performance outcomes such as increasing productivity or reducing turnover or absenteeism.

Authentic leaders are driven by internalized regulatory processes in the pursuit of an integrated set of goals that reflect their personal standards of conduct. Authentic leaders are undergoing what Csikszentmihalyi (2003, p. 18) calls 'flow' which is 'a subjective experience of full involvement with life'.

In sum, authentic leaders become true to themselves through broadening their self-awareness. Authentic leaders have greater congruence between their current and possible selves (Avolio and Luthans, 2006). In the authentic leadership development process, discrepancies between a leader's current and possible selves will narrow as they achieve heightened levels of self-awareness. In particular, authentic leaders will be true to their core values, know their identity, experience greater positive emotions, and become effective in attaining their goals when the authentic self reflects congruence between the actual and possible selves (Kernis, 2003).

Self-awareness to self-regulation

In conjunction with self-awareness, authentic leaders are proposed to have the capacity to self-regulate (Avolio and Luthans, 2006; Luthans and Avolio, 2003). Self-regulation involves self-control through (a) setting of internal standards, (b) evaluation of discrepancies between these standards and outcomes, and (c) identification of intended actions for resolving the discrepancies (Stajkovic and Luthans, 1998b). These regulatory processes are associated with maintaining congruence between ideal and possible selves, and thus becoming more authentic. Deci and Ryan's (1995) self-determination theory can be drawn upon for support. Self-determination theory states that authenticity is associated with internalized regulatory processes. It also lends support to Kernis's (2003) assertion that authenticity involves balanced (unbiased) processing, authentic behaviour, and relational transparency.

Self-determination theory is built upon a foundation of three fundamental needs: autonomy, relatedness, and competence (Ryan and Deci, 2003). The authentic self evolves as 'one acts volitionally (i.e. autonomously), experiences an inner sense of efficacy (i.e. competence), and is loved (i.e. feels related to) for who one is rather than for matching an external standard' (Deci and Ryan, 1995, p. 33). They offer four types of motivation that reflect progressively higher levels of internalization and integration: external regulation, introjected regulation, identified regulation, and integrated regulation. External regulation describes behaviours that are not yet internalized, but are prompted and sustained by external consequences. Introjected regulation involves behaviours driven by internal pressures (e.g. guilt or shame) arising from self-regulatory processes that have not been integrated within the self. Identified regulation occurs when a person sees the value and importance of an action. The most autonomous form of external regulation is integrated regulation, which is the complete integration of values into the one's self-system. This integrated regulation is perhaps most representative of authenticity.

Further support of the role that self-regulation plays in authentic leadership is found in Sheldon and Elliot's (1999) self-concordance model of goal striving, an extension of self-determination theory. This model suggests that people achieve higher levels of personal growth when goals are set that are appropriate for their actual values, needs, and interests. Self-concordant identities satisfy the Deci and Ryan (1995) basic needs for autonomy, competence, and relatedness. Self-concordant identities are authentic because they are internalized and operate at the integrated level of self-regulation, which we propose is indicative of authentic leadership.

The role of unbiased processing

Kernis (2003) offers the term unbiased processing as a basic component of authenticity. Unbiased processing refers to an absence of denials, distortions, exaggerations, or ignorance of internal experiences, private knowledge, and external evaluations of the self that characterize a subjective view of the self. In other words, authenticity is characterized by objectivity and acceptance of one's positive and negative qualities, which bolsters the authentic leader's self-awareness. Tice and Wallace (2003) offer evidence that people are biased information processors when it comes to self-relevant information. Therefore, the term 'balanced processing' becomes very relevant to authentic leadership.

Balanced processing is best understood by considering how people with low, or fragile high self-esteem, are motivated to select and interpret information (Kernis, 2003). Such individuals are loath to acknowledge personal shortcomings, e.g. a lack of skill, undesirable personal attributes, or negative emotions. Vaillant (1992) suggests that maladaptive or immature defence styles that involve information distortion, or failure to acknowledge and resolve negative emotions, contribute to a wide variety of psychological and interpersonal difficulties. On the other hand, those with optimal self-esteem process information much more objectively (Kernis, 2003).

We propose that authentic leaders with optimal self-esteem are able to more objectively process both relevant and non-relevant self-esteem information. They are more able to objectively evaluate and accept both positive and negative aspects, attributes, and qualities of themselves, including deficiencies, suboptimal performance, and negative emotions. The implication for authentic leadership development is that leaders who are more, as opposed to less, authentic will be driven by self-verification motives to make accurate self-assessments, as well as social comparisons (Swann, Rentfrow, and Guinn, 2003). Subsequently, authentic leaders act upon these assessments to pursue core beliefs and values and are not waylaid by dysfunctional ego-defence motives such as self-enhancement and self-protection.

Relational transparency

The benefits of leader transparency, specifically trust, are increasingly touted in both the popular and academic literatures. The dysfunctional nature of managerial decision making in which leaders hoard information to the exclusion of followers has always been recognized, but in recent times is receiving increased attention (Pagano and Pagano, 2004). In particular, relational transparency plays an important role in authentic leadership (Avolio and Luthans, 2005; Gardner et al., 2005; Luthans and Avolio, 2003). Gardner et al. (2005: in press) propose that authentic leaders will be 'relatively transparent in expressing their true emotions and feelings to followers [when appropriate], while simultaneously regulating such emotions to minimize displays of inappropriate or potentially damaging emotions'.

Transparency 'is relational in nature, inasmuch as it involves valuing and achieving openness and truthfulness in one's close relationships' (Kernis, 2003, p. 15). Relationally transparent authentic leaders are committed to helping followers see both positive and negative aspects of their true self through a genuine rather than deceptive self-presentation. This goal is accomplished through appropriate self-disclosure of the self-awareness categories of values, identity, emotions, and goals/motives, resulting in high levels of trust in the leader (Hughes, 2005).

Authentic behaviour

Kernis states that:

> behaving authentically means acting in accord with one's values, preferences, and needs as opposed to acting merely to please others or to attain rewards or avoid punishments through acting 'falsely'. Authenticity is not a compulsive effort to display one's true self, but is the free and natural expression of core feelings, motives and inclinations.
>
> (2003, p. 14)

Sometimes environmental contingencies call for behaviours that are inconsistent with authentic expressions. The result is internal conflict. The resolution of such conflict has implications for the integrity one feels. Where a person's values are incompatible with those valued within a given society (or organization), authenticity occurs when internal cues, rather than societal pressures, are responded to (Deci and Ryan, 1995; Ryan and Deci, 2003). In contrast, authentic leaders with optimal self-esteem possess genuine feelings of self-worth and will tend to resist external pressure to compromise their values.

THE ROLE OF PSYCHOLOGICAL CAPITAL IN AUTHENTIC LEADERSHIP

Drawing from the initial model of authentic leadership development (Luthans and Avolio, 2003) and Luthans and colleagues' emerging theory, research, and practice on positive organizational behaviour (Luthans, 2002a, 2002b) and psychological capital (Luthans, Luthans, and Luthans, 2004; Luthans and Youssef, 2004; Luthans, Youssef, and Avolio 2007), we now turn to the role that psychological capital or simply PsyCap plays in authentic leadership. Along with a highly developed, supporting strength-based organizational context (covered next), PsyCap is an important antecedent to an authentic leader's self-awareness and regulation for performance impact in today's organizations.

Drawing from the recent positive psychology movement (Seligman and Csikszentmihali, 2000; Snyder and Lopez, 2002), positive organizational behaviour (POB) is defined as 'The study and application of positively oriented human resource strengths and psychological capacities that can be measured, developed, and effectively managed for performance improvement in today's workplace' (Luthans, 2002b, p. 59). After first expanding on this definition of POB, we examine the major POB criteria meeting states of hope, optimism, resiliency, and self-efficacy/confidence. When combined into the core construct of PsyCap, these positive states can be invested in for authentic leadership and followership development and leveraged for performance impact and competitive advantage.

Positive organizational behaviour

Positive organizational behaviour (POB) is essentially translating and applying positive psychology to the workplace. Although similar to positive psychology in its orientation and theory and research basis, POB does also differ from positive psychology in that it identifies measurable and developable state-like strengths rather than more fixed, trait-like characteristics and virtues as does most of positive psychology (e.g. see Peterson and Seligman, 2004). Although some theorists believe that there is a clear dichotomy between states and traits, we take the position that they fall more along a continuum. The states we identify as being PsyCap for authentic leaders are relatively malleable and thus can be influenced by interventions (Luthans *et al.*, 2004; Luthans and Youssef, 2004; Luthans, Youssef, and Avolio, 2007).

In addition to being based on theory and research and open to development, POB states must also be validly measured. Therefore, these measured POB states can provide feedback to individuals and also evaluate the effectiveness of development programmes and performance management interventions. Finally, the POB states are unique to organizational behaviour. To date, the constructs of hope, optimism, resiliency, and self-efficacy have been judged to best meet these POB criteria (Luthans, 2002a).

Hope

Hope is rooted in the positive psychology research largely conducted by the late C. Rick Snyder and his colleagues (Snyder, 2000; Snyder and Lopez, 2002; Snyder, Irving, and Anderson, 1991). Snyder defines hope as 'a positive motivational state that is based on an interactively derived sense of successful (1) agency (goal-directed energy) and (2) pathways (planning to meet goals)' (Snyder, Irving, and Anderson, 1991, p. 287). Thus, hope includes both the will (goal-directed energy or motivation), and the way (alternative plans for accomplishing the goal). While its origins have been in educational and sports arenas, hope is beginning to receive attention in organizational leadership (Peterson and Luthans, 2002), even at the country level (Luthans, van Wyk, and Walumbwa, 2004).

Optimism

The recognized father of positive psychology Martin Seligman (1990) defines optimism as a cognitive process that involves favourable outcome expectancies. He has found it to be linked to positive organizational outcomes such as work motivation, performance, morale and satisfaction, and perseverance. In addition, there are countless examples of optimistic leaders who have had a positive effect on organizational outcomes (Luthans and Avolio, 2003).

Resiliency

Resiliency also meets the POB criteria and its application is largely based on the work of positive psychologist Ann Masten and colleagues (Masten, 2001; Masten and Reed, 2002). Resiliency refers to one's ability to bounce back from adversity, and recent research and theory-building has shown that resiliency can be developed (Coutu, 2002; Masten and Reed, 2002; Youssef and Luthans, 2005). Given the turbulent organizational environment present today, resiliency is an especially critical component in authentic leadership. In these new times, leaders who are better able to respond favourably to negative situations or goal-directed obstructions will be more successful and their resiliency may have a contagion effect on their followers.

Self-efficacy

Self-efficacy perhaps best meets the POB criteria (Luthans, 2002a) and is grounded in the considerable theory and research of Albert Bandura (1997). He defines self-efficacy as the belief of how well individuals can execute the necessary action required to deal with situations they are faced with (Bandura, 1982). Adapting this definition to the workplace and leadership is: 'Self-efficacy refers to an individual's conviction (or confidence) about his or her abilities to mobilize the motivation, cognitive resources, and courses of action needed to successfully execute a specific task within a given context' (Stajkovic and Luthans, 1998b, p. 66). Authentic leaders are confident and more likely to take 'calculated' risks that can lead to success for themselves, their followers, and their organizations. However, as per the definitions of efficacy, the context becomes critical to authentic leadership development (Luthans and Avolio, 2003).

HIGHLY DEVELOPED, STRENGTH-BASED ORGANIZATIONAL CONTEXT

While the PsyCap states are critical antecedents (and outcomes), they are not sufficient for our proposed authentic leadership development (Luthans and Avolio,

2003). Authentic leadership is a process and requires a highly developed organizational context. This context can be very complex and integrated and thus for understanding can draw from a comprehensive theoretical foundation from social psychology, leadership, and organizational behaviour.

The selection process

From the perspective of authentic leadership, the organizational context consists of a process that begins early in the relationship and interaction between the leader, followers, and others and continues throughout the tenure of this relationship and interaction. The starting point would be the selection process. In particular, careful selection would help ensure the fit between the new hire and the organization, which will increase the probability of both individual and organizational success. For example, the Gallup Organization has effectively utilized a targeted and specific hiring system that has accounted for high levels of employee retention and engagement (Clifton and Harter, 2003).

Such selection processes could be aimed at the POB states instead of the Gallup strengths and talents. By selecting those with high levels of PsyCap, the opportunities for attaining authentic leaders and followers would be enhanced and the contagion effect may in turn result in a more supportive, strength-based organizational context.

Socialization and norms

To date, much of the work in person–organization (P–O) fit has focused on the attraction–selection–attrition (ASA) model (Cable and Parsons, 2001; Schneider, 1987). Although an effective selection process can help establish P–O fit, it also evolves and can be strengthened though socialization (Cable and Parsons, 2001). Socialization refers to the process by which newcomers in an organization acquire the appropriate behaviour, attitudes, and knowledge needed to be successful as an organizational member (Cable and Parsons, 2001). Socialization involves sharing experiences and establishes mental models. It converts tacit knowledge among members into explicit knowledge (Nonaka and Takeuchi, 1995). In other words, an effective socialization process can be another way to contribute to a desired supportive context for authentic leadership.

Closely related to socialization are social norms that have been said to be at the core of organizational culture (Schein, 1983; Smith and Vecchio, 1993). Transmission of norms and appropriate behaviour can occur deliberately through active instruction, rituals, and so on, or more passively through non-verbal behaviours, or inferred from others around us (Cialdini and Trost, 1998). Norms as examined in relation to a supportive context for authentic leadership are shared belief systems. These norms must be examined from the perspective of both the individual psychological system and the sociocultural system in which the individual is embedded (Pepitone, 1976). Thus, there is a large social component involved in the creation and maintenance of group or organizational norms. Especially norms around transparency and respect can have a significant impact on authentic leadership.

Social capital

Still another dimension of a highly developed, strength-based organizational context supporting authentic leadership is social capital. Social capital is a concept that is rooted in sociology and network analysis. Although social capital has been interpreted many ways, the most common view is that it involves group members (actors) securing some benefit as a result of their membership in social networks or related social structures (Brass, 2001; Portes, 1998). Thus, members of the group benefit from the relationships (their social networks) that are both personal and social (Coleman, 1988; Nahapiet and Ghoshal, 1998). These social networks can also carry organizational benefits (Baker, 1990; Burt, 2004; Nahapiet and Ghoshal, 1998; Sparrowe, Liden, and Kraimer, 2001) and additionally we would suggest contextual support for authentic leadership.

Social capital can be a supportive contextual factor for authentic leadership not only inside the organization, but outside as well. Given that a large source of innovation comes from the outside (Cohen and Levinthal, 1990), social capital that is developed outside the organization is also important to authentic leadership. Thus, social capital, both inside and outside the organization can be a key element when examining organizational support.

The power of social capital supporting authentic leadership can be found in two sources. First, the idea of social capital focuses positively on the consequences of social interaction. This parallels the focus on both positive psychological capital and authentic leadership. Second, the idea of social capital revolves around the value of non-financial forms of capital and its role in power, influence, and success (Portes, 1998). That is, there is value in looking at the positive influence that other forms of capital can have on groups and organizations (Nahapiet and Ghoshal, 1998; Sparrowe, Liden, and Kraimer, 2001) and we would propose authentic leadership.

Contagion effect

Still another component of a highly developed, supportive organizational context are contagion effects. There has been increased attention given to social contagion and it has been empirically supported in various situations (Brett and Stroh, 2003; Levy and Nail, 1993; Pastor and Mayo, 1994; Williamson and Cable, 2003). Though the roots of social contagion are based in attribution theory (Brett and Stroh, 2003;

Pastor and Mayo, 1994), it has also been studied in diverse disciplines such as sociology, social learning, psychoanalysis, and social psychology (Levy and Nail, 1993). Le Bon has been credited with introducing the idea of contagion into social behaviour studies over 100 years ago when he described crowd behaviour as being influenced by both contagion and suggestibility (Levy and Nail, 1993). This conception contains both factors external to the individual (contagion) and factors internal to the individual (suggestibility).

More relevant to authentic leadership, including the effects of contagion discussed earlier, is the classic work of the sociologist Blumer. Over 50 years ago he defined social contagion as involving interpersonal communication that is more circular in nature, where people behave in unison with others' states (Levy and Nail, 1993). Thus, this definition of social contagion is parallel with our assertion that a leader's positive psychological states such as hope, optimism, resiliency, and self-efficacy, as well as their authenticity, can be perceived by others (e.g. followers). The perceiver (e.g. the follower) takes on the states of the person (i.e. the model or leader) they are interacting with and then acts in parallel with these states. Thus, this social contagion effect not only has implications for the supporting context for authentic leadership, but also authentic followership.

DEVELOPMENT OF AUTHENTIC FOLLOWERSHIP

We have proposed so far that authentic leaders are key role models for positive values, high moral standards, transparency, and PsyCap states. However, the personal histories of followers, including both their work and personal experiences, also contribute to the development of their conception of their self (Hoyle et al., 1999). Some followers, cynical as a result of organizational politics, change, opportunistic leaders, and unfulfilled promises, may actually be wary of a leader who espouses authentic values (Dean, Brandes, and Dhwardkar, 1998). By the same token, an encounter with an authentic leader may serve as a trigger event that helps them to shed their cynicism, rediscover lost idealism, and renew ambition. Again, authentic leaders focus on developing their followers (Avolio et al., 2004; Gardner et al., 2005; Luthans and Avolio, 2003).

As presented here, authentic followership can be formally defined as:

> the process whereby the positive organizational context, positive interactions with the leader, and the authenticity and integrity modelled by the leader combine to produce heightened levels of follower self-awareness, positive psychological capacities, positive self-regulated behaviours, and positive follower outcomes (trust, engagement, workplace well-being) in a continuous cycle of self-development.
>
> (Gardner et al., 2005)

The authentic followership process

Self-awareness, as previously discussed in authentic leadership is equally as critical to the authentic followership process (Kernis, 2003). Followers' knowledge of their own values, identity, emotions, and motives/goals are again key to their self-awareness. Through modelling of authentic values and behaviour, and actively encouraging and facilitating follower self-development, authentic leaders can enhance their followers' self-awareness. However, the effectiveness of such follower development is dependent upon the congruence between the leader's and followers' values, identity, emotions, and motives/goals. Self-concept clarity and value congruence are relevant to building the authentic leader–follower relationship (Weierter, 1997).

By definition, authentic leaders are follower building (Avolio *et al.*, 2004; Gardner *et al.*, 2005; Luthans and Avolio, 2003). This is proposed to be accomplished primarily via the modelling process. However, the authentic follower needs to identify with the leader's core values or the collective values of the group or organization rather than with the leader on just a personal level. This value congruence discriminates the authentic leadership and followership development construct from more socially influential constructs such as charismatic leadership (Weierter, 1997).

The means whereby leaders can foster a collective identity include an emphasis on the shared values of the organization and linking the organization's mission, goals, and desired behaviours to the collective (Kark and Shamir, 2002; Shamir, House and Arthur, 1993). This process should result in the followers' internalization of core organizational values, thus allowing the follower to achieve a high level of self-clarity and autonomy that both accompany authenticity (Deci and Ryan, 1995; Kernis, 2002). Conversely, those with low self-clarity could be prone to defensiveness and become threatened by a leader's authenticity (Campbell *et al.*, 1996). Consequently, followers may initially reject the authentic leader as a source of influence. However, over time the authentic leader will serve to model consistent and genuine behaviour for followers. The authentic leader serving as a model may evoke trust, which facilitates for followers the process of self-discovery, identification, and value internalization.

Self-discrepancy theory suggests the cognitive, affective, and motivational effects of discrepancies between an individual's normative and ideal selves. Robins and Boldero (2003) use the term 'commensurability' to account for the extent to which self-aspects are shared by both members of the dyad (i.e. leader–follower). While two individuals may share an attribute or state as a self-aspect, discrepancies arise from differences in the quantity or level of a particular attribute or state.

Authentic leaders who seek to develop authentic followers will help them move from external and introjected regulation to more internalized (e.g. integrated) forms of regulation (Deci and Ryan, 1995; Ryan and Deci, 2003). Positive modelling by authentic leaders will help followers develop authentic and self-concordant identities (Sheldon and Elliott, 1999; Sheldon et al., 2004). Authentic leaders can also help followers fulfil their needs for competence and autonomy by helping them discover their talents, develop these talents into strengths, and empower them to engage in tasks at which they can excel (Clifton and Harter, 2003; Liden, Wayne, and Sparrowe, 2000).

Although a wide variety of outcomes may accrue for the followers of authentic leaders, our attention is focused on three outcomes that have been consistently linked to authenticity: trust, engagement, and well-being (Erickson, 1995; Harter, 2002; Harter, Schmidt, and Hayes, 2002; Harter, Schmidt, and Keyes, 2003). Although each of these outcomes may be treated separately, there is mutual interdependence among them. Specifically, high levels of one will contribute to the other two, and vice versa (Avolio et al., 2004).

The role of trust in authentic followership

Trust is a central premise of classic social exchange theory. An important antecedent to a trust relationship is openness, which in turn is a component of relational transparency previously discussed under self-awareness. Therefore, because authentic leaders recognize the importance of relational transparency, which leads to trust in leader–follower relationships, the resulting psychological contract (Rousseau, 1995) that authentic leaders establish with followers has a stronger foundation. Once established, this psychological contract offers a common understanding about future action and each party's responsibilities. When the leader and follower meet each other's expectations, the foundation for trust is established and additional growth is fostered. The ultimate result is sustainable performance.

Early in the authentic leader–follower relationship, relational transparency is emphasized by words. Over time, however, followers come to learn what the authentic leader values and how these values match their own. Thus, relational transparency becomes emphasized by actions. To the extent that an authentic leader takes the needs of all stakeholders into consideration, and is considered fair in his or her actions, conditional trust will evolve to a deeper, relational trust.

As these higher levels of trust emerge among followers, they will become willing to trust in the leader's intentions, transcending a transactional basis for trust (Avolio et al., 2004). A follower's willingness to trust a leader without question is a dangerous transition point if the leader's intentions are harmful. History has seen charismatic leaders, who build deep trust among followers, then violate it for their own selfish interests. However, when trust in a leader is well placed, meta-analysis has shown it to be related to elevated levels of follower job satisfaction, organizational citizenship behaviours, commitment, and job performance (Dirks and Ferrin, 2002).

The role of engagement in authentic followership

Follower engagement is a key factor that mediates the relationship between the authentic leader, followers, and sustained, veritable performance. Nakamura and Csikszentmihalyi (2003, p. 87) use the term vital engagement to describe 'a relationship to the world that is characterized both by experiences of flow (enjoyed absorption) and by meaning (subjective significance)'. As previously discussed, flow occurs when individuals achieve a level of complete absorption in their interactions with the world and this experience unfolds organically (Csikszentmihalyi, 1990, 2003). The state of flow is entered when a person's perceived capabilities are balanced against perceived challenges, and this state is maintained as long as the balance is sustained.

However, flow is insufficient to achieve vital engagement in and of itself. For an activity to be considered meaningful, it must either provide new and deepening insights and/or make a valuable contribution to others. When work is experienced as being vitally engaging, it is often referred to as a 'calling' (Nakamura and Csikszentmihalyi, 2003). Authentic leaders can facilitate vital engagement in their followers by helping them to develop and draw upon their reserves of PsyCap and a positive moral perspective. They will thus become more, rather than less, authentic and vitally engaged in their work.

The term employee engagement is a more specific form of engagement and 'refers to the individual's involvement and satisfaction with as well as enthusiasm for work' (Harter, Schmidt, and Hayes, 2002, p. 269). Harter and colleagues' (2002) meta-analysis demonstrates that employee engagement is positively and strongly related to critical business performance outcomes, including customer satisfaction, productivity, profit, employee retention, and safety, all of which are indicators of sustained, veritable performance.

The role of workplace well-being in authentic followership

Eudaemonic well-being is a construct that is closely related to vital engagement. Eudaemonic well-being involves self-congruence, vital functioning, life satisfaction, and psychological health (Ryan and Deci, 2001; Ilies, Morgeson and Nahrgang, 2005). This construct can be distinguished from hedonic well-being (Kahneman, Diener, and Schwartz, 1999), which is distinguished by pleasure and pain with the goal of maximizing felt happiness, or subjective well-being. Eudaemonic well-being calls on people to live in accordance with their true self (Waterman, 1993), which provides an important linkage between authenticity and well-being (Ilies, Morgeson and Nahrgang, 2005). Also, mounting empirical evidence is providing documentation for the causal relationships between authenticity, vital engagement, and eudaemonic well-being (see Kahneman, Diener, and Schwartz, 1999; Kernis, 2003; Ryan and Deci, 2001; Sheldon and Elliot, 1999).

Given this theoretical support and empirical findings, we argue that a consequence of authentic leadership and followership is increased workplace well-being (Harter, Schmidt, and Keyes, 2003), organizational commitment, job satisfaction, and performance. Through modelling and encouraging authenticity, PsyCap, and a positive moral perspective, the authentic leader will foster self-concordance and vital engagement, and subsequently well-being authenticity in followers.

A FINAL WORD

The premise of this chapter has been that the new times we live in requires a new approach to organizational leadership. This new time is not only characterized by an apparent ethical and moral breakdown, but also a time in which followers are more sceptical of their leaders than ever before. Followers are often as well educated as their leaders and are privy to the same information as their leaders – oftentimes possessing it prior to their leaders. We have proposed and briefly outlined in this chapter that the challenge of these new times can perhaps be best met by our newly emerging authentic leadership.

REFERENCES

Ashkanasy, N. M. and Daus, C. S. (2002) Emotion in the workplace: The new challenge for managers. *Academy of Management Executive*, 16(1): 76–86.

Ashkanasy, N. M. and Tse, B. (2000) Transformational leadership as management of emotion: A conceptual review. In C. E. J. Hartel and W. J. Zerbe (eds) *Emotions in working life: theory, research and practice*. Westport, CT: Quorum Books, pp. 221–35.

Avolio, B. J. (2004) Examining the full range model of leadership: Looking back to transform forward. In D. V. Day, S. J. Zaccarro and S. M. Halpin (eds) *Leader development for transforming organizations: growing leaders for tomorrow*. Mahwah, NJ: Lawrence Erlbaum Associates, pp. 71–98.

Avolio, B. J. and Gardner, W. L. (2005) Authentic leadership development: Getting to the root of positive forms of leadership. *The Leadership Quarterly*, 16(3): 315–38.

Avolio, B. J. and Luthans, F. (2006) *The high impact leader: moments matter for accelerating authentic leadership development*. New York: McGraw-Hill.

Avolio, B. J., Gardner, W. L., Walumbwa, F. O., Luthans, F., and May, D. R. (2004) Unlocking the mask: A look at the process by which authentic leaders impact follower attitudes and behaviors. *The Leadership Quarterly*, 15: 801–23.

Baker, W. (1990) Market networks and corporate behavior. *American Journal of Sociology*, 96: 589–625.

Bananji, M. R. and Prentice, D. A. (1994) The self in social contexts. *Annual Review of Psychology*, 45: 297–332.

Bandura, A. (1997) *Self-efficacy: The exercise of control*. New York: Freeman.

Bandura, A. (1982) Self-sufficiency mechanism in human agency. *American Psychologist*, 37 (2): 122–47.

Brass, D. J. (2001) Social capital and organizational leadership. In Steven J. Zaccaro and Richard J. Klimoski (eds) *The nature of organizational leadership: understanding the performance imperatives confronting today's leaders*. San Francisco, CA: Jossey-Bass Publishers, 132–52.

Brett J. M. and Stroh, L. K. (2001) Working 61 plus hours a week: Why do managers do it? *Journal of Applied Psychology*, 88(1): 67–78.

Burt, R. S. (2004) Structural holes and good ideas. *American Journal of Sociology*, 110(2): 349–99.

Cable, D. M. and Parsons, C. K. (2001) Socialization tactics and person-organization fit. *Personnel Psychology*, 54: 1–23.

Campbell, J. D., Trapnell, P. D., Heine, S. J., Katz, E. M., Lavallee, L. F., and Lehman, D. R. (1996) Self-concept clarity: Measurement, personality correlates, and cultural boundaries. *Journal of Personality and Social Psychology*, 70: 141–56.

Cialdini, R. B. and Trost, M. R. (1998) Social influence: Social norms, conformity, and compliance. In D. T. Gilbert, S. T. Fiske and G. Lindzey (eds). *The Handbook of Social Psychology – Vol. II*, (4th edn), New York: McGraw Hill, pp. 151–92.

Caruso, D. R. and Mayer, J. D. (2001) Emotional intelligence and emotional leadership. In R. E. Riggio and S. E. Murphey (eds) *Multiple intelligences and leadership*. Mahwah, NJ: Erlbaum, 2001, pp. 55–74.

Clifton, D. O. and Harter, J. K. (2003) Investing in strengths. In K. S. Cameron, J. E. Dutton, and R. E. Quinn (eds) *Positive organizational scholarship*. San Francisco, CA: Berret-Koehler, pp. 111–21.

Cohen, W. M. and Levinthal, D. A. (1990) Absorptive capacity: A new perspective on learning and innovation. *Administrative Science Quarterly*, 35: 128–52.

Coleman, J. S. (1988) Social capital in the creation of human capital. *American Journal of Sociology*, 94: 95–120.

Coutu, D. L. (2002) How resilience works. *Harvard Business Review*, 80 (5): 46–55.

Csikszentmihalyi, M. (1990) *Flow*. New York: Harper & Row.

Csikszentmihalyi, M. (2003) *Good business: Leadership, flow, and the making of meaning*. New York: Penguin Books.

Dean, J. W., Brandes, P., and Dhwardkar, R. (1998) Organizational cynicism. *Academy of Management Review*, 23: 341–52.

Deci, E. L. and Ryan, R. M. (1995) Human autonomy: The basis for true self-esteem. In M. H. Kernis (ed.) *Efficacy, agency, and self-esteem*. New York: Plenum Press, pp. 31- 49.

Deci, E. L. and Ryan, R. M. (2000) 'What' and 'why' of goal pursuits: Human needs and the self-determination of behavior. *Psychological Inquiry*, 11: 227–68.

Dirks, K. T. and Ferrin, D. L. (2002) Trust in leadership: Meta-analytic findings and implications for research and practice. *Journal of Applied Psychology*, 87: 611–28.

Erickson, R. J. (1995) Our society, our selves: Becoming authentic in an inauthentic world. *Advanced Development*, 6: 27–39.

Gardner, W. L., Avolio, B. J., and Walumbwa, F. O. (2005) Authentic leadership development: Emergent themes and future directions. In W. L. Gardner, B. J. Avolio and F. O. Walumbwa (eds) *Authentic Leadership Development: Monographs in Leadership and Management Series* (vol. 3), Boston, MA: Elsevier, JAI Press.

Gardner, W. L., Avolio, B. J., Luthans, F., May, D. R., and Walumbwa, O. F. (2005) Can you see the real me?: A self-based model of authentic leader and follower development. *The Leadership Quarterly*, 16(3): 343–72.

George, J. M. (2000) Emotions and leadership: The role of emotional intelligence. *Human Relations*, 53(8): 1027–55.

Goleman, D. (1995) *Emotional intelligence*, New York: Bantam.

Harter, J. K., Schmidt, F. L., and Hayes, T. L. (2002) Business-unit level relationship between employee satisfaction, employee engagement, and business outcomes: A meta-analysis. *Journal of Applied Psychology*, 87(2): 268–79.

Harter, J. K., Schmidt, F. L., and Keyes, C. L. M. (2003) Well-being in the workplace and its relationship to business outcomes: A review of the Gallup studies. In C. L. M. Keyes and J. Haidt (eds) *Flourishing: Positive psychology and the life well-lived*. Washington, DC: American Psychological Association, pp. 205–24.

Harter, S. (2002) Authenticity. In C. R. Snyder and S. Lopez (eds) *Handbook of positive psychology*, Oxford: Oxford University Press, pp. 382–94.

Hogg, M. A. (2001) A social identity theory of leadership. *Personality and Social Psychology Review*, 5(3): 184–200.

Hoyle, R. H., Kernis, M. H., Leary, M. R., and Baldwin, M. W. (1999) *Selfhood: Identity, esteem, regulation*. Boulder, CO: Westview Press.

Hughes, L. W. (2005) Developing transparent relationships through humour in the authentic leader-follower relationship. In W. L. Gardner, B. J. Avolio and F. O. Walumba (eds) *Authentic Leadership Development: Monographs in leadership and management series* (vol. 3). Boston, MA: Elsevier, JAI Press.

Ilies, R., Morgeson, F. P., and Nahrgang, J. D. (2005) Authentic leadership and eudaemonic well-being: Understanding leader-follower outcomes. *Leadership Quarterly*, 16(3): 373–94.

Kahneman, D., Diener, E., and Schwartz, N. (eds) (1999) *Well-being: The foundation of hedonic psychology*. New York: Russell Sage Foundation.

Kark, R. and Shamir, B. (2002) The dual effect of transformational leadership: Priming relational and collective selves and further effects on followers. In B. J. Avolio and F. J. Yammarino (eds) *Transformational and charismatic leadership*, vol. 2, Boston, MA: Elsevier, JAI Press, pp. 67–91.

Kernis, M. H. (2003) Toward a conceptualization of optimal self-esteem. *Psychological Inquiry*, 14: 1–26.

Levy, D. A. and Nail, P. R. (1993) Contagion: A theoretical and empirical review and reconceptualization. *Genetic, Social, and General Psychology Monographs,* 119(2): 233–84.

Liden, R. C., Wayne, S. J., and Sparrowe, R. T. (2000) An examination of the mediating role of psychological empowerment on the relations between the job, interpersonal relationship, and work outcomes. *Journal of Applied Psychology,* 85(3): 407–16.

Lord, R. G., Brown, D. J., and Freiberg, S. J. (1999) Understanding the dynamics of leadership: The role of follower self-concepts in the leader/follower relationship. *Organizational Behavior and Human Decision Processes,* 78(3), 1999, 167–203.

Luthans, F. (2002a) The need for and meaning of positive organizational behavior. *Journal of Organizational Behavior,* 23: 695–706.

Luthans, F. (2002b) Positive organizational behavior: Developing and managing psychological strengths. *Academy of Management Executive,* 16: 57–72.

Luthans, F. and Avolio, B. J. (2003) Authentic leadership development. In K. S. Cameron, J. E. Dutton, and R. E. Quinn (eds) *Positive Organizational Scholarship.* San Francisco, CA: Barrett-Koehler, pp. 241–61.

Luthans, F. and Youssef, C. M. (2004) Human, social, and now positive psychological capital management: Investing in people for competitive advantage. *Organizational Dynamics,* 33(2): 143–60.

Luthans, F., Luthans, K. W., and Luthans, B. C. (2004) Positive psychological capital: Beyond human and social capital. *Business Horizons,* 47(1): 45–50.

Luthans, F., Van Wyk, R., and Walumbwa, F. O. (2004) Recognition and development of hope for South African organizational leaders. *Leadership and Organization Development Journal,* 25 (6): 512–27.

Luthans, F., Youssef, C. M., and Avolio, B. J. (2007) *Psychological capital,* Oxford: Oxford University Press.

Markus, H. R. and Wurf, E. (1987) The dynamic self-concept: A social psychological perspective. *American Review of Psychology,* 38: 299–337.

Masten, A. S. (2001) Ordinary magic: Resilience processes in development. *American Psychologist,* 56: 227–39.

Masten, A. S. and Reed, M. G. J. (2002) Resilience in development. In C. R. Snyder and S. Lopez (eds) *Handbook of Positive Psychology,* Oxford: Oxford University Press, pp. 74–88.

May, D. R., Chan, A., Hodges, T., and Avolio, B. J. (2003) Developing the moral component of anthentic leadership. *Organizational Dynamics,* 32: 247–60.

Nahapiet, J. and Ghoshal, S. (1998) Social capital, intellectual capital, and the organizational advantage. *Academy of Management Review,* 23(2): 242–66.

Nakamura, J. and Csikszentmihalyi, M. (2003) The construction of meaning through vital engagement. In C. L. M. Keyes and J. Haidt (eds) *Flourishing: Positive psychology and the life well-lived.* Washington, DC: American Psychological Association, pp. 83–104.

Nonaka, I. and Takeuchi, H. (1995) *The knowledge-creating company.* Oxford: Oxford University Press, pp. 56–94.

Pagano, B. and Pagano, E. (2004) *The transparency edge: How credibility can make or break you in business.* New York: McGraw-Hill.

Pastor, J. C. and Mayo, M. C. (1994) An empirical test of the social contagion theory of charismatic leadership. *Academy of Management Proceedings*, 259–64.

Peterson, C. and Seligman, M.E. (2004) *Character strengths and virtues.* Oxford: Oxford University Press.

Peterson, S. J. and Luthans, F. (2002) The positive impact and development of hopeful leaders. *Leadership and Organization Development Journal*, 24: 6–31.

Pepitone, A. (1976) Toward a normative and comparative biocultural social psychology. *Journal of Personality and Social Psychology*, 34: 641–53.

Portes, A. (1998) Social capital: Its origins and applications in modern sociology. *Annual Review of Sociology*, 24: 1–24.

Robins, G. and Boldero, J. (2003) Relational discrepancy theory: The implications of self-discrepancy theory for dyadic relationships and for the emergence of social structure. *Personality and Social Psychology Review*, 7(1): 56–74.

Rousseau, D. M. (1995) *Psychological contracts in organizations: Understanding written and unwritten agreements.* Newbury Park, CA: Sage.

Ryan, R. M. and Deci, E. L. (2001) On happiness and human potentials: A review of research on hedonic and eudaimonic well-being. *Annual Review of Psychology*, 52: 141–66.

Ryan, R. M. and Deci, E. L. (2003) On assimilating identities to the self: A self-determination theory perspective on internalization and integrity within cultures. In M. R. Leary and J. P. Tangney (eds) *Handbook of self and identity,* New York: Guilford, pp. 253–72.

Schein, E. (1983) The role of the founder in creating organizational culture. *Organizational Dynamics*, Summer, 13–28.

Schbenker, B. R. (ed.) (1985) *The self and social life.* New York: McGraw-Hill.

Schneider, B. (1987) The people make the place. *Personnel Psychology*, 40: 437–53.

Schwartz, S. H. (1999) A theory of cultural values and some implications for work. *Applied Psychology: An International Review*, 1(1): 23–47.

Seligman, M. E. P. (1990) *Learned Optimism,* New York: Pocket Books.

Seligman, M. E. P. and Csikszentmihalyi, M. (2000) Positive phychology. *American Psychogist*, 55: 5–14.

Shamir, B., House, R. J., and Arthur, M. B. (1993) The motivational effects of charismatic leadership: A self-concept based theory. *Organization Science*, 4: 577–94.

Sheldon, K. M. and Elliot, A. J. (1999) Goal striving, need satisfaction, and longitudinal well-being: The self-concordance model. *Journal of Personality and Social Psychology*, 76(3): 482–97.

Sheldon, K. M., Elliot, A. J., Ryan, R. M., Chirkov, V., Kim, Y., Wu, C., Demir, M. and Sun, Z. (2004) Self-concordance and subjective well-being in four cultures. *Journal of Cross-Cultural Psychology*, 35(2): 209–33.

Smith, C. G. and Vecchio, R. P. (1993) Organizational culture and strategic management: Issues in the management of strategic change. *Journal of Managerial Issues*, 5(1): 53–70.

Snyder, C. R. (2000) *Handbook of Hope*, San Diego, CA: Academic Press.

Snyder, C. R. and Lopez, S. J. (eds) (2002) *Handbook of positive psychology*. Oxford: Oxford University Press.

Snyder, C. R., Irving, L. M., and Anderson, J. R. (1991) Hope and health. In C. R. Snyder (ed.) *Handbook of social and clinical psychology*. Oxford: Oxford University Press, pp. 295–305.

Sparrowe, R. T., Liden, R. C., and Kraimer, M. L. (2001) Social networks and the performance of individuals and groups. *Academy of Management Journal*, 44(2): 316–25.

Stajkovic, A. D. and Luthans, F. (1998a) Self-efficacy and work-related performance: A meta-analysis. *Psychological Bulletin*, 124: 240–61.

Stajkovic, A. D. and Luthans, F. (1998b) Social cognitive theory and self-efficacy: Going beyond traditional motivational and behavioral approaches. *Organizational Dynamics*, 126: 62–74.

Swann, W. B. Jr, Rentfrow, P. J., and Guinn, J. S. (2003) Self-verification: The search for coherence. In M. R. Leary and J. P. Tangney (eds) *Handbook of self and identity*, New York: Guilford Press, pp. 367–83.

Tice, D. M. and Wallace, H. M. (2003) The reflected self: Creating yourself as (you think) others see you. In M. R. Leary and J. P. Tangney (eds) *Handbook of self and identity*, New York: Guilford Press, pp. 91–105.

Vaillant, G. (1992) *Ego Mechanisms of Defense: A Guide for Clinicians and Researchers*. Washington, DC: American Psychiatric Press.

Waterman, A. S. (1993) Two conceptions of happiness: Contrasts of personal expressiveness (eudaimonia) and hedonic enjoyment. *Journal of Personality and Social Psychology*, 64: 678–91.

Weierter, S. J. M. (1997) Who wants to play 'follow the leader?' A theory of charismatic relationships based on routinized charisma and followers characteristics. *Leadership Quarterly*, 8(2): 171–93.

Williamson, I. O. and Cable, D. M. (2003) Organizational hiring patterns, interfirm network ties, and interorganizational imitation. *Academy of Management Journal*, 46 (3): 349–59.

Youssef, C. M. and Luthans, F. (2005) A positive organizational approach to ethical performance. In R. A. Giacalone, C. Dunn and C. Jurkiewicz (eds) *Positive psychology in business ethics and corporate social responsibility,* Greenwich, CT: Information Age.

Chapter 5

The inspirational nature of level three leadership

James G. Clawson

Companies often have annual report and strategic planning meetings. At one such three-day event recently, the first day schedule consisted of a series of presentations by the general managers of various lines of businesses. The quality of the presentations varied, as one might expect. One participant noted though that one session was particularly anaesthetizing. 'We kept nodding off', he offered. 'It was awful'. Furthermore, the financial data being presented on the large screen was so tiny as to be unreadable. This is odd only in that these annual meetings are intended to have just the opposite effect; executives planning them hope the sessions will be both informative (what are they doing in that line of business) and inspiring (let's get pumped up for the New Year). In this case the results were quite mixed.

At another similar event, the organizers were very concerned about the 'inspiring' part. They hired famous celebrity look-alikes (in this case, 'Marilyn Monroe'), had clouds of carbon dioxide floating across the stage, and the local high school band playing in the background. Clearly, it was an attempt to fire people up and get them motivated for the New Year.

These two examples of executive attempts to inspire their employees raise difficult and interesting questions about how people in leadership positions can inspire their people. By 'inspire' typically, executives mean get people to have high energy and to be 100 per cent committed to reaching the corporation's annual goals.

But these approaches, which we might call the 'business review' and the 'cheerleading' alternatives, have some obvious flaws – they may neither well inform nor well inspire. Part of the problem lies with the assumptions executives make about how humans are motivated – or in the superlative case, inspired. The assumption underlying the business review model is something like 'managers will be eager to see how other businesses are being managed and will learn and gain energy from that'. The assumption underlying the cheerleading approach is something like 'humans need to be touched emotionally in order to perform well'. Neither alone seems sufficient in a sophisticated, global, modern business world.

Consider, for example, all of the people you've met at work during the course of your lifetime. On average what level of engagement in their work do they seem to have? Over the last several years, I've asked this question of hundreds of practising managers. The answers seem to revolve around 50–70 per cent. Gallup published a poll recently estimating levels of engagement as measured by the bare minimum (not looking for work elsewhere) and reported as much as half of employees were not engaged at work (Gallup, 2002). What manager hiring new people would be satisfied with half of his or her employees being engaged? Would you? Further, I wonder that individuals who will spend roughly two-thirds of their waking life at work would tolerate employment that only engages half of their energy and talent. What an indictment of modern work systems!

So, I assert with regard to leadership in general and inspirational leadership in particular, *leadership is about managing energy, first in one's self and then in the people around*. Executives continue to strive to find ways to 'inspire' their people, that is, to 'pump up their energy level', and often come up short.

Part of the problem is that executives often have a relatively simple set of beliefs and assumptions about what it takes to motivate people. Some may believe that 'people either have it or they don't', in which case the corresponding implication is that corporate success is all about recruiting. Others believe that 'the cream will rise to the top' which makes it easier to be more lax in recruiting and then to just sit back and watch who performs well. Others believe 'you have to pump people up' like an old-fashioned hand water pump or a bicycle air pump – apparently because they all have inside-out (not outside-in caused by the company) energy leaks that drain their enthusiasm over the course of a year.

LEVELS OF HUMAN BEHAVIOUR

These assumptions, often tacit, unexplored and unexamined, drive the enormous amounts of energy that go into the planning and delivery of corporate planning – including among other things the annual business meeting and efforts to develop the next generation of leaders. They also overlook a series of important insights about what it means to be an inspiring leader.

Human behaviour occurs at at least three levels (Schein, 1985). At Level One is visible behaviour, the things that people say and do that you can capture on a camera. Level Two is conscious thought, the things that people are aware that they are thinking but which they choose whether or not to reveal at Level One. At Level Three are the often semi-conscious or pre-conscious core values, assumptions, beliefs, and expectations (VABEs for short) about the way the world is or should be. Level One behaviour is 'above the line' because it is visible and can be captured on camera. See Figure 5.1.

Levels of human behaviour
1. VISIBLE BEHAVIOUR (SAY AND DO)
2. CONSCIOUS THOUGHT
3. VALUES, ASSUMPTIONS, BELIEFS, and EXPECTATIONS (VABEs)

Figure 5.1
Influence between and among levels of human behaviour.

Given this layered perspective of human behaviour, a number of interesting and important questions and implications arise. First, when one attempts to influence (lead) others, what level does one target? Throughout much of the Industrial Era (1790–1950) most of the worldwide corporate leadership systems attempted to influence Level One. Henry Ford reputedly once said, 'I keep trying to hire a pair of hands and they keep coming with heads and bodies attached.'

Clearly, much of the educational systems of the world target Level Two, trying to change the way people think. The underlying assumption there is 'if an expert tells you or shows you volumes of data, you will make the same conclusions as the experts'. The evidence over the years suggests this is not necessarily so. Thomas Kuhn (1996), for example, described how even among natural scientists, trained to stick to the data, this may not occur. In some cases, it may take a whole generation to literally die off before a new set of data-based conclusions may take hold (Kuhn, 1996).

The religions of the world obviously focus on Level Three, attempting to shape people's beliefs and values. It would seem apparent that business managers who want to be inspiring should rethink their propensity to focus on Levels One and Two and spend more attention attempting to influence Level Three.

What about the influences that seep between these levels? What's your theory about the connections between and among the three levels? Behaviourists, proponents of B. F. Skinner, target Level One. They believe 'it's not my right nor is it functional to try to influence what's inside, we can only deal with behavior'. Skinnerians believe that if you can get a person to do what you want them to do, the repetitive *doing* of a thing will make it seep into the person's consciousness and core values. What do you think? If you tell a subordinate to do something at Level One, what will happen when you leave the room? What would it take for a desired change to persist in another's behaviour when the requirement to behave in that way was not supervising? See Figure 5.2.

These questions become more complicated because much of what humans do is habitual. That is, people tend to repeat their behaviour in patterned ways, and this occurs at each of these three levels. What are your guesstimates given all of the people you've observed at work over the course of your lifetime? That is, how

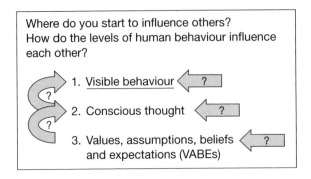

Where do you start to influence others?
How do the levels of human behaviour influence each other?

1. Visible behaviour ◁ ? ▭

2. Conscious thought ◁ ? ▭

3. Values, assumptions, beliefs ◁ ? ▭
   and expectations (VABEs)

Figure 5.2
Two key translations in level three leadership communication I.

much of visible human behaviour do you believe is habitual? How much of the way people think is habitual? And how much of what they value, assume, believe, and expect is habitual? See Table 5.1.

Hundreds of my executive education and consulting clients on average believe that about 80 per cent of human behaviour at Level One is habitual, that about 90 per cent of the way people think is habitual, and that nearly 99 per cent of people's underlying VABEs are habitual. If they are accurate, then, leadership is about the effort to change what people do or are doing in largely *habitual ways* in order to achieve some other or new objective. By its nature, leadership bumps up against this enormous inertia of human habit.

Consider this quote from a Cossack lieutenant in Southern Russia:

> We Cossacks are Christians. So we'll never be friends with Muslims –
> *never.* We won't let them build mosques here. . . . we've always lived with
> this religious tension – with this state of semi-war with the Muslims that
> you Americans only discovered after September 11. We long ago learned
> what you're just learning now: never flirt with those who despise you for
> your religion.
>
> (Valerii Alyokhin quoted by Tayler, 2005, p. 201)

Table 5.1 *Habituality of human behaviour*

Levels of human behaviour	Degree of habituality (What's your guesstimate?)
Visible behaviour	
Conscious thought	
Values, assumptions, beliefs, and expectations about the way the world is or should be (VABEs)	

How many generations have these VABEs been passed down? How habitual have these assumptions become? Leaders who hope to change behaviour must understand that, at Level Three, most people are repeating what they have had reinforced to them for a long time. The result is that countless leaders and managers have been frustrated because they seem unable to get people to do what they want them to do, particularly when they are not around to supervise. More often than not, people seem to regress or 'bounce back' to their original behaviour when the supervising force disappears. Level Three dominates the symptoms that appear at Level One.

The concern that Level Two and Level Three habits are too difficult to deal with is may be one of the primary reasons why people in positions of authority tend to focus on Level One. Part of the reason for this focus is the desire to keep things simple. Further, many managers are distinctly uncomfortable 'playing god' by 'mucking around' in people's lives at Levels Two and Three. The legal perspective reinforces this view. The law imposes restrictions on what people do, but not what they think or believe; managers tend to apply the same approach. They eschew attempts to 'get inside a person's head' or to 'muck around in their beliefs'. The problem with this approach is that it is distinctly uninspiring.

INSPIRING LEADERSHIP

Inspirational leadership involves influence at all three levels. In essence, this means that inspiring leaders connect with people at the core values level in a way that makes sense to them and propels them to high-energy action. When managers target primarily Level One in their attempts to lead, they are managing in a superficial way that frequently leads to an obligatory response that may get an organization to 'good enough' but not likely to 'world class'. The challenge is to influence people at all three levels. And that means connecting with, matching, or stimulating employees' core VABEs.

There are a number of objections to this approach. First, many say, 'It's only work, and work is *not* inspiring.' These managers give little if any thought to how if at all the work they offer might connect with a person's core VABEs. To them, for example, mission statements are trite clichés with little or no meaning. Working people will spend the majority of their waking lives at work. Managers can either choose to make that experience an engaging, even inspiring one, or not. Individuals who work can make the same choice. Many, most, choose to make it a dreary obligation and exclaim with a sigh at the end of the week, 'thank God it's Friday'.

There are a number of organizations in the world, however, who reject this objection. They believe and argue that work is dignified and dignifying especially if it is put in a worthy context. One company for example could present its employment options to the work as 'financial services' involving collecting, bundling, and reselling loan commitments. They chose instead to declare that the business is about 'making education affordable for everyone'. And that simple statement can, if presented with sincerity and a desire to touch people at Level Three, make a difference for people everywhere in the organization. Whether one is selling, processing, coordinating, or collecting, one can, if given the opportunity and the interest, connect to this noble, even inspiring, purpose.

Another company declares that its purpose is 'to protect those who protect us'. They could eschew the inspiring approach, and offer engineering positions in a project-oriented firm working with leading edge technology. Instead, whether an employee is writing code, building prototypes, training end users, or managing budgets, in the back of his or her mind are the images of young countrymen flying jet fighters in harm's way. This is a much more Level Three approach, and I've seen it presented by a former Marine (is there such a thing?) in that way.

Another objection is that people, especially 'professionals' will do what they have to accomplish the organization's goals so inspiring leadership is not necessary. There's no need, the argument goes, for getting inside people's heads and hearts, they will do what they have to do. The underlying assumption of this view is based on obligation or duty. And working out of obligation and duty is a formula for mediocrity, certainly not for world-class performance. People will put more into an endeavour they choose to do than one they would rather not but are obligated in some way to do. The evidence for this assertion has piled up over the last 30 years (Kohn, 1999).

For example, if you develop two randomly selected equivalent groups to play a board game over two hours with an announced break in the middle and *pay* one of the groups to play, what do you think will happen? The group you don't pay will play through the break with energy and have to be shooed out of the room at the end of the time. The group you paid will take their break, come back late, and leave early. Same game, same setting, equivalent groups. There's something about obligation that stifles people's engagement and performance. Tom Weiskopf, the professional and well-known golfer, made the statement once and the point, 'I stopped loving golf at exactly the time I decided to turn pro' (Weiskopf, 2004, p. 133).

Bill Zierden, a former colleague, once proposed a model of organizational 'glue' that held organizations together.[1] He posited that if an organization persisted it was 'held together' by a mixture of four major bonds: charismatic leadership, rules and regulations, rewards, and shared values. Consequently, one could assess the relative proportions of these bonds and then the implications of that mix. See Table 5.2. Practitioners can assess the impact of various mixes of 'glue' on their organizations' energy and engagement. The organization that relies heavily on charismatic or inspirational leadership, for example, may have difficulties in succession planning, in leveraging that influence in larger systems, and in inculcating commitment to rules and rewards (for consistency and fairness) rather than the more mercurial hero worship.

Table 5.2 *Types of organizational glue*

Types of organizational glue	Relative proportion (%)
Charismatic leadership	
Rules and regulations	
Rewards	
Shared values	
Total glue	100

The third objection to the attempt to influence people at Level Three is that management uses measurable goals rather than unmeasurable feelings to 'manage' their businesses. In fact, goal orientation has probably been the major management tool for centuries. The argument is that people are goal oriented and goals for growth will motivate them to produce more. It seems reasonable to conclude that human beings have an innate drive to acquire more, and that this is manifest in comparative, goal-oriented behaviour in business (Lawrence and Nohria, 2001). And it seems clear that goals motivate people some of the time. Yet goals have a dark side; they can create an obligation and in so doing, undermine a person's energy and engagement. In other words, goals can be 'exspiring' instead of inspiring.

A colleague and I were once teaching a weeklong one-company seminar to a group of 50 or so financial services upper mid-level managers. On the fourth day of the programme, the number two executive in the company flew the corporate jet to visit the class and speak to the troops. My colleague and I were in the back row eager to hear what he had to say since he wasn't really aware of what we'd been doing all week. He came in after lunch, leaned up against the blackboard, and said, 'It's the end of June. The stock price is at $95. If the stock price doesn't get to $125 by the end of the year, the CEO and I don't get our annual bonuses. You need to get your rears in gear!' We were flabbergasted. The giant sucking sound you could hear was the energy of the group draining out into the hallway. The executive then flew back to company headquarters, and we went to dinner with the participants. They were utterly demoralized. This executive clearly didn't come out to try to demoralize the troops, rather, his intention no doubt was to do just the opposite – to inspire them. He did just the opposite. The company was later acquired by another larger firm.

Goals *can* be inspiring, but they are tricky things. Another company I know weathered the dot.com bust very well, and in fact, was growing in double digits for more than five years during that period. Seminars I conducted were bubbling over with enthusiasm and energy. Recently, in my annual work with them, participants had begun to complain that the biggest challenge they faced was not the competition or the market, rather how to keep up with double digit growth goals year after year. There had been a sea change in the morale of the people. Some time in the last year, without fanfare or even recognition, the culture of the organization nosed over from their upward energy trajectory and had begun a nose down descent. Whether it will be corrected remains to be seen. If management is disconnected from the Level Three VABEs of their people, and focused primarily on Level One financial results, the odds are they won't know the *impact* of their goals stops energizing and begins de-energizing their people; they'll be oblivious to the sea tide changes in organizational energy.

This phenomenon, the early inspiring nature of good goals and the later 'exspiring' nature of them creates what I have come to call the 'motivator's dilemma'. How does a management team know when their motivational goal-oriented structures have left off being inspiring and become 'exspiring'? David McClelland identified this dilemma in his work with Indian children and the rope ring toss experiment (McClelland, 1988). Jim Collins acknowledged that his early presentation of big, hairy, audacious goals (BHAGs) was a bit off centre. In *Good to Great*, he noted that BHAGs are only motivating if they take place within the 'hedgehog concept', the intersection of a person's passion, skill, and economic possibilities.[2] Goals, in fact, do have a dark side (Clawson, 2002).

Dave Scott, the 50-year-old six time winner of the Hawaii Ironman Triathlon[3] once noted, 'During a race, I never wear a wristwatch, and my bike doesn't have a speedometer. They're distractions. All I work on is finding a rhythm that feels strong and sticking to it' (Scott, 2003, p. 122). What Scott has recognized is that even goals you set yourself can become obligatory to you and drain your energy. The reason is this. Most competitors set goals to try to improve their performance. But what happens when a racer gets to the first checkpoint, checks his watch, and realizes that he's behind 'schedule'. He says to himself, 'I *have to* go faster' and he tries harder – and this drains energy. The very act of placing one's self under obligation drains energy. So, I'll note again, leadership is about managing energy – first in yourself and then in those around you. Dave Scott has figured out how to manage his energy in one of the world's most competitive arenas – and he does better without setting goals, even his own.

SUGGESTIONS

So how can leaders become more inspiring? Here are some suggestions that seem to help:

Do your strategic homework. Unless a person has a grand, expansive vision about where the organization or the work unit should go, one has no 'story' to tell, no reason for people to get fired up. In the end, one's vision must touch a chord, that is, be congruent with the semi-conscious VABEs that one's audience holds, but first, one must have something to say. Have you thought about where the organization should be in ten years? Or in the case of Konosuke Matsushita, the founder of Panasonic Electronics, 250 years? Can you articulate without a moment's notice where you think 'we' should go? If you can't, no matter how eloquent you are, you won't move people. You won't have anything to fall back on except short-term operating goals – and that's where most managers spend all of their leadership effort.

Authenticity. Some people can fake inspiration for a while. They figure out what the people want to hear and then deliver that to them, even though they don't believe in it. Why? For fame, power, and self-aggrandizement. In my experience, there are two kinds of leaders in the world (well, at *least* two). The first are those who want to be leaders for the perks, the power, the fancy cars and offices, and the personal benefits. The second kind aren't interested in that, they'd rather fix something and the accoutrements of leadership power are secondary annoyances. The first, you cannot trust as far as you can throw them; the second you can hang your hat on. So, if you're thinking about trying to be a more inspirational leader, and you're thinking about that in terms of a bandage that you'll apply to your outer veneer (Level One), it won't work. Truly inspiring leaders are authentic, that is, they have done their strategic homework, they have a vision that matches the people they are working with, and they believe in that vision deeply. They are not faking it.

Clarity. The leader's most effective tool is language. Your ability to speak clearly, to articulate in the right words what you're trying to say is extremely important. If you hem and ha, and fumble around and can't find the words, or you use too many space fillers like 'um' and 'ah' and 'you know' and 'sort of' the effectiveness of your delivery declines. The reason is that these fillers convey a message to the audience that the speaker doesn't really know what he's trying to say. Inspiring leaders are very clear on what they are trying to say. It's far too common in business meetings that participants leave a session and are still wondering what the main point or key message of the last speaker were. If you want to inspire, you have to be able to find the words. Carl Rogers described this in terms of two translations – from an awareness of what you're experiencing or feeling that translates into thoughts, and then the translation of those thoughts into words.[4] See Figure 5.3. Inspiring leaders are able to look inward, recognize their experience (Goleman, 1995), and translate that with clarity to those around. If there's not passion when one looks within, fancy phrases won't carry the day.

Memorable. If you wish to inspire, your communication has to be memorable. Many executives who plan their presentations never seem to even think about this aspect of inspirational communication. Who can forget Martin Luther King's

'I Have a Dream' speech? Most of us can quote lines from it even today, decades later. The odds are that the people in the audience are not going to remember facts, figures, and charts. But the right phrase, the right story, the right turn of a phrase can last for months, even years.

There are a number of ways to add 'memorability' to your communications. First, people love good stories. In fact, the prehistoric tradition of the human race was clearly oral story telling. And that tradition persists even to today. What kind of stories can you tell that would be memorable? You might first consider stories about your self and how you got to be where you are and why you believe what you do. We worked with one CEO of a major financial services firm to get him to share a personal story at a reception. He was the kind of guy who believed at Level Three that you didn't mix business with personal life and had kept his 'professional distance' from the employees communicating with them at Level One.

After considerable nudging and discussion about the impact of Level Three communications, though, he relented and with significant reluctance, stepped forward at the reception that night and got everyone's attention. Then, a little nervously, he talked about his childhood, the poverty in which he grew up, how he developed his core values, and why he believed so strongly in what the company was trying to do. You could have heard a pin drop the entire time. His innate dry

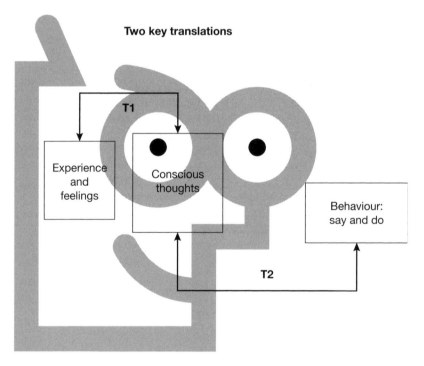

Figure 5.3 *Two key translations in level three leadership communication II.*

humour surprised them. Employees were knocked off their feet. For a moment, I thought they were going to burst into spontaneous applause – but the situation dictated otherwise. That event has become something of a story in and of itself around the company, about the 'old man' and why we're doing what we do.

Although personal stories give the employees a better chance of connecting with you, the stories don't have to be about you. Stories about significant and emotional events that involve your values and beliefs and strategy for the company can also move people. And stories are much easier remembered than numbers, charts, and data sets.

The attempts to create memorability by using the cheerleading approach may have some excitement at the time, and they may be recalled, but only as 'remember the time we had Marilyn Monroe at the annual meeting?' and not for the substance of what you're trying to communicate.

Respect. Some of the inspirational leaders in history have been bad people. Adolf Hitler's impassioned deliveries for example clearly 'inspired' millions of people – but to what end? For me, respect for the audience and for others is a key component of inspirational leadership. Leadership that degrades and detracts from people will not ultimately inspire them. John Kennedy's famous inaugural comment, 'Ask not what your country can do for you, ask what you can do for your country!' is a good example. It was in large part inspirational because it communicated the underlying (Level Three) message that 'you have value and we need that'. You won't inspire people if you do it out of hate; in the end, it will come back to haunt you and those who responded.

CONCLUSION

Inspirational leadership is leadership that influences people at Level Three at the level of their core beliefs. Without that core VABE connection, leadership is merely pinging the surface of human energy by appealing to the mundane motivations of mercenary exchange or behavioural modification. To connect with people at Level Three, the level of their core values, assumptions, beliefs, and expectations about the way the world is or should be, you have to be willing to share your values and beliefs with them, to be personal in your communications. Professional distance has little place in the attempt to inspire. But first, the inspirational leader must have done his or her strategic homework. With no story to tell, with no vision of what could – nay, *should* – be, the leader has no substance to package in his or her enthusiasm. That vision may come from intuition, from hard analysis, from a lifetime of learning and accumulation of wisdom, or a combination of all of the above, but wherever it comes from, you have to believe in it and be willing to extend your language and communication style to touch the hearts of others. Anything less would be just plain leadership, or worse, managerial maintenance.

NOTES

1 In his teaching at the Darden Graduate School of Business, before he became vice president of human resources at Circuit City Stores.

2 BHAGs were introduced in *Built to Last* (1999) and then Collins revised his perspective on them in *Good to Great* (2001).

3 A race consisting of a 2.2 mile swim in open sea, a 112 mile bicycle loop, and a 26.2 mile marathon run.

4 Summarized in a chapter in Athos (1978).

REFERENCES

Athos, A. G. (1978) *Interpersonal behavior: communication and understanding in relationships*. Englewood Cliffs, NJ: Prentice Hall.

Clawson, J. (2002) The dark side of goals. http://www.darden.edu/varoom/archive/biz Buzz/archive/bizbuzz082602.htm

Collins, J. (with J. Porras) (1999) *Built to last*. New York: HarperCollins.

Collins, J. (2001) *Good to great*. New York: HarperCollins.

Gallup Management Journal (8 August 2002) Start Worrying About 'Not Engaged' Employees,' Half of your workforce may be 'checked out.' Here's how great managers inspire, refocus, and re-engage these low-performing employees, A GMJ QandA with Curt Coffman, co-author of *First, break all the rules* (Simon & Schuster, 1999) and *Follow this path* (Warner Books, 2002). http://gmj.gallup.com/content/default.asp?ci=142, accessed 30 January 2005.

Goleman, D. (1995) *Emotional intelligence*. New York: Bantam.

Kohn, A. (1999) *Punished by rewards: The trouble with gold stars, incentive plans, A's, praise, and other bribes*. Boston, MA: Houghton Mifflin.

Kuhn, T. S. (1996) *The structure of scientific revolutions*. Chicago, IL: University of Chicago Press.

Lawrence, P. and Nohria, N. (2001). *Driven*. San Francisco, CA: Jossey-Bass.

McClelland, D. (1988) *Human motivation*. Cambridge: Cambridge University Press.

Schein, E. S. (1985) *Organizational culture and leadership*. San Francisco, CA: Jossey-Bass.

Scott, D. (2003) Quoted by Tim Sohn, 'Bodywork: Bulletins from the fitness frontier', in *Outside* Magazine, September, p. 122.

Tayler, J. (2005) Russia's Holy Warriors. *The Atlantic*, January–February, pp. 201ff.

Weiskopf, Tom (2004) Quoted by Peter Kessler, 'Wised Up', in regular feature 'Golf Talk', in *Golf Magazine*, June.

Part II

Qualities of effective and successful leaders

Chapter 6

Leadership competencies

Richard E. Boyatzis

The study of leadership has taken many twists and turns over the decades, but one persistent theme is inquiry into the type of person that is a great or effective leader. The best leaders inspire others around them. They feel inspired themselves. To understand how they bring out the best in people, it is important to understand that the essence of leadership is a relationship between the leader and the people around him or her, which we call a resonant relationship (Boyatzis and McKee, 2005; Goleman, Boyatzis, and McKee, 2002). But what allows or enables a person to initiate or sustain such a relationship?

Research published over the last 30 years or so shows us that outstanding leaders appear to require three clusters of talent as threshold abilities and five clusters of competencies as distinguishing outstanding performance:

1 expertise and experience is a threshold level of competency;
2 knowledge (i.e. declarative, procedural, functional and metacognitive) is a threshold competency; and
3 an assortment of basic cognitive competencies, such as memory and deductive reasoning are threshold competencies.

There are five clusters of competencies differentiate outstanding from average performing leaders and managers in many countries of the world (Boyatzis, 1982; Goleman, 1998; Goleman, Boyatzis, and McKee, 2002; Howard and Bray, 1988; Kotter, 1982; Luthans, Hodgett, and Rosenkrantz, 1988; Spencer and Spencer, 1993; Thorton and Byham, 1982). They are:

1 cognitive competencies, such as systems thinking and pattern recognition;
2 emotional intelligence self-awareness competencies, such as emotional self-awareness;

3   emotional intelligence self-management competencies, such as emotional self-control, adaptability, and initiative;
4   emotional intelligence social awareness competencies, such as empathy; and
5   emotional intelligence relationship management competencies, such as developing others and teamwork.

Are competencies enough for outstanding performance? No, so let's look at the larger picture for the role of competencies.

COMPETENCIES AS BEHAVIOURAL MANIFESTATIONS OF TALENT

An integrated concept of talent offers more than a convenient framework for describing human dispositions – it offers a theoretical structure for the organization of personality and links it to a theory of action and job performance. Goleman (1998) defined an 'emotional competence' as a 'learned capability based on emotional intelligence which results in outstanding performance at work'. In other words, if a competency is an 'underlying characteristic of the person that leads to or causes effective or superior performance' (Boyatzis, 1982), then an 'emotional or cognitive intelligence competency is an ability to recognize, understand, and use emotional information about oneself or others that leads to or causes effective or superior performance' (Boyatzis and Sala, 2004).

If defined as a single construct, the tendency to believe that more effective people have the vital ingredients for success invites the attribution of a halo effect. For example, person A is effective; therefore she has all of the right stuff, such as brains, savvy, and style. Like the issue of finding the best 'focal point' with which to look at something, the dilemma of finding the best level of detail in defining constructs with which to build a personality theory may ultimately be an issue of which focal point is chosen. With regard to emotional and cognitive intelligence, we believe the most helpful focal point allows for the description and study of a variety of specific competencies, or abilities, which can be empirically, causally related to effectiveness and describe the clusters within which these competencies are organized. But we must start with the competencies. The articulation of one overall emotional or cognitive intelligence might be deceptive and suggest a close association with cognitive capability (i.e. traditionally defined 'intelligence' or what psychologists often call 'g' referring to general cognitive ability). The latter would not only be confusing, but would additionally raise the question as to what one is calling emotional intelligence and whether it is nothing more than an element of previously defined intelligence or cognitive ability.

A competency is defined as a capability or ability. It is a set of related but different sets of behaviour organized around an underlying construct, which we call the 'intent'. The behaviours are alternate manifestations of the intent, as appropriate in various situations or times. For example, listening to someone and asking him or her questions are several behaviours. A person can demonstrate these behaviours for multiple reasons or to various intended ends. A person can ask questions and listen to someone to ingratiate him or herself or to appear interested, thereby gaining standing in the other person's view. Or a person can ask questions and listen to someone because he or she is interested in understanding this other person, his or her priorities, or thoughts in a situation. The latter we would call a demonstration of empathy. The underlying intent is to understand the person. Meanwhile, the former underlying reason for the questions is to gain standing or impact in the person's view, elements of what we may call demonstration of influence. Similarly, the underlying intent of a subtler competency like Emotional Self-Awareness is self-insight and self-understanding.

This construction of competencies as requiring both action (i.e. a set of alternate behaviours) and intent called for measurement methods that allowed for assessment of both the presence of the behaviour and inference of the intent. A modification of the critical incident interview was adapted using the inquiry sequence from the Thematic Apperception Test and the focus on specific events in one's life from the biodata method. The method, called the Behavioural Event Interview (BEI), is a semi-structured interview in which the respondent is asked to recall recent, specific events in which he or she felt effective (Boyatzis, 1982; Spencer and Spencer, 1993). Once the person recalls an event, he or she is guided through telling the story of the event with a basic set of four questions: (1) What led up to the situation? (2) Who said or did what to whom? (3) What did you say or do next? What were you thinking and feeling? and (4) What was the outcome or result of the event? Autobiographical research (Rubin, 1986) has shown the accuracy of recall of events is increased dramatically when the events are: (1) recent; (2) have a high valence or saliency to the person; and (3) the recall involves specific actions. All of these conditions were incorporated into the BEI.

The responses are audiotaped and transcribed and interpreted using a thematic analysis process (Boyatzis, 1998). Thematic analysis is a process for 'coding' raw qualitative information, whether in written, video, or audio form. Through the use of a 'codebook' articulating specific themes and how to identify them, the researcher is able to convert open-ended responses or unstructured responses and behaviour into a set of quantified variables for analysis. The method has been used in numerous studies showing predictive validity of the competencies demonstrated by the person during the events as coded from the interviews (Boyatzis, 1982; McClelland, 1998; Spencer and Spencer, 1993).

The anchor for understanding which behaviours and which intents are relevant in a situation emerges from predicting effectiveness. The construction of the specific competency is a matter of relating different behaviours that are considered alternate manifestations of the same underlying construct. But they are organized primarily or more accurately initially, by the similarity of the consequence of the use of these behaviours in social or work settings. For example, the competency called Empathy can be observed by watching someone listen to others or asking questions about his or her feelings and thoughts. If one is demonstrating Empathy, the person would be undertaking these acts with the intent of trying to understand another person. On the other hand, someone could show these acts while cross-examining a witness in a criminal trial where the intent is to catch them in a lie – which is likely also to be the demonstration of another competency, influence.

A theory of performance is the basis for the concept of competency. The theory used in this approach is a basic contingency theory, as shown in Figure 6.1. Maximum performance is believed to occur when the person's capability or talent is consistent with the needs of the job demands and the organizational environment (Boyatzis, 1982). The person's talent is described by his or her values, vision,

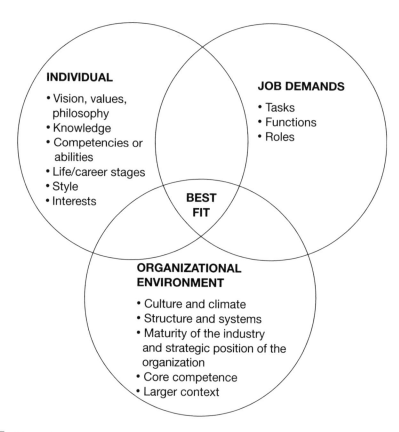

Figure 6.1 *Theory of action and job performance (best fit = area of maximum stimulation, challenge, and performance).*

and personal philosophy; knowledge; competencies; life and career stage; interests; and style. Job demands can be described by the role responsibilities and tasks needed to be performed. Aspects of the organizational environment that are predicted to have important impact on the demonstration of competencies and/or the design of the jobs and roles include culture and climate; structure and systems; maturity of the industry and strategic positioning within it; and aspects of the economic, political, social, environmental, and religious milieu surrounding the organization.

BEYOND COMPETENCIES TO BROADER VIEW OF TALENT

A basic contingency model of outstanding performance with the role of competencies is shown in Figure 6.1. It is an enhancement of the model shown in Boyatzis (1982). Beyond competencies, a person's talent can be said to include their values, vision, and philosophy (Boyatzis, Murphy, and Wheeler, 2000), as well as their life and career stage which will affect their desire to use abilities they have shown in the past or develop new ones. The job demands affect performance directly through roles and task responsibilities. Components of the organizational environment that relate to competencies to stimulate maximum performance include the culture and climate, structure and systems, strategic position within the industry or sector, and core competence of the organization; more accurately, these are the factors that relate to the clusters of competencies to create a best fit.

As suggested in Boyatzis (1982), clusters of competencies appear to hold more promise in understanding the 'best fit' than merely single competencies. Using one or two competencies from each of the clusters is far more effective than using all of the competencies in one or two clusters. This finding was cross-validated by McClelland (1998) in predicting performance of presidents of divisions of a food company and then by Boyatzis (2005) for leaders in a multinational professional service firm.

Empirically forming clusters is better than using theory or shared opinions. First shown in Boyatzis (1982), Boyatzis, Goleman, and Rhee (2000) contrasted different ways of discovering competency clusters. This paper related the competencies studied in this book to the concept of emotional intelligence. All but two of the 18 competencies shown in Boyatzis (1982) to predict outstanding leadership or management performance constitute one aspect or another of emotional intelligence (EI) (Goleman, 1998; Goleman, Boyatzis, and McKee, 2002); the other two are cognitive intelligence competencies. In this sense, the Self-Awareness cluster of EI includes Accurate Self-Assessment and Self-Confidence. The Self-Management cluster of EI includes: Efficiency Orientation, Proactivity (now known as Initiative), Stamina and Adaptability (now known as Adaptability), and Self-Control. The Social Awareness cluster of EI includes Perceptual Objectivity (now known as part of Empathy). The Relationship Management or Social Skills cluster of EI includes: Use of Unilateral Power (now known as Influence), Concern with Impact (now known as Influence), Managing Group Process (now known as Inspirational Leadership and Teamwork), Use of Socialized Power (now known as Building Bonds or Networking), Developing Others, and Oral Presentations (now known as Communications). The remaining two competencies were the two cognitive ones, Systems Thinking (called Analytic Thinking in Boyatzis, 1982) and Pattern Recognition (called Conceptual Thinking in Boyatzis, 1982).

SHIFTING IMPORTANCE OF COMPETENCIES FOR LEADERS

Competency studies in the last ten years reveal a growing importance of Empathy, Social Objectivity, Teamwork, and Adaptability. The diversity of the workforce has increased dramatically in the industrialized world over the last 20 years. With globalization of many markets, the diversity of customers and vendors has increased. To work with people who are different, we need an advanced ability to be sensitive to others. Empathy and Social Objectivity are more essential than they were to leaders in the 1980s.

The use of teams has increased. Downsizing and delayering organizations meant more interdependence on fewer people. To address customer needs and improve quality, multi-functional, project, and self-managing teams were developed as essential work units. Working with others across geographic distances, asynchronously with computer-based systems has provoked the need for more sophisticated skills in working with others. All of these factors have propelled the Teamwork competency to primary importance in managing and leading today.

The myriad changes in our society and work, and even the increase in the rate of change conspire to make life less certain. It inspires a belief that the future, even the near future, will be dramatically different than the present. It is no wonder that Adaptability and the ability to tolerate uncertainty have also become essential competencies in guiding others.

TIPPING POINTS FOR OUTSTANDING LEADERS

A major advancement in understanding the effect of competencies on performance came from catastrophe theory, which is now considered a subset of complexity theory. Instead of only asking the typical question, 'Which competencies are needed or necessary for outstanding performance?' David McClelland, in a paper published posthumously in 1998 posed the question, 'How often do

124

you need to show a competency to "tip" you into outstanding performance?' In other words, how frequently should a competency be shown to be sufficient for maximum performance? He reported that presidents of divisions of a large food company using competencies above the tipping points received significantly higher bonuses, which were proportional to the profitability of their divisions, as compared to their less profitable peers (McClelland, 1998).

Using this method, Boyatzis (2005) replicated significant findings regarding tipping points in an international consulting firm. The profits from accounts of senior partners were analysed for seven quarters following assessment of their competencies. Senior partners using competencies above the tipping point more than doubled the operating profits from their accounts as compared to the senior partners below the tipping point. The measure of competencies was the average perceived frequency of use of each competency by others around the senior partner, using a 360-degree competency questionnaire. He showed that this method was superior to a simple median split or continuous analysis of the relationship between the frequency of competencies shown and financial performance of the senior partners, leaders, of this firm.

Knowing the point at which a person's use of a competency tips them into outstanding performance provides vital guidance to managers and leaders. It helps those coaching others know which competencies are the closest to added value in stimulating outstanding performance. The tipping point is sometimes referred to as a trigger point.

The tipping point for each competency would be a function of the organization environment. For example, the manager of an office of a strategy consulting company would have a tipping point of Adaptability at the maximum level. To show sufficient Adaptability to be outstanding, he/she would have to be using it 'frequently and consistently'. Their business, projects, and clients change each year. They typically have high turnover in consulting staff as well. Meanwhile, the manager of a basic chemical processing plant may have a tipping point of only 'occasional or often' of Adaptability. The certainty of their product line and predictability of their production processes does not create as much uncertainty as the consulting business. They probably have less turnover in the chemical plant as well, requiring even less adaptation to new staff. Analysis of tipping points should become a standard feature of competency assessment studies in the future.

Boyatzis (2005) also confirmed the earlier argument about the importance of clusters. It was shown that the dramatic increase in profit contributed to the company occurred when senior partners were using an assortment of the competencies from each cluster above the tipping point. It did not seem to matter which of the competencies were being using above the tipping point form each cluster. This allows for the differences in style observed from outstanding leaders while confirming the importance of competencies as predictors of performance.

CHANGES IN PERSONALITY THEORY

Another important change in the last 30 years has been the insight into adult behaviour from neuroscience and endocrine research. Earlier competency models were based on personality theories where the deepest level of the human organism addressed was unconscious motives and traits (Boyatzis, 1982; Howard and Bray, 1988; Kotter, 1982; Thornton and Byham, 1982). Synthesis of research from many fields has enabled us to offer an image of the neural and hormonal basis of many of the competencies (Boyatzis and McKee, 2005; Boyatzis, Smith, and Blaize, in press; Goleman, Boyatzis, and McKee, 2002).

The emotional intelligence competencies can be defined as the abilities that enable a person to manage himself/herself and others. It can also be defined as those abilities that are driven by a neural circuit stemming from the limbic system, through the cingulated to the prefrontal cortex (Goleman, 1998; Goleman, Boyatzis, and McKee, 2002).

In Boyatzis, Goleman, and Rhee (2000), a refinement on the personality theory offered in Boyatzis (1982) included the neural and hormonal basis of the motivational and trait dispositions, the values and operating philosophy, and then the clusters of competencies. Each of these levels, in turn has an impact on the other levels, and in particular has an effect on neural and hormonal functioning. Now that we know that adult humans can grow new neural tissue, we believe people can develop competencies by building new neural pathways. Some of this comes from rerouting prior pathways (i.e. old habits) and some of the change comes from new pathways. But such change takes time.

COMPETENCIES CAN BE DEVELOPED

Although the understanding of competencies themselves has been extended, perhaps the most important contributions in the last 30 years have addressed how competencies are developed. Decades of research on the effects of psychotherapy (Hubble, Duncan, and Miller, 1999), self-help programmes (Kanfer and Goldstein, 1991), cognitive behaviour therapy (Barlow, 1988), training programmes (Morrow, Jarrett, and Rupinski, 1997), and education (Pascarella and Terenzini, 1991) have shown that people can change their behaviour, moods, and self-image. But most of the studies focused on a single characteristic, like maintenance of sobriety, reduction in a specific anxiety, or a set of characteristics often determined by the assessment instrument, such as the scales of the MMPI. But there are few studies showing sustained improvements in the sets of desirable behaviour that lead to outstanding performance.

The 'honeymoon effect' of typical training programmes might start with improvement immediately following the programme, but within months it drops precipitously. Only 15 programmes were found in a global search of the literature by the Consortium on Research on Emotional Intelligence in Organizations to improve emotional intelligence. Most of them showed impact on job outcomes, such as number of new businesses started, or life outcomes, such as finding a job or satisfaction (Cherniss and Adler, 2000), which are the ultimate purpose of development efforts. But showing an impact on outcomes, while desired, may also blur *how* the change actually occurs. Furthermore, when a change has been noted, a question about the sustainability of the changes is raised because of the relatively short time periods studied.

The few published studies examining improvement of more than one of these competencies show an overall improvement of about 10 per cent in emotional intelligence abilities three to eighteen months following training (for example Latham and Saari, 1979; Noe and Schmidt, 1986; and others summarized in Goleman, Boyatzis and McKee, 2002). More recent meta-analytic studies and utility analyses confirm that significant changes can and do occur, but not with the impact that the level of investment would lead us to expect, nor with many types of training (Burke and Day, 1986; Morrow, Jarrett and Rupinski, 1997). There are, undoubtedly, other studies which were not found and reviewed, or not available through journals and books and, therefore, overlooked. We do not claim this is an exhaustive review, but suggestive of the percentage improvement as a rough approximation of the real impact. This approximation is offered to help in the comparison of relative impact of management training, management education, and self-directed learning.

The results appear no better from standard MBA programmes, where there is no attempt to enhance emotional intelligence abilities. The best data here comes from a research project by the American Assembly of Collegiate Schools of Business. They found that the behaviour of graduating students from two highly ranked business schools showed only improvements of 2 per cent in the skills of emotional intelligence compared to their levels when they began their MBA training (DDI, 1985). In fact, when students from four other high-ranking MBA programmes were assessed on a range of tests and direct behavioural measures, they showed a gain of 4 per cent in self-awareness and self-management abilities, but a *decrease* of 3 per cent in social awareness and relationship management (Boyatzis and Sokol, 1982).

A series of longitudinal studies underway at the Weatherhead School of Management of Case Western Reserve University have shown that people can change on this complex set of competencies that we call emotional intelligence that distinguish outstanding performers in management and professions (Boyatzis, Stubbs, and Taylor, 2002). And the improvement lasted for years. These changes occurred because of the use of Intentional Change Theory in the design of a course to stimulate use of and development of emotional and cognitive competencies (Boyatzis, 2001 and in press; Boyatzis, Cowen, and Kolb, 1995).

127

A visual comparison of the percentage improvement in behavioural measures of emotional intelligence from different samples is shown in Figure 6.2.

MBA students, averaging 27 years old at entry into the programme, showed dramatic changes on videotaped and audiotaped behavioural samples and questionnaire measures of these competencies as a result of the competency-based, outcome oriented MBA programme implemented in 1990 (Boyatzis, Stubbs, and Taylor, 2002). Four cadres of full-time MBA students graduating in 1992, 1993, 1994, and 1995 showed 47 per cent improvement on self-awareness competencies like Self-confidence and on self-management competencies such as the Drive to Achieve and Adaptability in the one to two years to graduation compared to when they first entered. When it came to social awareness and relationship management skills, improvements were even greater: 75 per cent on competencies such as Empathy and Team Leadership.

Meanwhile with the part-time MBA students graduating in 1994, 1995, and 1996, the dramatic improvement was found again, in these students who typically take three to five years to graduate. These groups showed 67 per cent improvement in self-awareness and self-management competencies and 40 per cent improvement in social awareness and social skills competencies by the end of their MBA programme.

That's not all. Jane Wheeler (1999) tracked down groups of these part-timers two years *after* they had graduated. Even all that time later, they still showed improvements in the same range: 63 per cent on the self-awareness and self-management competencies, and 45 per cent on the social awareness and relationship management competencies. This is in contrast to MBA graduates of the WSOM of the 1988 and 1989 traditional full-time and part-time programme who showed improvement in substantially fewer of the competencies

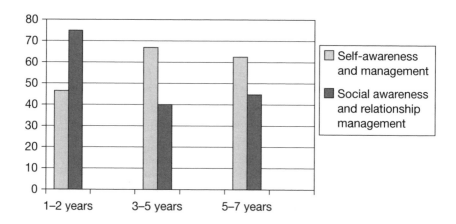

Figure 6.2 *Percentage improvement of emotional intelligence competencies of different groups of MBA graduates taking the Competency Development Course.*

The positive effects of this programme were not limited to MBAs. In a longitudinal study of four classes completing the Professional Fellows Program (i.e. an executive education programme at the Weatherhead School of Management), Ballou *et al.* (1999) showed that these 45- to 55-year-old professionals and executives improved on Self-confidence, Leadership, Helping, Goal Setting, and Action skills. These were 67 per cent of the emotional intelligence competencies assessed in this study.

CONCLUDING THOUGHT

Competencies are a critical ingredient to outstanding performance of leaders. Although our understanding of competencies has expanded dramatically in the last 30 years, the most inspiring insights have come from research showing we can develop these competencies. This holds promise for the holy grail of leadership development. As leaders, we can only create environments in which others want to use their capabilities and competencies if we are authentic and consistent in our own demonstration of these behaviours. Through the intentional change process, we have the opportunity to truly make a difference. Whether applied in universities or companies, government agencies or not-for-profits, this process can help us coach each other to create the social environments we want and find so conducive to making a difference.

REFERENCES

Ballou, R., Bowers, D., Boyatzis, R. E., and Kolb, D. A. (1999) Fellowship in lifelong learning: An executive development program for advanced professionals, *Journal of Management Education*, 23(4): 338–54.

Barlow, D. H. (1988) *Anxiety and disorders: The nature and treatment of anxiety and panic*. New York: The Guilford Press.

Boyatzis, R. E. (1982) *The competent manager: A model for effective performance*. New York: Wiley.

Boyatzis, R. E. (1998) *Transforming qualitative information: Thematic analysis and code development*. Thousand Oaks, CA: Sage.

Boyatzis, R. E. (2001) How and why individuals are able to develop emotional intelligence. In C. Cherniss and D. Goleman (eds) *The emotionally intelligent workplace: How to select for, measure, and improve emotional intelligence in individuals, groups, and organizations*. San Francisco, CA: Jossey-Bass, pp. 234–53.

Boyatzis, R. E. (2005) Using tipping points of emotional intelligence and cognitive competencies to predict financial performance of leaders. *Psicothema, 17*.

Boyatzis, R. E. (in press) Intentional change theory from a complexity perspective. *Journal of Management Development*.

Boyatzis, R. and McKee, A. (2005) *Resonant leadership: Sustaining yourself and connecting with others through mindfulness, hope, and compassion.* Boston, MA: Harvard Business School Press.

Boyatzis, R. E. and Sala, F. (2004) Assessing emotional intelligence competencies. In Glenn Geher (ed.) *The measurement of emotional intelligence* Hauppauge, NY: Novas Science Publishers, pp. 147–80.

Boyatzis, R. E. and Sokol, M. (1982) *A pilot project to assess the feasibility of assessing skills and personal characteristics of students in collegiate business programs.* Report to the AACSB (St. Louis, MO).

Boyatzis, R. E., Cowen, S. C., and Kolb, D. A. (1995) *Innovation in professional education: Steps on a journey from teaching to learning.* San Francisco, CA: Jossey-Bass.

Boyatzis, R. E., Goleman, D., and Rhee, K. (2000) Clustering competence in emotional intelligence: Insights from the Emotional Competence Inventory (ECI)s. In R. Bar-On and J. D. A. Parker (eds) *Handbook of emotional intelligence.* San Francisco, CA: Jossey-Bass, pp. 343–62.

Boyatzis, R. E., Murphy, A. J., and Wheeler, J. V. (2000) Philosophy as a missing link between values and behavior. *Psychological Reports.* 86: 47–64.

Boyatzis, R. E., Smith, M., and Blaize, N. (in press) Sustaining leadership effectiveness through coaching and compassion: It's not what you think. *Academy of Management Learning and Education.*

Boyatzis, R. E., Stubbs, L., and Taylor, S. (2002) Learning cognitive and emotional intelligence competencies through graduate management education. *Academy of Management Journal on Learning and Education,* 1(2): 150–62.

Burke, M. J. and Day, R. R. (1986) A cumulative study of the effectiveness of managerial training. *Journal of Applied Psychology,* 71(2): 232–45.

Cherniss, C. and Adler, M. (2000) *Promoting emotional intelligence in organizations: Make training in emotional intelligence effective.* Washington, DC: American Society of Training and Development.

Development Dimensions International (DDI) (1985) *Final report:Phase III.* Report to the AACSB (St. Louis, MO).

Goleman, D. (1998) *Working with emotional intelligence.* New York: Bantam.

Goleman, D., Boyatzis, R. E., and McKee, A. (2002) *Leadership and emotional intelligence.* Boston, MA: Harvard Business School Press.

Howard, A. and Bray, D. (1988) *Managerial lives in transition: Advancing age and changing times.* New York: Guilford Press.

Hubble, M. A., Duncan, B. L., and Miller, S. D. (eds) (1999) *The heart and soul of change: What works in therapy.* Washington, DC: American Psychological Association.

Kanfer, F. H., and Goldstein, A. P. (eds). (1991) *Helping people change: A textbook of methods,* 4th edn. Boston, MA: Allyn & Bacon.

Kotter, J. P. (1982) *The general managers.* New York: Free Press.

Latham, G. P. and Saari, L. M. (1979) Application of social-learning theory to training supervisors through behavioral modeling. *Journal of Applied Psychology*. 64(3): 239–46.

Luthans, F., Hodgetts, R. M., and Rosenkrantz, S. A. (1988) *Real managers*. Cambridge, MA: Ballinger Press.

McClelland, D. C. (1998) Identifying competencies with behavioral event interviews. *Psychological Science*. 9(5): 331–9.

Morrow, C. C., Jarrett, M. Q., and Rupinski, M. T. (1997) An investigation of the effect and economic utility of corporate-wide training. *Personnel Psychology*. 50: 91–119.

Noe, R. A. and Schmitt, N. (1986) The influence of trainee attitudes on training effectiveness: Test of a model. *Personnel Psychology*, 39: 497–523.

Pascarella, E. T. and Terenzini, P. T. (1991) *How college affects students: Findings and insights from twenty years of research*. San Francisco, CA: Jossey-Bass.

Rubin, D. C. (1986) *Autobiographical memory*. New York: Cambridge University Press.

Spencer, L. M. Jr and Spencer, S. M. (1993) *Competence at work: Models for superior performance*. New York: Wiley.

Thornton, G. C. III and Byham, W. C. (1982) *Assessment centers and managerial performance*. New York: Academic Press.

Wheeler, J. V. (1999) The impact of social environments on self-directed change and learning. Unpublished doctoral dissertation. Case Western Reserve University.

Chapter 7

Leadership and emotional intelligence

Cary Cherniss

American Express was one of the companies especially affected by the attack on the World Trade Center in New York City on September 11, 2001. Twelve employees were killed, and many others were injured. In addition to the loss of life and injuries, the company's world headquarters was completely destroyed. The company suffered economically as well. Amex had already seen a drop in revenues due to changes in the economy. Now, as a company heavily dependent on the travel industry, the employees faced even more difficult times.

The challenge would have been daunting for any leader; but it was even more so for the company's CEO, Kenneth Chenault. He had only assumed the top post the previous April. Also, while he was a popular choice, he was under particularly close scrutiny as one of the first African Americans to lead a major US corporation. In addition, he was 2,000 miles away in Salt Lake City, Utah at the time of the attack, and he could not return for several days due to the cessation of all air travel in the United States. Nevertheless, Chenault responded quickly and decisively.

Communicating with his people by telephone, email, and any other media still working, Chenault took charge. First, he arranged for a company call centre in North Carolina to contact every one of American Express's 6,000 employees who worked in downtown Manhattan to find out how they were doing and what they needed. Then he made sure that those who had become homeless were helped to find temporary living accommodations. When Chenault finally was able to return to New York, he personally visited the families of the 12 employees who died in the attack. And then he organized a 'town meeting' for 5,000 employees in Madison Square Garden.

Those who attended the meeting reported that it was one of the most remarkable displays of caring, compassion, and healing that they had ever seen from a corporate leader. Chenault sat open-shirted and alone on a stage, and he answered any question that the employees wished to pose. When an employee became overcome with emotion, which happened several times, Chenault came down from the stage to give the person a hug. Finally, Chenault ended the meeting by saying to the assembled group, 'You are my strength. I love you.'

Chenault's response to the 9/11 disaster illustrated how one leader used emotional intelligence to deal with a critical moment in his organization's history. Rather than ignore or downplay the emotional dimensions of the event, he was acutely aware of his own feelings and those of his employees. And he was not afraid to express those feelings openly. He also understood well how those feelings would ebb and flow during the coming days and weeks, and how they would impact the company. He instinctively responded in ways that helped people effectively manage those feelings. In short, Chenault understood that what was most critical during this difficult time was to recognize and connect with the feelings that engulfed all of the American Express family, including himself. In a speech just a month after the disaster, he said, 'The challenge at American Express was dealing with psychological and emotional trauma. Many people lost family and friends, and most witnessed horrific scenes right outside their windows' (Kunz, 2001).

Kenneth Chenault's sensitivity and skill in dealing with the emotional trauma of 9/11 helped American Express to make one of the most remarkable recoveries in corporate history. The travel sector of the American economy eventually dropped by 40 per cent in the weeks following the tragedy, and there was a $1 billion credit loss. Yet American Express not only survived, but within 18 months, the company had gained a relative advantage over others (Kattula, 2003).

Chenault's handling of the 9/11 disaster exemplifies what psychologists now call emotional intelligence. Mayer, Salovey, and Caruso (2000), who first used the term in a published scientific paper, define it as, 'The ability to perceive and express emotion, assimilate emotion in thought, understand and reason with emotion, and regulate emotion in the self and others' (p. 396). Goleman (2001) has suggested that emotional intelligence encompasses 'the abilities to recognize and regulate emotions in ourselves and others' (p. 14). Bar-On's definition is, 'A cross-section of emotional and social competencies that determine how well we understand and express ourselves, understand and relate with others, and cope with daily demands and pressures' (Bar-On, Handley, and Fund, 2005). Although these definitions differ, there appears to be a common core. Putting them together, emotional intelligence seems to involve *the abilities to perceive, understand, and manage emotions in oneself and others.*

The link between emotional intelligence and leadership has not always been obvious. There has been a tendency to view organizational leadership in more coldly rational terms and to see emotion as a potential danger rather than an aid to leadership. For instance, there was the senior executive at a major aviation company who often went into uncontrolled rages whenever someone gave him bad news. His subordinates were so intimidated by him that they often withheld important information; as a result, he negotiated a contract to sell 20 more planes than his plants could produce. The fallout was disastrous for the company, and the executive was fired (Cherniss and Adler, 2000). Examples like this one seem to suggest that 'becoming emotional' can get leaders into trouble.

However, the example of Kenneth Chenault demonstrates that becoming emotional and openly expressing one's feelings sometimes can be helpful for leaders. In Chenault's case, a warmer, more emotionally tuned response helped his employees to cope with their shock, grief, and fear. Also, the research of Damasio (1994, 1999) and other neuroscientists suggests that pure rationality, devoid of emotion, does not necessarily lead to effective leadership. Emotion provides important information that helps leaders to make decisions and make choices. Even a negative emotion such as anger can help a CEO to motivate and focus his efforts to address the problem, for example, when he becomes aware of a pattern of sexual harassment in a department. His anger also signals to the organization that this kind of behaviour should not be tolerated (George, 2000).

Thus, there are times when the expression of emotion is adaptive for leaders, and times when it needs to be kept in check. The most effective leaders are not coldly rational and unemotional, but they are able to manage emotions such as anger effectively. To paraphrase Aristotle, the effective leader is angry with the right person, to the right degree, at the right time, for the right purpose, and in the right way (quoted in Goleman, 1995). Such a leader has a high degree of emotional intelligence.

But what about traditional, cognitive intelligence? Many people have tended to regard cognitive intelligence as the primary factor in effective leadership. To be successful as a leader, according to this view, one should be smarter than others. However, while there is some empirical support for the notion that good leaders are smart, the actual relationship between general mental ability and leadership effectiveness is not very strong. In fact, a recent meta-analysis found that 'the relationship between intelligence and leadership is considerably lower than previously thought'. with a corrected correlation coefficient of only 0.27 (Judge, Colbert, and Ilies, 2004, p. 542). This finding suggests that IQ accounts for only about 8 per cent of the variability in leadership effectiveness, which leaves much of the variability in performance unexplained.

In 1973, McClelland proposed that we use a different approach in studying leadership. He suggested that researchers begin by identifying the superior performers and then compare them with typical or below average performers. The abilities that most strongly differentiated the two groups he called 'competencies' (McClelland, 1973). When McClelland and others began doing these competency studies, they found that most of the competencies critical for success had to do with social and emotional abilities (Spencer and Spencer, 1993). In leadership positions, 85 per cent of the competencies that emerged as critical for superior performance related to emotional and social intelligence (Goleman, 1998a).

Although some researchers and theorists have been slow to recognize the importance of emotional intelligence for leadership effectiveness, many of the most prominent practitioners have found it to be obvious. As Jack Welch, former CEO of General Electric, observed in the *Wall Street Journal,* 'Emotional intelligence is more rare than book smarts, but my experience says it is actually more important in the making of a leader' (Welch, 2004). Thus, while cognitive intelligence provides part of the package, it is the competencies most strongly linked to emotional intelligence that make the biggest difference for outstanding leadership.

HOW DOES EMOTIONAL INTELLIGENCE HELP LEADERS TO BE MORE EFFECTIVE?

Emotional intelligence is the foundation for many of the qualities associated with effective leadership. For instance, the classic Ohio State Leadership Studies isolated two factors that seemed to be at the root of effective leadership: initiating structure and consideration (Hemphill, 1959). Leaders who scored high in consideration were the ones who established 'mutual trust, respect, and a certain warmth and rapport' with members of their group (Fleishman and Harris, 1962). 'Consideration' requires emotional intelligence – i.e. an ability to tune in to others' feelings and to use that information to create a supportive environment.

In the 1950s, Douglas Bray and his colleagues at ATandT created the first assessment centre. Their longitudinal research showed that the way in which a manager performed on certain assessment centre tasks at the beginning of his or her career accurately predicted how successful that person was 20 years later (Bray, 1976). Most of those tasks involved abilities that depend on emotional intelligence, such as communication, sensitivity, and interpersonal skills (Gowing, 2001; Thornton and Byham, 1982).

The role of emotional intelligence becomes apparent when we examine the functions of leadership. For instance, a number of writers have proposed that leadership ultimately is about the ability to influence others (Zaccaro, 2002). A leader's influence seems to depend heavily on the way in which the leader manages emotion. As Murphy (2002) wrote, effective leaders influence others through the 'creative use of words that paint a compelling vision of the future for the organization or work group' (p. 174). Also, 'those people who feel that they are truly understood may be more likely to listen to the leader's ideas and implement his or her plans' (Murphy, 2002, p. 175). Emotional intelligence is the foundation for these aspects of the leadership role.

Leadership research and theory in recent years has focused on a set of leadership qualities associated with 'transformational leadership' (Bass, 2002). Transformational leaders excel because they develop clear and compelling visions, and they inspire their followers to work towards those visions through their use of language, story telling, and other communication devices. The ability to communicate in ways that evoke the desired emotional response requires emotional intelligence (Ashkanasy and Tse, 2000).

Along with their ability to create a compelling vision, transformational leaders also are sensitive to their followers' needs. They have the ability to identify those needs and then act in ways that inspire dedication and enthusiasm for the task. Here, too, emotional intelligence seems to play a prominent role because followers often do not communicate their needs in a clear or direct way. They express them indirectly through their emotions. Thus, transformational leadership requires that the leader be highly skilled in reading followers' emotions.

Leadership also requires the ability to mediate between conflicting individual and group demands. Zaccaro (2002) has argued that to be effective, leaders need to accommodate multiple constituencies both within the organization and in the external environment, and leaders often must deal with conflicting demands. A leader's ability to manage these conflicts effectively is strongly influenced by her or his skill in sensing when people care most about an issue, identifying their underlying concerns, and managing their emotions in ways that help them to come together and resolve their differences. The effective management of conflicting demands from diverse constituencies is another aspect of leadership that requires a high level of emotional intelligence.

Emotional intelligence has become even more important for leadership with increasing cultural diversity (Offerman and Phan, 2002). Leaders need high levels of emotional intelligence to understand and effectively manage those who are different, and the ability to respond effectively in a culturally diverse environment depends as much on self-understanding as it does on understanding others.

Awareness and effective management of one's own emotions seem to be especially important for effective leadership. Sternberg (2002) has proposed that leaders achieve success in part by capitalizing on their strengths and correcting or compensating for their weaknesses. This self-knowledge allows them to find, or create, good matches between the kind of leader they are and what the situation requires (Fiedler, 2002).

High levels of self-understanding are especially important in helping leaders to be more open to receiving corrective feedback. Murphy (2002) observed that corporate leaders who are less aware of their own motives and feelings are more likely to handle crises poorly. 'One of the major mistakes made by many top CEOs was that they were in denial about many aspects of their own actions, as well as those of their firms' (p. 168).

It is in the management of their own emotions that the importance of emotional intelligence for leaders becomes most clear. Researchers have found that high levels of stress and anxiety reduce one's capacity to handle information. The higher the degree of stress, the fewer bits of information can one handle in one's brain (Fiedler, 2002; Goleman, 1998b). Thus, leaders who are able to remain calm and composed in the midst of threatening situations are more likely to act effectively. 'By managing anxiety, maintaining a positive attitude, and successfully coping with stress, leaders and followers are more able to make use of the resources of knowledge and skill that they possess' (Chemers, 2002, p. 152). Confidence is especially important for effective leadership; and skill in handling stress, along with a high degree of self-awareness, form the basis for strong self-confidence.

Effective leadership requires the ability to regulate one's mood because a leader's mood affects her performance and that of her followers. Leaders who are in a positive mood make better decisions (Staw and Barsade, 1992). Groups led by leaders in a positive mood also perform better (Barsade, 1998; Sy, Cote, and Savedra, in press). For instance, one study found that groups whose leaders were more positive provided better customer service than those whose managers were more neutral or negative in mood (George, 1995).

The importance of emotional intelligence also becomes apparent when one considers some of the specific tasks that organizational leaders must routinely perform. For instance, consider the situation in which a leader is coaching a subordinate. In this potentially volatile situation, the leader must be skilful in using just the right degree of praise and criticism based on the mood and personality of the follower. As Chemers put it:

> It is at this deeper level of understanding that emotional intelligence becomes critical. The leader needs first to control his or her own emotional reactions to the coaching situation, both in terms of anxiety about delivering feedback, as well as in terms of threats to one's own sense of competence. Second, the ability to read and understand the emotions of others, i.e. empathy, forms the basis for truly individualized consideration.
>
> (2002, p. 151).

Emotional intelligence can be important even in situations that appear to be devoid of any emotional content. For instance, consider two managers who are not very good at flow charting projects. Each of them has a subordinate who is good at doing so. Manager number one goes to the subordinate and asks for his help whenever he needs to flow chart a project. Manager number two is afraid that he will 'look bad' if he turns to a subordinate for help, and so he tries to do it himself. Ultimately, manager number one is more effective and is eventually promoted. Manager number two is eventually laid off. In this case, manager number one is more emotionally intelligent – he is more aware of his strengths and weaknesses, and better able to manage his emotions. And this emotional intelligence helps him to perform more effectively and to succeed.

Thus, whether it is charting a grand vision for the future, mediating among diverse stakeholders, or providing corrective feedback to a struggling subordinate, leaders must draw on the abilities associated with emotional intelligence. There are few aspects of leadership that do not depend on emotional intelligence in one way or another.

WHAT DOES THE RESEARCH SAY ABOUT EMOTIONAL INTELLIGENCE AND LEADERSHIP?

During the last decade, a growing body of empirical research has documented the link between emotional intelligence and leadership effectiveness. One of the most compelling studies involved managers of Beefeater restaurants in the United Kingdom. Using the EQ-i, a popular measure of emotional and social intelligence developed by Bar-On (1997), Langhorn assessed 100 managers and then analysed how well their scores predicted various indices of effectiveness (Bar-On, 2004). He found a multiple R of 0.47 when emotional and social intelligence was used to predict annual profit increase. EQ-i scores also predicted guest satisfaction ($R = 0.50$). What is especially impressive about this study is that the performance measures were objective, 'bottom-line' outcomes.

Another study that used an objective measure of leadership effectiveness measured emotional intelligence with the Emotional Competence Inventory (ECI). The ECI, a multi-rater ('360') instrument, measures four basic dimensions of emotional intelligence: Self-Awareness, Self-Management, Social Awareness, and Relationship Management. This study found that for 92 college principals in the United Kingdom, a school's retention rate was significantly correlated with Self-Awareness ($r = 0.20$) and Social Awareness ($r = 0.18$) (Boyatzis and Sala, 2004).

Salary level was the performance measure used in another study involving the ECI. Boyatzis and Sala (2004) reported that all four dimensions of emotional intelligence as measured by the ECI were correlated with salary level in a group of 40 Turkish financial managers. The Pearson correlation coefficients were 0.30, 0.37, 0.43, and 0.40 for Self-Awareness, Self-Management, Social Awareness, and Relationship Management respectively.

Several other studies have found positive relationships between emotional intelligence and leadership effectiveness as measured by nominations or ratings of individuals who know the leader well (Dulewicz and Higgs, 2004; Slaski and Cartwright, 2002; Williams, 2004). One study looked at 302 individuals who participated in the Center for Creative Leadership's (CCL) Leadership Development Program (Ruderman et al., 2001). Leadership effectiveness was measured with CCL's Benchmarks, a widely used and well-validated multi-rater instrument. The researchers found that 10 out of 16 Benchmarks dimensions were significantly correlated with one or more aspects of emotional and social intelligence as measured by the EQ-i. Two derailers measured by Benchmarks were also correlated with the EQ-i dimensions.

Another study used the multi-rater ECI in a large corporate setting. The participants were 358 managers employed by Johnson and Johnson (Cavallo and Brienza, 2004). The managers were not only North American but also came from Europe, Asia, and other parts of the world. The results revealed that superior performers (based on annual performance ratings by their bosses) scored higher in all four emotional intelligence clusters (Self-Awareness, Self-Management, Social Awareness, and Relationship Management) when the emotional intelligence assessment was based on ratings by their superiors or subordinates. The superior performers scored higher in the Self-Awareness and Self-Management clusters when the emotional intelligence assessment was based on peer ratings.

Another study used the Mayer–Salovey–Caruso Emotional Intelligence Test (MSCEIT), which attempts to measure various aspects of emotional intelligence directly through tasks completed by the test taker. This study examined the impact of emotional intelligence on the performance of project managers (Leban, 2003). The managers were directing 24 projects in six organizations from varied industries. Project success was measured via rating forms completed by members of project teams and stakeholders, as well as interviews with organizational executives. The results indicated that the most successful projects were led by project managers who scored higher in EI.

In another study using the MSCEIT, the participants were management students working in small teams for a ten-week long course project. The researchers found that students scoring higher in emotional intelligence were rated by their teammates as proposing more compelling goals and ideas for the group project. The relationship was significant even when the researchers controlled for personality traits and demographic differences (Lopes, Cote, and Salovey, 2005).

Research suggests that emotional intelligence also is linked to effective leadership in schools. Stone, Parker, and Wood (2004) studied 464 school principals and vice principals in the Canadian province of Ontario. Emotional intelligence was measured with the EQ-i, and performance was measured by a 20+-item leadership questionnaire completed by the person's superior and up to three subordinates. The researchers found that top-performing leaders scored significantly higher than below average leaders on all four dimensions of emotional intelligence (Intrapersonal, Interpersonal, Adaptability, and Stress Management).

Emotional intelligence is also associated with leadership effectiveness in the military. In one study, recruits in the Israeli Defense Forces who were nominated most often by peers as having officer potential scored significantly higher on the EQ-i than those nominated least often (Bar-On, Handley, and Fund, 2005). The relationship accounted for 15 per cent of the variance. In a related study, recruits accepted for officer training scored significantly higher on the EQ-i than a random sample of recruits. In this case, the prediction model accounted for 24 per cent of the variance (Bar-On, Handley, and Fund, 2005).

One other study involving the military measured emotional intelligence with the ECI (Stubbs, 2005). The participants were leaders of US air force teams. The results indicated that the team leader's emotional intelligence was associated with the group functioning of the teams, which in turn was related to team performance measured both objectively (percentage of performance goals accomplished) and subjectively (ratings done by higher level leaders).

Some studies have looked at specific aspects of emotional intelligence and their link to leadership effectiveness. For instance, Murphy (2002) measured how sensitive leaders were to their own and others' feelings in a laboratory study, and found that sensitivity predicted member satisfaction with leader performance. The relationship was even stronger in a high stress condition. Byron (2003) looked at the impact of 'emotional decoding ability', another aspect of emotional intelligence, and found that managers who scored higher on a test of this ability received higher ratings from their subordinates.

In addition to examining the relationship between emotional intelligence and leadership performance directly, a number of researchers have looked at the link between emotional intelligence and variables that are known to contribute to leadership effectiveness. For instance, a number of studies have documented a strong link between emotional intelligence, measured in a variety of ways, and transformational leadership (Barling, Slater, and Kelloway, 2000; Burbach, 2004; Gardner and Stough, 2002; Hartsfield, 2003; Leban, 2003; Skinner and Spurgeon, 2005; Sosik and Megerian, 1999; Srivsastava and Bharamanaikar, 2004). Other research has demonstrated a strong relationship between a leader's emotional intelligence and organizational climate (Boyatzis and Sala, 2004) or organizational commitment of followers (Giles, 2001).

Thus, a number of different studies suggest that there is a significant link between emotional intelligence and leadership effectiveness. What is impressive about this body of research is that different studies have used different measures of EI. Some have used self-report measures such as the EQ-i or the EIQ. Others have used the ECI, a multi-rater assessment. And still others have used the MSCEIT or another ability measure. Similarly, these studies have used different measures of performance. A few have used relatively objective measures (e.g. annual profit increases in restaurants or student retention rates in colleges). Many others have used more subjective performance measures such as nominations or ratings by those who work with the leader.

However, interest in emotional intelligence has been fuelled in part by the claim that emotional intelligence is more important for effective leadership than cognitive abilities. Much less research has examined this issue, but there are some studies suggesting that social and emotional competencies are better predictors of leadership effectiveness than IQ or general mental ability. Grotas (2003) found that for 280 mid-level managers from a variety of organizations who participated in an assessment centre, the social and emotional competencies most closely associated with emotional intelligence were much better predictors of performance than was cognitive ability. In fact, cognitive intelligence, as measured by the Watson–Glaser Critical Thinking Appraisal and the Wesman Personnel Classification Test, accounted for none of the variance in assessment centre performance. And there was a negative relationship between cognitive ability and performance on the job as rated by co-workers.

Bass (2002) presented empirical research suggesting that social and emotional intelligences are better predictors of transformational leadership than cognitive intelligence, and emotional intelligence seems to be better than social intelligence.

Although the weight of evidence suggests that emotional intelligence is a strong predictor of leadership effectiveness, not all the research has been consistent with this interpretation. A few studies have failed to find such a relationship (Brooks, 2003; Schulte, 2003; Weinberger, 2003). For instance, Slaski and Cartwright (2003) used the EQ-i and EIQ to assess the impact of a training programme on a group of retail store managers. Increases in emotional intelligence did not result in improved performance as measured in the annual performance review process. However, measures of health and well-being did improve. In another study using the EIQ, Dulewicz and Higgs (2004) looked at skippers of yachts entered in a round-the-world yacht race. They found no relationship between emotional intelligence and race performance. And in a study using the MSCEIT, Collins (2001) found no relationship between emotional intelligence and performance as measured by multi-rater assessment, position, and salary in a group of 91 executives from a large corporation. However, in this last study there was some evidence that emotional intelligence did predict performance when other variables, such as personality and cognitive ability, were controlled.

A closer examination of these studies with negative findings suggests that in many cases, there were flaws or certain contextual factors that could account for the unexpected results. For instance, there was the laboratory study reported by Murphy (2002) in which the participants formed groups that engaged in a 'simulated personnel placement task'. The results showed that in a high stress condition, leaders high in social and emotional skills had groups that performed worse on the task. However, the simulation used in this study probably is not representative of typical or critical leadership situations.

Another study with negative results involved 11 team leaders who led 26 teams of claims adjusters (Feyerherm and Rice, 2002; Rice, 1999). Using the MEIS, a forerunner of the MSCEIT, the researchers found that total emotional intelligence was not related to overall team performance as rated by managers, and emotional intelligence was negatively correlated with accuracy and productivity as rated by team members. In this case, however, nine of the 26 teams were composed of only two people. Also, in several instances, one team leader led many teams. And the total number of participants was very small – there were only 11 team leaders in the study.

Thus, when all of the research is considered together, the evidence seems to support the claim that emotional intelligence is a significant factor in leadership effectiveness. The positive studies far outweigh the negative ones in number and methodological quality. Nevertheless, the few negative studies that have emerged suggest that the relationship between emotional intelligence and leadership effectiveness is a complex one. More research is needed to discover the contextual factors that influence the relationship. For instance, what are the kinds of leadership tasks and functions that are most affected by the leader's emotional intelligence? Are there certain kinds of followers who are more affected by the emotional intelligence of the leader than others? Hopefully, research in the future will address these more sophisticated questions about the connection between emotional intelligence and leadership.

EMOTIONAL INTELLIGENCE AND LEADERSHIP DEVELOPMENT

Programmes for helping leaders and would-be leaders to become more emotionally intelligent have mushroomed in recent years. Although many of these programmes are promising, few are designed in a way that is likely to lead to much change. Emotional intelligence and the competencies linked to it are based on neural pathways that have been used repeatedly since childhood. To become more socially and emotionally competent, one must change those neural pathways, and this is a task that requires months of concerted effort. One-day seminars or workshops can be valuable in educating people and raising awareness, but they cannot by themselves lead to the kind of neural reprogramming that is required for significant improvement (Cherniss and Adler, 2000).

Also, leadership development programmes that rely heavily on lectures, discussion, and demonstrations will probably have little impact on emotional intelligence because they do not target a part of the brain that is involved in emotional intelligence. The emotional centre of the brain is found in the limbic system, which is located just above the brain stem (Goleman, 1998b). The limbic system, one of the oldest parts of the brain in evolutionary terms, does not 'understand' words or concepts. Thus, any successful effort to improve emotional intelligence must be active and experiential, not just verbal and cognitive.

Put another way, increasing emotional intelligence is like learning to ride a bicycle. One can read books about bicycle riding. One even can master the physics involved. But none of this will help one to learn how to ride a bike because bike riding, a motor skill, also involves an ancient part of the brain that does not deal with words or concepts. Ultimately there is no substitute for getting on a bike, trying to ride, feeling what it is like to lose one's balance and fall off, getting on again, and repeating this process until the muscles and nerves learn to work in harmony. Just as one needs to use an active, experiential approach in learning to ride a bike, one needs such an approach in developing emotional intelligence.

Fortunately, it is possible for motivated individuals to become more emotionally intelligent leaders. In fact, there are two promising approaches that have been developed, with empirical evidence to back them up. These two approaches provide models that others can emulate.

The first is the Emotional Competence Training programme, developed at American Express Financial Advisors in 1992 and since used with thousands of managers in that company and several others in the US (Cherniss and Adler, 2000, Goleman, 1998b). There are a few different versions of the programme, but the one that has been found to be effective involves about 40 hours of training, divided into two group sessions of two or three days each, which are separated by a month or two. Carefully selected, doctoral-level psychologists who understand the special challenges involved in implementing such a programme in work organizations deliver the programme. Although there are some didactic segments of the programme, much of it involves highly experiential activity, such as role-plays, simulations, demonstrations, etc. The programme covers a number of topics, including the role of emotion in the workplace, different ways of expressing how we are feeling, the impact of 'self-talk' on feelings and behaviour, active listening, and norms for the expression of emotion at work.

Several studies have documented the effectiveness of the Emotional Competence Training programme. In one study, regional management teams went through the programme together, and the financial advisors who worked under the trained managers were compared to those who worked under managers who did not receive the training. The results indicated that advisors who worked under trained managers grew their businesses 18 per cent over a period of 15 months compared to a 16.2 per cent growth rate for the controls (Cherniss and Adler, 2000).

A second effective approach for helping people to become more emotionally intelligent leaders is 'Self-Directed Learning' (Boyatzis, 2001). In this strategy, the participants first learn about the social and emotional competencies most critical for effective leadership. This initial phase of the training not only teaches the participants about the competencies but also shows them in clear and vivid ways what the competencies look like in practice. Next, the participants are assessed on the competencies. Then they are given feedback and helped by a coach to develop a personal action plan for developing one or two competencies.

One of the earliest applications of Self-Directed Learning occurred at Case Western Reserve University's Weatherhead School of Management (Boyatzis, 1994). Students in the MBA programme participated in a course based on the Self-Directed Learning model during their first semester, and then researchers followed them as they completed their studies and embarked on their new careers. During the first two years following the course, the Weatherhead students improved 47 per cent on the competencies associated with self-awareness and self-management, and they improved 75 per cent on the competencies associated with social awareness and handling relationships. Students who attended two other highly ranked MBA programmes and did not go through the Self-Directed Learning programme showed only a 2 per cent improvement on skills related to emotional intelligence. Students at four other highly ranked MBA programmes showed improvements of only 4 per cent on the competencies associated with self-awareness and self-management, and they posted a decrease of 3 per cent in the social awareness and relationship management competencies (Boyatzis, 2002).

Even more impressive, the student gains in the Weatherhead programme continued for at least two years following graduation. At that point, they still showed improvements of 36 per cent on the self-awareness and self-management competencies, and 45 per cent on the social competencies (Boyatzis, 2002).

The Self-Directed Learning approach has also been effective with practising managers in a corporate setting. Spencer used it to develop emotional intelligence competencies in managers working in a firm that makes industrial controls (Spencer, 2001). The managers who received the training led groups that posted an additional profit of $1.5 million on average during the next year, which was twice the amount posted by a control group. Thus, well-designed leadership development programmes can bring about significant improvements in emotional intelligence, and these improvements pay off in bottom-line results.

CONCLUSION

True leadership involves more than cold, calculating logic. Leadership involves getting people to do things that they normally would not want to do, and this requires connecting with people on an emotional level. To motivate their followers, leaders must understand their own emotional reactions as well as those of their followers. To inspire their followers, leaders must create emotional responses in those followers, whether it is anger against the injustice of racism or excitement and anticipation over a new software design project. And in order to manage the emotions of others, leaders must be able to master their own emotions. It is not surprising, therefore, that the sort of cognitive intelligence measured by IQ tests, SATs, or GMATs does not count for much when it comes to acts of extraordinary leadership. What does count is a different kind of intelligence – emotional intelligence.

There is still much to learn about emotional intelligence. There are different models and measures, and too many programmes now being used to develop emotional intelligence are unproven. Some are so poorly designed that it is almost certain they will fall short. However, the good news is that we now can measure emotional intelligence with some degree of precision, and we have proven programmes to help people develop their emotional intelligence and use it to be more effective leaders. As research and practice in the field proceed, there is every reason to believe that our measures and methods will become even better.

REFERENCES

Ashkanasy, N. M. and Tse, B. (2000) Transformational leadership as management of emotion: A conceptual review. In Ashkanasy, N. M., Hartel, C. E. J., and Zerbe, W. J. (eds) *Emotions in the workplace*. Westport, CT: Quorum Books, pp. 221–35.

Bar-On, R. (1997) *Bar-On emotional quotient inventory: User's manual*. Toronto, ON: Multi-Health Systems.

Bar-On, R. (2004) Applying the power of emotional intelligence. Paper presented at the EQ Symposium, Golden, CO, 28 October.

Bar-On, R., Handley, R., and Fund, S. (2005) The impact of emotional intelligence on performance. In Druskat, V., Sala, F., and Mount, G. (eds) *Linking emotional intelligence and performance at work: Current research evidence*. Mahwah, NJ: Lawrence Erlbaum Associates, pp.3–20.

Barling, J., Slater, F., and Kelloway, E. K. (2000) Transformational leadership and emotional intelligence: An exploratory study. *Leadership and Organization Development Journal,* 21: 157–61.

Barsade, S. (1998) *The ripple effect: Emotional contagion in groups*. New Haven, CT: Yale University School Of Management.

Bass, B. M. (2002) Cognitive, social, and emotional intelligence of transformational leaders. In Riggio, R. E., Murphy, S. E., and Pirozzolo, F. J. (eds) *Multiple intelligences and leadership*. Mahwah, NJ: Lawrence Erlbaum Associates, pp.105–18.

Boyatzis, R. E. (1994) Stimulating self-directed learning through the Managerial Assessment and Development Course. *Journal of Management Education,* 18: 304–23.

Boyatzis, R. E. (2001) How and why individuals are able to develop emotional intelligence. In Cherniss, C. and Goleman, D. (eds) *The emotionally intelligent workplace*. San Francisco, CA: Jossey-Bass, pp. 234–53.

Boyatzis, R. E. (2002) Unleashing the power of self-directed learning. In Sims, R. (ed.) *Changing the way we manage change: The consultants speak*. New York: Quorum Books.

Boyatzis, R. E. and Sala, F. (2004) Assessing emotional intelligence competencies. In Geher, G. (ed.) *Measuring emotional intelligence: Common ground and controversy*. Hauppage, NY: Nova Science Publishers, pp. 147–80.

Bray, D. W. (1976) The Assessment Center Method. In Craig, R. L. (ed.) *Training and development handbook*. New York: McGraw-Hill.

Brooks, J. K. (2003) *Emotional competencies of leaders: A comparison of managers in a financial organization by performance level*. Unpublished doctoral dissertation, North Carolina State University.

Burbach, M. E. (2004) Testing the relationship between emotional intelligence and full-range leadership as moderated by cognitive style and self-concept. Unpublished doctoral dissertation, The University of Nebraska, Lincoln, NE.

Byron, K. L. (2003) Are better managers better at 'reading' others? Testing the claim that emotional intelligence predicts managerial performance. Atlanta, GA: Georgia State University.

Cavallo, K. and Brienza, D. (2004) Emotional competence and leadership excellence at Johnson and Johnson: The Emotional Intelligence and Leadership Study. New Brunswick, NJ: Consortium for Research on Emotional Intelligence in Organizations, Rutgers University.

Chemers, M. M. (2002) Efficacy and effectiveness: Integrating models of leadership and intelligence. In Riggio, R. E., Murphy, S. E., and Pirozzolo, F. J. (eds) *Multiple intelligences and leadership.* Mahwah, NJ: Lawrence Erlbaum Associates, pp.139–40.

Cherniss, C. and Adler, M. (2000) *Promoting emotional intelligence in organizations.* Alexandria, VA: ASTD.

Collins, V. L. (2001) Emotional intelligence and leadership success. Lincoln, NE: University Of Nebraska.

Damasio, A. (1994) *Descartes' error: Emotion, reason, and the human brain,* New York: Grosset/Putnam.

Damasio, A. (1999) *The feeling of what happens: Body and emotion in the making of consciousness.* New York: Harcourt Brace.

Dulewicz, V. and Higgs, M. (2004) Can emotional intelligence be developed? *International Journal of Human Resource Management,* 15: 95–111.

Feyerherm, A. E. and Rice, C. L. (2002) Emotional intelligence and team performance: The good, the bad, and the ugly. *International Journal of Organizational Analysis,* 10: 343–62.

Fiedler, F. E. (2002) The curious role of cognitive resources in leadership. In Riggio, R. E., Murphy, S. E., and Pirozzolo, F. J. (eds) *Multiple intelligences and leadership.* Mahwah, NJ: Lawrence Erlbaum Associates, pp. 91–104.

Fleishman, E. and Harris, E. F. (1962) Patterns of leadership behavior related to employee grievances and turnover. *Personnel Psychology,* 15: 43–56.

Gardner, L. and Stough, C. (2002) Examining the relationship between leadership and emotional intelligence in senior level managers. *Leadership and Organization Development Journal,* 23: 68–78.

George, J. M. (1995) Leader positive mood and group performance: The case of customer service. *Journal of Applied Social Psychology,* 25: 778–94.

George, J. M. (2000) Emotions and leadership: The role of emotional intelligence. *Human Relations,* 53: 1027–55.

Giles, S. J. S. (2001) The role of supervisory emotional intelligence in direct report organizational commitment. Sydney, Australia: University of New South Wales.

Goleman, D. (1995) *Emotional intelligence.* New York: Bantam.

Goleman, D. (1998a) What makes a leader? *Harvard Business Review,* 76: 92–102.

Goleman, D. (1998b) *Working with emotional intelligence.* New York: Bantam.

Goleman, D. (2001) Emotional intelligence: Issues in paradigm building. In Cherniss, C. and Goleman, D. (eds) *The emotionally intelligent workplace.* San Francisco, CA: Jossey-Bass, pp. 13–26.

Gowing, M. (2001) Measurement of individual emotional competence. In Cherniss, C. and Goleman, D. (eds) *The emotionally intelligent workplace.* San Francisco, CA: Jossey-Bass, pp. 83–121.

Grotas, J. (2003) To know thyself: The roles of accuracy of self-assessment, personality, and cognitive intelligence in assessment center performance. New Brunswick, NJ: Rutgers University, Graduate School of Applied and Professional Psychology.

Hartsfield, M. K. (2003) The internal dynamics of transformational leadership: Effects of spirituality, emotional intelligence, and self-efficacy. Virgina Beach, VA: Regent University.

Hemphill, J. K. (1959) Job description for executives. *Harvard Business Review, 37*: 55–67.

Judge, T. A., Colbert, A. E., and Ilies, R. (2004) Intelligence and leadership: A quantitative review and test of theoretical propositions. *Journal of Applied Psychology, 89*: 542–52.

Kattula, J. (2003) Kenneth Chenault on managing in volatile times. *Monroe Street Journal.* Retrieved 19 April 2005 from www.themsj.com/global_user_elements/printpage.cfm?storid=383457.

Kunz, C. (2001) American Express CEO Chenault speaks at Cornell. Retrieved from www.cornellbusiness.com/news/2001/11/13/JohnsonNews/American.Express.CEO.Chenault.Speaks.At.Cornell-143620.shtml.

Leban, W. V. (2003) The relationship between leader behavior and emotional intelligence of the project manager and the success of complex projects. Benedictine University, IL.

Lopes, P. N., Cote, S., and Salovey, P. (2005) An ability model of emotional intelligence: Implications for assessment and training. In Druskat, V., Sala, F., and Mount, G. (eds) *Emotional intelligence and workplace performance.* Mahwah, NJ: Lawrence Erlbaum, pp. 53–80.

Mayer, J. D., Salovey, P., and Caruso, D. R. (2000) Models of emotional intelligence. In Sternberg, R. J. (ed.) *Handbook of intelligence,* 2nd edn. New York: Cambridge University Press, pp. 396–420.

McClelland, D. C. (1973) Testing for competence rather than intelligence. *American Psychologist, 28*: 1–14.

Murphy, S. E. (2002) Leader self-regulation: The role of self-efficacy and multiple intelligences. In Riggio, R. E., Murphy, S. E., and Pirozzolo, F. J. (eds) *Multiple intelligences and leadership.* Mahwah, NJ: Lawrence Erlbaum Associates, pp. 163–86.

Offerman, L. R. and Phan, L. U. (2002) Culturally intelligent leadership for a diverse world. In Riggio, R. E., Murphy, S. E., and Pirozzolo, F. J. (eds) *Multiple intelligences and leadership.* Mahwah, NJ: Lawrence Erlbaum Associates.

Rice, C. L. (1999) A quantitative study of emotional intelligence and its impact on team performance. Malibu, CA: Pepperdine University.

Ruderman, M. N., Hannum, K., Leslie, J. B., and Steed, J. L. (2001) Making the connection: Leadership skills and emotional intelligence. *Leadership in Action, 21*: 3–7.

Schulte, M. J. (2003) Emotional intelligence: A predictive or descriptive construct in ascertaining leadership style or a new name for old knowledge? San Antonio, TX: Our Lady Of The Lake University.

Skinner, C. and Spurgeon, P. (2005) Valuing empathy and emotional intelligence in health leadership: A study of empathy, leadership behaviour and outcome effectiveness. *Health Services Management Research, 18*: 1–12.

Slaski, M. and Cartwright, S. (2002) Health performance and emotional intelligence: An exploratory study of retail managers. *Stress And Health,* 18: 63–8.

Slaski, M. and Cartwright, S. (2003) Emotional intelligence training and its implications for health, stress, and performance. *Stress And Health,* 19: 233–9.

Sosik, J. J. and Megerian, L. E. (1999) Understanding leader emotional intelligence and performance: the role of self-other agreement on transformational leadership perceptions. *Group and Organization Management,* 24: 367–90.

Spencer, L. M. (2001) The economic value of emotional intelligence competencies and EIC-based HR programs. In Cherniss, C. and Goleman, D. (eds) *The emotionally intelligent workplace.* San Francisco, CA: Jossey-Bass, pp. 45–82.

Spencer, L. M., Jr and Spencer, S. (1993) *Competence at work: Models for superior performance,* New York: Wiley.

Srivsastava, K. B. L. and Bharamanaikar, S. R. (2004) Emotional intelligence and effective leadership behaviour. *Psychological Studies, India,* 49: 107–13.

Staw, B. M. and Barsade, S. G. (1992) Affect and managerial performance: A test of the sadder-but-wiser vs. happier-and-smarter hypothesis. *Administrative Science Quarterly,* 38: 304–31.

Sternberg, R. J. (2002) Successful intelligence: A new approach to leadership. In Riggio, R. E., Murphy, S. E., and Pirozzolo, F. J. (eds) *Multiple intelligences and leadership.* Mahwah, NJ: Lawrence Erlbaum Associates, pp. 9–28.

Stone, H., Parker, J. D. A., and Wood, L. M. (2004) Report on the Ontario Principals' Council Leadership Study: Executive summary. Ontario Principals' Council.

Stubbs, E. C. (2005) Emotional intelligence competencies in the team and team leader: A multi-level examination of the impact of emotional intelligence on group performance. *Organizational behavior.* Cleveland, Case Western Reserve University.

Sy, T., Cote, S., and Saavedra, R. (in press) The contagious leader: Impact of leader's affect on group member affect and group processes. *Journal of Applied Psychology.*

Thornton, G. C. I. and Byham, W. C. (1982) *Assessment centers and managerial performance,* New York: Academic Press.

Weinberger, L. A. (2003) An examination of the relationship between emotional intelligence, leadership style and perceived leadership effectiveness. Minneapolis, MN: University Of Minnesota.

Welch, J. (2004) Four E's (a Jolly Good Fellow). *Wall Street Journal.* New York. Retrieved from www.opinionjournal.com/editorial/feature.html?id=110004596.

Williams, H. W. (2004) A study of the characteristics that distinguish outstanding urban principals: Emotional intelligence, problem-solving competencies, role perception and environmental adaptation. Cleveland, Case Western Reserve University.

Zaccaro, S. J. (2002) Organizational leadership and social intelligence. In Riggio, R. E., Murphy, S. E., and Pirozzolo, F. J. (eds) *Multiple intelligences and leadership.* Mahwah, NJ: Lawrence Erlbaum Associates, pp. 29–54.

Chapter 8

Leading through values and ethical principles

R. Edward Freeman, Kirsten Martin, Bidhan Parmar, Margaret Cording, and Patricia H. Werhane

The purpose of this chapter is to introduce a view of leadership that infuses ethics into its definition.* This chapter will demonstrate that previous conceptions of leadership within management literature define leadership as either amoral or only having an instrumental use for values. However, we are able to develop an ethical view of leadership from research outside the management literature. As we will demonstrate, the common principles that cross different types of leadership, situations, organizations, and goals are infused with moral implications – one could say that the only commonality across various types of leadership is ethics. The implications to theory, research, and practice are outlined based on these ethical leadership principles.

Our current maps and mental models about leadership are failing us. Changing economic, political, and social realities, like shifting sands are forcing us to re-examine where we are, how we got here, and where we are going. A variety of factors are reshaping the managerial landscape. Around the world governments are embracing market solutions and deregulating industries. Fifty years ago governments provided footholds and shelter for business expansion, today in countries across the globe, business is playing an increasing role in spreading democracy. In addition, business leaders are responsible for a larger diversity of decisions that impact a larger diversity of constituents.

Also, information technology is changing the way we live. There is greater autonomy in the workplace, with highly educated employees working from home or video conferencing in from the Paris office. Managers need new ways to think

* This chapter is the result of a number of collaborations over the years. Margaret Cording (Rice University), Patricia Werhane (Darden School UVA), and R. Edward Freeman (Darden School UVA) are developing the theoretical connections between ethics and leadership in a working paper, 'Connecting Ethics and Leadership'. Sections of this chapter are derived from that working paper and a paper given by R. Edward Freeman, titled, 'Ethical Leadership and Creating Value for Stakeholders'. We wish to thank our co-authors for their ideas and support.

about building consensus, meeting goals, and leading in a world where physical space has become less of a limitation. Technological advances have also made global business a fact in the twenty-first century. New contexts, cultures, and considerations can leave managers in a moral vertigo. Successful adaptation to the global marketplace requires a strong sense of 'who we are and what we stand for'.

Finally, the short-term character of business success creates tremendous pressure on leaders to be a panacea for all corporate crises. In a time where CEOs are referred to as 'saviors' and expected to be 'prophets for profit', our very standards for successful navigation in the business environment kicks action into overdrive. In the frenetic, short-term goal driven business environment, leaders can easily become myopic and lose sight of the larger landscape, thus opening themselves to ethical minefields.

The role of theorists in this journey is to keep the ways we talk and think about leadership current and useful, to make sure the 'territory always precedes the map'.[1] Good theory should be a reflection of and a guide for what is happening on the ground. The changing business landscape, calls for a revisiting and revising of the maps and metaphors that we use to think about leadership and business. It is in this spirit that we offer an overview and analysis of the last century's academic literature on leadership. We conclude that many of the leading theories offer only an isolated picture of leadership. We use the work done over the past century as important building blocks to draw a new holistic picture of the systems of leadership, one which fundamentally fuses ethics and leadership. This 'canonical model' is built up chronologically from the fragments of leadership theory developed throughout the twentieth century. Through this project we hope to revive the maps and models of leadership that we use and to separate out the minefields and obstacles that are of our own making.

The canonical model allows us to analyse various leadership theories on their approach to ethics. We will be able to see which critical elements are left out of certain leadership theories, and which ones become foundational. After introducing and developing the canonical model, we categorize the leadership literature into three basic types – Amoral, Values-based, and Ethical Leadership – according to the degree to which ethics and value judgements are featured. Finally, principles of ethical leadership are developed and implications to theory, research, and practice are explored.

THE CANONICAL MODEL

As we surveyed of the last 100 years of popular leadership literature, five core themes revealed themselves on the theoretical landscape. The 'leader', the 'followers', 'leadership process and skills', 'context', and 'outcomes' have all been in one theory or another the 'central' aspect of leadership. Scholars generally pick and choose among the different concepts and locate their theories among a few select spheres. Today, most leadership theories take some position on all of these variables even if it is to say that, for example context doesn't matter. The relationship between these five concepts is depicted in the canonical model below (Figure 8.1).

In the following sections we will chronologically survey the development of this model.

The leader

In the early twentieth century scholars set out to understand the traits and characteristics of great leaders. Armed with a love of reason and a penchant for overly deterministic models, these academics aimed to isolate leadership traits to (1) identify potential leaders early in life, and (2) enable people to develop and enhance critical leadership characteristics (Bernard 1926; Bingham and Davis 1927; Kilbourne 1935; Tead 1935). The 'traits' approach covers a large portion of the leadership literature. Studies on a wide variety of traits have been developed, from charisma and physical fitness to the amount a leader 'babbles', and how much time they spend in social interactions, Leadership trait theorists have left no traits unturned.

Over the course of the next few decades theorists became frustrated that no single set of traits could be isolated. In 1948 Stogdill published an in-depth analysis which concluded that no consistent set of traits and characteristics could explain why some are leaders and others followers. Despite its limited applicability, the traits approach is still very influential. As recently as 1991, Kirkpatrick and Locke claimed that 'it is equivocally clear that leaders are not like other people'.

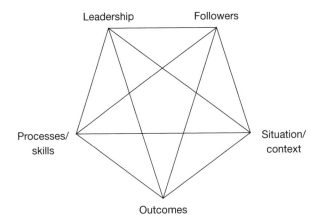

Figure 8.1 *The canonical model of leadership.*

Unfortunately, these approaches have failed to map the larger landscape of leadership. The myopic focus on just the leader and his or her personal and immutable traits has left many questions unanswered. The traits approach assumes that there are immutable traits that are useful for leaders in all contexts. It aims for an understanding of leadership that is abstracted from followers, processes, and context. It is also helpful to note the traits approach is unidirectional. Leaders produce outcomes but are not generally affected by them (Figure 8.2).

Based in part on the utopian view that science can perfect society, the tragedies of the holocaust and World War II, cracked the very philosophical foundations that were their precondition. Afterwards, the traits approach and other strictly empirical projects seemed somehow incomplete. For management scholars, it became impossible to square the assumptions of the traits approach with real-world leaders like Hitler and Stalin. For the next several decades scholars, in an attempt to understand what happened, branched out their research into a variety of different approaches.

Adding followers

The roots of a more robust leadership paradigm can be found in the psychodynamic theories of Freud. The psychodynamic theories and their theoretical progeny reconceptualize leadership not as a static thing, but as a dynamic relationship between leaders and followers. Critical research questions focus on how to manage this relationship and how to improve its health in order to achieve desirable outcomes (see Figure 8.3). Within the leader/follower group of theories we find that there is variation in the way that followers are depicted: as a parent–child relationship, or as an exchange relationship. In both cases, however, the dynamics between the leader and follower are viewed as 'good' or 'bad' based on their effectiveness in achieving the organization's goals.

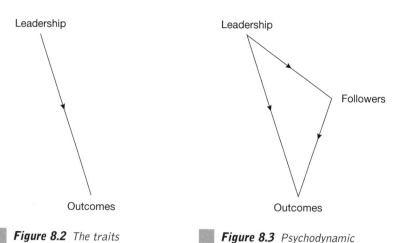

Figure 8.2 The traits approach to leadership.

Figure 8.3 Psychodynamic theories of leadership.

The psychodynamic theories frame leadership as a parent–child relationship. Our parents become our first leaders. In our early days we develop critical feelings about leadership, our role in it, and our reactions to it. Childhood experiences determine one's comfort level with paternal, maternal, and familial patterns of leadership. These theories claim that psychological development produces personality types, and the key to effective leadership is for the leader to be astute to his or her type, the types of the followers, how these followers will likely respond to the leader's type and the resulting impact on effectiveness. The consequence for followers is that they become typecast as 'child-like' with both the innocence and lack of rights that go with childhood.

Psychodynamic theories are also used to explain why a particular person emerges as a leader. Deveries (1977) examined the relationship of leaders and situation in times of crisis. He concluded that charismatic leaders arise in these times for two reasons: the leader's superego and the follower's sense of helplessness and dependency.

Another influential theory that links leaders and followers to outcomes is the leader–member exchange theory. Early proponents include Danserau, Graen and Haga (1975), Graen and Cashman (1975), and Graen (1976). Here leaders and followers are viewed as parties to an economic transaction. Early studies focused on the dyadic relationship between the leader and each of her followers. Effective leadership requires a fair and equitable relationship between the leader and the followers. The leader's job is to ensure that she 'gives as much as she gets', and that the follower is adequately compensated – financially and psychologically – for the efforts imparted. If followers feel that desired behaviour will result in a fair return, they conclude that the effort is worth it and participate in reaching the goals set by the leader. Here we see a more equitable relationship between the leader and followers. Unlike psychodynamic theories of leadership, the leader–member exchange theory assumes equal rights for followers, and builds theoretical implications if those 'rights' are not met. Early traces of moral behaviour can be found as the canonical model gains complexity.

Recently, Graen and Uhl-Bien (1995) explored the link between the health of leader–member exchanges and organizational effectiveness. They found that high-quality relationships resulted in less employee turnover, superior performance evaluations, higher frequency of promotions, greater organizational loyalty, greater participation, and higher job satisfaction.

Bass's work on transformational leadership is an excellent example of the leader/follower paradigm. He claims that highly effective leadership is one in which both the leader and the followers are profoundly changed. In contrast to other leader/follower theories, which assume that leaders only affect followers, Bass's approach explores the dialectic relationship between leaders and followers, meaning that both parties are interconnected and influence each other. Linking the leader and follower relationship to outcomes is a critical step in making leadership theory more robust and useful.

Adding processes and skills

After the 1950s another branch of researchers began to focus on what leaders do as opposed to who they are. This group of theories combines a focus on the leader/follower relationship with an examination of the tools and processes used by leaders (Figure 8.4). We still see a privileging of leaders in these models as no mention is made of skills and processes used by 'followers,' as agents, to build relationships with the leader and change outcomes. Little mention is made of how these skills and processes change outcomes in different physical and cultural contexts. This section will review three of these process- and skill-oriented theories.

Behavioural theorists from both Ohio State and the University of Michigan attempted to unearth how *leaders* could optimally combine task behaviours and relationship behaviours to achieve the maximum impact on employee satisfaction and performance. These researchers were seeking a universal theory of leadership that would explain leadership in every context (Northouse, 1997). Sadly, many of the results of this branch of research remain unclear and contradictory (Yukl, 1994).

Nonetheless, Blake and Mouton identified two factors that leaders use to create effective outcomes: concern for production and concern for people. Concern for production involves the activities of the leader that focused on helping followers meet organizational goals. Planning, scheduling, policy, new products, operational issues, etc. are among the leadership activities. Concern for people encompasses the efforts made by the leader in attending to the people engaged in production-oriented activities. The leader seeks to build trust, commitment, and meaning for her followers: the leader seeks to ensure a safe work environment, a fair salary structure, and good interpersonal relations.

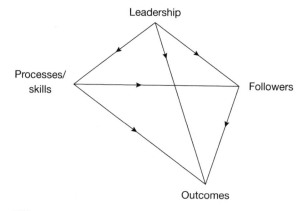

Figure 8.4 *Process- and skill-oriented theories of leadership.*

Combining these two research orientations led to Blake and Mouton's Managerial Grid, which is still widely used in consulting for organizational development (Northouse 1997). The grid describes five major managerial styles that are dependent on the nature of the organization's work, culture, and the needs of the followers. The styles range from authority-compliance to team management.

Similar to behavioural theories, significant research has occurred under the rubric of 'situational approached'. These leadership theories focus on the need for different leadership styles in different situations. Here 'situations' refers to the developmental needs of the employees, not the larger context in which the leadership occurs. These theories suggest that leaders must adapt their approach to their followers.

Hersey and Blanchard (1977) founded this view and have refined it several times throughout their careers. Their focus is placed squarely on two dimensions: the skills and processes of leadership, and the needs of the followers. The situational theories posit two main dimensions of leadership: directive behaviours and supportive behaviours. The role of the leader is to assess the development level of her employees and modify her style accordingly. The theory is silent on advice for followers to improve themselves.

Finally the work of Kouzes and Posner (1993, 1995) exemplifies the skills and processes view of leadership. Building on their survey and interview based research, the authors focus on the 'practices leaders use to turn challenging opportunities into remarkable successes' (Kouzes and Posner, 1995). Their five fundamental practices include:

1   Challenge the process – never accept the status quo.
2   Inspire a shared vision – focus on what could be, rather than on what is.
3   Enable others to act – empowerment and participation.
4   Model the way – provide personal example and dedicated execution.
5   Encourage the heart – individual recognition and group celebration.

Like Bass's writing on transformational leadership, Kouzes and Posner focus on the relationship of the leader and the led. 'Leadership is a reciprocal relationship between those who choose to lead and those who decide to follow. Any discussion of leadership must attend to the dynamics of this relationship.'

The processes and skills approach further fleshes out the leadership model, though authors in this branch of theory do not make much of context and situations. The canonical model of leadership, however, is starting to take shape.

Adding context

Later leadership literature increases the complexity of the canonical model by adding context as a critical factor (Figure 8.5). This section will review two

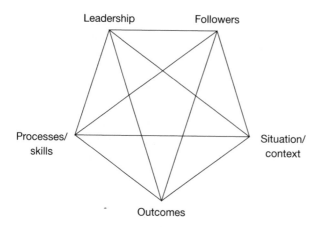

Figure 8.5 *The canonical model.*

theories of leadership that take context seriously: path–goal theory and contingency theory.

The path–goal theory emerged in the 1970s through the work of Evans (1970), House (1971), House and Dessler (1974), and House and Mitchell (1974). These theorists seek to find the optimal way to motivate employees to achieve the stated goals. Path–goal theory relies heavily on expectancy theory, which states that individuals will be more highly motivated if they believe that (1) they can accomplish the task, (2) their efforts will result in a certain outcome, and (3) the outcome is fair given the required effort. Here the job of the leader is to employ a style that best matches the motivational level of the follower. But in contrast to earlier leader–follower literature, the work situation plays a central role. 'Leaders provide subordinates with the elements they think that their subordinates need to reach their goals' (Northouse, 1997, p. 89). The theory claims that the way to do this is for the leader to select behaviours that are harmonious with or bolster the work environment. House and Mitchell (1974) claim that motivation can be increased in two ways: (1) increasing the quality and quantity of rewards and, more interestingly, (2) removing obstacles that can lead to frustration and thwarted efforts. The leader's job is in part to provide a smooth and clear path to the desired goals. In path–goal theory we see theorists beginning to take context and situation of performance into account.

Contingency theory claims that 'effective leadership is contingent on matching a leader's style to the right setting' (Northouse, 1997, p. 76). The most influential version of this theory was developed by Fiedler (1964, 1967). Unlike many theorists of the time Fiedler believed that any leadership style could be effective given the right situation. Hence, leaders must adapt the situation to their strengths. Three major situational variables will determine the leader's effectiveness:

1   leader–member relations – the degree to which followers trust and accept the leader as legitimate;
2   task structure – the degree to which the tasks and how to accomplish them are clear;
3   position of power – the authority held and the ability to exercise by the leader.

Leadership styles are either task or relationship motivated. Based on these research findings, contingency theory seeks to prescribe certain leadership styles with situational variables. Contingency theory – unlike path–goal theory – does not assert that a leader can or should alter her style to meet the needs of the situation. Rather, the leader's style is viewed as fixed. The theory places more emphasis on measuring a leader's style and the situational variables to determine if that particular leader will be effective in that particular situation.

Both theories of leadership integrate context into their complex models of leadership. It is interesting to note that the context is internal to the firm – the social, psychological, and organizational environment inside the team or firm. A wider net can be cast for context.

The canonical model

Despite its unabashed Greek aesthetic appeal, we believe the canonical depiction of leadership does actually work in helping leaders understand and manage their tasks better. In Figure 8.1 each concept is connected to the other four and each line represents a dialectic relationship. So for instance, leaders not only influence outcomes, but outcomes in turn have an effect on leaders. Followers are not just 'human means' to an end, as they were depicted in early leadership literature, but full agents who can and do affect all other aspects of the leadership system. This integrated systems analysis of leadership doesn't assume one variable to be supreme by default.

To apply this conceptual model practically we have to do considerable work. First, each concept must be fleshed out further. 'Followers' is not a simple catch all for 'non-leaders' but itself a large network of stakeholders with names and faces. Context can be different physical and temporal spaces, both internal to the firm and more broadly external. As the concepts are made more concrete, the diagram becomes infinitely more complex and useful to address real issues and connections. It enables leaders to see and think through links and connections that they may have taken for granted previously. It allows full agency for stakeholders and is adaptable to a variety of situations. It looks at leadership as part of an integrated whole, rather than an isolated piece. Finally it incorporates outcomes as a part of an ongoing process, rather than a separate result.

Rather than needlessly argue over which is more important – the context or the leader – this model grants legitimacy to each view and accepts that in different circumstances each concept will contribute to the overall balance differently. We do not mean to say that the previous approaches to leadership are not useful. Our issue is with the dominance of a small piece of the map for the entire globe. The larger narrative of the canonical model is built up from and embraces the local wisdom of the previous literature.

LEADERSHIP, VALUES, AND ETHICS

With this understanding of the leadership literature, we can now move on to understanding how leadership theories treat values and ethics. The canonical description of leadership allows us to understand where our theory and principles fit within the larger purview of management literature. In addition, by parsing out 'leader', 'followers', 'processes/skills', 'situation', and 'outcomes' in our analysis, we can now move on to analysing how these authors consider each facet of leadership ethically. The leadership literature does not separate 'the leader' from 'leadership processes and skills', however; making each piece of the theories explicit highlights common approaches and assumptions within disparate theories. This technique allows us, for example, to ask if there is a moral question about the choice of tools for the leader and their interaction with the leader, followers, and situation.

Furthermore, as we shall demonstrate, it is only within this canonical study of leadership that we have the opportunity to understand ethical leadership. What authors *do not* include in their approach to leadership is as important as what they *do* include. The authors are, in fact, determining the moral weight of each of the factors in deciding what factors to include in their analysis. For some, the processes and skills are not considered as important factors to understanding leadership – they are not treating the processes and skills as morally important to the outcome. For others, the situation is irrelevant causally and morally to the understanding of leadership. However, including all the facets of leadership does not necessitate the inclusion of ethics in theory. Rather, it is the starting point. Only by including all of the interwoven facets of leadership do we have the opportunity to give them each moral importance.

Typical views of leadership

We now move on to understand how the authors have connected leadership and ethics. We offer three ways to connect leadership, values, and ethics: (1) Amoral leadership, (2) Values-based leadership, and (3) Ethical leadership. We will focus first on amoral and values-based leadership models within management literature before introducing ethical leadership.

Amoral leadership

During the first 50 years of the twentieth century, as scholarly attention to leadership intensified, ethics and values played no role in understanding effective leaders. Indeed, 'effective leaders' were those viewed as capable of achieving 'effective outcomes'. And 'effective outcomes' were defined as attainment of organizational objectives, such as efficiency, low turnover, high profitability, innovation, client service, and so on. As long as the leader was judged by these measurable standards, the theories saw no need to understand how ethics and values might impact those outcomes.

For instance, the great man and trait theories sought simply to understand those (universal) characteristics that great leaders embody. This group of theories claims that if one wishes to understand why a particular person emerges as a leader in a particular situation, one must look to the personality traits of that person. While each theory's specific traits differ, all have some combination of intelligence, sociability, determination, and self-confidence. The extent to which a person is born with these traits – or acquires them through experience – determines the likelihood that that person will become a leader. This group of theories does not enable us to evaluate the goodness, or rightness, of leadership. Of the most common traits identified in effective leaders, only one – authenticity – could possibly be viewed as having an ethical or value-based component. However, a leader can be authentic and bad – she just needs to be authentically bad. There is no outside judgement on whether the authenticity is *good*.

Other theories are silent as well on ethical and value-based issues. Psychodynamic theories address the leader's and followers' most intimate and personal drives for success, and yet are silent on the appropriateness of manipulating these raw emotions for some organizational goal. Blake and Mouton's (1964) theory suggests that the leader selects her particular leadership style to match the needs of the followers. However, no mention is made on where this line moves from 'enabling' to 'manipulation'. In addition, situational theories of leadership move from the descriptive to the prescriptive, but they remain morally neutral. Their basic premise is that different situations demand different styles of leadership (e.g. Hersey and Blanchard, 1988). This approach's thrust demands that a leader matches her style to the competence and commitment of the subordinates. Effective leaders are those who can recognize what employees need and then adapt their own style to meet those needs. It is silent, however, on the ethics of those needs, the tools used to meet the needs, and the ends being sought.

We claim that these theories belong within amoral leadership as they make no claim as to whether the leader and her chosen outcomes are 'good' or 'bad'. This group of leadership theories has three main characteristics in common:

1   They focus narrowly on the leader and/or followers. No mention is made of the situation or the skills that the leader employs.

2   Each theory seeks to help the leader better motivate her constituents. An implicit assumption is made that workers need to be 'prodded' into being productive. These discussions occur outside any consideration of values or ethics.

3   Effective leadership is defined as the attainment of stated objectives, without concern as to the 'goodness' or the end or of the means.

Hence, in this group of theories, ethics and values are not a legitimate part of the study of leadership. Further, by ignoring the situation and skills of the leader, these theories give them no moral weight. These facets of the definition of leadership are not even important enough to consider. One can understand the outcomes produced by studying how the four variables (or some part thereof) interact, without addressing the ethical content of those variables. Hence, we can talk about effective leadership, but can make no statement of ethics or values.

These amoral theories of leadership do not enable to explore certain interesting questions, and therefore leave us unsatisfied:

■   Is the desired outcome desirable?
■   Are the tools used ethically sound?
■   Should followers be apprised as to how the leader is motivating them?
■   On what basis can we determine a 'good' leader from a 'bad' leader?

So while these leadership theories have helped advance the study of leadership – and perhaps represent the inevitable starting point for understanding this complex process – their limitations are significant, especially if we look to our organizations' leaders to help solve some of our societal problems.

Values-based leadership

The values-based view of leadership attempts to explicitly bridge the gap between ethics, values, and leadership. Here, values are taken as a central part of leadership: the argument is that if one wishes to understand how the outcome emerged, then one must understand also the values of the leaders and followers. This view's emphasis is on the description of values (such as honesty and trustworthiness) and the causal role those values play in the determination of desired outcomes. Ethics comes into play only in so far as the question for the leader or follower concerns authenticity and integrity. Since this values view is primarily concerned with a social scientific point of view, a hesitancy to pass moral judgements exists (see Table 8.1).

Much of the recent, popular leadership literature can be categorized as placing the leader and followers' values as front and centre in determining the effectiveness of leadership. These theories claim that in order to understand the outcome

Table 8.1 *Amoral and values-based leadership*

	Amoral leadership	Values-based leadership
Leader	Bernard (1926), Bingham and Davis (1927), Tead (1935) and Kilbourne (1935).	Esser and Strother (1962) Jensen and Morris (1960)
Leader-follower	Deveries (1977) Danserau, Graen and Haga (1975), Graen and Cashman (1975) and Graen (1976)	Kouzes and Posner (1993 and 1995), Bass (1995), Bennis and Nanus (1985, 1997) and Bennis (1989)
Leader-follower-situation	Evan (1970), House (1971), House and Dessler (1974), and House and Mitchell (1974)	Covey (1990)

– a highly successful business enterprise – one needs to determine if the values of the leader are aligned with those of the followers. Some of the more popular of these management texts include Kouzes and Posner (1993, 1995), Covey (1990), Bennis and Nanus (1985, 1997), and Bennis (1989.)

All of these works lament the absence of 'true leadership' in our era. They ascribe all types of social and business ills to this leadership vacuum. In so doing, the authors actively raise our anxiety level. The next observation made is the fact that the nature of leadership is a human *relationship*. In order to understand leadership, it is necessary to understand this relationship. And in order to understand the relationship, it is necessary to first understand oneself – one's own values, motives, ethics, strengths, weaknesses, etc. – and then to understand the values of the followers. By understanding and respecting the followers wants and needs, and providing what is wanted and what is needed, one gains the trust, loyalty, and commitment of the followers. They will then be empowered to achieve accomplishments heretofore undreamed of.

For these theories, the leader must at all times be seen as honest, trustworthy, attuned to the people's dignity and values, inspiring, and confident. Each of these texts provides prescriptions on what one must do to attain these qualities. Kouzes and Posner's *The Leadership Challenge* (1995) provide us with the 'Ten Commitments of Leadership'. Bennis (1989) claims that there are five 'ingredients' to leadership: integrity, dedication, magnanimity, openness, and creativity. And Covey (1990) gives us 'one 'P' and eight 'S's': people, self, style, skills, shared vision, structure and systems, strategy, and streams. Bennis and Nanus (1985, 1997) claim the need for five 'key skills': acceptance, forgiveness, courtesy, trust, and self-confidence.

The values-based leadership theories have certain aspects in common. These include:

- These works do not debate the appropriateness of the goals; they do not query the rightness of the followers' values. They simply say that values are central to the leadership process in either a descriptive or prescriptive manner.
- The values-based view of leadership focuses attention on the values of the leader and on the skills and processes used to affect the desired outcome.
- Gone are potentially manipulative strategies to elicit desired behaviours, as these authors make the assumption that followers are fully autonomous, ethical beings. Rather, focus is on the observation that followers seek an honest leader above all else (Kouzes and Posner, 1993).
- The relation between the leader's and followers' values is paramount to achieving the stated goals of the organization and understanding the effectiveness of leadership.

However, these theories also share some limitations:

- The role that the situation plays in determining the outcome may not be adequately dealt with in moral terms.
- Ethics is treated as authenticity. The theories are more concerned with internal matching of values rather than meta-analysis of the rightness of the skills/processes, leaders, outcomes, followers, and situation.

While the values-based leadership theories have made strides by including values in both descriptive and prescriptive manner, they have left us with additional unanswered (and unasked) questions:

- Are constituents truly free to exit the situation if their ethics require that?
- Is it sometimes morally correct for the leader to withdraw from the leadership role?
- Is the leader ethical?
- Are the goals legitimate?

Below we have listed examples of the different approaches and theories of leadership. Some have attempted to include more facets of leadership, yet still relegate values to a causal role in achieving goals. Missing from each of these approaches are the overall questions of 'good' or 'bad' leadership.

Ethical leadership

The typical views of leadership outlined above leave ethics outside the definition and research. While values may be instrumentally advantageous to use (as in the values-based view of leadership), we can also speak of leadership without ethics. We turn now to the work of two political scientists – John W. Gardner and James

MacGregor Burns – for a description of what integrated, ethical leadership might look like in the business environment.

While Gardner's (1990) focus is on government, world problems, and community disintegration, much of what he has to say is applicable to the business executive. Gardner claims that, 'attention to leadership alone is sterile – and inappropriate. The larger topic of which leadership is a subtopic is the *accomplishment of group purposes . . .*' (Gardner, 1990, p. xvi). Factors influencing the achievement of group purposes include the availability of resources, the degree of agreement as to basic values and objectives, the situation faced by leaders and followers, their willingness to adapt and renew, and issues of moral and social cohesion. The study of leadership, therefore, should be seen in the broader context of achievement of group goals.

For Gardner, the morally acceptable leader must have, at a minimum, the following objectives:

- releasing human potential of constituents;
- balancing the needs of the individual and the community/organization;
- defending the fundamental values of the community/organization;
- instilling in individuals a sense of initiative and responsibility.

A leader, for Gardner, goes beyond attempting to achieve their goals. While a leader has a hand in influencing the purpose of the organization with others, she also has goals for the organization with respect to the individuals within and the community outside.

Note also that Gardner is not focused solely on 'followers' as a means to the goals of the group. Rather, individuals and constituents are ends in and of themselves who deserve rights of autonomy. Understanding leadership is not relegated to questions of the leader–follower relationship. The leader must work to eliminate or reduce some of the more dehumanizing aspects of large organizations. A key task of leadership, according to Gardner, is to devise ways to offset the inevitable tensions between largeness and control vitality and creativity. Job redesign, autonomous working groups, schemes for performance feedback, and so on should be used to ensure that the constituents can find meaning in their work. Gardner characterizes these leadership tasks not as one means to enhancing organizational effectiveness, but rather as a way to ensure the soundness of the organizational moral climate.

Like all leadership theorists, Gardner places an emphasis on the leader's role in setting a vision for the organization. Even in this fundamental task, we cannot separate leadership and values:

> Leaders today are familiar with the demand that they come forward with a new vision. But it is not a matter of fabricating a new vision out of

whole cloth. A vision relevant for us today will build on values deeply embedded in human history and in our own tradition . . . The materials out of which we build the vision will be the moral strivings of the species, today and in the distant past.

(Gardner, 1990, p. xi)

The leader, in this scenario, is tasked with influencing the organization's purpose and incorporating the needs and goals of both internal individuals and external constituents. No longer is the leader given a goal to achieve and measured by her effectiveness and efficiency in meeting that goal. The leader is expected to work from within a network of constituents with, assumingly, different values and beliefs.

Similarly, James MacGregor Burns's seminal work on transformational leadership is also considered an ethically integrated view of leadership. However, Burns places more emphasis on power and authority in relationship to leadership. He states:

I hope to demonstrate that the processes of leadership must be seen as part of the dynamics of conflict and of power; that leadership is nothing if not linked to collective purpose; that the effectiveness of leaders must be judged not by their press clippings but by the actual social change measured by intent and by the satisfaction of human needs and expectations; that political leadership depends on a long chain of biological and social processes, of interaction with structures of political opportunity and closures, of interplay between the calls of moral principles and the recognized necessities of power; that in placing these concepts of political leadership centrally into a theory of historical causation, we will reaffirm the possibilities of human volition and of common standards of justice in the conduct of people's affairs.

(Burns, 1978, p. 3)

While Burns's writing was concerned with political leadership, if we acknowledge that a business is simply a mini-community — with all the aspirations and emotions of people, and inevitable impact on them — then we can certainly translate his teachings to the business community. Take, for instance, Burns's definition of leadership and compare it with that of the management scholars:

Leadership over human beings is exercised when persons with certain motives and purposes mobilize, in competition or conflict with others, institutional, political, psychological, and other resources so as to arouse, engage and satisfy the motives of followers.

(Burns, 1978, p. 18)

For Burns, legitimate leadership necessitates a leader coming into position 'in competition or conflict with others . . .' The individuals in the group must have a real choice in who they mobilize behind. This is similar to Gardner's argument that 'leaders by choice' is the only interesting concept. Burns grounds the moral legitimacy of his transformational leadership theory in '*conscious choice among real alternatives.* Hence leadership assumes competition and conflict, and brute power denies it' (Burns, 1978, p. 36). The key difference in both Gardner's and Burns's definition is that of mobilizing others when they have a choice in whom to follow.

We can build on these ideas of Gardner, Burns, and others to offer a view of an 'ethical theory of leadership'. On this view, little can be said about leadership without at least implicitly making moral or value judgements. Skills and processes cannot be divorced from the outcomes they produce, and hence cannot be seen as morally neutral. Followers' make judgements and choices, project their wishes and dreams onto the leaders, and hold them accountable. And, situations are ripe with moral meaning, depending in part on how such contextual factors are framed.

Ethical leadership also notes the social legitimacy (and hence the implicit value judgement) that is conferred on someone simply by calling her a leader. So the very idea of leadership cannot be stated without ethical judgement. Presumptively, leaders are legitimate – in business as well as the political sphere – and social legitimacy begins with the idea that one is acting from an ethical point of view.

Ethical leadership takes three steps forward from the values-based view. First, we have dropped the hesitancy to pass judgement on leadership. Where values-based leadership can describe values and their instrumental worth, we can now add prescriptive questions in addition to the descriptive and instrumental studies that exist (see implications to research below). Second, values, morals, and ethics have more than mere instrumental worth to a leader. In values-based leadership, a leader's values can be congruent with those of her followers, which can be an effective tool to achieving goals. Ethical leadership does not view values as merely instrumental but as having moral worth in and of themselves regardless of whether they achieve the goal or not. The third difference is really a combination of the first two. An ethical leader uses frameworks that stand tests of time and of their own consensus. She does not only hold her decisions and actions up to internal standards, but also incorporates societal mores and personal ethics. Ethical leadership moves the analysis of values and decisions from a test of internal consistency to an understanding within the organization's community standards and morals.

PRINCIPLES OF ETHICAL LEADERSHIP

This leads us to the question of principles of ethical leadership. What are the core principles of leadership? While authors have rightfully focused on certain types of leaders, certain types of situations, certain types of organizations, certain types of followers, we have a vacuum of information on principles of leadership that integrate each of the facets of leadership and approach theories on ethics and leadership (See Table 8.2). We can learn from the commonality across different contexts to form principles of ethical leadership. In developing the principles of ethical leadership, we build on the canonical understanding of leadership and include each facet of leadership as outlined above. These principles should be seen as a revision to the map we currently have of leadership.

The principles of ethical leadership are those concepts and rules of engagement that leaders can and should follow to be considered true leaders. These principles build on the definition of ethical leadership above:

Leader principle: A leader is first and foremost a member of her own organization and stakeholder group. As such, her actions, goals, and interactions are for the benefit of the entire group of stakeholders.

Constituents principle: Leaders see their constituents as more than followers but rather as stakeholders to the common purpose and vision. They have their own individuality and autonomy, which is respected in order to maintain a moral community.

Outcome principle: A leader embodies the purpose and values of the organization and of the constituents within an understanding of ethical ideals. A leader connects the basic value proposition to stakeholder support and societal legitimacy. She connects the goals of the organization with that of the internal individuals and external constituents.

Processes/skills principle: A leader works to create an open, two-way conversation thereby maintaining a charitable understanding of different views, values, and opinions of her constituents. She is open to others' opinions and ideas.

Situation/context principle: A leader sees particular values and ethical principles as being useful within certain spheres. She uses *moral imagination*[2] to make difficult decisions to cross the boundaries of those spheres and the frontiers of knowledge.

Ethics principle: A leader frames actions and purposes in ethical terms. A leader does not understand leadership without ethics, but rather thinks in terms of consequences, principles, rights, as well as character in her actions, beliefs, and behaviours.

166

Table 8.2 Ethical leadrship compared with values-based and amoral approaches

	Ethical leadership	Values view	Amoral view
Leader	A leader is first and foremost a member of her own organization and stakeholder group. As such, her actions, goals, and interactions are for the benefit of the stakeholder group.	The leader must maintain an effective relationship with followers in order to achieve goals.	A leader attains goals. No judgement if the leader is good or bad. A bad leader would be one that is ineffective.
Constituents	Leaders see their constituents as more than followers but rather as stakeholders to the common purpose and vision. Constituents make judgements and choices, project their wishes and dreams onto the leaders, and hold them accountable.	Followers have an instrumental role in attaining the goals as defined by the leader. No other stakeholders are mentioned in theory.	Followers are viewed as docile and requiring 'prodding' to attain goals.
Outcomes	A leader embodies the purpose and values of the organization and of followers within the understanding of basic value proposition to stakeholder support and societal legitimacy. She connects the goals of the organization with that of the internal constituents and external stakeholders.	Goals are judged to be either consistent or not consistent to the values and beliefs of the organization. Internal consistency is paramount.	Goals are considered self-evident or given. No judgement is made on the purpose of the organization or its outcome.
Processes/skills	A leader works to create an open, two-way conversation thereby maintaining a charitable understanding of different views, values, and opinions. Skills and processes cannot be divorced from the outcomes they produce, and hence cannot be seen as morally neutral.	The nature of leadership is a human relationship. In order to understand eadership, it is necessary to understand this relationship.	Theory focuses narrowly on the leader and/or followers. No mention is made of the situation or the skills that the leader employs.
Situation/context	Situations are ripe with moral meaning, depending in part on how such contextual factors are framed. There is no one set of leadership principles that work in all situations or all organizations. A leader sees values and ethical principles as being useful within certain spheres. She uses moral imagination to make difficult decisions to cross the boundaries of those spheres and frontiers of knowledge.	A leader's values and personality are either a good or bad fit with the situation.	No mention is made of the situation or changing situations.
Ethics	On this view, leadership is seen as a full player in the moral discourse. Little can be said about leadership without at least implicitly making moral or value judgements.	Ethics come into play only in so far as the question for the leader or follower concerns authenticity and integrity. There exists a hesitancy to pass moral judgements.	No mention of ethics. We can only talk about effective leadership as attaining the goals of the leader.

IMPLICATIONS FOR RESEARCH

By integrating ethics within the view of leadership, we change the language we use and the assumptions we make in research. We have, in fact, changed the map that guides us in research and practice. We now move to understanding how the new model and maps impact the questions we use to approach the territory of leadership. In theory, we are open to understanding more than just the traits needed to prod a group into behavioural modification. We look at the entire system or network as an interaction to understand. Where we once focused on effective leadership without regards to internal or external morality (amoral leadership) or effective leadership which utilizes internally consistent values to attain objectives (values-based leadership), we can now ask questions around the role of ethics and values in leadership theories and practice. How should a leader incorporate personal, organizational, and societal ethics into her leadership? Now, each factor of leadership has moral worth and the research questions will reflect our need to understand how each facet of ethical leadership should be treated.

As ethical leadership builds on the canonical understanding of leadership, we can ask questions from the perspective of each of the five facets of leadership. As we outline below, researchers will broaden the types of questions asked in research.

IMPLICATIONS FOR BUSINESS

Its time to put together the analysis of the previous sections into some concrete tasks for executives who must manage in the turbulent world of today – who must devote their time and energy into leading the process of value creation. The argument has been that such a process has ethics and values present at a number of levels. In fact, it would be disingenuous to try and separate out which tasks are 'ethical tasks' and which are 'business tasks', for the idea behind 'managing for stakeholders' is that one can't and shouldn't separate 'business' from 'ethics'. Ethical leadership frees leaders to incorporate and be explicit about their own values and ethics (See Table 8.3).

Ethical leadership is about 'raising the bar', helping people to realize their hopes and dreams, creating value for stakeholders, and doing these tasks with the intensity and importance that 'ethics' connotes. That said, there must be room for mistakes, for humour, and for a humanity that is sometimes missing in our current leaders. Ethical leaders are ordinary people who are living their lives as examples of making the world a better place while reaping benefits for themselves.

The following set of tasks is based on the observations of and conversations with a host of executives and students over the past 25 years, and on a reading of the business literature, both popular and scholarly. However, it should be seen as

Table 8.3 *Research questions arising from ethical leadership*

	Previous research questions		New research questions
	Amoral view	Values view	
Leader	What type of leader is effective with the organization?	What type of leader and values fits with the organization and/or situation?	On what basis can we determine a 'good' leader from a 'bad' leader? Is it sometimes morally correct for the leader to withdraw from the leadership role?
Processes/ skills	Do the skills and processes used reach the objective of the leader?	Do the skills and processes used match the needs of the organization?	Are the tools used ethically sound?
Constituents	How can a leader effectively motivate her followers to reach her goals?	How does a leader's values, motives, ethics, strengths, weaknesses, etc. – match the needs of the followers? How much of a 'match' of values between leader and follower is needed to accomplish goals?	Are constituents truly free to exit the situation if their ethics require that? Should followers be apprised as to how the leader is motivating them? To what degree are the constituents able to disagree and voice dissent?
Outcomes	Did the leader reach her goal? How can the leader reach her goal effectively and efficiently?	How does the congruence of values between leader and follower play into the outcome of the organization? How do the values of the organization impact the purpose of the organization?	Is the goal of the organization desirable to all impacted parties? Are the outcomes ethical according to internal and external standards?
Situation/ context	No questions around situations.	Does the leader's skills and values match the needs as determined by the situation?	What are the moral implications of the situation? What language are we (researchers) using to frame the situation? What language does the leader use to frame the situation?
Ethics	No mention or concern as to the 'goodness' of the skills, processes, values, outcomes, or leader.	Is the leader authentic in her beliefs? How does the integrity of the leader impact the achievement of her goals? Do the values of the organization help in attaining the goals?	How do the values of the leader fit within the greater community? Is the leader ethical? How do the values of the organization fit within the greater community?

tentative and open to revision. The set of tasks is from the perspective of the leader – what the leader should do to incorporate the principles from above and embody ethical leadership. The tasks are displayed through the lens of the canonical model to demonstrate how the ethical leader deals with each facet of ethical leadership, as follows.

Leader

The ethical leader articulates and embodies the purpose and values of the organization. It is one thing to tell a good story – to tell a compelling and morally rich story. But, it is another to embody it and live it. Ethical leaders must do both, and it is difficult to do so in today's business environment where everyone lives in a fishbowl – on public display. So many political leaders fail to embody the high-minded stories they tell at election time, and more recently, business leaders have produced the same kind of cynicism through the revelations of numerous scandals and bad behaviours.

The ethical leader separates criticism from ego. The ethical leader understands her place within the larger network of constituents and stakeholders. It is not about the leader as an individual, it is about something bigger – the goals and dreams of the organization.

Constituents

The ethical leader finds the best people and develops them. This task is pretty standard for all models of leadership. The ethical leader pays special attention to it precisely because she sees a moral imperative to developing people – helping them to lead better lives that create more value for themselves and for others.

Process/skills

The ethical leader creates a conversation about ethics, values, and the creation of value for stakeholders that is alive. Too often business executives think that having a 'values card' or a compliance approach to ethics has solved the 'ethics problem. Suffice it to say that Enron and other troubled companies had all of this apparatus. What they didn't have was a conversation across all levels of the business where the basics of value creation, stakeholder principles, and societal expectations were routinely discussed and debated. There is a fallacy that values and ethics are the 'soft, squishy' part of management. Nothing could be further from the truth. In organizations that have a live conversation about ethics and values, people hold each other's feet to the fire about whether they are really living the values; and they expect the leaders of the organization to do the same. Having a live conversation means that people must have knowledge of alternatives, must choose every day to stay with the organization and its purpose because it is important and inspires them. How to bring to life such a conversation is a long story beyond the scope here, but it is essential to do, if one is to lead ethically.

The ethical leader creates mechanisms of dissent. Most people know the story of Johnson and Johnson's Jim Burke and the Tylenol incident in the 1980s. But, the background is that JandJ had held a series of 'challenge meetings' all around the world, where managers sat and debated their 'Credo', a statement of their purpose and principles. There was an explicit way to 'push back' if someone thought that a particular market, region, or internal process was out of line with the principles. Other companies have used anonymous e-mail and telephone processes to give employees a way around the levels of management that inevitably spring up as barriers in large organizations. Most of the current scandals could have been prevented if only there were more creative ways for people to express their dissatisfaction with the actions of some of their bosses and others in the companies. Creating these mechanisms of dissent will vary by company, by leadership style, and by culture, but it is a crucial task in leading the creation of value for stakeholders in today's world.

The ethical leader takes a charitable understanding of other's values. Ethical leaders can understand why different people make different choices, but still have a strong grasp on what they would do and why.

Situation

The ethical leader makes tough calls while being imaginative. The ethical leader inevitably has to make a lot of difficult decisions, from reorienting the basic value proposition to working with people to exit the organization. There is no way for the ethical leader to duck these decisions since 'I'm doing this for the business' is not an excuse. The ethical leader must put together 'doing the right thing' and 'doing the right thing for the business'. And, as Patricia Werhane has so eloquently argued, sometimes exercising 'moral imagination' is the most important task. The idea that 'ethical leadership' is just 'being nice' is very far from the truth.

The ethical leader knows the limits of the values and ethical principles they live. All values have limits, spheres in which they don't work as well. This may be a different context, with different people, etc. Ethical leaders have an acute sense of the limits of the values they live and are prepared with solid reasons to defend their chosen course of action.

Outcomes

The ethical leader frames actions in ethical terms. In short, the ethical leader sees her leadership as a fully ethical task. This entails taking seriously the rights claims of others, the effects of one's actions on others (stakeholders), and how acting (leading) in a certain way will have effects on one's character and the character of others. There is nothing amoral about the ethical leader, and she recognizes that her own values may well sometimes turn out to be a poor guidepost. The ethical leader takes responsibility for using sound moral judgement.

The ethical leader connects the basic value proposition to stakeholder support and societal legitimacy. The ethical leader must think in terms of enterprise strategy, not separating 'the business' from 'the ethics'. Linking the basic *raison d'être* of the enterprise with the way that value gets created and society's expectations is a gargantuan task. But, the ethical leader never hides behind, 'Its just business'.

NOTES

1   The metaphor of map and territory comes from the opening pages of Jean Baudrillard's *Simulations*. Our usage of the metaphor is fashioned in a markedly different and more pragmatic tone than the one in Baudrillard's text.

2   'Moral imagination refers to the ability to perceive that a web of competing economic relationships is, at the same time, a web of moral relationships. Developing moral imagination means becoming sensitive to ethical issues in business decision making, but it also means searching out places where people are likely to be hurt by decision making or behaviour of managers. This moral imagination is a necessary first step, but because of prevailing methods of evaluating managers on bottom-line results, it is extremely challenging' (Werhane, 1999, p. 5).

REFERENCES

Bass, B. M. (1995) Concepts of leadership: The beginnings. In J. T. Wren (ed) *The leaders companion: Insights on leadership through the ages,* New York: The Free Press, pp. 49–52.

Baudrillard, J. (1983), *Simulations.* Boston, MA: Semiotext MIT Press.

Bennis, W. and Nanus, B. (1985) *Leaders.* New York: HarperCollins.

Bennis, W. and Nanus, B. (1989) *Why leaders can't lead.* San Francisco, CA: Jossey-Bass.

Bennis, W. and Nanus, B. (1997) *Leaders: Strategies for taking charge* (2nd edn). New York: Harper Business.

Bernard, L.L. (1926) *An Introduction to social psychology.* New York: Holt.

Bingham, W. V. and Davis, W. T. (1927) Leadership. In H. C. Metcalf (ed.) *The psychological foundations of management,* New York: Shaw, pp. 56–74.

Blake, R. R. and Mouton, J. S. (1964) *The managerial grid.* Houston, TX: Gulf Publishing.

Covey, S. R. (1990) *Principle-centered leadership.* New York: Fireside.

Dansereau, F., Graen, G. G. and Haga, W. (1975) A vertical dyad linkage approach to leadership in formal organizations. *Organizational Behavior and Human Performance,* 13: 46–78.

DeVries, M. F. (1977) Crisis leadership and the paranoid potential: An organizational perspective. *Bulletin of the Menninger Clinic,* 41: 349–65.

Esser, N. J. and Strother, G. B. (1962) Rule interpretation as an indicator of style management. *Personnel Psychology,* 15: 375–86.

Evans, M. G. (1970) The effects of supervisory behavior on the path-goal relationship. *Organizational Behavior and Human Performance,* 5: 277–98.

Fiedler, F. E. (1964) A contingency model of leadership effectiveness. In L. Berkowitz (ed.) *Advances in Experimental Social Psychology,* New York: Academic Press, vol. 1, pp. 149–90.

Fiedler, F. E. (1967) *A theory of leadership effectiveness.* New York: McGraw-Hill.

Freud, S. (1921) Group psychology and the analysis of the ego. *Civilization, Society and Religion,* Pelican Freud Library, London, 12: 91–178.

Gardner, J. W. (1990) *On leadership.* New York: The Free Press.

Graen, G. (1976) Role making process within complex organizations. In M. D. Dunnette (ed.) *Handbook of industrial and organizational psychology.* Chicago, IL: Rand McNally.

Graen, G. and Cashman, J.F. (1975) A role making model of leadership in formal organizations: A developmental approach. In J. G. Hunt and L. L. Larson (eds) *Leadership frontiers.* Kent, OH: Kent State University Press.

Graen, G.B. and Uhl-Bien, M. (1995) Relationship-based approach to leadership: Development of leader-member exchange (LMX) theory of leadership over 25 years: Applying a multi-level multi-domain perspective. *Leadership Quarterly,* 6(2): 219–47.

Hersey, P. and Blanchard, K. H. (1977) *Management of organizational behavior: Utilizing human resources* (4th edn). Englewood Cliffs, NJ: Prentice Hall.

House, R. J. (1971) A path-goal theory of leader effectiveness. *Administrative Science Quarterly,* 16: 321–8.

House, R. J. and Dessler, G. (1974) The path goal theory of leadership; Some post-hoc and a priori tests. In J. G. Hunt and L. L. Larson (eds) *Contingency approaches to leadership.* Carbondale, IL: Southern Illinois University Press.

House, R. J. and Mitchell, T. R. (1974) Path-goal theory of leadership. *Journal of Contemporary Business,* 3: 81–97.

Jensen, M. B. and Morris, W. E. (1960) Supervisory ratings and attitudes. *Journal of Applied Psychology,* 44: 339–40.

Kirkpatrick, S. A. and Locke, E. A. (1991) Leadership: Do traits matter? *The Executive,* 5: 48-60.

Kilbourne, C. E. (1935) The element of leadership. *Journal of Coast Artillery,* 37: 45–8.

Kouzes, J. M. and Posner B. Z. (1993) *Credibility: How leaders gain and lose it, why people demand it.* San Francisco, CA: Jossey-Bass.

Kouzes, J. M. and Posner, B. Z. (1995) *The leadership challenge.* San Francisco, CA: Jossey-Bass.

Northouse, Peter G. (1997) *Leadership: Theory and practice.* Thousand Oaks, CA: Sage.

Solomon, R. (2001) The one-minute moralist. In *The new world of business.* New York: Rowman and Littlefield, pp. 9–12.

Stogdill, R. M. (1948) Personal factors associated with leadership: A survey of the literature. *Journal of Psychology,* 25: 35–71.

Tead, O. (1935) *The art of leadership.* New York: McGraw-Hill.

Werhane, P. (1999) *Moral imagination and management decision making.* New York: Oxford University Press.

Yukl, G. (1994) *Leadership in organizations.* Englewood Cliffs, NJ: Prentice Hall.

Chapter 9

Strength of character

Exceptional leadership in a crisis

Cary L. Cooper CBE, James Campbell Quick,
Jonathan D. Quick, and Joanne H. Gavin

Business crises are not everyday occurrences, yet every leader should be prepared in the course of his or her career to encounter a professional crisis, or a personal tragedy. One never quite knows how one will respond until adversity presents itself in the form of a crisis or a tragedy. In the midst of a discussion of the attributes of great leaders, Aaron Batchelor's team in the Goolsby Leadership Academy identified 'the experience of adversity' as one characteristic that provides the groundwork for the leader's growth and development. While some adversity befalls a leader in the form of a professional crisis, other adversity is wittingly or unwittingly self-caused in nature. Regardless of the origin of the crisis, we address in this chapter the alternative responses that leaders may display. Our thesis is that the exceptional leader displays great strength of character, acting with excellence in the context and circumstance in which s/he finds her/himself. We approach the topic of crisis mindful of the Chinese symbol for the word 'crisis', which is composed of two primary symbols: one for danger and the other for opportunity. We define strength of character as excellence of action in circumstances that would otherwise place pressure on the leader to act in a self-serving manner. Excellence of action is characterized by a concern for the well-being of all impacted by the conflicted and confusing circumstance of the crisis.

THREE CASES OF BUSINESS CRISES

We open the chapter with three case examples of business crises. These are from the Enron Corporation, the Great Texas Banking Crash, and Otis Engineering, a Halliburton Company. In the first case, we discuss the responses of the three top leaders to the crisis. In the second case, we discuss the response of the Chairman and CEO of Texas American Bancshares. In the third case, we discuss the response of the Chairman and CEO. The very different responses of these five leaders sheds light on the strength of character, or lack thereof, of each of these five different leaders who found themselves in the midst of crises.

The Enron Corporation

The first case example is that of Enron Corporation based in Houston, Texas (Nelson and Quick, 2003). In early 2000 and the first half of 2001, Enron was one of the top Fortune 50 corporations in American whose stock price was skyrocketing up and whose chairman Ken Lay was spreading largesse throughout Houston. However, there were not solid business fundamentals underlying Enron's business model but rather a fraudulent set of 'clever' bookkeeping and financial dealing in large part orchestrated by Andy Fastow, former Chief Financial Officer of Enron. In the fall of 2001, a financial firestorm broke out over Enron and the world saw the collapse of a giant business corporation with widespread damage throughout the Houston community and sectors of the financial markets. How did three of Enron's leaders respond to this business crisis? The three leaders we consider are ex-CEO Jeffrey Skilling, ex-Chairman Ken Lay, and the late Vice Chairman J. Clifford Baxter.

Mr Skilling's response was one of flight and displayed a notable lack of character. He attempted to extricate himself from the emerging crisis by resigning his position in August 2001. His self-serving actions were short lived and he was indicted in Houston, Texas on 19 February 2004, subsequently going to prison and being assessed $80 million in fines. As the crisis at Enron began to emerge and the stock price began to drop dramatically, Mr Skilling was one of the Enron leaders selling Enron stock at the same time that the company was preventing employees from unloading their stock, which was becoming increasingly worthless. Flight is one natural physiological response to high stress situations, even if it is not the right action to take.

J. Clifford Baxter also displayed a flight response but of a very different kind (Quick *et al.*, 2002). In his case, he was overwhelmed by the blame and responsibility that were associated with the emerging crisis. Cliff Baxter did accept responsibility for what was transpiring, in contrast to Jeff Skilling who attempted to shirk all personal responsibility. While Enron collapsed into bankruptcy and left many creditors, shareholders, and employees penniless, the company's top executives cashed in their stock and walked away with an estimated $1.1 billion between October 1998 and November 2001. Cliff Baxter was among the 29 past and current executives and board members named as defendants in a federal lawsuit filed in January 2002. The plaintiffs claimed that Baxter had sold 577,436 shares of Enron stock for $35.2 million. Unable or unwilling to face these charges, Baxter took his own life on 25 January 2002.

The third leading executive at Enron was Chairman Kenneth Lay. His response to the crisis was not the same as either Skilling's or Baxter's. While Skilling sought flight and the denial of personal responsibility and Baxter fled through suicide due to an overwhelming sense of responsibility, Lay's response was one of denial of knowledge, and therefore denial of responsibility. Even though he was chairman of the corporation and had a PhD in economics, Mr Lay claims to this day that he simply did not know what was going on inside the shop. He resigned his position in January 2002 and claims that all of Enron's problems were attributable to a renegade group within the company under CFO Andy Fastow. During that era, there were board members at other companies in the industry who were questioning Enron's reported profit levels since these board members doubted whether there was that much money in the industry. If board members external to Enron were asking such questions, why was not Mr (Dr) Lay asking those questions of his own senior staff (Nelson and Quick, 2006)?

None of these three Enron leaders displayed strength of character or excellence of action in the face of a very legitimate business crisis. They displayed either self-serving or self-destructive actions, which benefited no one and deepened the crisis rather than helping to resolve it. We turn next to two case examples where senior leaders displayed strength of character in the midst of business crises.

The Great Texas Banking Crash

The US Congress passed two legislative acts, one in 1981 and one in 1986, which precipitated the Great Texas Banking Crash. During this financial crisis, all of the leading banks of Texas went under except for Frost Bank. Bank after bank was taken over by the FDIC and/or out-of-state banks with the capital and reserves to support the deeply troubled institutions. As the crisis broke, Dr Joseph M. Grant was chairman and CEO of Texas American Bancshares (TAB) in Fort Worth, Texas. Under Dr Grant, TAB struggled to find capital and a plan to save the bank. However, these were not forthcoming and the bank was liquidated and its bankruptcy was dismissed on 26 June 1990 (Grant, 1996). It was not until the crisis was resolved that Dr Grant moved on to become CFO at Electronic Data Systems Corporation (EDS) and then chairman and CEO of Texas Capital Bank (TCB) in Dallas, Texas.

The strength of character displayed by Dr Grant is notable in at least two ways. First, he chose not to flee TAB during its period of worst distress (Grant and Mack, 2004). With a very significant amount of his personal net worth tied up in TAB stock, it was very difficult personally to watch the stock price run down to zero. In contrast to the actions of Skilling, Baxter, and Lay, Grant did not sell off his stock in an effort to extricate himself from a deepening financial crisis. Second, Dr Grant provided the kind of exceptional leadership that bonded a team of TAB executives and managers to do the very best they were able to do during this financial crisis. As a testament to his excellence as a leader, Grant maintains continuing and positive relationships with former colleagues both at TAB and EDS, which he left to form TCB at the time EDS spun-off from General Motors Corporation.

177

Otis Engineering, a Halliburton company

The business crises in real estate and the financial markets were not the only ones to hit Texas during the 1980s. The mid-1980s also saw a crisis in the oil sector, with adverse effects throughout the industry. Purvis Thrash was a petroleum engineer who had risen to the become chairman and CEO of Otis Engineering, an oil field service company with operations around the world, including very severe arctic climates (Quick, Nelson, and Quick, 1990). When he became chairman and CEO, Mr Thrash looked forward to several years of relatively uncomplicated service at the helm, akin to his predecessors. However, it was not long into his tenure that the bottom fell out and oil prices dropped dramatically. This is not what he had bargained for, but it was his responsibility.

Like Grant, Thrash displayed strength of character and exceptional leadership to bring Otis through the crisis. Staying on as chairman for about twice the tenure he anticipated, he had to engage in some significant downsizing of the company and restructuring activities to ensure the long-term viability of Otis. The work was substantively more difficult and challenging than he anticipated, but he neither shirked his responsibilities nor became overburdened as did Baxter at Enron.

Lessons to learn

These three case examples of business crises offer a view of the different responses that leaders may display in the midst of crises. Exceptional leaders display strength of character and excellence in action, as did Jody Grant and Purvis Thrash during their periods of adversity, trial, and tribulation. In contrast, the leaders of Enron (Lay, Baxter, and Skilling) failed to display strength of character or excellence in action. Theirs were self-serving and self-centred routes which ultimately were dead ends, in one case quite literally so. In his research with the men in the Grant Study, Vaillant (1977) found that every life had experienced some crisis or tragedy. However, the crisis, tragedy, or adversity was not the distinguishing feature of these lives. Strong people rose above the crisis or tragedy. This chapter addresses the wide variety of crises and tragedies that challenge leaders to be the best that they can be by displaying strength of character and excellence in action. Gilbert (2000) suggests that crises are often best managed through collaborative efforts rather than by a single leader acting alone. In the next two sections of the chapter we address both professional crises and personal tragedies.

PROFESSIONAL CRISES

There are at least five categories of professional crises that can challenge a leader. These include political turmoil, terrorism and military action, industrial restructuring activities, labour strife, and industrial accidents. Threats to the business or organization vary in the degree to which they are also, at a more personal level, threats to individual executives or managers. Executives' and managers' health is interdependent with the health of their organizations. While a manager or executive may stay healthy and productive in an unhealthy work environment, to maintain one's health in these environments requires external relationships, anchors, and resources.

Executives, managers, and their families should consider crossover and spillover effects too. While some managers and executives may be able to compartmentalize work, home, and other life spheres, the boundaries between these spheres of living are never completely sealed. This means that the effects and threats in one sphere, either at work or at home, can spillover into the other. The primary concerns in this chapter are with the spillover effects of professional crises into one's home and family environment and of personal tragedies into one's work and professional life.

Political turmoil

National and international politics affect business operations, exposing an executive to risk, frustration, and even danger. For example, Jack Welch and General Electric saw their plans to acquire Honeywell frustrated during 2001 because of questions and reservations expressed by European regulators, not because of any questions raised within the US government. The relationship between governmental bodies and business organizations is markedly different in the European Community and in the United States. These differences are not as extreme as is the case between developing and underdeveloped countries where executives and managers work. The health and well-being of executives is at greater risk in the latter.

The political turmoil and change of governments in Iran at the end of the 1970s created special risks and threats for two American executives. In 1975, EDS learned that the Ministry of Health in Tehran was looking for a data-processing company experienced in health insurance and social security work. The company made a successful proposal to the ministry and had an agreed-upon contract in August 1976 (Follett, 1983). Paul Chiapparone then became the country manager for the company, as president of EDS Corporation Iran. The internal political context in which Mr Chiapparone and other EDS employees worked began to change dramatically during 1978. The Ayatollah Khomeini was committed to the destruction of the Shah of Iran and his Pahlavi dynasty. By late 1978, the political situation in Iran had deteriorated significantly, and the Shah did not have firm control of the country. The political turmoil in the country culminated in the seizing of the United States Embassy in Tehran on 4 November 1979 and the taking of 52 Americans as hostages for over a year. The entire episode in Tehran deeply scarred the end of Jimmy Carter's term as President of the United States when the rescue effort he mounted came to an ignominious end in the deserts of central Iran.

It was in this context that Mr Chiapparone and his deputy, Bill Gaylord, began what became a harrowing and potentially life-threatening experience at the hands of militant Iranians. The two American executives had their US passports seized; they were arrested and were imprisoned by the Iranian government in December 1978. The US Embassy was of little help in securing their release, due in part to the political turmoil within Iran. President Carter made the decision to send one of his senior US Air Force generals on a secret mission to Tehran (Huyser, 1986). General Huyser entered Tehran in early January 1979 during the last days of the Shah of Iran, saw the transition of power to the Bakhtiar government and the Regency Council, and departed after the return of the Ayatollah Khomeini in early February 1979.

EDS chairman Ross Perot took it upon himself to secure the release of his imprisoned executives, choosing retired Colonel Bull Simons to lead the effort. In contrast to the subsequent, failed rescue attempt of the hostages in the US Embassy in Tehran, Colonel Simons was able to secure the release of the two EDS executives and see them walk safely across the north-west border of Iran into Turkey. A number of senior Iranian military officers followed suit, given the risks to their own lives, evidenced by the fact that other senior Iranian military leaders from the Shah's government were tried and executed in secret proceedings beginning at midnight and ending before a firing squad at sunrise. Given this history, it is no wonder that when EDS spun off from General Motors in 1996, the company was still spending $250,000 annually on personal security systems for Mr Chiapparone, who was by then an executive vice president of EDS (Mack and Quick, 2002).

The political turmoil in Vietnam posed very different pressures and threats for senior American government executives, such as Secretary of Defense Robert McNamara. The threats to McNamara were not personal and immediate in the same way as they were for Chiapparone and Gaylord, and McNamara's personality influenced the health effects of his situation. Robert McNamara was always characterized as a cold and calculating intellect without emotion. He communicated an emotional distance that may have made him a carrier for stress, tension, and health problems, although he did not experience immediate personal health problems. His case is an excellent example of crossover effects at work. Crossover effects occur when a person under stress experiences no signs of distress or strain while the spouse sympathetically does. In McNamara's case, his wife's health failed when she got the stomach ulcer that was rightfully his.

The pressures of the political turmoil and military failure of the Vietnam War scarred the United States and many who were involved in the war. McNamara almost appeared inhuman in the way he approached the war effort, speaking always in clipped businesslike tones and discussing body counts in logical and impersonal ways. While this clearly was a crisis situation for many Americans, American military members, and for the nation, one never quite got that sense from McNamara, who always communicated a sense of control. While he may have bypassed many of the emotions at the time, passing the emotional burden to his wife, he did engage in a soul-searching re-examination of the Vietnam era over 20 years later (McNamara and Vandemark, 1996). Emotions do not necessarily abate with time, and the risk of unexamined and unresolved emotion can always reverberate years and decades later in the life cycle. Hence, there is great value in personally confronting and addressing feelings and emotions as they arise.

Terrorism

The crisis that hit the World Trade Center on September 11, 2001 was a surprise to many, yet there had been an early warning call eight years earlier when one of the towers had been bombed. Morgan Stanley used the 1993 scare as a learning opportunity to prepare for the future. That decision, coupled with the subsequent planning done within the company, as well as the time lag between when the aircraft hit the tower and its collapse, may well have saved the lives of thousands of executives, managers, and employees. The majority of civilian executives, managers, and employees do not have the expectation that they are targets for militant armed forces. However, it is precisely the commercial and financial centres that terrorists target, given the fear it engenders and the economic damage it causes. The Dow Jones Industrial Average had its worst one-week decline, over 1,300 points and nearly 14 per cent, during the week following the bombing in New York City.

Executives and managers working in less developed parts of the world are more accustomed to the threats posed by terrorism, thus developing strategies for protection and defence. For example, senior executives living in Nairobi, Kenya, never travel in a single vehicle to the airport at night; instead they always travel with two or more cars at a time. Armed guards and locked family quarters are among the precautionary measures that enhance safety and security, along with 24-hour guards at the perimeter of one's property. Threat assessment, threat monitoring, and planned responses offer some element of preventative action for terrorism.

The aims of terrorists are to intimidate, create fear, cause damage, and potentially extract a price through ransom. The latter occurred in the case of John Paul Getty and his family when one of his grandsons was kidnapped and held for ransom. The threats and the severing of the grandson's ear ultimately came to naught when Getty refused to negotiate, reasoning that this would place his other grandchildren at risk. Fortunately, the grandson was returned alive, and no subsequent attempts were made to terrorize Mr Getty or his family.

One of the ways in which terrorists strike fear into an organization or a government is to target the senior leadership. Such was the case for the militant Irish extremists who killed Lord Mountbatten, a distinguished member of the House of Windsor, great-grandson of Queen Victoria, and a highly decorated English naval officer. Admiral Earl Mountbatten of Burma served in both World War I and II and was First Sea Lord from 1955 to 1959, when he became chief of the United Kingdom Defence Staff and chairman of the Chiefs of Staff Committee. While sailing near his holiday home in County Sligo, Ireland, on 27 August 1979, Mountbatten was murdered by an IRA bomb, which also killed two young boys. Lord Mountbatten's death was a serious psychological blow to the British royal family, yet it did not deter the British government in its policy with regard to the Irish (Ziegler, 1987, 1988, 2001).

Industrial restructuring activities

Industrial restructuring activities, and in particular employment downsizing, have taken a toll on executives and managers in select industries. These activities began during the mid-1980s in the United States and have continued unabated through the present. Employment downsizing occurs when an organization reduces its workforce by more than 5 per cent. The majority of American businesses are not currently downsizing, but some industries and sectors of the economy are more vulnerable than are others. Employment downsizing or redundancy is increasingly common in the United Kingdom since Margaret Thatcher began to Americanize the British economy at the beginning of the present period of globalization. Health care and banking are two sectors of the US economy that have seen dramatic restructuring activities, in many cases with unpredictable impacts on individual executives.

Labour strife

The relationship between management and labour has a complex, at times conflicted, history in which executives, managers, and workers alike may be at risk. During the contentious era of labour–management strife in the US steel industry during the 1920s and 1930s, executives and managers at US Steel were issued .32 calibre pistols for the purpose of self-defence. Both labour and management have at times carried weapons into places of work, placing many at risk of workplace violence. Fortunately, armed conflict is the exception rather than the norm in the history of labour–management relationships.

A major professional crisis for John D. Rockefeller Jr was the Ludlow massacre, which occurred in October 1913 at the Rockefeller-controlled Colorado Fuel and Iron (CFI) (Chernow, 1998). The Rockefellers' ill-fated involvement with CFI dated back to 1902 when John D. Senior took a 40 per cent interest in the company with windfall profits from selling iron ore to US Steel. John D. Senior was militantly anti-union and a major confrontation between CFI's management and its coal workers emerged in 1913 as a result of worker complaints concerning mine safety, pay, and housing conditions. Over 400 miners died in mining accidents during the year. When CFI's management failed to respond to worker concerns, 11,000 of the nearly 14,000 miners struck before the end of September. Both miners and management's guards were heavily armed. The governor sent in Colorado National Guard troops to control the situation. Unfortunately, one shot led to workers being machine-gunned and their tents burned, killing over a dozen women and children.

President Wilson intervened with federal troops, who did not leave Colorado until the end of 1914, and John D. Junior was required to testify before the US Congress. There were unsuccessful attempts on his life during this period, but the experience was a touchstone that transformed his attitude toward and relationship with labour. Up until the 1913 labour crisis, John D. Junior had spent much of his life working diligently to rehabilitate the very tarnished family name through the generous philanthropic work of the Rockefeller Foundation. The crisis led him to create a new Department of Industrial Relations at the foundation, transforming both his attitude and behaviour in labour–management relationships. For example, when US Steel was unrelenting in its harsh stand on working hours with labour in 1920, John D. Junior sold all his US Steel stock.

Contemporary workplace violence is not divided as much along labour–management lines, and the FBI estimates that 85 to 90 per cent or more of workplace violence is preventable, often being triggered by a stressful event. Labour and management continue to have different objectives and a competitive relationship, yet they must have the capacity for cooperation and collaboration to avoid the kind of crisis experienced by the Rockefellers in 1913. That cooperation is based on open communication and negotiation, on interdependent relationships, and on mutual support. These were illustrated in the both the way John D. Junior worked through the CFI crisis and the way in which Lee Iacocca invited UAW union leader Douglas Frazier onto the Chrysler Corporation Board of Directors. Building relationships and negotiating conflicts reduces tensions, stress, and risk for all concerned.

Industrial accidents

Industrial accidents are a fifth category of professional crisis that challenge the strength of character of leaders. Many industrial and manufacturing operations require safe operating procedures along with protective clothing, eyewear, and other safety equipment. Danger from heavy equipment and moving parts, while risky for well-trained operators highly familiar with the work environment may be especially risky for executives or managers unaccustomed to these working conditions. Managers who fail to ensure strict compliance with safety regulations and procedures may ultimately place their own health at risk. Such was the case for a manager in a railcar overhaul facility that failed to discharge an employee after his second safety violation. The manager intervened with senior executives and, rather than terminate the employee, protected his job. Subsequently, the employee committed another safety violation; in this case failing to hook the two sides of a railcar together with a safety chain during overhaul operations. When the manager was in the work area to inspect the operation, one half of the railcar weighing several tons came loose and crushed him to death. Sadly, he had unwittingly contributed to his own death.

The immediate and physical threats from workplace accidents are not the only ones for executives and managers, especially senior executives. Possibly the most lethal industrial accident on record occurred at Union Carbide's Bhopal operations in India on 3 December 1984, where the death toll was approximately 2,500 people (Shrivastava, 1987). Earlier in the century, the explosion of a ship with a cargo of ammonium nitrate in Texas City had been the most lethal, resulting in over 500 deaths. While the government of India labelled the Bhopal crisis an 'industrial accident', it was characterized by Union Carbide as an 'incident', by the injured victims as a 'disaster', and by social activists as a 'tragedy' or a 'massacre'. These very divergent perspectives on the industrial circumstances and events in Bhopal led to equally divergent responses with their associated conflicts, potentially exacerbating an already difficult situation.

The plant managers of Union Carbide (India) Ltd were arrested on criminal charges, as were other Union Carbide officials, including Chairman Warren M. Anderson, when they rushed to Bhopal on 7 December. Rather than view Anderson's trip to Bhopal as motivated by concern and sympathy, with clear personal risk to him, Indian officials and residents perceived his trip as a pre-emptive effort to minimize Union Carbide's legal responsibility. Anderson did accept moral responsibility for the accident and made significant efforts to enhance communication throughout the crisis.

A less violent form of professional crisis results from economic turmoil and the collapse of a business. The economic turmoil and collapse of Enron, beginning in the fall of 2001, is a sad example of a corporation that at one point stood in seventh position in the Fortune 500 list and then experienced a dramatic decline. The decline, beginning with the announcement of a $1 billion write-off and continuing through subsequent revelations of accounting irregularities, led the corporation into bankruptcy court. One of the early casualties in this crisis was J. Clifford Baxter, a senior executive of the corporation who resigned in early 2001 over questions about business irregularities, only to commit suicide, as ruled by the medical examiner, within a year of his departure.

PERSONAL TRAGEDIES

Loss of family, friends, financial resources, and health problems are among the personal tragedies that may befall a leader and test his or her character. All executives and managers are vulnerable to such losses and problems, regardless of how well prepared they are. The John Wayne myth suggests that strong men are not vulnerable. The myth is false and a fantasy. The myth was embodied in Harold Geneen's comment when he was chairman of ITT: 'If I had enough arms and legs and time, I would do it all myself.' Many believe the myth, however, and employees often look to their managers, executives, and leaders to be strong, sure, and secure. The dependency needs of followers lead many executives and managers into the trap of secrecy and lack of disclosure when it comes to personal matters. Franklin D. Roosevelt was a true master at disguising his polio disability, projecting a powerful image of a strong, healthy chief executive.

Loss of loved ones

The loss of loved ones is a personal tragedy that may throw an executive's life out of balance at several levels. Such a life-changing event happened to Hewlett-Packard Chairman Lew Platt with the death of his first wife Susan in 1981 (Nelson and Quick, 2003). In retrospect, the personal tragedy became a growth opportunity for Mr Platt with positive ramifications for Hewlett-Packard as an organization and important effects on HP policies within a decade. At the time of Susan's death, Mr Platt was a general manager for the company. For several months following her death, he struggled with the demands of work coupled with caring for his two daughters, aged nine and eleven. He began to realize that many of the struggles of women managers at HP were not of their own making. Prior to her death, Susan Platt had taken the leadership role in all home and family responsibilities. Lew Platt struggled.

Within two years of Susan's death, Lew Platt met and married his second wife Joan, who restored balance to his work and personal life. However, his period of struggle had changed Mr Platt, who continued to empathize with the plight of the women managers and employees at HP who had family and child responsibilities in addition to demanding jobs. In 1992, when Mr Platt was HP's chief executive, he discovered a near mass exodus of women managers from the company, many never to return, with few women rising to senior executive ranks. He also discovered that HP's policies were not flexible enough to accommodate executives' lives outside the workplace. By instituting family-friendly policies, HP became a much more egalitarian work environment for people like Brenda Vathauer, a female marketing manager who returned to work after her maternity leave because HP gave her freedom to set her own agenda.

The positive outcomes from Lew Platt's personal tragedy took time. This was also the case for Lee Iacocca when his wife Mary died. He too was thrown out of balance and struggled in his personal life, marrying twice and briefly over the several years following her loss before finding a new equilibrium in life.

Loss of financial and material resources

We discussed earlier the Great Texas Banking Crash of the 1980s and the financial loss that Joseph M. Grant and other banking leaders experienced during that crisis. Dr Graut was able to recover through his years as chief financial officer for EDS and now as chairman and CEO of Texas Capital Bancshares in Dallas, Texas. To recover from loss while displaying strength of character and excellence in action is rare, and admirable.

Others' personal tragedies

In her autobiography, Katharine Graham, the late chairman of *The Washington Post*, describes the pain in the workplace caused by the manic-depressive episodes of her late husband Philip during his tenure as president and publisher of the *Post* (Graham, 1997). He ultimately shot himself to death in 1963, leaving his wife Katharine ill-equipped to assume responsibility for the paper her father had established and then brought Philip Graham in to run. As did Lew Platt, Katharine Graham turned a personal tragedy into a positive growth experience, if a difficult one. Through years of challenge and growth, she left a life legacy of personal strength and professional integrity. She is not alone as a leader who came to grips with personal tragedy, rose above it, grew stronger, and ultimately realized the potential within herself only previously imagined.

Health problems

Vulnerabilities can become problems in difficult economic times. This was the case for Theodore John 'Ted' Arneson, who founded Professional Instruments Corporation, an engineering firm, in 1946 (Tanouye, 2001). Mr Arneson experienced a serious depression in 1969 as a result of a financial crisis in which interest rates rose, banks called in loans with lower rates, and big clients cancelled contracts. These business reverses overwhelmed him, though he was able to see himself and the business through safely. However, this was just an early-warning indicator, and when times got tough seven years later, Mr Arneson attempted to commit suicide. Fortunately, his failed attempt led to psychological intervention as well as support from family and friends. Although he was still chairman of the board in 2001, his three sons were running the business, and much of his personal time was devoted to suicide prevention.

Mike Welch's experience during his tenure as Chairman and CEO of Tenneco was not as fortunate. Mr Welch developed brain cancer and continued his leadership role in the company during a period of very rigorous, challenging treatments. His battle with cancer was one he finally lost.

THE SILVER LINING?

Zaleznik (1990) points out the importance of leadership and the power of inspiring leaders. Professional crises and personal tragedies are the storms that test a leader's strength of character. Every storm cloud does not have a silver lining, and it would be unrealistic to think so. These are experiences with which few of us are comfortable, yet they are experiences that all executives must be prepared to cope with and manage. While the last thing a good soldier wants to do is go to war, it is the first thing that he or she is prepared to do. By the same token, the last thing an executive wants to manage is a professional crisis or personal tragedy, yet in the framework of preventative health management, it is one of the first experiences he or she should be prepared to confront. As we have seen, it is sometimes in the midst of professional crisis or personal tragedy that we discover more of who we are and what our real strengths are, so as to grow more fully into adulthood. In the words of Rudyard Kipling:

> If you can meet with Triumph and Disaster,
> And treat these two impostors just the same;
> . . .
> Or watch the things you gave your life to broken,
> And stop and build 'em up with wornout tools;
> . . .
> Yours is the Earth and everything that's in it,
> And – which is more – you'll be a man, my son!

ACKNOWLEDGEMENTS

The authors thank Monisha Adhikary, Richard Aston, Aaron Batchelor, Christopher Ballenger, Julius Berotte, Mehomood (Mike) Charania, Meredith Faltermeier, Danielle Georgiou, Kevin Ghassemi, Morris Hill, Farah Khan, Reza Magdon-Ismail, Sophia Morris, Beatrice Mjuguna, Juanita Nunez, Eric Pace, Parcus Rave, Jessica Rios, Richard (Richie) Stuart, and other members of the Goolsby Leadership Academy for their contributions to the development of this chapter. We thank too John and Judy Goolsby for their generous gift that established the Academy in 2003, and whose motto is: Integrity, Courage, Impact.

REFERENCES

Chernow, R. (1998) *Titan: The life of John D. Rockefeller, Sr.* New York: Random House.

Follett, K. (1983) *On wings of eagles.* New York: Penguin Books.

Gilbert, R. E. (ed.) (2000) *Managing crisis: Presidential disability and the Twenty-Fifth Amendment.* New York: Fordham University Press.

Graham, K. (1997) *Personal history.* New York: Alfred A. Knopf.

Grant, J. M. (1996) *The great Texas banking crash: An insider's account.* Austin, TX: University of Texas Press.

Grant, J. M. and Mack, D. A. (2004) Preparing for the battle: Healthy leadership during organizational crisis. *Organizational Dynamics,* 33: 409–25.

Huyser, R. E. (1986) *Mission to Tehran.* New York: Harper & Row.

Mack, D. A. and J. C. Quick (eds) An inside view of a corporate life cycle transition. *Organizational Dynamics,* 31: 281–93.

McNamara, R. S. and Vandemark. B. (1996) *In retrospect: The tragedy and lessons of Vietnam.* New York: David Mckay.

Nelson, D. L. and Quick, J. C. (2003) *Organizational behavior: Foundations, realities and challenges,* 4th edn. Mason, OH: South-Western/Thompson.

Nelson, D. L. and Quick, J. C. (2006) *Organizational behavior: Foundations, realities and challenges,* 5th edn. Mason, OH: South-Western/Thompson.

Quick, J. C., Cooper, C. L. , Quick, J. D., and Gavin, J. H. (2002) *The Financial Times guide to executive health: Building strength, making risks.* London: *Financial Times.*

Quick, J. C., Nelson, D. L. and Quick, J. D. (1990) *Stress and challenge at the top: The paradox of the successful executive.* Chichester: Wiley.

Shrivastava, P. (1987) *Bhopal: Anatomy of a crises.* Cambridge, MA: Ballinger.

Tanouye, E. (2001) Mental illness: A rising workplace cost. *Wall Street Journal,* 13 June 13, B1–B6.

Vaillant, G. E. (1977) *Adaptation to life.* Boston, MA: Little, Brown.

Zaleznik, A. (1990) The leadership gap. *Academy of Management Executive* 4: 7–22.

Ziegler, P. (ed.) (1987, 1988) *The diaries of Admiral the Lord Louis Mountbatten* (2 vols). London: Collins.

Ziegler, P. (2001) *Mountbatten.* Pompano Beach, FL: Phoenix Press.

Part III

Leading teams and organizations

Chapter 10

A strategic contingency model of team leadership*

Tjai M. Nielsen and Terry R. Halfhill

Tom Smith felt his team leadership approach wasn't as effective as he had hoped. Though he thought of himself as an effective leader and skilful coach, efforts with his new leadership team were backfiring. Tom heard through the grapevine that his team members were unclear about their roles and seemed to be demoralized. He couldn't understand this because he spent a considerable amount of time explaining his priorities and strategy for moving forward. He also tried his best to get his team excited about their future. Frustrated, he decided to think through his problems during a round of golf.

Tom recently assumed the role of vice president of operations for EZ Bank, an investment bank with locations up and down the Eastern seaboard of the US. While Tom had been with EZ Bank for eight successful years, he was in a new position with a relatively new senior leadership team. Only one of five team members had significant experience in position when he arrived. Moreover, Tom knew from experience that EZ Bank was less experienced managing teams as they were implemented within the last three years. However, Tom had worked effectively with new teams in the past and because he was regularly recognized for his relationship-oriented and tactful leadership style, felt confident moving forward. He also believed his coaching ability would be an important asset in getting his team off to a strong beginning.

What factors are working against this senior leadership team's success? While Tom has a good track record, experience, and a solid approach to team leadership, his team is struggling. What must Tom do to turn the team around and start them on the right path? The answer lies in the nature of his leadership approach. Tom concentrated on communicating his strategy for the future and assigning individual team roles. While this is an obvious and oft recommended approach, it fails to account for three important contingencies: (1) context factors (Sundstrom

* In an effort to maintain anonymity, all names used are pseudonyms.

et al., 1990) at *EZ Bank*; (2) team support systems provided by *EZ Bank* (Sundstrom, 1999); and (3) management team dynamics (Nielsen, Sundstrom, and Halfhill, 2005). Tom Smith should have assessed each of these carefully before formulating his leadership approach. Without considering these important contingencies, Tom Smith is essentially 'flying blind' as he develops his team leadership strategy.

This chapter focuses on helping team leaders improve their effectiveness by identifying specific team leadership strategies that are contingent upon organization context factors, support systems, and the type of team being led. First, we describe a general model of team leadership based partially on the work of Sundstrom *et al.* (1990), Sundstrom (1999), and Hackman and Wageman (2005); second, we suggest effective team leader approaches aligned with the three critical team functions; third, we describe organizational context factors that limit and improve team leaders' opportunities to impact team effectiveness; next, we consider organizational support systems necessary for team success; then, we review varying dynamics for different types of teams; and finally, we suggest a contingency model of team leadership that will help team leaders develop effective leadership strategies.

A MODEL OF TEAM LEADERSHIP

Work groups have received increasing levels of empirical attention (Cohen and Bailey, 1997; Kozlowski and Bell, 2003) and coverage in the management press (Edwards and Wilson, 2004; Nielsen *et al.*, 2003). Attention to teams has coincided with their increased application in organizations. In 1996, by one estimate, as many as 78 per cent of *Fortune 1000* companies used self-managing work teams (Lawler, Mohrman, and Ledford, 1998), in a sharp upward trend from previous years that apparently continues today. Yet, while organizations embrace work groups, many questions remain unanswered. For example, how do team leaders improve their own leadership skills while promoting group effectiveness? Though research on leadership (Bass, Avolio, Jung, and Berson, 2003; Yukl, 1989) and factors related to the effectiveness of work teams (for a recent review see Nielsen, Sundstrom, and Halfhill, 2005) has been significant, research on team leadership has been limited (Pearce and Herbik, 2004).

Before attempting to address these questions it is necessary to provide operational definitions for several key terms used throughout the chapter.

Definitions

We define 'work group' and 'work team' as interdependent collections of individuals who share responsibility for specific outcomes for their organizations

(Sundstrom *et al.*, 1990). While some authors (Katzenbach and Smith, 1993) have argued for distinguishing work groups from work teams, we use the terms interchangeably. A distinction has yet to be widely accepted among researchers or practitioners (Guzzo and Shea, 1992; Kozlowski and Bell, 2003). While the definition of a team has achieved some level of agreement among practitioners and researchers, agreement on the definition of team effectiveness has been more tenuous.

Team effectiveness

It is important to define team effectiveness for two reasons. First, it is necessary to distinguish team viability from team performance, and second to distinguish those outcomes associated with team leadership and those driven by the organization. In many instances the team leader may have little or no control over certain criteria. Group effectiveness consists of two components: group performance and group viability. *Performance* entails the successful delivery of an output (i.e. products, decisions, performance events, services, or information) to customers inside or outside the organization. The concept of *viability* (Sundstrom *et al.*, 1990) has existed for nearly 15 years, and until recently there has been no attempt to define the construct operationally. The concept of *group viability* is future oriented and includes *continuity* (ability to maintain a core group membership), *commitment* (to a shared group purpose), *cohesion* (commitment to and liking of team members), and *capability* (to accomplish the shared purpose) (Halfhill and Huff, 2004). Successful team leaders must attend to both *performance* and *viability* to maximize effectiveness.

Team type

While it may seem obvious, team leaders must consider the types of teams they manage to select the most effective leadership strategy. Identifying different types of work groups aids in understanding team effectiveness in various contexts. Ideally, a taxonomy of work groups uses mutually exclusive and exhaustive categories, while maximizing between-category variance and minimizing within-category variance (Devine, 2002). For present purposes, we distinguish six types of work teams: (1) production groups (e.g. assembly groups, paper mill work crews); (2) service groups (e.g. airline attendant teams, maintenance groups, and telecommunications sales groups); (3) management teams (e.g. corporate executive teams, regional steering committees); (4) project groups (e.g. product development groups, strategy teams); (5) action and performing groups (e.g. surgery teams, terrorist response units); (6) advisory groups (e.g. task forces, quality circles).

Team leadership

Team leadership typically takes two forms in organizations. One includes a team leader who occupies a higher-level position in the organizational hierarchy and to whom team members report. A second form is found in semi-autonomous teams consisting of members who occupy the same hierarchical level with one member identified as the team leader. In this second form, the designated team leader can be appointed or elected and typically reports to an external manager who monitors team and leader effectiveness.

Definitions of leadership effectiveness in team settings have been based on leadership style and the ability of the leader to address the multiple interpersonal demands that exist in group settings. For the purposes of this chapter we focus on a functional approach to leadership, stated concisely by Hackman and Wageman (2005): 'If a leader manages, by whatever means, to ensure that all functions critical to group performance are taken care of, the leader has done his or her job well' (p. 273). The functions that are most critical to team effectiveness fall into three categories: (1) effort; (2) strategy; and (3) knowledge, skills, and abilities (KSAs) (Hackman and Morris, 1975; Hackman and Walton, 1986). Teams who are able to put forth the appropriate amount of effort, formulate strategies in line with key task demands, and whose team members possess sufficient KSAs will likely perform more effectively compared to those who are not. However, there are organizational context factors that may impact the relevance and impact of effort, strategy, and KSAs.

Organization context

Organization context factors include elements such as culture, task design and technology, autonomy, performance feedback, rewards, training, and physical environment (Sundstrom *et al.*, 1990). For the purposes of this chapter, we will focus on task design, autonomy, and input control (a dimension of autonomy). *Task design* involves the degree to which team tasks are complex, unpredictable, and dynamic versus simple, predictable, and stable. *Autonomy* is defined as the degree to which team leaders control *how* their teams approach work. *Input control* refers to the control over work inputs utilized by teams to perform their tasks. Each of these three contextual elements may constrain or improve the impact of effort, strategy, and KSAs on effectiveness. Moreover, the particular mix of contextual factors present in an organization indicates the importance of team leaders focusing on one, some, or all of the critical team functions (i.e. effort, strategy, KSAs). The benefit of team leaders focusing on: (1) effort is sensible only if team leaders have a significant level of control over work inputs (e.g. supply, materials, etc.); (2) strategy is sensible only if they have some degree of autonomy in how they do their work; and (3) KSAs makes sense only if the team's task is complex and unpredictable (Hackman and Wageman, 2005).

For example, consider a store inventory team (SIT) working in a big-box retailer such as Wal-Mart, Best Buy, or Home Depot. This team's primary responsibilities include unloading delivery trucks, cataloguing inventory as it is unloaded, organizing and storing inventory, and placing inventory in stores for purchase. SITs do not control what is delivered or when it is delivered (no control over work inputs), as it is determined by inventory availability, customer demand, and delivery logistics. Therefore, SIT leaders would gain little advantage by focusing on work inputs. On the other hand, most SITs have flexibility (i.e. autonomy) regarding the strategy they employ in accomplishing their job once inventory arrives at the store. So SIT leaders would contribute more to increasing team effectiveness by focusing on strategy. On the other hand, if SITs had to follow strict parameters for how they did their job (i.e. lack of autonomy), then an emphasis on strategy would make little sense.

Organization support systems

In order to maximize effectiveness, teams need organizational support from several key systems. Sundstrom and colleagues (1999) identify these systems as, 'a structure compatible with teamwork; leaders' roles that foster cooperation; complementary systems for selection, measurement, information, training, and compensation; and facilities with communication technology that facilitates needed interaction within and among teams' (p. 4). The challenge for team leaders is identifying what specific support systems are most important for fostering their teams' effectiveness, which currently exist within the organization, and what strategies to employ when needed support systems are not available. The complexity of leading teams is significant, but team leaders who focus on high impact behaviours, those with the greatest impact on their teams' success within a temporal environment of organization context factors and support systems – will have the greatest chance of overcoming this complexity.

Team leaders must recognize the dynamics of the type of team they lead, organizational context factors, and support systems directly affecting their team. Then, considering these contingencies, they must identify the most appropriate strategic course of action. This model for leading teams (see Figure 10.1) focuses on leader behaviour guided by team function and task performance (Wageman, 2001), as opposed to individual and team personality (Halfhill, et al., 2005) or interpersonal issues. The first component on which team leaders should focus is strategic leader behaviour.

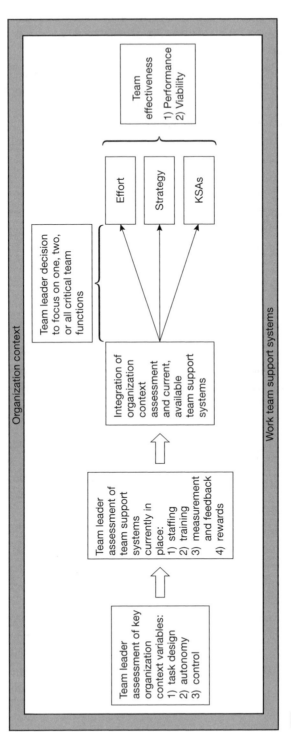

Figure 10.1 A strategic contingency model of team leadership.

STRATEGIC TEAM LEADER BEHAVIOURS

The three functions most critical to team performance include effort, strategy, and KSAs (Hackman and Wageman, 2005). Team leaders must focus on behavioural approaches that will have the greatest impact on each of these three functions and then based on organization context, team support, and team type, decide on which function to concentrate. This process, executed successfully, demonstrates the key points of this chapter.

Effort

Leader behaviours promoting individual and group motivation are key to improving team effort. The most direct way for team leaders to increase motivation is to develop an environment where team members are treated fairly, expected to contribute equally, and are mutually committed to accomplishing team goals. Creating group norms around each of these three facets should be an important area of focus for team leaders. In his seminal paper on the development of group norms, Feldman (1984) states, 'Group norms are the informal rules that groups adopt to regulate and regularize group members' behavior' (p. 84). One key method for group norm development involves explicit statements and behaviours from team leaders. A group norm of fair treatment will develop when team leaders consistently enforce rules uniformly and avoid favouritism and inconsistent reinforcement. A group norm focusing on equal contribution will develop more quickly and powerfully when team leaders consistently provide feedback to individual team members and the team as a whole regarding task performance and the expectation of extraordinary effort. Mutual commitment to team goals is a group norm that develops when team leaders engage each member of the team in the development of those goals. Objectives created in the absence of team input will be less likely to engender mutual commitment. In addition to fair treatment, equal contribution, and mutual commitment, it is important for team leaders to focus on the development of team level citizenship behaviour.

Team citizenship behaviour (TCB) refers to a general set of behaviours performed by team members that are helpful, discretionary, and go far beyond normal job requirements (Nielsen *et al.*, 2003). Specifically, TCB has been defined as, 'individual behavior that is discretionary, not directly or explicitly recognized by the formal reward system, and that in the aggregate promotes the effective functioning of the organization' (Organ, 1988, p. 4). Behavioural examples of TCB include:

- an employee staying late to help a team-mate finish his or her part of an important project;
- an experienced manager helping a new manager 'learn the ropes,' even though this activity is not part of the experienced manager's job description and takes much time;

- an office employee exerting the extra effort to come to work during a snow-storm, even when other employees use the storm as an excuse to stay home.
- a team member spending many hours helping to resolve a conflict between other team members.

Such team behaviour will increase work team performance by promoting self-management, increasing the team's ability to accomplish goals, and improving the efficiency and coordination of the team (Podsakoff and MacKenzie, 1994). More importantly, team leaders who make the expectation of TCB known to team members and regularly support TCBs through reinforcement and reward will have teams who more quickly develop TCB as a team norm.

Team norms of fair treatment, equal contribution, mutual commitment, and team citizenship behaviour will result in teams capable of putting forth maximum effort to accomplish their tasks. However, significant team effort without sufficient strategy may result in wasted effort.

Strategy

Teams depend on effective strategy to know where they are going, adapt to changes in their environment, and maintain the alignment of team processes with task requirements. Team leaders must consistently and effectively communicate expectations to help their teams stay goal focused. Without this, team members tend to lose sight of their goals and suffer efficiency losses. In addition, it is difficult for team members to accomplish appropriate tasks when they are unclear about the team's ultimate objective. Another important component of the strategy function is adapting to change. An inability to adapt to change at the group level puts the team at a distinct disadvantage.

One benefit of teamwork is the ability to adapt, shift, and realign based on changes in the environment (West, 1994). Changes in the environment could entail a number of different things such as team member turnover in an action team, shifts in the competitive landscape for a sales team, or a reduction of funding for a new product development team. The advantage of a team-based structure can only be realized when team leaders assist team members in identifying impending changes and then provide the appropriate support to adjust work processes in an effort to meet new demands. A final element of team strategy on which team leaders must concentrate is alignment of team processes and task demands.

Aligning what a team does with the tasks they must accomplish seems obvious, but remains challenging for many teams. Consider *Tom Smith's* management team discussed at the beginning of this chapter, whose primary task is to ensure the long-term success of *EZ Bank's* operations. One important process for accomplishing this task is leadership development. If members of the management team do not develop the abilities of those below them to take their place, long-term success will be less likely. However, like many management teams, *Tom Smith's* team at *EZ Bank,* spends less than 5 per cent of its time on leadership development. In this example, *Tom* must ensure the alignment of team processes with team tasks by refocusing his team members on their leadership development responsibilities. Another key function of team effectiveness that deserves team leaders' attention is team members' knowledge, skills, and abilities (KSAs).

Knowledge, skills, and abilities

A common term used in place of the words knowledge, skill, and ability is talent. The importance of talent to team leaders in their drive for effectiveness is ubiquitous. However, the level of talent in teams varies widely. Therefore team leaders must concentrate on ways to increase the availability, importance, and applicability of continuing team member education. The first challenge team leaders face is the identification of talent gaps. What KSAs does my team lack that impairs their ability to perform tasks and achieve goals? This question should also be posed to team members since the impact of any specific talent deficit will likely be experienced by them first. While identification of talent gaps goes a long way toward adding importance to acquiring the proper KSAs, it remains the least challenging task.

Team leaders' ability to provide necessary resources to meet team members' needs is a vital function. In many large organizations, educational resources are available internally in the form of training, workshops, and seminars. However, the extent of those resources is often not readily known by team members. Team leaders must be aware of these resources and educate team members. On the other hand, many medium and small organizations do not have sufficient internal resources to satisfy KSA gaps. The leadership challenge in these organizations is to identify external or alternative methods for acquiring access to education resources. One possibility in this area involves the team leader acquiring the needed training and then training team members.

ORGANIZATION CONTEXT FACTORS

Organization context factors include task design, autonomy, and input control (Sundstrom *et al.*, 1990). Task design involves the degree to which team tasks are complex, unpredictable, and dynamic versus simple, predictable, and stable. Autonomy is defined as the degree to which team leaders control: (1) *how* their teams approach work; and (2) the work inputs utilized by their teams to perform their tasks. Each of these contextual elements may constrain or improve team effectiveness. Specifically, the particular mix of contextual factors present in an organization indicates the importance of team leaders helping their teams focus on one, some, or all of the critical team functions (i.e. effort, strategy, KSAs). The benefit of team leaders focusing on: (1) effort is sensible only if the task design permits them to have some control over work inputs (e.g. supply, materials, etc.); (2) strategy is sensible only if they have some degree of autonomy in how they do their work; and (3) KSAs makes sense only if the teams' task is complex and unpredictable (Hackman and Wageman, 2005).

If we analyse the contextual elements of a surgery team whose task is highly complex, fast-paced, and volatile (Edmondson, 2003), we begin to see the impact of certain contextual factors. Consider a surgery team operating on a patient with a rare AB– blood type. If the hospital supply of AB– is very low due to issues with a local blood bank and the surgery team runs out during an operation, increased effort will not significantly impact performance. The management team for a consumer electronics store can put forth as much effort as possible, but if its supply of plasma televisions runs out it will not matter. Thus, the context factors present in these situations require team leaders to focus on team functions other than effort. These examples illustrate task design factors limiting the impact of team effort and the importance for team leaders to recognize this limitation. However, if we examine the same types of teams and consider strategy, the impact on effectiveness changes.

During certain procedures surgery teams have a significant amount of autonomy in deciding how to complete their work (Edmondson, 2003). Therefore, developing the most effective strategy for approaching the task of surgery could potentially have a significant impact on effectiveness. In procedures where surgery teams have specific parameters to follow and have less latitude, team leaders would focus less on strategy because it is constrained (Hackman and Wageman, 2005). Similarly, most management teams have latitude to decide how to recruit talent, whom to hire, and other personnel-related decisions. This exacerbates the importance of strategy in achieving positive outcomes. These examples illustrate organization context (i.e. autonomy) increasing the impact of strategy and the importance for team leaders to recognize this positive impact. Extending these examples, let us consider the importance of KSAs.

The work of management teams and surgery teams is complex and unpredictable (Barsade *et al.*, 2000; Edmondson, 2003). This work context intensifies the importance of team members' KSAs (Campion, Medsker, and Higgs, 1993) compared to a manufacturing team working on an assembly line whose work context is simple and predictable. Thus, leaders of surgery and management teams will improve team effectiveness by focusing on doing what is necessary to improve team member KSAs, as opposed to leaders of some manufacturing teams who would benefit far less.

Team leaders must consider organization context factors in deciding the best way to improve team effectiveness. Depending on what contextual elements exist

200

in a given organization, one, two, or three of the critical team functions (effort, strategy, KSAs) we have discussed will serve as opportunities for increasing team effectiveness. Team leaders must take responsibility for diagnosing their organization's contextual matrix to help them identify the appropriate leadership strategy to pursue. Regardless of whether organization context factors facilitate or restrain specific team functions, current team support systems will play an important role in team effectiveness (Sundstrom, 1999).

ORGANIZATION SUPPORT SYSTEMS

Team-based structures offer the potential advantages of flexibility, superior performance, and dramatically improved creativity. However, teams must be supported properly to perform optimally. Sundstrom and colleagues (1999) argue that support systems must be implemented and also meet the needs of specific types of teams. 'Within types, each team has unique needs. The management challenge is to design, implement, and maintain organizational support systems to meet the needs of the type of team, with flexibility to accommodate each team's unique features' (p. 5). There are four essential support systems necessary for promoting team effectiveness: (1) team staffing; (2) training; (3) measurement and feedback; and (4) reward system. Just as team leaders must recognize organization context factors that impact their teams, they must also consider the extent to which their organizations have and effectively utilize the four support systems. More importantly, team leaders must formulate alternative methods in the absence of these systems. The following descriptions should assist team leaders in knowing what to look for.

Team staffing

Team staffing is an important support element contributing to effectiveness because it ensures that team members have an appropriate blend of experience, knowledge, skills, and abilities. Let's consider our *EZ Bank* example again. *Tom Smith* knows that *EZ Bank* began implementing teams only recently. One consequence of *EZ Bank's* lack of experience using teams is the absence of an effective team staffing support system which may prevent the organization from selecting team members with sufficient teamwork skills and putting together a team with complementary KSAs. *Tom Smith* must consider *EZ Bank's* team support systems to more accurately identify the proper leadership approach to employ.

Hiring people for work in teams is different than hiring people for individual work because team members share responsibility for the completion of team tasks with each member having specific roles and responsibilities. Team members depend on each other to make unique contributions according to their specific mix of

KSAs. It is up to the organization to support team staffing by creating teams with individuals who will perform well collectively (Borman, Hanson, and Hedge, 1997). For example, some new product development project teams require team members with expertise in marketing, sales, engineering, manufacturing, and product development (Sarin and Mahajan, 2001). Those responsible for staffing must focus on creating a team with complementary skills in each of those areas, as opposed to simply staffing the team with five intelligent, individually effective people. Another important component in staffing is a focus on teamwork skills. Creating teams with individuals who don't possess effective teamwork skills is a recipe for mediocrity. While a focus on teamwork skills seems obvious, many organizations do not perform teamwork skill assessments during the selection process. Team leaders whose organizations do not have a team staffing support system in place will have to overcome this barrier to effectiveness. The degree to which this can be done depends largely on the amount of autonomy team leaders have with regard to selection. If a team leader has the authority to make selection decisions, he or she can focus on selecting individuals whose unique KSAs complement the team and whose teamwork skills are well developed. However, when this is not possible other support systems such as training can help fill KSA gaps among team members.

Training

Team members who require additional knowledge and skills are often exposed to training. In fact, team training is widely used (Bassi, Cheney, and Van Buren, 1997) and has benefited organizations adopting team-based structures such as Motorola and Xerox (Gronstedt, 1996; Henkoff, 1993, respectively). In the event that team leaders do not have an effective team staffing support system and have people with significant KSA gaps, an effective training support system can help. Effective team training involves closing KSA gaps, but should also include a significant focus on the many facets of teamwork. Stevens and Yarish (1999) analysed the use of team training during the implementation of teams at a copper refinery. The training support system at the refinery created multiple training modules around different facets of teamwork: (1) introduction to the team concept; (2) managing group dynamics; (3) conducting effective team meetings; (4) team quality training; (5) goal setting for teams; and (6) collaborative decision-making (Stevens and Yarish, 1999, p. 130). In some instances, training may be the only viable support system available to team leaders. In the copper refinery team leaders were unable to change rewards, had almost no turnover which limited the impact of team staffing, and measurement and feedback systems were unchanged. That left training as the only viable support system available. If team leaders find themselves without suitable organization training support, they must assume this responsibility. If a team leader doesn't have enough expertise to provide training, he or she must gain access to individual training that can then be taught to team-mates. If no access to training is possible, team leaders must focus on teaching what they know and working within the organization to create team-based training opportunities. In some organizations measurement and feedback systems are primary choices for team leaders wishing to impact team effectiveness.

Measurement and feedback

Performance measurement and feedback provide essential information to teams and team leaders. Team leaders must know how their teams are doing in order to provide the support they need for improvement or continued success. Moreover, research has demonstrated that team effectiveness increases when team members are given feedback on objective measures of their performance (Pritchard and Watson, 1991). Measurement systems not only provide information for teams to improve their performance, they also provide tangible examples of success in which teams can take pride. This motivational aspect of feedback is very important and should be considered when measurement and feedback systems are designed. Let us consider a sales team working in the insurance industry. A partial list of daily feedback the team receives includes total sales, sales as a percentage of target goals, new customer acquisitions, number of sales calls, average customer acquisition cost, and running averages of profit margin across customers. These data allow team members to track performance very closely and concentrate on areas where performance is lagging. Team leaders must decide what feedback is most pertinent to their team based on business strategy and team motivation. In some cases leaders of insurance sales teams will emphasize specific metrics because of alignment with their teams' strategic goals. At other times, team leaders will have greater impact by concentrating on metrics representing exceptional performance as a way of boosting motivation. Team leaders will increase their impact on overall effectiveness when they link team performance to rewards.

Rewards

Many team-based organizations continue to support reward structures created for individuals. That is, team members are rewarded for individual performance rather than collective performance. This can have a significant and detrimental impact on team performance (Lawler and Cohen, 1992). Organizations with team-based reward systems in place are far more prepared to support team effectiveness. Depending on their position within the organization, team leaders may or may not have influence regarding the reward structure used by their organizations. However, team leaders may have discretion regarding bonuses and other incentives. In the absence of team-based rewards, team leaders should utilize incentives under their control to reward team performance. Otherwise they run the risk of having team members more concerned with individual performance at the expense of team effectiveness. Similar to staffing, training, and measurement, reward support systems should be tailored to specific types of teams (Sundstrom, 1999).

LEADERSHIP OF DIFFERENT TYPES OF TEAMS

A third contingency that team leaders must consider when developing their leadership strategy is the type of team they lead. How do we differentiate one type of work group from another? Do different factors across varying types of teams have differential effects on team effectiveness? Are certain team functions and subsequent leadership approaches more vital with certain teams subject to specific organization contextual factors? The answer is yes. In the following section we differentiate and identify critical team functions and subsequent leadership approaches based on organization context, support systems, and team type.

The classification of different types of work groups aids in understanding team effectiveness in various contexts. Sundstrom *et al.* (2000), building on earlier typologies, identified six types of work groups: (1) production groups (consist of front-line employees who repeatedly produce tangible output such as automobile assembly groups or paper mill work crews); (2) service groups (consist of employees who cooperate to conduct repeated transactions with customers, as in airline attendant teams, maintenance groups, and telecommunications sales groups); (3) management teams (consist of an executive or senior managers who coordinate work units, through joint planning, policy-making, budgeting, staffing, and logistics); (4) project groups (consist of members who tend to come from different departments or units such as product development groups or strategy teams); (5) action and performing groups (consist of individual experts and support staff who conduct complex, time-limited performance events involving audiences, adversaries, or challenging environments such as surgery teams or search and rescue teams; (6) advisory groups (consist of different employees, sometimes from multiple levels within the organization, who solve problems and recommend solutions such as task forces and quality circles).

Different teams, based on their primary tasks and responsibilities, interact differently with the three organization context variables (i.e. task design, autonomy, input control) and four team support systems (i.e. staffing, training, measurement/feedback, and rewards) we have discussed. Identifying the appropriate team function on which to focus should be contingent on organization context, available support systems, and team type.

Action teams (e.g. surgery team; terrorist response units) have complex tasks, varying degrees of autonomy, and a high degree of input control. Therefore, none of the critical team functions and opportunities for team leader influence (i.e. effort, strategy, KSAs) are significantly constrained. Key support systems for action teams are staffing, training, and rewards. Action teams require team staffing support to ensure they are comprised of individual specialists who work well together. Training is important due to the complexity and challenging nature of the task action teams engage in. Whether it is an airline cockpit crew, terrorist response unit, or professional sports team, an appropriate reward structure is key to ensuring continued effectiveness. Based on Table 10.1, action team leaders should concentrate on: (1) their teams' effort and KSAs; (2) strategy depending on the degree of autonomy; and (3) staffing, training, and reward support systems.

Advisory teams (e.g. task forces) have tasks of varying complexity, varying degrees of autonomy, and low control over work inputs. These factors differentially constrain the relative impact of team leaders focusing on effort, strategy, and KSAs. Advisory team leaders must consider the level of task complexity and autonomy for their specific team in an effort to identify team functions that should receive their attention. Advisory teams have relatively few needs, work apart from the primary functions of the organization and are usually temporary. Therefore, the reward support system is most important for advisory teams. Team members typically participate in addition to their normal work duties. Specific incentive packages to motivate team members for this 'extra work' are important.

Management teams (e.g. senior leadership) complete complex tasks, have a high degree of autonomy, and a high degree of input control. These features do not constrain the impact of effort, strategy, or KSAs. Staffing, measurement, training, and reward support systems are most vital to management team effectiveness. A well-designed reward system is essential for management teams as they often have naturally conflicting goals due to their disparate areas of responsibility (e.g. operations, marketing, and engineering). Measurement systems to support the reward structure are important as members of management teams have a plethora of performance indicators to monitor. The challenge for management team leaders is significant due to the number of areas (team functions and support systems) that offer opportunities for increasing team effectiveness.

Production teams (e.g. car assembly teams; paper mill work crews) complete relatively simple tasks, have a low degree of autonomy, and a low degree of input control. These factors constrain the importance of effort, strategy, and KSAs. Therefore, it is essential for production team leaders to focus on the support systems important for their success. Team-based rewards help maintain motivation for production teams who typically have repetitive, less stimulating tasks. As with management teams, appropriate measurement systems are necessary to reward production teams effectively. These measurement systems could potentially track a variety of performance indicators involving quantity and quality. The importance of training increases as technology advances the complexity of the processes used by production teams.

Project teams (e.g. product development teams) engage in tasks of varying complexity, have a high degree of autonomy, and a low degree of control over work inputs. These factors differentially constrain the relative impact of team leaders focusing on effort, strategy, and KSAs. Project team leaders must consider the level of task complexity for their specific team in an effort to identify team functions that should receive their attention. For example, if a project team has a highly complex task such as developing an entirely new product for their organization, the team leader would have a great impact on effectiveness by focusing on KSAs. Project teams' high degree of autonomy regarding how they approach their work offers team leaders an opportunity to increase effectiveness by focusing on strategy. Project team leaders can also benefit their teams by focusing on staffing and reward support systems. Because project teams require a diversity of expertise and experience, team staffing is particularly important. As with each other type of team, a reward structure specifically designed for project teams will also enhance performance and deserves the team leader's attention.

Service teams (e.g. airline attendant teams) have a relatively lower degree of task complexity (due to repetition), a low degree of autonomy, and a variable degree of input control. The repetitive nature of service teams' tasks contribute to relatively lower degrees of complexity. This constrains the impact of team leaders focusing on KSAs. A low degree of autonomy in service teams' approach to completing their work constrains the relative importance of team leaders emphasizing strategy. Team leaders will benefit from identifying their teams' degree of input control. If it is high, team leaders would be well served to focus on team effort. The key support systems contributing to service team effectiveness are measurement and staffing. Service teams often deal with customers repeatedly and benefit from measures focusing on customer satisfaction. Because service team members often interact directly with an organization's customers, staffing these teams with extroverted, agreeable, and teamwork oriented individuals is important. Team leaders will positively impact their service teams' performance by concentrating on these support systems.

EFFECTIVE TEAM LEADERSHIP STRATEGIES

Identifying the appropriate team function on which to focus should be contingent on organization context, available support systems, and team type. In Table 10.1, we present a strategic contingency matrix that identifies the most important team

Table 10.1 *Strategic contingency matrix for determining effective team leadership approaches*

Team type and organization context factors

Team support systems	Action			Management			Advisory			Production			Project			Service		
	TD	Auto.	Control	TD	Auto.	Control	TD	Auto.	Control	TD	Auto.	Control	TD	Auto.	Control	TD	Auto.	Control
	+ −	+ −	+ −	+ −	+ −	+ −	+ −	+ −	+ −	+ −	+ −	+ −	+ −	+ −	+ −	+ −	+ −	+ −
+Staffing	K	S E,K	E S,K	K	S	E	S	S E,S	E	+	+	−	+	E	K	S	K	E,S S
+Training	K	S E,K	E S,K	K	S	E	S	S E,S	E	+	+	−	+	E	K	S	K	E,S S
+M&F	K	S E,K	E S,K	K	S	E	S	S E,S	E	+	+	−	+	E	K	S	K	E,S S
+Rewards	K	S E,K	E S,K	K	S	E	S	S E,S	E	+	+	−	+	E	K	S	K	E,S S
−Staffing	K	S E,K	E S,K	K	S	E	S	S E,S	E	+	+	−	+	E	K	S	K	E,S S
−Training	K	S E	S	K	S	E	S	S E,S	E	+	+	−	+	E	K	S	K	E,S S
−M&F	K	S E	E −	K	S	E	S	S E,S	E	+	+	−	+	E	K	S	K	E,S S
−Rewards	K	S K	E S	K	S	E	S	S E,S	E	+	+	−	+	E	k	S	k	E,S S

Notes: TD = task design; Auto. = degree of autonomy; Control = degree of work input control; M & F = measurement and feedback; TD+ = complex, unpredictable, and dynamic task; TD− = simple, predictable, and stable task; Auto.+ = high degree of autonomy; Auto.− = low degree of autonomy; Control+ = high degree of input control; Control− = low degree of input control; +Staffing = strong staffing support; +Training = strong training support; +M & F = strong measurement and feedback support; +Rewards = strong team–based rewards; −Staffing = weak or no staffing support; −Training = weak or no training support; −M & F = weak or no measurement and feedback support; −Rewards = individually–based rewards; E = effort; S = strategy; K = KSAs; **E** = positive interaction between an organization context contingency and an organization support contingency indicating the importance of **effort**; **S** = positive interaction between an organization context contingency and an organization support contingency indicating the importance of **strategy**; **K** = positive interaction between an organization context contingency and an organization support contingency indicating the importance of **KSAs** .

functions for team leaders' attention based on the context, support, and team type contingencies.

The most efficient way to read this table is to identify the type of team you lead, then move down one level and decide what organization context factors either constrain or facilitate the functioning of your team. Next, look in the left-most column and identify what team support systems are in place in your organization (indicated by a plus sign) and/or what support systems do not exist in your organization (indicated by a minus sign). Using this information, look for the appropriate cells in order to identify the critical team functions that deserve your attention. A bold letter (**E**, **S**, or **K**) within a cell indicates, as a result of the three contingencies interacting, that a specific functional area is most vital and deserves your immediate attention. For example, if we examine management teams in this matrix we see that due to the dynamics of management teams, the three elements of organization context are each in plus columns indicating that management teams deal with complex and dynamic tasks (task design), have autonomy to determine how they approach their work (autonomy), and often control work inputs (control). The minus sign column for each organization context factor is darkened because management teams typically do not: (1) encounter simple, repetitive tasks (task design); (2) lack control over how they do their work (autonomy); and (3) lack control over work inputs (control). If you examine the task design column and assume a strong staffing support system, KSAs would be the vital team function on which the team leaders should focus. The task design contingency interacts with the strong staffing support contingency to highlight the importance of team KSAs. In other words, in a scenario where a management team's tasks are highly complex and it has a strong staffing support function, focusing on team member KSAs would likely contribute significantly to team effectiveness. The key leadership challenge is the continuous process of assessing the organization context and team support systems to determine the most effective team leadership strategy.

CONCLUSION

In this chapter we identify leadership strategies for specific types of teams by providing a model of team leadership that integrates organizational context, organizational support systems, type of team, and leader behaviours. Team leaders must recognize the dynamics of the type of team they lead, organizational context factors, and support systems directly affecting their team. Then, considering these contingencies, they must identify the most appropriate strategic course of action. The model developed in this chapter focuses on leader behaviour guided by team function and task performance, as opposed to individual and team personality or interpersonal issues. Without considering the key contingencies of organization context, team support systems, and team type, team leaders will not have the information they need to develop an effective team leadership strategy.

REFERENCES

Barsade, S. G., Ward, A. J., Turner, J. D. F., and Sonnenfeld, J. A. (2000) To your heart's content: A model of affective diversity in top management teams. *Administrative Science Quarterly,* 45(4): 802–36.

Bass, B. M., Avolio, B. J., Jung, D. I., and Berson, Y. (2003) Predicting unit performance by assessing transformational and transactional leadership. *Journal of Applied Psychology,* 88(2): 207–18.

Bassi, L. J., Cheney, S., and Van Buren, M. (November, 1997) Training industry trends 1997. *Training and Development,* pp. 46–59.

Borman, W. C., Hanson, M. A., and Hedge, J. (1997) Personnel selection. *Annual Review of Psychology,* 48: 299–337.

Campion, M. A., Medsker, G. J., and Higgs, A. C. (1993) Relations between work group characteristics and effectiveness: Implications for designing effective work groups. *Personnel Psychology,* 46: 823–50.

Cohen, S. G. and Bailey, D. (1997) What makes teams work: Group effectiveness research from the shop floor to the executive suite. *Journal of Management,* 23, 239–90.

Devine, D. J. (2002) A review and integration of classification systems relevant to teams in organizations. *Group Dynamics,* 6(4): 291–310.

Edmondson, A. C. (2003) Speaking up in the operating room: How team leaders promote learning in interdisciplinary action teams. *Journal of Management Studies,* 40(6): 1419–52.

Edwards, A. and Wilson, J. R. (2004) *Implementing virtual teams: A guide to organizational and human factors.* Aldershot: Gower.

Feldman, D. C. (1984) The development and enforcement of group norms. *Academy of Management Review,* 9(1): 47–53.

Gronstedt, A. (1996) Integrated communications at America's leading total quality management corporations. *Public Relations Review,* 22(1): 25–42.

Guzzo, R. A. and Shea, G. P. (1992) Group performance and intergroup relations in organizations. In M. D. Dunnette and L. M. Hough (eds) *Handbook of industrial and organizational psychology,* 2nd edn, Vol. 3. Palo Alto, CA: Consulting Psychologists Press, pp. 269–313.

Hackman, J. R. and Morris, C. G. (1975) Group tasks, group interaction processes, and group performance effectiveness: A review and proposed integration. In L. Berkowitz (ed.) *Advances in experimental social psychology,* vol. 8. New York: Academic Press, pp. 45–99.

Hackman, J. R. and Wageman, R. (2005) A theory of team coaching. *Academy of Management Review,* 30(2): 269–87.

Hackman, J. R. and Walton, R. E. (1986) Leading groups in organizations. In P. S. Goodman (ed.) *Designing effective work groups.* San Francisco, CA: Jossey-Bass, pp. 72–119.

Halfhill, T. and Huff, J. (2004) *Defining group viability.* Roundtable presented at the 19th annual meeting of the Society for Industrial and Organizational Psychology, Chicago, IL.

Halfhill, T., Nielsen, T. M., Sundstrom, E., and Weilbaecher, A. (2005) Group personality composition and performance in military service teams. *Military Psychology,* 17(1): 41–54.

Henkoff, R. (March 22, 1993) Companies that train best. *Fortune,* p. 62.

Katzenbach, J. R. and Smith, D. K. (1993) *The wisdom of teams: Creating the high-performance organization.* Boston, MA: Harvard Business School Press.

Kozlowski, S. W. J. and Bell, B. S. (2003) Work groups and teams in organizations. In W. C. Borman, and D. R. Ilgen, and R. Klimoski (eds) *Handbook of psychology: Industrial and organizational psychology*, vol. 12. New York: Wiley, pp. 333–75.

Lawler, E. E. and Cohen, S. G. (1992) Designing pay systems for teams. *ACA Journal,* 1(1): 6–19.

Lawler, E. E., Mohrman, S. A., and Ledford, G. E. (1998) *Strategies for high perform-ance organizations: Employee involvement, TQM, and reengineering programs in Fortune 1,000 corporations.* San Francisco, CA: Jossey-Bass.

Nielsen, T. M., Sundstrom, E., and Halfhill, T. (2005) Group dynamics and effectiveness: Five years of applied research. In S. A. Wheelan (ed.) *Handbook of Group Research and Practice.* Thousand Oaks, CA: Sage, pp. 285–311.

Nielsen, T. M., Sundstrom, E., Soulen, S. K., Halfhill, T., and Huff, J. (2003) Corporate citizenship in team-based organizations: An essential ingredient for sustained success. In M. Beyerlein, D. Johnson and S. Beyerlein (eds) *Advances in interdis-ciplinary studies of work teams.* Greenwich, CT: JAI Press, pp. 169–87.

Organ, D. W. (1988) *Organizational citizenship behavior: The good soldier syndrome.* Lexington, MA: Lexington Books.

Pearce, C. L. and Herbik, P. A. (2004) Citizenship behavior at the team level of analysis: The effects of team leadership, team commitment, perceived team support, and team size. *Journal of Social Psychology,* 144(3): 293–310.

Podsakoff, P. M. and MacKenzie, S. B. (1994) Organizational citizenship behavior and sales unit effectiveness. *Journal of Marketing Research,* 31: 351–63.

Pritchard, R. D. and Watson, M. D. (1991) Understanding and measuring group produc-tivity. In S. Worchel, W. Wood, and J. A. Simpson (eds) *Group Process and Productivity.* Thousand Oaks, CA: Sage, pp. 251–75.

Sarin, S. and Mahajan, V. (2001) The effect of reward structures on the performance of cross-functional product development teams. *Journal of Marketing,* 65: 35–53.

Stevens, M. J. and Yarish, M. E. (1999) Training for team effectiveness. In E. Sundstrom (ed.) *Supporting Work Team Effectiveness.* San Francisco, CA: Jossey-Bass, pp. 126–56.

Sundstrom, E. (1999) Challenges of supporting work team effectiveness. In E. Sundstrom (ed.) *Supporting work team effectiveness*. San Francicso, CA: Jossey-Bass.

Sundstrom, E., DeMeuse, K. P., and Futrell, D. (1990) Work teams: Applications and effectiveness. *American Psychologist,* 45: 120–33.

Sundstrom, E., McIntyre, M., Halfhill, T. R., and Richards, H. (2000) Work groups: From the Hawthorne studies to work teams of the 1990s and beyond. *Group Dynamics,* 4: 44–67.

Wageman, R. (2001) How leaders foster self-managing team effectiveness. *Organization Science,* 12(5): 559–77.

West, M. (1994) *Effective teamwork: Practical lessons from organizational research.* Malden, MA: Blackwell.

Yukl, G. (1989) Managerial leadership: A review of theory and research. *Journal of Management,* 15(2): 251–89.

Chapter 11

Leadership and organizational culture

Marc J. Schabracq

INTRODUCTION: WHAT IS ORGANIZATIONAL CULTURE?

In a superficial way, organizational culture can be described as 'how we do things here'. Organizational culture then amounts to how the members of an organization deal with the recurrent problems of their company. Apart from the routines to solve these problems, it involves such things as the housing and layout of the organization and the common reality stemming from all that, with its blueprints for behaviour, perception, thought and feeling. Its actual forms may have come about in somewhat coincidental ways, but other possibilities have been excluded by the appearance of the first ones, simply because something can take only one form at a time. This is called 'autopoiesis' (Maturana and Varela, 1980), a state resulting from a self-organizing system. The result is a highly predictable way of doing things, a solid shared reality in which its members can firmly belief. Because of this unquestioned belief, they keep on enacting its forms, which makes this reality even more solid. They usually see this reality as the only possible one and as long as they act on this belief, it actually is: a typical case of a self-fulfilling prophecy.

Jointly enacting this reality each time anew implies a shared investment of much effort by all concerned. However, this investment has its yields. It enables the members of the culture to do their thing. As these routines are enacted without much awareness, they can keep their minds free for what they deem important. The fact that until now these automatisms have done the trick most of the time implies a powerful reinforcement for those automatisms. As this reinforcement is partial as well as random, the resulting responses are hard to extinguish (for example Deese, 1952). Moreover, these routines have become so familiar to those involved that they are felt to be a part of their identities. Lastly, all of this happens more or less outside of awareness.

All these factors — the unquestioned beliefs underlying reality, the investment of effort, the positive outcomes for all involved, the partial and random reinforcement scheme, the tacit or even unconscious nature of all of this – make organizational culture a very stable datum, which is hard to change at will. As a result, leaders' attempts to change organizational culture usually evoke strong resistance from its members. Though this resistance seems to be ill-directed and illogical, it often turns out to be surprisingly well-concerted and effective in fighting off the proposed change.

The effectiveness of this resistance has led to the idea that culture cannot be changed at all in a preferred direction. References to organizational culture have even become a habitual excuse to avoid the responsibility to intervene: it is just culture. Some support for this stance stems from structure-oriented ways of theorizing about organizational culture. By highlighting the unaware and unconscious aspects of crucial parts of organizational culture, these approaches stress the difficulties inherent in changing it. Though useful as a warning, such approaches may lead to an obviously counterproductive paralysis of all attempts to change culture.

In this chapter, it is defended that culture can be changed by a competent leader or a team of leaders – though not easily – and also that the unconscious nature of much of that culture even can be used to bring about intended change. Changing culture can be done best when a direct and an indirect approach are combined. Of these two, the latter is the more decisive. Essentially, this approach rests on principles described by Sun Tzu's 'Art of War', a Chinese treatise probably from the fifth century BC, as elucidated by McNeilly (2001).

First, an exemplary structural approach, the one by Schein (1985), is examined. Then, some alternative ideas are discussed, which do allow for some planned change: the direct approach mentioned above. Then some functionalistic ideas about organizational culture are introduced, derived from Talcott Parsons. These functionalistic ideas provide us with the building blocks for the indirect approach.

SCHEIN'S STRUCTURAL APPROACH

Schein (1985) distinguishes four 'layers' of organizational culture, where the next one each time is farther removed from awareness than the previous one:

1. the *forms* of the physical layout, personal appearance, and behaviour, with its standard routines and approaches;
2. the lore of tales, notions, and images, known as *mythology*;
3. the *rules and norms* that shape organizational functioning;
4. the *underlying assumptions*.

The *forms* are, at least in principle, open to inspection, though usually nobody inspects them. As long as they are properly displayed and do not deviate too much from the normal, the members do not pay much conscious attention to them.

When the members are fully socialized, the forms are just experienced as self-evident parts of reality. More out of awareness, the forms provide the members with a multitude of cues signalling what is the case (the play at hand), the ongoing activities and their integration (the roles in the play and their interaction), and where they are in the play (the scene and the lines at hand). These cues enable the others to display the proper behaviour, which in its turn provides cues for the next step. So one's posture and movements imply proposals of a certain relation and directives how to take it from there (Schabracq, 1991).

The *mythology* gives the members some casuistry about good and bad actions and characters (see pp. 219–21 for more about heroes) in that culture, portraying in this way its most relevant virtues and vices. By setting examples, the mythology serves as a frame of reference, providing standards and guidelines for what to do and what is normal. As such, it influences the display of actual behaviour. Moreover, mythology helps to give meaning to the behavioural forms and integrates them in a historical context. The stories and images inherent in the mythology are of course open to inspection, but can't be exchanged for other ones at will. They are felt to be data from the past and the past cannot be changed. So, mythology has a stabilizing effect on the culture.

The forms to be enacted or the plays to be played follow certain standardized formats, sets of tacit *rules and norms*. These make up the next layer of organizational culture, which operates outside awareness most of the time, though it is in principle accessible to reflection. These rules take the form of 'if . . ., then . . .' As such, they link the cues inherent in the afore-mentioned forms to well-specified responses. They are the result of a long history of modelling and self-conditioning (Schabracq, 1991), and shape both mythology and the forms. By shaping and tending our environment and by automatically adhering to the proper behavioural forms, we ourselves install these cues. Usually, these rules and norms only enter our awareness when such a rule is openly transgressed. Harold Garfinkel (1967) has even made purposefully transgressing such rules into a part of sociological methodology.

The deepest layer is the one of the *underlying assumptions*. These involve notions about what is and should be real and what is not and should not be real, as well as about what we shall and shall not accomplish in the future. As such, they steer our attention, focusing it on what is meant to be and ignoring what is not meant to be. According to Schein, these assumptions determine the rule system, are not open to conscious reflection, and are hard to put into words. As such, they are seen as the most important factor in the culture's resistance to change.

Schein's approach gives the impression that it is an objective, even value-free description of organizational culture. It is a classical way to look at organizations, which gives you some idea about resistance to change and the continuity of organizational culture. Culture is seen as the inevitable result of a historical development. By taking its forms, all other forms are more or less excluded. Changing culture becomes a matter of modifying these inevitable results, which surely will evoke strong resistance. Moreover, this view can be supported by a long history of failures in changing organizational culture.

Though the distinction of these four layers and their interrelations are attractive, the nature of the underlying assumptions has remained somewhat unclear. How do we acquire them? Are they abstractions of the rule structure that develop later in life? I think not.

ASSUMPTIONS AND POSTURES

In this section, the underlying assumptions are related to attitudes, both in their physical and mental meaning. By assuming an attitude, people show what they assume to be the case: assuming an attitude or posture, literally, reflects their assumptions. This is not only so in English, but also in German and Dutch. As their assumptions reflect their beliefs about reality, their posture indicates that they assume that this belief is at least of use to them and maybe even true. These are well-tried beliefs, because they have successfully assumed those attitudes many times before. These beliefs enable them to make sense of their reality. In the words of Anselm of Canterbury around AD 1100: I believe in order to understand ('credo ut intelligam', in Störig, 1971, p. 230).

This relation between assumptions and attitudes or postures is important because people took most of their attitudes, without knowing it, from the ones to whom they were exposed, especially during their first two years. Imitating and simulating attitudes are an automatic process, ontogenetically older than speech, which is a normal and necessary part of paying attention to another person (e.g. Davis, 1982; Gibson, 1979; Schabracq, 1987, 1991). This is probably an outcome of the activity of 'mirror neurons', nerve cells that at the same time are involved in the perception of other persons' movements and controlling one's own movements. Experiences are less separated from actions than Descartes taught us. My experiences are embodied.

Since their earliest childhood, imitating posture and movement helped people to take part in the world of the others, a world they progressively came to share in this way. Gradually, they mastered it, from within. While this started out without any sense of meaning and without words, meanings and words developed slowly within the reality made up of mutual postures, in close cooperation with the ones who felt responsible for them. After their second birthday, people usually exchange full-blown imitation for subliminal simulation, without the actual muscular activity inherent in actual posture and movements.

As their posture reflects the reality that they believe to be the case, this posture embodies a proposal to the others present how they want to see that reality and how they, based on that, want to relate to them. The proposal is about the definition of the situation: what is going on and what is in it for all involved. This activates shared formats about who is going to do what, the division of power, the emotional tone of the relation, and the degree of involvement. In short, attitude serves as an effective relation proposal. This effectiveness has several reasons.

First, by assuming an attitude or posture, all other possible attitudes are off. One's attitude and its inherent assumptions now have tacitly become part of the reality of all involved. Assuming a complementary attitude is the habitual thing to do for the others, at least as long as the proposal doesn't go against the others' wishes and interests and falls within the limits of normality. So assumptions operate as a self-fulfilling prophecy: by assuming that they are true, they actually become true.

Another point is that an appropriate relation proposal is not an individual but a cultural phenomenon. By showing an appropriate attitude, one acts as if a certain culturally determined play, an utterly familiar situation, is the case. One does so by submitting to the situational rules. This play provides situated roles for everybody involved. The results feel so real and self-evident that the others are inclined to go along without a thought. They have been here numberless times and it gave them what they came for, namely the outcomes of the situations.

Moreover, simulating others' attitudes and drumming up shared situations are more or less automatic activities. As a result, the other persons experience the situational assumptions inherent in my attitude as coming from themselves, and not as coming from me.

All in all, person and culture coincide in attitudes. Personal behaviour can be described as a string of attitudes through time, in which each attitude is reinforced by the gains from the plays or situations of which these attitudes are part. At the same time, our culture can be regarded as the whole of the standardized configurations of these attitudes in definite plays or situations, which each offer a solution for an ever-recurring problem.

As these plays are governed by ethical principles as well, displaying our attitudes is an ethical matter also. It is no coincidence that the Greek term 'ethos' (ηθος) means 'habit' or 'usual place to be', such as it still is used in 'ethology', the study of animal behaviour. This ethical component gives an adequate attitude a definite moral glow, which can make it to the others involved even more irresistible to display a complementary attitude.

When a refined or new attitude develops, it can spread quickly to the degree that it contributes to better solutions, making the solutions used up to then obsolete. This can be described as an evolutionary process. Here, attitudes serve as units of – or even vehicles for – the transfer of personal and cultural information. Considering the ease of imitating and simulating attitudes and how their use is reinforced in situations, they act as Dawkins's (1976) 'memes', a kind of non-hereditary genes which shape cultures, as well as personalities. As transferable units of our identities and culture, our attitudes succeed each other in periodical ways, attuned in standardized ways to others' attitudes, making up what can be called a 'periodic system of attitudes'.

ATTITUDE AND LEADERSHIP

What is said about attitude in the previous section has important implications for leadership. The contagiousness of attitudes enables leaders to act as strong role models, the more so as people attend more to leaders then vice versa, a pattern we share with other primate species (Chance and Larsen, 1976). This exposes them to their leaders' attitudes, and to simulating or imitating these attitudes. As such, leaders' attitudes are a powerful instrument for influencing their followers' motivation and behaviour. The other way around, a leader who displays inadequate attitudes can have a devastating effect on employees' motivation. So leaders should be aware of their modelling function. They should walk their talk, strongly and perceivably.

In an exaggerated form, this pattern occurs in the Stockholm syndrome: the phenomenon that hostages take over the attitudes and opinions of the ones who hold them hostage, without being aware of it. Anna Freud (1964) described this as a defence mechanism, calling it 'identification with the aggressor'. The same occurs in small children who walk and behave exactly like their same-sex parent. In this respect, one should realize that small children are completely dependent upon their parents as well.

In order to be maximally effective in this respect, an attitude should be energetic and show clear intent. High energy makes attitudes more vivid (Nisbett and Ross, 1980) and salient (Taylor and Fiske, 1978) – that is, more likely to attract attention – because it appeals more strongly to the observer's emotions (James, 1890/1950). The most distinguishing characteristic of Mao Zedong, for instance, appears to have been his unbridled energy (Spence, 2000). Clear intent refers to being undivided in one's attitude, that is not showing mixed objectives or restraining oneself too much. It also means displaying a clear focus and purpose, being determined, certain and optimistic. Unclear or mixed intent has a self-disqualifying effect: don't look at me, I don't know either. Clear intent is perceived also as a sign of sincerity and authenticity (Heidegger, 1962; May, 1969), of being the same on and off the job (Bennis and Thomas, 2002).

Being authentic is foremost a matter of knowing and being convinced of your own suppositions and goals. Gandhi, for example, put in a lot of effort and reflection to be as clear and undivided as possible (Nair, 1998).

Essentially, this is a special case of a more general pattern: the leader as a hero (Campbell, 1988; Smit, 1997). Heroes enter the stage when things are not good. An exemplary hero usually retreats from society to a secluded place for some time, where he doesn't need his intellect for everyday concerns. Some – Jesus, Moses, Muhammad – preferred deserts. Ignatius of Loyola chose a grotto. A prison-like environment, such as in the cases of Sadat, Lenin, and Mandela, and even a desolate garret – Hitler – can do the trick as well (Schabracq, 2003a). In such an environment, the hero has the room to face the painful difference between how it

217

is and how it ought to be. His hero-like capacities manifest themselves foremost in his enduring this discrepancy and all its inherent aversive feelings, as long as needed. To this end, he descends to the level of the assumptions. Here he slays his dragon and finds the seeds of the new approach, which takes him up to visionary heights, where the new vision can fully unfold. Most of the time, this vision is a vigorous new recombination of well-known elements, which turn out not to be completely obsolete after all. Lastly he steps down again to the world of everyday life, with the blueprint of a new approach to overcome the discrepancy under his arm. Once returned to his society, the hero tries to implement this vision there. Though this sounds as a purely individual affair, it doesn't need to be. As the stories about the Argonauts and the Trojan War demonstrate, heroes can band together. A group, a management team for example, can do the same thing also.

When a leader knows his modelling power, he can use his attitude deliberately to propose to his people what he wants them to do. This implies that he must pay special attention to his own attitudes. The first step here may consist of looking into the mirror and inspecting his habitual attitudes. What relation proposals do they imply? Do they communicate what he wants them to communicate? By carefully modifying one's habitual attitudes and experimenting with them, it is possible to be more in control over one's attitudes, i.e. to display the attitudes that one wants to display. This enables one to take more responsibility for one's attitudes and to be more precise and effective in what one wants to get across. The main guideline here is to be honest with oneself.

Some leaders exaggerate their attitudes, make them bigger than life, and support them with elaborate gesturing, in order to make them more salient. Infamous examples are Mussolini and Hitler, as caricatured by Charlie Chaplin in *The Great Dictator*. Hitler also put up a display of near frenzy when addressing big crowds. A modern variant can be seen in the performances of pop stars, though spreading frenzy there appears to be more of an objective in itself.

Energy and clear intent are part of charismatic leadership, energizing and steering followers in an immediate way. In an organization, this implies a direct confrontation with the organization members. Charismatic leadership then represents the classical, frontal approach of leadership. This approach is characterized by much repetition: displaying the positions one wants to display time after time in all relevant situations. It also involves advertising a strong moral stance: I act as I do, because this is the best way to act. However, what is the best way to act? This is about the line of action that maximally furthers the *raison d'être* of the organization in a morally sound way, its mission.

An important instrument here is a convincing story (Postman, 1999), preferably one with catchy metaphors, acting as a self-fulfilling reality and indicating action guidelines. So, a good leader is a more than averagely successful storyteller, casting himself as a protagonist. A good mission must also apply to the longer term and picture a destiny worth taking risks for. When embedded in history too, it gets a sense of logic and self-evidence. Furthermore, it usually provides a visual component – such as the word 'vision' already implies – as well as a feeling of adventure and challenge. Moreover, its success is partly a function of its novelty, triggering curiosity and creativity. A good mission lastly leaves enough room for personal interpretation, adaptation, and transformation; is flexible enough to be applicable in a changing environment; and allows for a choice to take or leave it.

Essentially, championing a mission is an incremental approach, a serial, remedial, and fragmented process that takes much effort and stamina. The implementation of a mission is discussed on pp. 222–3. In everyday practice this keeping on pushing boils down to the following rules of thumb.

Being aware of yourself

■ Be yourself and be aware of your modelling role; know what optimism, trust, decisiveness, passion and hope, as well as despair, indifference, reticence and reluctance can do. Just be there and learn to deal with the limitations for your personal freedom.

■ Put your credibility at stake, stay personally involved, and try to remain consistent and honest: do not ever lie (Hammer, 2001)!

■ Don't block experience and be aware of this: try to experience everything that is relevant and don't suppress intuitions and hunches (Schabracq and Cooper, 2003).

■ Explore your feelings and reflect regularly. Overcome your apathy to do so. Learn to know your suppositions (Schabracq, 2003a).

■ Try to identify the causes of your moods. Cope with your frustration, anger, uncertainties, and your need to be liked (Schabracq and Cooper, 2001). Deal with ascribed stardom. Don't strive against all cost for popularity and harmony. Know that you can't always be sure or invulnerable (Lencioni, 1999).

■ Deal with your own stress. Apart from regular reflection, planning, and establishing priorities, this involves actual coping with your stressors and the suppositions underlying your stress reactions. In addition, this is about taking enough pauses, practising a healthier lifestyle, organizing your social support, and establishing a good work–life balance involving enough leisure time and holidays. Lastly, it takes some thought-stopping and assertiveness skills and being able to bring about 'thinking of nothing special', such as by breathing, relaxation, meditation, or running (Schabracq and Cooper, 2001).

Being aware of what is happening and steering

■ Prepare things. Know where you want to go, go for it in a wholehearted and undivided way; and if you are successful, know what you want to do next.

Know also what the others want to do, why they want to do that, and who will support them (Sun Tzu, 1993).

- Don't change too much at a time. See to it that all change can be labelled by one concept (Hammer 2001).
- Don't do the work of your employees, not even when they do it badly. Just provide clear direction.
- Stress the common interests. Speak in terms of 'we'.
- Define your goals in clear and positive, but general and generic terms. Stress their importance by showing a vista of what would happen if these are not accomplished, time after time. Create a sense of urgency.
- Build awareness about the mission in the organization by advocacy, as well as by questioning, challenging, and probing (Senge *et al.*, 1994).
- Make what you do a symbol of the mission and let the mission be an explicit guideline and touchstone in your decision-making, as well as in the selection of new personnel.
- Support and reward as explicitly as possible what adds to the mission and make that legitimate.
- Give protagonists enough room and authority, and – if appropriate – put them in key positions.
- Initiate model projects in order to further the mission.
- Don't attack resistance. Ask people who resist what they want and how that can be accomplished.
- Acknowledge that accomplishing the mission is no linear process and that different approaches are feasible: let people find out themselves what the mission implies for them and make enough room to discuss this in work progress meetings.
- Celebrate and feed success, starve failure. Acknowledge industry and toil, show sympathy and give tokens of appreciation. Generate a short-term success. Consolidate success by anchoring it in the organizational culture (Kotter, 2001).
- Take ample time to reflect on how you are doing and how you can improve things. Take from time to time a longer period to think things over.
- Learn from your errors.

Essentially this is all about the direct approach, following what seems to be the shortest way. It is for example in line with the list of leaders' characteristics from the 'Field Manual of the US Army'.[1] However, as Sun Tzu teaches us, the shortest way is not always the best one, and not even the quickest one either, even though direct approaches may be an indispensable element of the overall strategy (McNeilly, 2001). What is meant here is that a frontal approach organizes the attitudes of the people you are confronting: they imitate it or subliminally simulate it, and tend to act accordingly. When this is done successfully, this leaves them exposed to the more indirect approaches that are examined in the next sections. A combination of direct and indirect approaches then is the most likely route to overcoming resistance and preventing conflicts and damage (McNeilly, 2001).

PARSONS' FUNCTIONAL APPROACH

Parsons, a founding father of sociology, put less emphasis on the structural aspects of organizational culture, but saw an organization more in terms of its functions, the solving of recurring problems in order to survive and flourish (Parsons, 1960; Smit, 1997). Changing organizational culture then becomes improving these solutions.

Parsons' approach does not pretend to be as objective and value-free as Schein's more structural approach seems to be. Parsons' approach implies that a leader looks at the organizational functions from the perspective of the organization, which of course is not value-free. Secondly, changing organizational culture then becomes improving how these functions are realized. As this is essentially in line with the existing culture, it probably evokes less resistance. Improving these functions is what I, following Sun Tzu, call the indirect way (McNeilly, 2001).

The approach used here is a cascade-like one. It starts at the top of the organization, to descend step by step to the lower levels. All departments and levels have to translate the different functions to their own functioning. What does it mean for us, what does it mean for me and how can we accomplish this in the best possible way for all parties involved?

A useful first step here is discussing the present state of affairs and how it has come into being. This is about the goals, plans, and aspirations that led to the present state, as well as about what has gone wrong and what factors played a part. The next step then is examining what this has meant personally for everybody involved. How did it affect their work and private life? What did they feel? Frustration, anger, grief? As an effective outlet for counterproductive feelings, this accelerates the so-called transition process, inherent in all significant change (Marris, 1974; Schabracq, 2003a). It also provides an opportunity to learn more about what actually has happened. Moreover, sharing these experiences and finding out that one is not the only one contribute to team building.

The next step consists of consulting the persons directly involved. What do they see as the causes for the present state of affairs? What can be done about these causes? What possibilities do they see to improve the function at hand? What pitfalls do they expect and what can be done in this respect? What is worthwhile to them, how can things be made better, and how can it best be implemented? Essentially, this is a probing technique to learn about their resistance, to get to its suppositions and to transform it into the motor of the change process.

221

Essentially, this is about clarifying the assumptions of the others as well as about your own ones, to come to a real dialogue (Bohm, 2004), characterized by advocating your own assumptions and inquiring about those of the others (Senge *et al.*, 1994). The underlying idea is that most assumptions in themselves strive to accomplish something good. The sought solution then is the one that reflects a joint optimization of the assumptions of everyone involved, a so-called win–win solution. In practice, such a solution often stems from formulating the different assumptions in the form of dilemmas, as sharply as possible, in order to brainstorm about syntheses at the level of everyday practice that serves both assumptions (see for instance Hampden-Turner, 1994, and Trompenaars and Hampden-Turner, 2002). From a completely different angle, Altshuller, a Russian scientist who examined tens of thousands patent applications, calls this the best way to do inventions (http://www. trizexperts. net/). Goldratt (1990), a theorist in logistics who aims at making organizations more functional, here speaks about 'evaporating clouds'. In terms of game theory, all of this is about creating interdependence and striving for non-zero solutions (Wright, 2001), solutions that benefit all players involved.

The great gain of these – so-called – indirect approaches is that they create optimal solutions as well as maximal support for these solutions, especially when it is combined with the more direct approach mentioned in the previous section. The next step then consists of the leader asking all involved to monitor how things are going, to report on everything that still goes wrong and to devise possible solutions, which can be discussed later on. A last point is that there are big opportunities here for the elderly, more experienced employees.

Parsons (1960) defined the following four categories of functions:

1 goal attainment
2 adaptation
3 integration
4 latency and pattern maintenance.

These four categories of functions are the focal points on which the leader's efforts to bring about culture change are concentrated. In the next sections, each of these categories is examined separately.

GOAL ATTAINMENT

An organization must have a valid reason for being there. This reason must have importance and meaning inside as well as outside the organization. The organization must integrate the goals of its members with needs that exist in its environment in a non zero-sum way (Wright, 2001), i.e. in a way that benefits all parties involved: it must have a mission (see pp. 224–6). This involves a 'vision', a picture of an ideal future to be realized within a certain time span. Mission and vision give the organization its purpose and direction: an organization must have definite goals. If not, they are in trouble. Losing goals affects vitality, just as it does in individuals. Goals connect an organization with outer reality and a possible future. They give meaning to its existence. As such, goals are an crucial condition for staying alive, and this essentially is a matter of taking responsibility (Frankl, 1978), not only for individuals but for organizations as well, put in Frankl's own words: goals are not only a matter of what we expect from life, but what life expects of us. Absence of clear goals implies sterility, its essence being uselessness, described by May (1969) as living in the land of the dead. As goals imply a beginning and an end, as well as a perimeter and a middle zone, they give us means to orientate ourselves in time and space. They lay out our reality at the level of assumptions and goals (see pp. 223–4), though these assumptions and goals here appear to be a little more malleable than as seen from Schein's perspective. So, this section is about sharing – and adjusting – goals.

On pp. 219–22, mission was mentioned as the outcome of a hero's journey. However, this is not necessarily so. Not all leaders are heroes. Put more strongly, hero-leaders are relatively rare, most missions are handed down by previous leaders, and many, if not most organizations have only a vague idea why they exist and what they want to accomplish.

In this section, mission is treated as something given, which may need improvement and maintenance, and must be shared by all members. This sharing is here explicitly treated as a group accomplishment. So, this section is about making the mission more articulate, developing and maintaining it, and customizing it to the different levels and departments so that all involved can influence its final form.

On the one hand, the mission is about what the organization wants to accomplish for the outer world, such as manufacturing certain products or rendering certain services. This is about providing something that the environment needs. These needs must be so essential that their fulfilment justifies the organization's existence. What problems does your organization help to solve? What improvements does it bring about? How can it do that more effectively and efficiently? In short, how can your organization offer your customers the greatest possible surplus value? In practice, this can amount to doing what you do best and cooperating with other organizations, which perform best in the other links of a chain delivering the greatest surplus value to the end customer in the shortest time and at the lowest price (Hammer, 2001).

On the other hand, mission is concerned with the inner world of the organization. A good mission must make sense of and give meaning to what the employees are doing too. To that end, the work must be sufficiently attuned to what they are best at and want to do. Ideally, the mission also helps them to develop themselves, leading them to a promising future, on a journey of adventure and discovery, without jeopardizing their safety and well-being, making their work a self-evident and logical line of action. This leads to questions such as: does the work offer them sufficient meaning, challenge, opportunities for development and pleasure; can they live from it as they like it?

Essentially, this implies that organizations concentrate on core competencies, which give them potential access to a broad variety of markets, contributing to what clients want in a way that is difficult to copy by the competition (Prahalad and Hamel, 1990)

All in all, the goal-directedness of your organization is a matter of the degree to which it succeeds in doing something that is attractive and self-evident to all parties involved. This implies, of course, that those goals have to be in line with the law and the usual ethical norms also. All of this leaves leaders with the following rules of thumb:

- Try to define together core competencies and let your people devise the best possible products stemming from that. Let them try to innovate, create and develop.
- Learn about the needs of potential clients that your product may fulfil, try to see the world through your client's eyes and make this the guideline for forming new alliances. Find out how you can improve the added value of your product for them in terms of quality, delivery time, price, and service (Hammer, 2001).
- Don't neglect the longer term.
- Determine how all of this contributes to the actualizations of the needs and goals of your employees, as well as how this can be improved.
- Encourage the development of your people, not only by training and formal education, but also by learning from experimenting and taking risks. Point out the necessity of errors and make them into learning experiences.
- Determine how all of this contributes to the actualizations of your own needs and goals, as well as how this can be improved.

ADAPTATION

Logically speaking, every organization has an environment. Adaptation refers to the success of how an organization interlocks with that environment. This environment is not so much a matter of the physical surroundings as of the members of the surrounding culture. Adaptation then is about how the organization succeeds in attuning to the situations in which its employees can interact with the different stakeholders to reach mutual goals. This is not only about clients, but also about suppliers, neighbours, fellow organizations in the trade, including the competition, and the government and its rules. This also should be a non zero-sum game

(Wright, 2001), though now at the levels of rules and forms (see pp. 220–1). In principle, the environment can provide the organization with everything it needs to survive and flourish, such as a location, safety, energy, and raw materials, while it also can provide the money to pay expenses, make a profit, and grow.

To that end, an organization must become to all stakeholders an attractive, easily accessible, inexpensive, and self-evident partner to interact with. This also means earning trust, respect, and prestige, as well as guarding these earnings. To this end, you first need to know your stakeholders. What do they need? What do they want to know from you? Relations with suppliers for instance can focus on quality, work flow, and delivery time. Partnership means building stable relationships with each of these parties, resulting in mutual trust and loyalty (Reichheld, 1996). Consciously managing the contacts with these partners and making your people thoroughly aware of their relevance then become important leadership tasks.

As organizational environments have become more turbulent and variable (Schabracq and Cooper, 2000), adaptation has increasingly become adaptation to change. This involves creating an early warning system for change, involving all employees, but especially the ones in the frontline. Make detectives or journalists out of your employees. Let them develop a deep insight into your stakeholders, especially your 'end clients', as they are paying for everything. Let them dig up information about what your stakeholders find new, interesting, and exciting, about the changes they want and foresee, as well as about what they think your organization can do best in this respect. Specify to your employees what you want to know. The next steps then are bringing the information together, categorizing and analysing it, interpreting it so that it can be used to act on, and seeing to it that it is used. Monitoring and operating this system should be a well-managed process (Hammer, 2001; Sun Tzu, 1993). Responding to change can also imply that your organization itself has to change in a more or less radical way. This will be dealt with in the next section.

Adaptation can also consist of making accounting a joint operation with your customers, such as banks do with their cash machines and banking by internet. Another form is collaboration with other companies in different trades, for example by sharing distribution channels, shops, and storage facilities. Still another form is integrating yourself in the product development and production processes of your suppliers, distributors, and clients, for instance by seconding your own employees to the other company (Hammer, 2001; Schabracq, 2003c).

Adaptation can also be a matter of joining forces in one production chain with other organizations. Each organization then may take care of that part of the production chain at which it is best. This would enable you to serve the end customer in the best, cheapest, and quickest possible way. This should become a well-managed process, not overly liable to coincidences and independent of much improvisation and extraordinary performances, a process also from which all double work, for instance in accounting, is removed (Hammer, 2001).

Another issue in adaptation is how to deal with competition. Apart from competing with them, you can use them as a source of information. For example, ask your customers about their strong and weak points (Hammer, 2001). When there are mutual interests, cooperation and alliance, temporal or permanent, are definite possibilities. Often, this demands adjusting your suppositions. Examples are the possibility of complementing each other and sharing facilities, increasing market share in this way, as well as preventing a third party from becoming too powerful. Sometimes, this may just be a matter of disrupting or preventing another alliance that threatens your survival (McNeilly, 2001). Lastly, the competition is always an incitement to do better.

All of this leads to the following rules of thumb:

- Know your stakeholders.
- Make your organization a self-evident, respected, and reliable partner for all stakeholders. Make it pleasurable, easy, and inexpensive to do business with your organization. Determine what you can do for your stakeholders as well as what they can do for you in this respect (Hammer, 2001).
- Determine how you can better attune your information system and production process to the needs of your stakeholders.
- Try to have a broader scope.
- Monitor and respond to relevant change.

INTEGRATION

Integration refers to the coordination of all activities of the departments and individual employees within the organization, in order to accomplish goal-directedness and adaptation to the environment. The need for integration stems from the specialization inherent in organization development, leading to role differentiation. Integration is then about staying aware of the interconnectedness of all contributions, in order to serve the customers optimally, in such a way also that the employees can work effectively and pleasantly and changes can be implemented smoothly.

Integration essentially means acting as one organism, a whole that has more to offer than the sum of its separate parts. An organization that does not create such synergy usually has no reason to exist. Again, this is about a non zero-sum game (Wright, 2001), at the levels of rules and forms, this time within the organization. This implies that everybody involved must understand the overall goals and organization as well as their own contributions. So it is a leader's task to keep on emphasizing this interconnectedness. The main concern here is preventing dividedness and fruitless conflicts stemming from pursuing departmental and individual interests. Another issue here consists of clarifying and adjusting expectations between departments, as well as between individuals, aiming at a smooth workflow and a pleasurable work climate, in which all involved, if needed, will help and support each other.

Integration also involves implementing organizational change. Though organizational change generally is difficult and often leads to much stress, it is possible to build up skill in this respect: people can learn to cope with change. First, people can learn to consciously confront the losses inherent in the transition, instead of avoiding them. The intended result here is that they come out of this stronger for now and better prepared for new changes in the longer term (Schabracq, 2003a). Second, dealing with change is made easier and more rewarding when the employees are given real influence in shaping the change and get more time, information and attention (Schabracq et al., 2001). Third, people can learn to bring about change in a more standardized way. This implies distinguishing its consecutive stages and learning to pay attention to what is important in each stage (Schabracq, 2003b). This may involve digging up your underlying assumptions and those of the other persons involved. This can help to come to a real dialogue resulting in a new, more productive reality, based on less limiting and more suitable assumptions (Bohm, 2004; Senge et al., 1994). A fourth approach is developing different scenarios (de Geus, 1997) and business games (McNeilly, 2001) to learn about goals and suppositions by role-playing, trying out different strategies. Lastly, it is important to realize that one should not change things just for the sake of changing: change should only be implemented when it is really needed (Schabracq, Cooper, and Winnubst, 2003).

In order to realize integration, the following rules of thumb are important:

■ Pay sufficient attention to what goes on in the organization and don't be focused exclusively on the outer world. See to it that you get all information you need. Ask everybody involved questions, explain the necessity of that information, make people responsible for sharing relevant information with you, and make it a two-way process. Sometimes, however, it may be better to appoint an extra manager with sufficient mandate to this task, resulting in a form of leadership called co-management (Schabracq, 2005a).

■ If possible, try to establish team leadership, leadership as a team task, so that different issues can be dealt with by the specialist within the team. Such an approach demands following a kind of 'constitution' for collective decision-making, focusing on the interests of the whole organization and the customer (Schabracq, 2005b).

■ See to it that people find out how to collaborate and communicate, and emphasize the greater good of the goal. Show approval for good collaboration and communication.

■ Improve coordination between departments and organize around end-to-end processes. For example, improve coordination between independent strategic business units. Try to present one face to the external client, as well as shared service centres, and standardized approaches (Hammer, 2001).

- Don't throw work over the fence. See to it that departments and individuals communicate about expected work-flow effectively and habitually. Solve inter-group communication problems and confront stereotypes and prejudices.

- Solve constraints in the end-to-end process, focusing each time on the main constraint (Goldratt, 1990), such as bottlenecks in equipment, information, or personnel.

- Pay sufficient attention to the implementation of organizational change. Give the employees sufficient time to change and keep them well-informed.

LATENCY AND PATTERN MAINTENANCE

Latency refers to the joint realization of the previous three functions in a self-evident everyday reality. As most of these problems stem from permanent or recurrent causes, they tend to be solved in non-problematic, habitual ways. This is a characteristic of all cultures: providing recurrent solutions for recurrent problems. People continuously re-enact, re-construct, re-cognize, re-present and re-cite the forms and meanings of culture, and abstain from other possibilities (Moscovici, 1984). People even re-create themselves. Much of this repetitious character stays out of awareness. It submerges in everyday, self-evident ways of doing things. Though essentially a never-ending form of hard labour, a real Sisyphus labour, people just do it, do not pay attention to other possibilities, and ignore that they do not pay attention. So they create a reality that provides stability and continuity, as well as normality and perceived safety. As far as this takes effect, one can lose oneself in one's work without being unnecessarily distracted and disturbed, blissfully ignoring all the effort involved, while everybody knows what he must do, what he must attend to, and whom he must involve in it.

To the degree that this latency function is not realized, the functionality of the organization is diminished, and stress and alienation ensue. Of course, stress and alienation are undesirable, but they also serve an important signal function: they clearly indicate that something is definitely wrong.

Latency and pattern maintenance can be divided into four domains: the work itself, its physical environment and conditions, its social embedding, and the fit between the values and goals of individual employees and those of the organization. In each of these domains, disturbances can arise that can be described as a 'too much' or 'too little' of what in itself is a good thing. These disturbances result in a situation in which the individual must do something that he cannot do and/or doesn't want to do, which results in a loss of control, as well as stress and alienation (Schabracq, 2003a).

Guarding the latency function in an organization usually is a full-time job. Still many managers are more focused on the external world than on the internal organization affairs (see pp. 226–8). As it is, managers are seldom selected or rewarded for minding what goes on within the organization, while their ambitions are also usually focused elsewhere. Appointing a co-manager, who is responsible for the internal affairs, as mentioned in the previous section, can be the solution for guarding the latency function as well (Schabracq, 1995a).

In order to realize latency and pattern maintenance, the following rules of thumb can be followed:

- See to it that jobs are challenging but workable.
- See to it that the physical layout of workplaces enables employees to work effectively and efficiently.
- Try to create a climate of trust and pleasant contacts, which allows employees to belong, prove themselves, and establish rewarding relations, without being disturbing or too overwhelming.
- Take care that the organization's values and goals don't deviate too much from the personal ones. See to it also that they are in a position to guard their own limits.
- Periodically assess things by observation and questioning, as well as by surveying variables such as work satisfaction, work stress, alienation, and commitment with the help of (online) questionnaires, such as ASSET (Faragher, Cooper, and Cartwright, 2004). Recognize stress risks as early as possible. Use stress-reactions and alienation (apathy, indifference) as signals. Be alert to phenomena such as harassment, scapegoating, and stereotyping too. Break the taboo on talking about these phenomena and talk about them with your employees at an early stage. Know when to refer to or call in a specialist.
- Ask about problems, their causes, and their possible solutions. See to it that people take responsibility for reporting problems and thinking about solutions, even when this does not seem to be their first responsibility. Gather enough knowledge about the department's or team's past (from different sources!) and the problems that occurred in it. Find out who the opinion leaders are.
- Engage in sessions to improve things. Really put problems on the agenda and discuss these in a constructive, problem-solving way in work progress meetings and in individual talks with the people with whom one has difficulties.
- Inform employees as early as possible in face-to-face interactions, about impending radical changes. Let them have an active say in the ultimate design of the change. Be alert to emotions evoked by change. Give bad news in such a way that you are there to deal with the emotions evoked.
- Know what to do in case of crisis and traumatic events (hold-ups, accidents, lay-off, etc.). Give extra time and attention to employees who have experienced traumatic events, especially to let them talk about it.

229

- Keep in touch with ill employees, preparing their return to the department or team; and invest extra time and attention in them after their return.
- In times of reorganization and merger, discuss things periodically during work progress meetings. Ask explicitly about rumours during meetings and comment on these as openly as possible to prevent needless worry.
- Assist and protect your employees and offer emotional support, if needed.
- Serve as a coach, who gives employees the room they need to function properly and really listens to them, also when this concerns critique of you. Apart from creating the proper conditions, this implies stimulation of self-steering and giving advice if necessary.
- Interview employees regularly about their individual functioning and career, and, if needed, offer training, coaching, or mentoring.
- Show approval for good performances and taking responsibility.

CONCLUSION

To the degree that the approach sketched above is successful, it will positively influence the corporate results. This leads to shareholder satisfaction and a satisfied management that reinforces the employees to go on in this way. This can evoke a positive spiral, the so-called 'loyalty effect' (Reichheld, 1996), a phenomenon characteristic of successful companies. Similar patterns are described by Rosenbluth and McFerrin Peters (1992) and de Geus (1997). Though all this may sound overly optimistic, such a positive spiral is a well-documented phenomenon, even though many of us may work in organizations where such a spiral is not very prominent.

All in all, there are big gains to be made when management pays more attention to the organizational culture, even when that involves appointing a separate co-manager.

NOTE

1 Integrity, will, flexibility, endurance, coolness under stress, justice, assertiveness, sense of humour, bearing, tact, maturity, self-discipline, confidence, decisiveness and initiative (McNeilly, 2001).

REFERENCES

Bennis, W. G. and Thomas, R. J. (2002) *Geeks and geezers. How era, values and defining moment shape leaders*. Boston, MA: Harvard Business School.

Bohm, D. (2004) *On dialogue*. London/New York: Routledge Classics.

Campbell, J. (1988) *The power of myth*. New York: Doubleday.

Chance, M. R. A. and Larsen, R. R. (eds) (1976) *The social structure of attention.* London: Wiley.

Davis, M. (ed.) (1982) *Interaction rhythms.* New York: Human Sciences Press.

Dawkins, R. (1976) *The selfish gene.* Oxford: Oxford University Press.

Deese, J. (1952) *The psychology of learning.* New York: MacGraw-Hill.

Faragher, E. B., Cooper, C. L., and Cartwright, S. (2004) A shortened stress evaluation tool (ASSET). *Stress and Health,* 20: 189–201.

Frankl, V. E. (1978) *De zin van het bestaan* (Man's search for meaning). Rotterdam: A. Donker.

Freud, A. (1964) *Das Ich und die Abwehrmechanismen* (The I and the defence mechanisms). München: Kindler Verlag.

Garfinkel, H. (1967) *Studies in ethnomethodology.* Englewood Cliffs, NJ: Prentice-Hall.

Geus, A. de (1997) *The living company.* New York: Longview.

Gibson, J. J. (1979) *The ecological approach of visual perception.* Boston, MA: Houghton Mifflin.

Goldratt, E. (1990) *What is this thing called theory of constraints and how should it be implemented?* Croton on Hudson, NY: North River Press.

Hammer, M. (2001) *The agenda.* New York: Crown Business.

Hampden-Turner, C. (1994) *Corporate culture.* London: Piatkus.

Heidegger, M. (1962) *Being and time* (translated by J. Macquarrie and E. Robinson). New York: Harper & Row.

James, W. (1890/1950) *The principles of psychology, part II.* New York: Dover.

John Kotter, J. (2001) *Leiderschap bij verandering* (Leadership at change). Amsterdam: Academic Service.

Lencioni, P. (1999) *De vijf verleidingen voor topmanagers.* (The five temptations of top leaders). Amsterdam: Contact.

Marris, P. (1974) *Loss and change.* New York: Pantheon.

Maturana, H. R. and Varela, F. J. (1980) *Autopoiesis and cognition.* Dordrecht, Holland: D. Reidel.

May, R. (1969) *Love and will.* New York: Norton.

McNeilly, M. (2001) *Sun Tzu and the art of modern warfare.* Oxford: Oxford University Press.

Moscovici, S. (1984) The phenomenon of social representation. In R. M. Farr and S. Moscovici (eds) *Social representations.* Cambridge: Cambridge University Press, pp. 3–69.

Nair, K. (1998) *Waarde[n]vol leiderschap* (Valuable leadership). Schiedam: Scriptum.

Nisbett, R. E. and Ross, L. (1980). *Human inference.* Englewood Cliffs, NJ: Prentice-Hall.

Parsons, T. (1960) *Structure and process in modern societies.* Glencoe, IL: Free Press.

Postman, N. (1999) *Building a bridge to the eighteenth century: How the past can influence the future*. New York: Vintage.

Prahalad, C. K. and Hamel, G. (1990) The competence of the organization. *Harvard Business Review*, 68(3): 79–91.

Reichheld, F. F. (1996) *The loyalty effect*. Boston, MA: Harvard Business School Press.

Rosenbluth, H. F. and McFerrin Peters, D. (1992) *The customer comes second*. New York: W. Morrow and Co.

Schabracq, M. J. (1987) Betrokkenheid en onderlinge gelijkheid in sociale interacties (Involvement and mutual similarity in social interactions. Dissertation. Amsterdam: University of Amsterdam.

Schabracq, M. J. (1991) *De inrichting van de werkelijkheid*. (The design of reality). Amsterdam/Meppel: Boom.

Schabracq, M. J. (2003a) *De droomfabriek* (The dream factory). Utrecht: Kosmos.

Schabracq, M. J. (2003b) Organisational culture, stress and change. In M. J. Schabracq, J. A. M. Winnubst, and C. L. Cooper (eds) *The handbook of work and health psychology* (2nd edn) Chichester: Wiley, pp. 37–62.

Schabracq, M. J. (2003c) What an organisation can do about its employees' well-being and health: An overview. In M. J. Schabracq, J. A. M. Winnubst, and C. L. Cooper (eds) *The handbook of work and health psychology* (2nd edn) Chichester: Wiley, pp. 585–600.

Schabracq, M. J. (2005a) Well-being and health: What HRM can do about it. In R. J. Burke and C. L. Cooper (eds) *Reinventing HRM. Challenges and new directions*. London and New York: Routledge, pp. 187–206.

Schabracq, M. J. (2005b) Stress, alienation and shared leadership. In A.-S. G. Antoniou and C. L. Cooper (eds) *Research companion to organizational health psychology*. Cheltenham, UK/Northampton, MA: Edward Elgar, pp. 122–31.

Schabracq, M. J. and Cooper, C. L. (2000) The changing nature of work and stress. *Journal of Management Psychology*, 15: 227–41.

Schabracq, M. J. and Cooper C. L. (2001). *Stress als keuze* (Stress as a choice). Schiedam: Scriptum.

Schabracq, M. J. and Cooper C. L. (2003) To be me or not to be me. About alienation. *Counselling Psychology Quarterly*, 16: 53–79.

Schabracq, M. J., Cooper, C. L., and Winnubst, J. A. M. (2003). Epilogue. In M. J. Schabracq, J. A. M. Winnubst, and C. L. Cooper (eds) *The handbook of work and health psychology* (2nd edn) Chichester: Wiley, pp. 601–4.

Schabracq, M. J., Cooper, C. L., Travers, C., and Van Maanen, D. (2001). *Occupational health psychology: The challenge of stress*. Leicester: British Psychological Society.

Schein, E. H. (1985) *Organizational culture and leadership*. San Francisco, CA: Jossey-Bass

Senge, P. M., Kleiner, A., Roberts, C., Ross, R. B., and Smith, B. J. (1994) *The fifth discipline fieldbook*. London: N. Brealey.

Smit, I. (1997) Patterns of coping. Dissertation. Utrecht: Universiteit van Utrecht.

Spence, J. (2000) *Mao*. Amsterdam: Balans.

Störig, H. J. (1971) *Geschiedenis van de filosofie I* (History of philosophy I). Utrecht: Het Spectrum.

Sun Tzu (1993) *The art of war*. Ware: Wordsworth Reference.

Taylor, S. E. and Fiske, S. T. (1978) Salience, attention and attribution. In: L. Berkowitz (ed.) *Advances in experimental social psychology*. Vol 11. London/New York: Academic Press, pp. 250–88.

Trompenaars, F. and Hampden-Turner, C. (2002) *21 leaders for the 21st century*. New York: McGraw-Hill.

Wright, R. (2001) *Nonzero. History, evolution and human cooperation*. London: Abacus.

Part IV

Flawed leaders

Chapter 12

Why leaders fail

Exploring the dark side*

Ronald J. Burke

Perhaps the single most important indicator of potential executive failure is the one that is hardest to precisely define – the question of character. A person who has high ethical standards and deep competence, who desires to succeed by helping others to be better than they would otherwise be on their own, who can face reality even when it's unpleasant and acknowledge when something is wrong, and who engenders trust and promotes honesty in the organizations they create and lead.

(Finkelstein, 2003, p. 263)

Leadership has been a heavily researched topic for over 50 years. As a result, over 15,000 articles and books have been published on this topic. We know a lot about the characteristics of successful leaders. And based on this knowledge, organizations spend an estimated $50 billion a year on the development of leaders.

In spite of this knowledge and investment, most organizations feel they have a shortage of effective leaders. It has been estimated that between 50 and 75 per cent of leaders are not performing well (Hogan and Hogan, 2001). The number of leaders that get fired for failing to perform has increased over the past decade and the tenure of organizational leaders has steadily dropped (Hogan, 1999).

Why have we not done better in understanding leader performance and in developing effective leaders (Lipman-Blumen, 2001)? Kellerman (2004) believes that there has been a positive bias in leadership research and writing. The early writing and research on leadership was carried out in the United States, a country that holds optimism, progress, and growth as core values. Writers use a language

* Preparation of this manuscript was supported in part by the Schulich School of Business, York University. I thank Lisa Fiksenbaum for help with the literature review.

that equates a leader with a good leader. The United States also had a need to improve business performance to hold off competitors from other countries; this was more likely to occur if they developed good leaders. This spawned a huge leadership industry based on the assumption the leadership was a skill that could be taught and good leaders produced as a result.

This paper suggests that taking a more accurate view of leadership given the prevalence of bad leadership, might contribute to our understanding of both leadership effectiveness and the development of leaders (Charan and Colvin, 1999). One can learn as much from leadership successes as from leadership failures – the dark side of leadership (Clements and Washbush, 1999). But continuing to ignore the dark side will lead to an incomplete understanding of leadership; it is confusing, misleading, and limiting to development of good leaders (Hogan, Raskin, and Fazzini, 1990).

Leadership failure has typically been considered in the context of career derailment (Leslie and VanVelsor, 1996; VanVelsor and Leslie, 1995). Derailment in a leadership or executive role is defined as being involuntarily plateaued, demoted, or fired below the level of expected achievement or reaching that level but unexpectedly failing.

There are some common notions about leadership failure:

- Failing leaders were stupid and incompetent – lacking in talent. Most leaders are very intelligent and have considerable industry-specific knowledge.
- Failing leaders were caught by unforeseen events. The available evidence does not support this as a cause of leadership failure.
- Failing leaders exhibited a failure to execute.
- Failing leaders weren't trying or working hard enough.
- Failing leaders lacked leadership ability. All were able to get people to follow the course of action that was set.
- The company lacked the necessary resources. Not supported in fact.
- Failing leaders were a bunch of crooks.

These common notions however were not sufficient to understand business failures. CEOs are almost always smart, savvy, hard working, and experienced business leaders with track records of success. But CEO tenure is shortening; many talented leaders are failing.

Kellerman (2004) focuses on two basic categories of bad leadership, ineffective and unethical, identifying seven types of bad leaders that are most common. Type, here, refers to a pattern of leader and follower behaviour that is maintained over time:

1 *incompetent* – lack will or skill to create effective action or positive change;
2 *rigid* – stiff, unyielding, unable or willing to adapt to the new;

3   *intemperate* – lacking in self-control;
4   *callous* – uncaring, unkind, ignores the needs of others;
5   *corrupt* – lies, cheats, steals; places self-interst first;
6   *insular* – ignores the needs and welfare of those outside the group;
7   *evil* – does psychological or physical harm to others.

The first three types of bad leaders are incompetent; the last four types are un-ethical. Incompetent leaders are the least problematic (damaging) while evil leaders are the most problematic (damaging). One must also consider both means and ends. Ineffective leaders fail to achieve the desired results or to bring about positive changes due to the means falling short. Unethical leaders fail to distinguish between right and wrong. Ethical leaders put followers' needs before their own, exhibit private virtues (courage, temperance), and serve the interests of the common good.

Hogan and Hogan have written extensively on leadership failure. They conclude (2002), based on a review of the work of others and their own research, that when leaders fail they do so because they are unable to understand other people's perspectives. They lack socio-political intelligence. This produces an insensitivity to others that limits their abilities to get work done through others. Work colleagues do not like or do not trust (or both) the leader.

Hogan and Hogan (2002) list the following components of socio-political intelligence: accurately reading interpersonal cues, accurately communicating intended meanings, conveying trustworthiness, building and maintaining relationships with others, and being a rewarding person to work with. They present results from six studies indicating a relationship of socio-political intelligence (defined and measured in different ways) and managerial performance.

Dotlich and Cairo (2003) show that even great leaders can derail their careers by exhibiting flawed behaviours, which are often closely related to the factors that made them successful so far. Leadership failure is primarily a behavioural issue. Leaders fail because of who they are and how they act, particularly when they are under stress. They identify eleven leader behaviours that derail careers of formerly successful executives:

1   *arrogance* – you think you're right and everyone else is wrong;
2   *melodrama* – you need to be the centre of attention;
3   *volatility* – you are subject to mood swings;
4   *excessive caution* – you are afraid to make decisions;
5   *habitual distrust* – you focus on the negative;
6   *aloofness* – you are disengaged and disconnected;
7   *mischievousness* – you believe that rules are made to be broken;
8   *eccentricity* – you try to be different just for the sake of it;

239

9 *passive resistance* – what you say is not what you believe;

10 *perfectionism* – you get the little things right and the big things wrong;

11 *eagerness to please* – you try to win the popularity contest.

All leaders are vulnerable to the eleven derailment factors; these are deeply ingrained personality traits that affect their leadership style and behaviours. But identifying and managing these derailers is possible; failure can be prevented.

It is who people are – not what they know or how bright they are – that leads to success or failure, how well they work with others, and how well they understand themselves. Some effective and successful leaders have many derailers – some derailers are both strengths and weaknesses. Dotlich and Cairo (2003), based on their consulting and research data, believe that the average manager has two or three derailers. Derailers are most likely to emerge under stress. It is hard to eliminate derailers – a part of one's personality for a long time. It may take years before these derailers become a liability. A major difficulty is that these people rarely get adequate feedback to understand their own personalities.

Fulmer and Conger (2004), in their book on best practices in succession planning, list five derailers from the Bank of America's leadership competence model:

1 *Failing to deliver results*
   – fails to hold self and others accountable for results;
   – overpromises and underdelivers;
2 *Betraying trust*
   – says one thing and does another;
   – makes excuses or blames others;
   – shades, manages, withholds information to promote his/her personal or functional agenda;
3 *Resisting change*
   – has trouble with adapting to new plans, programmes, or priorities;
   – being exclusive vs inclusive;
   – fails to understand and take into account others' perspectives;
   – devalues the opinions and suggestions of others;
   – fails to engage others with different perspectives or skills than him/herself;
4 *Failing to take a stand*
   – is indecisive;
   – stays on the fence on tough issues; won't weigh in until the boss weighs in;
5 *Over leading and under managing*
   – lets details fall through the cracks;
   – Fails to get involved with the day-to-day workings of the business unit.

Executive failings include:

- overreaching strategically;
- being risk-averse;
- running roughshod over subordinates;
- being cold and aloof;
- focusing on empire building and other kinds of self-aggrandizement;
- being inordinately concerned with getting ahead;
- not distinguishing clearly enough between high and low priority items;
- pushing themselves too hard and burning out;
- pushing their people too hard and burning them out;
- being rigid or difficult to influence.

McCall and Lombardo (1983) identified the ten most common causes of leadership derailment:

1 an insensitive, abrasive, or bullying style;
2 aloofness or arrogance;
3 betrayal of personal trust;
4 self-centred ambition;
5 failure to constructively address an obvious problem;
6 micromanagement;
7 inability to select good subordinates;
8 inability to take a long-term perspective;
9 inability to adapt to a boss with a different style; and
10 overdependence on a mentor.

Bentz (1985) reported that executive level failures lacked managerial skills in one or more areas as well as a characteristic, usually a personality defect, that derailed their careers (lack of administrative skills, unable to deal with complexity, failed leadership – unable to deal with problem subordinates or build an effective team, overly emotional, lack of knowledge of the business on overriding personality deficit).

Finkelstein (2003) considers why businesses fail and breakdown and the people behind these failures. The key to business failure were the people that created, managed and led the company. Finkelstein identified seven habits of spectacularly unsuccessful people, the personal qualities of leaders, who presided over major business failures. These people obviously had a lot of admirable qualities to have reached senior leadership roles. They were highly intelligent, talented, and personable, but they took a small failure and made it into a large one.

1 They saw themselves and their companies as dominating their environments. They had an over-optimistic and overestimated view of how much control

they have over events. They thought that they and their organization were successful because of them.

2　There was no clear boundary between their personal interests and their organizational interests. The organization was an extension of themselves.

3　They thought they had all the answers. They were crisp, decisive, often fixated on being right. Such leaders had the final say on everything that their companies did. They were control freaks. They listened badly and would not accept advice or suggestions. Any dissent then was then pushed underground.

4　They eliminated anyone not 100 per cent behind them. They disliked critics intensely.

5　They were the consummate company spokespersons. They were obsessed with the company's image in the public eye.

6　They underestimated major obstacles, and increased escalation of efforts when obstacles emerged and were acknowledged. Why? Because they felt an enormous need to be right. Sometimes other staff even wanted leaders to be right. If leaders are wrong, this raised doubts in the minds of staff.

7　These leaders stubbornly clung to what worked for them in the past.

Lombardo, Ruderman, and McCauley (1988) developed a quantitative measure of eight derailment factors and had managers rate 86 successful managers and 83 managers who had derailed. These factors were: handling business complexity; directing, motivating and developing subordinates; honour (ethical behaviour, integrity, loyalty), drive for excellence; organizational savvy; composure; sensitivity; and staffing. Supervisors' ratings of the successful senior managers were significantly higher on these eight dimensions than those of managers who had derailed.

Najar, Holland, and Von Landuyt (2004), using Hogan and Hogan's (1997) Hogan Development Survey, examined the relationship of leaders dysfunctional interpersonal tendencies and multi-rater evaluations. The sample included 295 high potential senior executives from a Fortune 500 company. Raters included immediate supervisors and a composite group of peers and others familiar with the individuals job performance. Criteria included four leadership factors (business results, people, self) and eleven interpersonal factors (e.g. trusting, resilient, dependable). Four broad hypotheses were considered:

1　Characteristics associated with arrogance will be associated with lower peer ratings.

2　Characteristics associated with cautiousness will be associated with lower supervisor and peer ratings.

3　Characteristics associated with excitability will be associated with lower supervisor and peer ratings.

4   Characteristics associated with scepticism and distrust will be associated with lower peer ratings.

The Hogan Development Survey contains eleven scales measuring behavioural tendencies that may cause failure:

1   excitable – moody, easily annoyed, hard to please, and emotionally volatile;
2   sceptical – distrustful, cynical, sensitive to criticism, and focused on the negative;
3   cautious – unassertive, resistant to change, risk averse, and slow to make decisions;
4   reserved – aloof, indifferent to the feelings of others, and uncommunicative;
5   leisurely – overtly cooperative, but privately irritable, stubborn, and un-cooperative;
6   bold – overly self-confident, arrogant, with inflated feelings of self-worth;
7   mischievous – charming, risk taking, limit testing, and seeking excitement;
8   colorful – active, energetic, entertaining, dramatic, and attention seeking;
9   imaginative – creative but thinking and acting in unusual or eccentric ways;
10 diligent – meticulous, precise, conscientious, hard to please, and perfectionistic;
11 dutiful – eager to please and reluctant to act independently or against popular opinion.

Their results showed that dysfunctional behaviours associated with arrogance, cautiousness, volatility, and scepticism negatively affected performance ratings and these effects differed between supervisors and peers.

Chidester *et al.* (1991) examined the personality characteristics of more and less effective commercial airline flight crew. Effectiveness was defined by the number and severity of errors made by the crew. Captains of crews with the fewest errors were described as warm, friendly, self-confident, and coped well with pressure. Captains of crews with the most errors were described as arrogant, hostile, boastful, egotistical, dictatorial, and passive aggressive.

McCall and Lombardo (1983) noted that weaknesses could override strengths; an early strength can become a weakness (technical skill becomes less important as one progresses), some deficiencies – inability to work with peers matters; and bad luck such as a business recession – can play a role in failure.

But many questions remain unanswered. Do certain deficiencies (e.g. arrogance) matter more later in one's career than earlier? Can a strength become a weakness (strong leadership of subordinates leading to a narrow focus)? Are some patterns of strengths and weaknesses acceptable while others are fatal (brilliant but insensitive might derail while organizational savvy, but insensitive might not)? Are there some flaws that transcend any combination of strengths (person can't be trusted)? And do flaws operate in the same way at upper and lower organizational levels (success and derailment)? Some flaws (emotional instability, arrogance, abrasiveness) may be more critical at upper levels because the jobs are larger and more complex, the stakes higher and the costs of failure greater.

Some themes emerge in the writing on leader failure. First, failure was associated with inability to develop effective interpersonal relationships (arrogant, stubborn, egocentric). Second, some leaders were afraid to take risks and make errors (cautious, avoid responsibility). Third, excitable individuals were found to have difficult relationships (impatient, moody, negative, volatile, emotional instability). Fourth, as Lubit (2002) observes, scepticism and distrust will reduce leaders effectiveness in motivating others (cynical, untrustworthy).

CAN DARKSIDE CHARACTERISTICS BE CHANGED?

Hogan, Curphy, and Hogan (1994) believe that darkside characteristics can be changed but that this requires more intensive development than currently found in most leader training programmes. They cite evidence from the Coaching for Effectiveness Program at Personnel Decisions Inc. (Peterson 1993; Peterson and Hicks, 1993), based on work with 370 managers over a five-year period, which showed that most managers were able to change a number of targeted behaviours.

The leader's character determines how he or she leads the organization, though business knowledge and managerial skill also matter. The higher one rises in an organization the more self-awareness lies at the centre of leadership development. Yet most people have mixed feelings about knowing themselves better and the organizational environment compounds the problem. Most leaders believe they cannot show weakness; individuals are afraid to 'talk straight' with the leader.

Why do managers get so little feedback? There are several barriers at executive levels: their power stops criticism; isolation; they do not get regular performance appraisals; and they use their power and pressure to intimidate others. Their egos make them resistant to criticism and many feel a need to justify themselves and their actions (Kaplan, 1991).

Some solutions to this lack of feedback are possible. These include minimizing power differences, locating the leader's office close to those of other managers, formalizing feedback mechanisms, supporting constructive critics who are willing to take risks and confront the executive, and encouraging examination of the forces in the executives themselves. They must be willing to have their behaviour and motives described and criticized. Executives need to have confidence, to believe in themselves but not be arrogant.

Derailers at the CEO level obviously have greater consequences. CEOs may also feel more vulnerable to these derailers than lower level leaders; the higher one is in the organization, the less feedback the individual receives. Personal awareness is critical for these individuals. Possible solutions to identify and reduce these derailers include the following:

- Identify the stressors that trigger your derailers (environments, events, problems, decisions).
- Analyse your potential derailers (your business failures, are any common behaviours involved in these?).
- Get feedback on what you can do to be a better leader.
- Get a confidant.
- Talk about derailers in one's management team.
- Get a coach.
- Use small failures to prompt awareness, learning, and change.

Events this decade raise new challenges for leaders on several fronts. First, the war for talent and increased competitive pressures will create demands for higher quality leadership. Second, increased performance pressures will lead to greater scrutiny of leaders' performance. Third, the move to a service economy will change the skills and practices of leaders. Fourth, leaders will more often have to manage for innovation and creativity. Fifth, increasing use will be made of personality measures – both bright and dark side – in leader assessment and selection. A consideration of the dark side of leadership is likely to increase our ability to effectively develop the leaders organizations will need in the twenty-first century.

REFERENCES

Bentz, J. V. (1985) A view from the top: A thirty year perspective of research devoted to the discovery description and prediction of executive behavior. Paper presented at the 92nd Annual Convention of the American Psychological Association, Los Angeles, August.

Charan, R. and Colvin, G. (1999) Why CEOs fail? *Fortune*, 39: 69–78.

Chidester, T. R., Helmreich, R. L., Gregorich, S. R., and Geis, C. E. (1991) Pilot personality and crew coordination. *International Journal of Aviation Psychology*, 1: 25–44.

Clements, C. and Washbush, J. B. (1999) The two faces of leadership: Considering the dark side of leader-follower dynamics. *Journal of Workplace Learning: Employee Counselling Today*, 11: 39–48.

Dotlitch, D. L. and Cairo, P. (2003) *Why CEOs fail: the 11 behaviors that can derail your climb to the top and how to manage them*. San Francisco, CA: Jossey-Bass.

Finkelstein, S. (2003) *Why smart executives fail and what we can learn from their mistakes*. New York: Portfolio.

Fulmer, R. M. and Conger, J. A. (2004) *Growing your company's leaders*. New York: AMACOM.

Hogan, J. and Hogan, R. (2002) Leadership and sociopolitical intelligence. In R. E. Riggio, S. E. Murphy, and F. J. Pirozzolo (eds) *Multiple intelligences and leadership*. Mahwah, NJ: Lawrence Erlbaum, pp. 75–88.

Hogan, R. (1999) Trouble at the top: Causes and consequences of managerial incompetence. *Consulting Psychology Journal*, 46: 1061–87.

Hogan, R. and Hogan, J. (1997) *Hogan Development Survey Manual*. Tulsa, OK: Hogan Assessment Systems.

Hogan, R. and Hogan, J. (2001) Assessing leadership: A view of the dark side. *International Journal of Evaluation and Assessment*, 9: 40–51.

Hogan, R., Curphy, G. J., and Hogan, J. (1994) What we know about leadership: Effectiveness and personality. *American Psychologist*, 49: 493–504.

Hogan, R., Raskin, R., and Fazzini, D. (1990) The dark side of charisma. In K. E. Clark and M. B. Clark (eds) *Measures of leadership*. Greensboro, NC: Center for Creative Leadership, pp. 174–97.

Kaplan, R. E. (1991) *Beyond ambition: How driven managers can lead better and live better*. San Francisco, CA: Jossey-Bass.

Kellerman, B. (2004) *Bad leadership*. Boston, MA: Harvard Business School Press.

Leslie, J. and VanVelsor, E. (1996) *A look at derailment today: North America and Europe*. Greensboro, NC: Center for Creative Leadership.

Lipman-Blumen, J. (2001) Why do we tolerate bad leaders – magnificent uncertitude, anxiety, and meaning. In W. Bennis, G. M. Spreitzer, and T. C. Cummings (eds). *The future of leadership: Today's top leadership teachers speak to tomorrow's leaders*. San Francisco, CA: Jossey-Bass, pp. 125–38.

Lombardo, M. M., Ruderman, M. N., and McCauley, C. D. (1988) Explanations of success and derailment in upper-level management positions. *Journal of Business and Psychology*, 2: 199–216.

Lubit, R. (2002) The long term impact of destructively narcissistic managers. *Academy of Management Executive*, 16: 127–38.

McCall, M. and Lombardo, M. (1983) *Off the track: why and how successful executives get derailed*. (tech, Rep. No. 21) Greensboro, NC: Center for Creative Leadership.

Najar, M. J., Holland, B. D., and VanLandayt, C. R. (2004) Individual differences in leadership derailment. Paper presented at the SIOP Conference. Chicago, IL. April.

Peterson, D. B. (1993) Measuring change: A psychometric approach to evaluating individual training outcomes. In V. Arnold (Chair), *Innovations in training evaluation: New measures, new designs*. Symposium conducted at the Eighth Annual Conference of the Society for Industrial and Organizational Psychology, San Francisco, CA.

Peterson, D. B. and Hicks, M. D. (1993, May) *How to get people to change*. Workshop presented at the Eighth Annual Conference of the Society for Industrial and Organizational Psychology, San Francisco, CA.

VanVelsor, E. and Leslie, J. B. (1995) why executives derail: Perspectives across time and cultures. *Academy of Management Executive*, 9: 62–72.

Chapter 13

Perfectionism as a detrimental factor in leadership

A multidimensional analysis

Gordon L. Flett and Paul L. Hewitt

How would you describe the perfect, ideal leader? Is this person high or low in perfectionism? Ironically, the ideal leader is probably someone who is not very high in perfectionism. This is unfortunate because perfectionists have many character- istics that would suggest high leadership aspirations. Perfectionists by nature are very achievement-oriented and they are attentive to detail and have high aspira- tions. Also, perfectionists often are very capable people, and their talents and abil- ities will often make them eligible for leadership positions. Finally, perfectionists are high in the need for control and assuming a leadership position is one way of satisfying this need.

Although perfectionists are likely to have leadership aspirations and the perfec- tionist in a leadership role may strive to be the ultimate leader, it is unlikely that he or she will achieve this goal. As noted by Conway (2000), it is important to make the distinction between the desire to do something and the effectiveness in actually doing it. Many perfectionists are idealists who likely crave the opportunity to lead but they may not be very good at it. Accordingly, in the current chapter, we describe the characteristics of perfectionism that detract from effective leader- ship. Perfectionism is described as a complex, multidimensional construct with both personal and interpersonal factors, and both types of factors will be exam- ined in terms of their negative impact on leadership behaviours. Deleterious factors that are associated with perfectionism will be described with a particular focus on the destructive elements associated with narcissistic perfectionism. We will also discuss the need to distinguish between extreme perfectionism (hyper- conscientiousness) and more adaptive forms of trait conscientiousness. Our analysis of the destructive aspects of perfectionism will incorporate an overview of existing research on perfectionism in the work context. Finally, we conclude our analysis with an outline for future research on perfectionism and leadership.

We will preface our review with the statement that, at present, there is a paucity of research on perfectionism and leadership *per se*. Thus, much of the current chapter will examine perfectionism and leadership from a conceptual perspective. However, we will describe research findings on several factors associated with perfectionism that should undermine leadership behaviours. Our discussion of perfectionism and leadership is based on the premise that an effective leader is someone who is proficient at 'getting ahead' and 'getting along' (see Conway, 2000) and the negative interpersonal style of perfectionists undermines the effectiveness of their leadership.

Clearly, our analysis of the role of perfectionism as a personality construct in leadership is consistent with renewed interest in the ability of personality traits to differentiate effective and ineffective leaders. Critical articles by Stogdill (1948) and Mann (1959) are credited with undermining interest in research on person-ality traits and leadership for the next three decades. This occurred even though Stogdill (1948) suggested that despite some problems, there was still clear evidence that personality traits such as self-confidence and dominance were associated with effective leadership.

Fortunately, research on the role of personality traits in leadership has increased over the past 15 years or so, in part due to the recovery of the personality field in general from the criticisms raised by Mischel, and the growing popularity of the five-factor model and related schemes. Several authors have provided contemporary reviews of the literature on personality and leadership (see Bono and Judge, 2002; Ford and Oswald, 2003; Judge et al., 2002; Spangler, House, and Palrecha, 2004). The paper by Judge et al. (2002) is a meta-analysis of the personality correlates of various leadership styles. They found in general that better leadership was associated with extraversion, conscientiousness, openness to experience, and low neuroticism. Extraversion was the personality factor that was identified as the most consistent predictor of leadership across various settings. A subsequent meta-analysis by Bono and Judge (2004) compared the personality correlates of transformational versus transactional leadership. These two different types of leadership were described initially by Burns (1978) and elaborated by Bass (1985). Tranformational leadership is more desirable and involves such positive attributes as idealized influence, inspirational motivation (i.e. charisma), intellectual stimulation, and individualized consideration so that the growths and needs of each employee are recognized. Transactional leadership is less desirable and involves motivating employees via con-tingent rewards, management by exception, and passive forms of leadership. The overall results suggested that the traits assessed by the five-factor model were relatively weak predictors of both types of leadership, though extraversion was linked once again with transformational leadership. The authors suggested, given the overall weak predictive associations, a focus on narrower more specific traits might be useful. It is our contention that perfectionism is one such trait.

Spangler, House, and Palrecha (2004) evaluated these data and other existing data and concluded that future research on personality and leadership effectiveness should be guided by the following formula:

Leadership effectiveness =

f (implicit power, achievement, affiliation motivation) +

f (neuroticism, extraversion, openness, agreeableness, conscientiousness) +

f (interactions of implicit motives and traits).

This formula signifies that traits reflecting the five-factor model and individual differences in psychological needs should both be considered.

A notable absence in these recent reviews is any mention whatsoever of the possible role of perfectionism in leadership and this is due to the paucity of research on perfectionism and leadership. The relevance of personality traits in terms of the five-factor model in leadership should be kept in mind because in a subsequent section on the correlates of perfectionism, we discuss research on perfectionism and the five-factor model. First, however, we discuss the history of perfectionism theory and research in general, including the shift from studying perfectionism as a unidimensional construct to the contemporary focus on perfectionism as a multidimensional construct.

PERFECTIONISM AS A MULTIDIMENSIONAL CONSTRUCT

A common pattern in the personality literature is that personality constructs are first regarded as unidimensional and then specific facets or dimensions are eventually discovered. Indeed, the perfectionism construct was conceptualized and assessed as a unidimensional, monolithic construct for many years. Perfectionism was regarded by depression researchers such as Burns and Beck (1978) as a type of dysfunctional attitude along the lines of 'I must be perfect in order to be loved'. Burns (1980) used this as his main emphasis when he developed the unidimensional ten-item Burns Perfectionism Scale to assess perfectionism as a cognitively based measure. Researchers interested in the study of eating disorders also assessed perfectionism as a unidimensional construct. Garner, Olmstead, and Polivy (1983) included a six-item perfectionism subscale as part of their broader measure called the Eating Disorders Inventory. This subscale consisted of a mix of items that tapped perfectionism in terms of exceedingly high personal goals and in terms of perceived parental pressure to be perfect.

The unidimensional approach prevailed for many years, but it is now recognized that the perfectionism construct consists of several dimensions that reflect personal and interpersonal concerns. Frost and associates conducted seminal work in this area. They constructed the Multidimensional Perfectionism Scale to assess six components of perfectionism (see Frost *et al.*, 1990). Various dimensions of perfectionism were identified after pooling together perfectionism items from existing scales and by writing some new items. Factor analyses confirmed that perfectionism is multidimensional. This scale assesses the personal aspects of perfectionism (i.e. personal standards, concern over mistakes, doubts about actions, organization) and the familial aspects of perfectionism (i.e. unrealistic parental expectations and parental criticisms). Frost and associates (Frost *et al.*, 1990; Frost *et al.*, 1993) have shown that the concern over mistakes subscale is the element of the Frost scale that is linked most consistently with symptoms of depression. Two factors (i.e. excessive concern over mistakes, doubts about actions) have some obvious negative implications for the perfectionist's leadership potential. Perfectionists with an excessive concern over mistakes tend to ruminate obsessively about past mistakes and are hesitant to act for fear of making new mistakes (Frost *et al.*, 1997).

At the same time, Hewitt and Flett (1990) also began exploring different dimensions of perfectionism and this culminated in the development of another multifaceted measure of perfectionism that is also called the Multidimensional Perfectionism Scale (see Hewitt and Flett, 1991, 2004). This scale taps three dimensions of perfectionism—self-oriented perfectionism, other-oriented perfectionism, and socially prescribed perfectionism. These dimensions are described below.

Self-oriented perfectionism

Self-oriented perfectionism is a personal dimension involving perfectionistic behaviours that both derive from the self and are directed toward the self. The important facets of self-oriented perfectionism include a strong motivational drive for the self to be perfect, a tendency to maintain unrealistic self-expectations in the face of failure, and stringent self-evaluations that focus on one's flaws and short-comings. It is also important to acknowledge that in order to be considered a self-oriented perfectionist, the unrealistic standards are generalized across behavioural domains. That is, the extreme perfectionist is someone who demands perfection from the self and wants to be perfect at work, at home, in social situations, and so on. It is somewhat natural and understandable for people to want to be perfect in the one domain of most importance to them, but when the focus is on perfectionism as a personality trait, the demand for personal perfection cuts across situations and life roles.

Other-oriented perfectionism

Whereas self-oriented perfectionism entails a striving for personal standards of perfection, other-oriented perfectionism involves a focus on the need for other people to be perfect. Other-oriented perfectionism entails setting unrealistic standards for others and rewarding them only if standards are attained. Whereas self-oriented perfectionism is focused on self-directed affect and cognitions, other-oriented perfectionism is hypothesized to involve externally directed affect and cognitions reflecting hostility toward others, authoritarianism, and dominating behaviour. Other-oriented perfectionism does not appear to be related to depression, but it is related to certain adjustment difficulties such as dramatic cluster personality disorders (Hewitt and Flett, 1991).

The most commonly used measure of this aspect of the construct is the other-oriented perfectionism scale from the Multidimensional Perfectionism Scale (see Hewitt and Flett, 1991, 2004). However, this measure was pre-dated by an earlier measure that was described by Hewitt and Flett (1990). The items relating to other-oriented perfectionism were as follows:

- If I do not set very high standards for people I know, they are likely to end up second-rate people.
- I think less of people I know if they make mistakes.
- If someone I know cannot do something really well, they shouldn't do it at all.
- I cannot help getting upset if someone I know makes mistakes.
- It is shameful for people I know to display weakness or foolish behavior.
- An average performance by someone I know is unsatisfactory
- When someone I know fails at something important, it means they are probably less of a person.
- If I scold others for their failure to live up to expectations, it will help them in the future.

Even a cursory examination of the item content of this initial measure identifies a number of themes that are problematic in terms of the implications for someone who is high in this tendency yet desires to be an effective leader. The scale content implies that other-oriented perfectionists believe that the demands they place on others are in the best interests of these people or 'they are likely to end up second-rate people'. Other themes reflect a dogmatic orientation and the clear message that mistakes made by other people will not be tolerated.

This other-oriented perfectionism often comes in the form of other-directed 'should' statements and this could foster a very authoritarian form of leadership. Problems ensue when other people don't live up to expectations or it is perceived that they don't live up to expectations.

Socially prescribed perfectionism

The third dimension of perfectionism – socially prescribed perfectionism – is the component of perfectionism that is related most consistently to maladjustment. Socially prescribed perfectionism is a stable trait that is based on the perception that others have unrealistic standards and perfectionistic motives for one's own behaviours and that others will be satisfied only when these standards are attained. It involves a sense of pressure stemming from the view that others have imposed perfectionistic demands on the self. Clearly, this is a highly neurotic orientation that is antithetical to leadership aspirations.

This perfectionism dimension is related to numerous social interaction variables including fear of negative social evaluation, belief in the external control of reinforcement, and need for the approval of others (Hewitt and Flett, 1991). Although these perfectionistic standards are believed to emanate from outside the self, it should be noted that attributing control to outside or external forces can result in depressive symptoms involving an element of self-blame (see Krantz and Rude, 1984; Rude, 1989). Hence, a lack of perceived control and subsequent learned helplessness and depressive symptomatology appear to be important consequences of socially prescribed perfectionism (e.g. Hewitt and Flett, 1991).

One question that is often addressed to us is whether it is possible to identify people who are high in only one dimension of perfectionism but low in the other dimensions of perfectionism. This is indeed possible. The test manual for our Multidimensional Perfectionism Scale (see Hewitt and Flett, 2004) contains actual case examples of people who are elevated in only one or two aspects of perfectionism. When considering the personality attributes of leaders, given all of the negative characteristics of socially prescribed perfectionism, it makes more sense to focus on potential leaders with high levels of self-oriented and other-oriented perfectionism. However, it is important to preface this focus with the caveat that research with a variety of samples has shown consistently that all three perfectionism dimensions are intercorrelated. Thus, it is typically the case that a person with a high score on one perfectionism dimension tends to have elevated scores on all three dimensions. As such, the self-oriented perfectionist who is made to feel defensive may respond with the negative emotional reactions that have been associated more commonly with socially prescribed perfectionism.

PERFECTIONISM VERSUS CONSCIENTIOUSNESS

When contemplating the issue of perfectionism and leadership, some readers might be thinking 'But aren't perfectionists conscientious people? Aren't they the reliable and goal-directed people who make effective leaders?' Tests of the link between these perfectionism dimensions and the five-factor model have confirmed that self-oriented perfectionism is associated positively with trait conscientiousness, while other-oriented perfectionism is associated primarily with low agreeableness, and socially prescribed perfectionism is associated primarily with neuroticism (see Hewitt and Flett, 2004; Hill, McIntire, and Bacharach, 1997). Although there are predictable links with the traits in the five-factor model, these associations are not so strong as to suggest that the perfectionism construct is subsumed and is redundant with the five-factor model.

Nevertheless, the link between self-oriented perfectionism and conscientious-ness is potentially quite important in terms of leadership potential. Research on perfectionism and conscientiousness indicates that not only is self-oriented perfectionism linked with the broad conscientiousness domain, self-oriented per-fectionism is also associated with the various facets of conscientiousness, including competence, order, dutifulness, achievement striving, self-discipline, and delibera-tion (Hill, McIntire, and Bacharach, 1997).

This finding is potentially relevant to the link between perfectionism and leader-ship because there is extensive evidence suggesting that conscientiousness is a highly positive attribute in job settings and achievement contexts. However, it is our contention that self-oriented perfectionism and conscientiousness should not be equated and it is important to identify those individuals who are conscien-tiousness yet not extreme perfectionists. We regard self-oriented perfectionism as an extreme form of striving that is related to but goes well beyond conscien-tiousness. It involves a hyperconscientiousness that is motivated by a defensive orientation toward the self. One indication that self-oriented perfectionism is distinct from conscientiousness is that a tendency to be organized is a key com-ponent of the conscientiousness construct (Hogan and Ones, 1997). Frost *et al.* (1990) included an organization subscale as part of their perfectionism measure, but they recommended that this organization subscale should not be included when computing a total score on their inventory because the organization subscale has low correlations with the other perfectionism dimensions assessed by their measure. This reiterates that perfectionism is more than a need or desire for order and organization. It is the relentless pursuit of exceedingly high standards and it is an achievement-based construct.

We have stated elsewhere that items that assess self-oriented forms of perfec-tionism need to be evaluated carefully to determine whether they enable researchers to make the subtle but important distinction between people with a high level of conscientiousness versus other people who take it one step further and demand absolute perfection from the self (see Flett and Hewitt, 2002). Although we believe it is vitally important to distinguish perfectionism and consci-entiousness, there is an increasingly proliferation of measures that seem to blur this distinction. For instance, the HEXACO Personality Inventory by Lee and Ashton (2004) includes a perfectionism subscale as part of the broader conscien-tiousness trait. Similarly, the newly created Perfectionism Inventory by Hill *et al.* (2004) contains perfectionism subscales that assess planfulness and organization. People can be both planful and organized without necessarily being a relentless perfectionist, yet this possibility was not acknowledged by Hill *et al.* (2004). It is important for future researchers to keep these scale content issues in mind when assessing the link between perfectionism and leadership. Does a scale really assess perfectionism or is it tapping a more adaptive form of conscientiousness? Those involved in personnel selection would also be well advised to keep this distinction in mind. As we will illustrate below, perfectionism is more than conscientiousness. Ideally, someone selected for a leadership position will be high in conscientiousness, but not extremely high in perfectionism. And it needs to be pointed out that it is possible to empirically distinguish perfectionism and conscientiousness. This point was demonstrated by a recent study on eating behaviours in which the investigators identified a group of perfectionists who were relatively low in conscientiousness (see O'Connor and O'Connor, 2004).

It is our view that while conscientiousness is a desirable trait in general, clearly, there are aspects of self-oriented perfectionism that hinder rather than help the perfectionist and these features are highly relevant to an understanding of why perfectionists may not make for effective leaders. These features include a negative cognitive style that includes a tendency toward categorical, all-or-none thinking whereby only absolute success or abject failure exist as possible outcomes (see Hewitt and Flett, 1991) and a tendency to overgeneralize negative feedback so that it is seen as reflecting the entire self (see Hewitt et al., 1991). The standards of self-oriented perfectionists can become so high that it impairs their ability to acquire a sense of self-satisfaction. Hamachek (1978) has suggested that this lack of satisfaction is the essence of neurotic perfectionism. Empirical work has shown that even among people with exceptional levels of skill who perform at high levels, self-oriented perfectionism is linked with performance dissatisfaction (Enns et al., 2001; Mor et al., 1995). This could be a reflection of the tendency for self-oriented perfectionists to be high in dispositional levels of self-criticism. Robinson (2000) has observed that among perfectionistic workaholics, this harsh self-criticism is often accompanied by harsh criticism of significant others. He noted that:

> Perfectionistic workaholics are difficult to work for, and even more difficult to live with. Lives are narrowed to only those things at which the workaholic can excel. Both the self and others are judged unmercifully . . . Because of these superhuman standards, failure and anger at others for not meeting high standards are constant companions.
>
> (Robinson, 2000, p. 49)

It is evident from this description that the perfectionism of workaholics seems to have both personal and interpersonal manifestations.

Perfectionistic self-presentation

Although most of our analysis will focus on self-oriented and other-oriented perfectionism, we would be remiss if we did not mention a newly identified aspect of the perfectionism construct known as perfectionistic self-presentation. Perfectionistic self-presentation is a style that has clear implications for leadership potential. Some people are overly invested in projecting an image of flawlessness to others. This attribute is found among a subset of perfectionists who feel a pressure to be perfect, and instead of rejecting this pressure, they try to project and protect a public image of flawlessness. Hewitt *et al.* (2003) created the Perfectionistic Self-Presentation Scale (PSPS) to assess perfectionistic self-promotion (i.e. the need to appear perfect to others), the non-display of imperfection (i.e. the need to avoid appearing imperfect to others), and non-disclosure of imperfection (i.e. the need to avoiding disclosing imperfections to others). Research has established that perfectionistic self-presentation is empirically distinguishable from trait perfectionism and has incremental validity in terms of predicting unique variance in psychological distress (Hewitt *et al.*, 2003).

Perfectionistic self-presentation is a highly neurotic style that should be antithetical to effective leadership behaviour. People high in perfectionistic self-presentation are defensive and unwilling to acknowledge when a mistake has been made. This is reflected by one of the PSPS scale items: 'Admitting failure to others is the worst possible thing.' This perfectionistic self-presentation can be revealed in many different tendencies among leaders. For instance, this unwillingness to acknowledge mistakes in judgement could contribute to a form of decisional rigidity. In addition, leaders high in perfectionistic self-presentation may simply be unwilling to tackle problems and projects that are highly visible to others and are threatening because of the possibility of failure.

Leadership implications of neurotic versus narcissistic perfectionism

Socially prescribed perfectionism and perfectionistic self-presentation are characteristics that typically apply to people who would be considered neurotic perfectionists. This type of perfectionistic individual is highly anxious and interpersonally sensitive. They are fearful of criticism and report that they are frequently the targets of negative social interactions (Flett *et al.*, 1997). This type of perfectionist would be too defensive and would lack the resiliency to be an effective leader.

Contrast the neurotic perfectionist with the narcissistic perfectionist. Unfortunately, relatively few authors in the perfectionism field have considered the narcissistic perfectionist. Narcissistic perfectionism refers to an individual who not only strives for perfection, he or she also defensively regards himself or herself as perfect or close to perfect and having the capability of being perfect.

Research on perfectionism and narcissism has yielded some useful information about perfectionism and leadership. Empirical research has not only confirmed a link between perfectionism and narcissism, it has also pointed to the possible leadership aspirations of narcissistic perfectionists. Watson, Varnell, and Morris (1999/2000) examined the link between the Multidimensional Perfectionism Scale and the various factors of the Narcissistic Personality Inventory as described by Emmons (1984, 1987). Emmons identified four factors, including a leadership/authority factor. Watson, Varnell, and Morris (1999/2000) found that both self-oriented and other-oriented perfectionism were associated with the leadership/authority factor. These same perfectionism dimensions were also associated with other indices of narcissism, including superiority/arrogance, self-absorption, and exploitativeness. Hewitt and Flett (1991) had shown earlier that both self-oriented and other-oriented perfectionism were associated with narcissism.

Research on the narcissism factors identified by Emmons (1984, 1987) has yielded several findings suggesting that the leadership/authority component is a relatively adaptive aspect of narcissism. This component has been linked with characteristics such as optimism, high self-esteem, and low social anxiety (for a review, see Sturman, 2000). One problem with much of this research is that it is based on self-report measures. Narcissistic individuals may have little awareness of their impact on other people who may not share their positive views. The need for including informant ratings in general was shown recently in one of our studies on perfectionism, defence styles, and depression (see Flett, Besser, and Hewitt, 2005). Reports provided by peers found that other-oriented perfectionism was linked with maladaptive defence styles in terms of peer ratings but not in terms of self-reports. This is an important point in general because future research on perfectionism and leadership would be bolstered considerably by the inclusion of observer ratings of both perfectionism and leadership qualities. If ratings are provided by co-workers in organizational settings, it would be advisable to distinguish the ratings provided by superiors versus ratings provided by subordinates; the willingness of other-oriented perfectionists to express disappointment and impose their demands should be more evident to subordinate employees.

The negative attributes of narcissistic perfectionists was hinted at by Porter (2001), who incorporated a focus on perfectionism as part of her analysis of workaholism. Data gathered with a four-item perfectionism measure created for her study led Porter (2001) to conclude that perfectionists question the value of co-workers and this has a detrimental impact on relationships with co-workers. The narcissistic elements of perfectionists were clearly evident here. Perfectionists believed that they were more conscientious, more responsible, more attentive to detail, and better workers than other people. If the perfectionist openly expressed this sense of superiority, then it would likely undermine attempts by the perfectionistic leader to motivate others.

Perhaps the biggest concern about narcissistic perfectionists in leadership positions is that they seem to have a negative interpersonal style that would only serve to alienate other people over time. At present, two empirical investigations have been conducted of the association between perfectionism and the interpersonal styles that comprise the interpersonal circumplex. The interpersonal circumplex is a circle of interpersonal styles that involves two major dimensions. The first one involves themes of love, warmth, and nurturance. This dimension is represented by cold and quarrelsome at one end or pole versus warm and agreeable at the other end. The other main axis or dimension reflects being dominant and ambitious at one end or pole versus lazy and submissive at the other end. The interpersonal circumplex is further divided into eight major octants that represent blends of varying degrees of the nurturance and dominance dimensions. Hill, Zrull, and Turlington (1997) administered the Multidimensional Perfectionism Scale (Hewitt and Flett, 1991) and two interpersonal circumplex measures to a sample of male and female university students. Unfortunately, this study is seldom cited by authors who wish to argue that self-oriented and other-oriented perfectionism are adaptive dimensions. The Hill, Zrull, and Turlington (1997) study found both self-oriented and other-oriented perfectionism in men were associated with hostile and dominant interpersonal traits. As for women, self-oriented perfectionism was associated with an overly nurturant interpersonal style, while other-oriented perfectionism was associated with the same hostile and dominant interpersonal tendencies found in men. The magnitude of the findings for both men and women suggested that these interpersonal styles are extreme and rigid.

Another study conducted in our laboratory examined the interpersonal circumplex correlates of the Hewitt and Flett (1991) and Frost et al. (1990) inventories when administered to students (see Flynn et al., 1998). The findings are described in detail in Habke and Flynn (2002). Self-oriented and other-oriented perfectionism in both women and men were associated with hostile and dominant tendencies. A more fine-grained analysis of the circumplex octants showed that both perfectionism dimensions were associated with a maladaptive interpersonal style involving extreme and rigid arrogance (see Habke and Flynn, 2002, p. 162). Thus, although people with self-oriented and other-oriented perfectionism rate themselves as being good and effective leaders when they complete a narcissism inventory, their other self-reports suggest an arrogant and hostile interpersonal style that would undermine attempts at leadership.

Perhaps it is these negative interpersonal characteristics that account for an intriguing result from research on astronaut selection. The suitability of perfectionists was addressed indirectly as part of a testing programme designed to select the most effective astronauts (see Rose et al., 1994). The astronauts were classified into two groups described as 'more effective' versus 'laggards' with respect to interpersonal competence. A scatterplot analysis revealed that all of the astronauts deemed to be 'laggards' were moderate to high in perfectionistic tendencies. All of the astronauts with lower levels of perfectionism were considered to be substantially more effective in interpersonal competence.

In the next section, we examine perfectionism as a defensive orientation designed to compensate for possible weaknesses and shortcomings in the self. It is argued that perfectionists are highly sensitive to failure to the extent that they would have difficulty when exposed to constructive criticism. Perfectionism is also examined in terms of feelings of self-worth and how these feelings get translated into a workaholic orientation that can lead to substantial stress, both for the self and others.

PERFECTIONISM AS A DEFENSIVE ORIENTATION

Fear of failure and inability to tolerate failure

One of the defining aspects of effective leadership is the ability to tolerate failures while finding ways to stop further failures from happening. Farson and Keyes (2002) have provided a detailed description of 'the failure tolerant leader.' Failure tolerant leaders are able to foster an environment in which people are not afraid to make mistakes and instead acknowledge that important new insights can come from carefully considering the mistakes that are made. Failure intolerance can stifle creativity and the willingness to take chances.

Numerous authors have suggested that perfectionists have an excessive preoccupation with the possibility of failure along with a demonstrated need to avoid censure from others (Burns, 1980; Hamachek, 1978; Missildine, 1963; Pacht, 1984). Missildine (1963) has observed that extreme perfectionists 'are motivated not so much by a desire for improvement as they are by a fear of failure' (p. 28).

To what extent is this hypersensitivity to failure associated with the various perfectionism dimensions? As part of an investigation of dimensions of perfectionism and self-actualization, Flett et al. (1991) administered the Multidimensional Perfectionism Scale (Hewitt and Flett, 1991) and the Short Index of Self-Actualization (Jones and Crandell, 1986) to a sample of 164 undergraduate students. The Short Index of Self-Actualization has three identifiable factors, including a measure of the inability to tolerate failure. The inability to tolerate failure was correlated significantly with all three MPS perfectionism dimensions (rs ranging from 0.22 to 0.47). Research on perfectionism, procrastination, and fear of failure in achievement situations has found consistent evidence linking both self-oriented and socially prescribed perfectionism with a fear of failure (see Flett, Hewitt and Martin, 1995; Onwuegbuzie, 2000).

We have conducted a new study on perfectionism, fear of failure, and psychological distress that evaluated this issue with a multidimensional measure of fear of failure. The Performance Appraisal Inventory (Conroy, 2001) assesses fear of failure in five areas: (1) fear of shame and guilt due to inadequate performance; (2) fear of loss of self (i.e. devaluing one's self-estimate); (3) fear of loss of plans for the future; (4) fear of loss of social influence and upsetting important others; and (5) fear of having an uncertain future. Recent analyses of our unpublished data have shown that the five subscales combine to form a latent fear of failure construct, and both self-oriented and socially prescribed perfectionism are associated positively and significantly with this latent construct.

258

Given this fear of failure, what happens when perfectionists receive failure feedback? Besser, Flett, and Hewitt (2004) conducted a unique experiment that examined perfectionists' responses to failure versus success. The impetus for this study was our interest in exploring how self-oriented perfectionists react when they experience failure feedback after performing a challenging task. The diathesis-stress model of perfectionism and depression is based on the premise that perfectionists are vulnerable to dysphoria if they experience failure feedback (Flett *et al.*, 1995; Hewitt and Flett, 1993; Hewitt, Flett, and Ediger, 1996). The Besser, Flett, and Hewitt (2004) study was unique because, to our knowledge, it was the first experimental test of how perfectionists respond to ego-involving feedback that differed in valence. The results confirmed that self-oriented perfectionists were debilitated, both in terms of cognition and affect, when they received negative feedback about their performance on a challenging task. The analyses showed that self-oriented perfectionists engage in excessive cognitive rumination, place irrational importance on performance outcomes, experience various forms of negative affect, and make negative social comparisons. Besser, Flett, and Hewitt (2004) also reported that self-oriented perfectionists were particularly disappointed with their performance when they received negative feedback. In many respects, the negative characteristics of self-oriented perfectionism described by Besser, Flett, and Hewitt (2004) are very much in keeping with Hamachek's (1978) insightful description of neurotic perfectionists. The essence of neurotic perfectionists is their self-dissatisfaction.

One of the by-products of the defensiveness of perfectionists is a tendency to engage in self-handicapping behaviour as a way of protecting a vulnerable sense of self-worth. Experimental work by Hobden and Pliner (1995) established that self-oriented and socially prescribed perfectionism are both associated with self-handicapping behaviour. The self-defensiveness of perfectionists is described in more detail below.

Vulnerable self-worth

Adler (1956) suggested originally that perfectionism is a response to perceived feelings of inferiority and, as a result, vulnerable self-esteem is at the root of perfectionism. More recently, as part of his self-worth model of achievement motivation, Covington discussed perfectionists at length (see Covington, 2000; Covington and Mueller, 2001). He described perfectionists as overstrivers. Perfectionistic overstrivers are seeking to protect their self-worth, which is at risk because of the unattainability of the goal of being perfect. Although perfectionists desperately want to outperform others and be recognized for doing so, they also have a strong defensiveness due to their need to avoid failure and the horrible implications that failure would have in terms of self-characteristics. Covington

(2000) suggested that perfectionists engage in slavish overpreparation as a way of trying to redirect their feelings of anxiety and personal conflict. Two clear implications follow from Covington's description of perfectionism as a reflection self-worth. First, as we discuss below, perfectionists should suffer from a conditional sense of their self-worth. Second, if perfectionists do indeed engage in 'slavish over-preparation' (Covington, 2000, p. 187), then perfectionists should be prone to a form of workaholism that could undermine their leadership aspirations. Both of these possibilities are analysed in the following sections.

Recent research with measures of conditional self-worth seems to bear these observations out. Flett et al. (2003) investigated the link between trait perfectionism and a measure of unconditional self-acceptance in a sample of university students. All three dimensions assessed by the Multidimensional Perfectionism Scale were associated negatively with unconditional self-acceptance (rs ranging from -0.29 to -0.47), and low unconditional self-acceptance mediated the link between perfectionism and depression.

Other research by Hallsten, Josephson, and Torgen (2005) evaluated the association between Hallsten's newly created measure of performance-based self-esteem and measures of positive perfectionism and negative perfectionism. Performance-based self-esteem was of interest in general because of its established link with burnout in work contexts. Positive and negative perfectionism are terms that were introduced by Slade and Owens (1998), who postulated a dual process that includes a normal, healthy form of perfectionism they describe as 'positive perfectionism', and there is a maladaptive, pathological form of perfectionism that they describe as 'negative perfectionism'. The notion of positive versus negative perfectionism is related to earlier descriptions of normal versus neurotic perfectionists (see Hamachek, 1978). Hallsten, Josephson, and Torgen (2005) found that performance-based self-esteem was associated significantly with positive and negative perfectionism.

Independently, DiBartolo et al. (2004) created a revised version of the high personal standards subscale from the Frost et al. (1990) Multidimensional Perfectionism Scale. They also created new measures of success-based conditional self-worth (i.e. self-esteem is contingent on successful performance) and activity-based conditional self-worth (i.e. self-esteem is contingent on being very busy and maintaining a high activity level). They found that the high personal standards subscale was correlated with elevated scores on both the activity-based and success-based conditional self-worth measures. That is, perfectionists characterized by exceptionally high personal standards also tend to have a conditional sense of self-worth, and these perfectionists ought to be vulnerable to ego-involving performance feedback and outcomes which suggest that they are not meet standards.

Additional pilot data gathered in our laboratory have been obtained to evaluate conditional self-worth and the trait dimensions assessed by the Hewitt and Flett

(1991) Multidimensional Perfectionism Scale. This research with a sample of 100 university students has confirmed that self-oriented, other-oriented, and socially prescribed perfectionism are all correlated significantly with both measures of conditional self-worth. We have also examined the link between dimensions of perfectionism and self-worth contingencies as assessed by the multidimensional measure created recently by Crocker and associates (see Crocker *et al*. 2003). This measure assesses contingencies of self-worth in seven different areas reflecting factors internal and external to the self, including self-worth contingent on other's approval (e.g. I can't respect myself if others don't respect me) and self-worth based on outdoing others in competition (e.g. I feel worthwhile when I perform better than others on a task or a skill). Once again, analyses conducted on data from over 500 students confirmed that all three perfectionism dimensions were associated with almost all of the self-worth contingency domains described by Crocker and her associates. These data signify that the self-esteem of perfectionists is highly conditional and if contingencies are not met, then perfectionists will be highly vulnerable to low self-esteem and attendant feelings of dysphoria. In many respects, this need for validation seems to be antithetical to the notion of resilient leaders.

Given that perfectionists tend to evaluate themselves in terms of contingencies, it is quite possible that perfectionists who are given free reign in leadership roles will display a transactional form of leadership that incorporates this approach. That is, they should promote a sense of contingent reward with rewards being allocated on the basis of whether high expectations are met. This can become problematic if there is too much of an emphasis on this to the extent that intrinsic interest in work and achievement is undermined.

Perfectionism and workaholism

Descriptions of perfectionists as driven overstrivers who relentlessly pursue their goals suggest that perfectionists suffer from workaholism. An extreme work orientation would be one way of fending off the negative implications for the self when performance is inferior. Theory and research on workaholism by Spence and Robbins (1992) is highly relevant to an understanding of perfectionism because they included a measure of perfectionistic work behaviours as one of the subscales of their workaholism inventory. The three primary measures from this inventory were work involvement, drive, and work enjoyment. Perfectionism was among the other subscales (i.e. job stress, job involvement, non-delegation of responsibility, and time commitment). The eight items used to tap perfectionism reflect a specific form of self-oriented perfectionism with respect to work (e.g. I am satisfied with nothing short of perfection in my work. My high standards sometimes makes it difficult for me to get everything done).

A survey sent to a sample of social workers by Spence and Robbins (1992) showed that the perfectionism subscale was associated with a sense of being driven.

261

It was also found for both men and women that perfectionism was associated with greater work and job involvement, and it was associated with an inability to delegate responsibilities to others and higher levels of job stress. Perhaps not surprisingly, given the inherent stressfulness of striving for absolute perfection, and its link with job stress, both men and women high in perfectionism also reported greater health complaints. Health complaints could also reflect a form of self-handicapping or excuse-making that would lessen concerns about how a failure to attain perfection would be viewed by other people. Whatever the case, other research suggests that perfectionists with low levels of self-efficacy suffer from health problems (see Martin *et al.*, 1996).

Burke (1999) tested the replicability of the Spence and Robbins (1992) findings in a sample of 530 managers. Once again, perfectionism was associated with a sense of being driven, greater job involvement, and an inability to delegate. Comparison of six different workaholism types showed that workaholics were among several different types of workers with elevated perfectionism.

Recently, Flett, Strongolos, and Hewitt (2005) examined the link between the various trait dimensions of perfectionism and elements of workaholism and work addiction. A study with 106 employees from an insurance company involved assessing the associations among trait perfectionism, perfectionistic work behaviours assessed by Spence and Robbins (1992) and the elements of work addiction as described by Robinson (1999). The work involvement, work enjoyment, and driven subscales were the other subscales from the Spence and Robbins (1992) workaholism inventory included in this investigation. Regarding the measure of work addiction, in addition to the total score, the measure provides brief subscales assessing compulsive tendencies, need for control, inability to delegate, a focus on self-worth, and impaired communication/self-absorption. First, our results confirmed a strong association between trait self-oriented perfectionism and the Spence and Robbins (1992) measure of work-related self-oriented perfectionism ($r = 0.80$). The results involving the other subscales are displayed in Table 13.1. Both self-oriented and socially prescribed perfectionism were associated with greater work involvement, but there was no link with work enjoyment. All three perfectionism trait dimensions were correlated with a sense of being driven and greater overall work addiction. All three perfectionism trait dimensions were also associated with compulsion and need for control. The self-worth issues involved in perfectionism were reflected by significant correlations involving the self-worth factor and all three perfectionism dimensions. Finally, both self-oriented and socially prescribed perfectionism were linked with an inability to delegate. Other-oriented perfectionism was not associated with an inability to delegate.

The results with self-oriented perfectionism provide several new insights about the nature of this dimension. Clearly, people high in this dimension are driven and may be compulsive in their work style. This relentless approach suggests that they have internalized dictates about the need to keep working toward their goals.

Table 13.1 *Correlations between perfectionism and measures of workaholism and work addiction*

Work variable	Perfectionism dimension		
	Self	Other	Social
Perfectionism – work	.80**	.46**	.36**
Drive	.42**	.23**	.30**
Work involvement	.32**	−.01	.23*
Work enjoyment	.17	−.04	−.15
Work addiction – total	.48**	.27**	.59**
Work compulsion	.54**	.24*	.55**
Control	.38**	.34**	.47**
Self-absorption	.15	.02	.44**
Self-worth	.30**	.27**	.24*
Inability to delegate	.27**	.02	.27**

Note: ** $p < .05$, * $p < .01$. The following abbreviations were used: Self (Self-oriented perfectionism), Other (Other-oriented perfectionism), and Social (Socially prescribed perfectionism).

Perfectionism and stress

It is clear from research with the Spence and Robbins (1992) measure that perfectionists are among those people who believe that they should do things themselves if they want things to get done in a proper manner. The apparent inability of self-oriented perfectionists to delegate is in keeping with research on perfectionism and the desire for control. Flett *et al.* (1995) tested the hypothesis that perfectionism is associated with higher levels of desired and actual control. They found that both self-oriented perfectionism and other-oriented perfectionism were associated significantly with higher scores on the Desire For Control Scale. Moreover, both perfectionism dimensions were associated with greater sense of personal control, which is often conceptualized as a perceived personal efficacy over the events in one's life.

Flett *et al.* (1995) suggested that the repeated experience of negative life events may be particularly threatening to the perfectionist's need for personal control. A sensitivity to the experience of uncontrollable events fits with the model of perfectionism and stress outlined by Hewitt and Flett (2002). This model will now be examined briefly because of its implications for the role of perfectionism in leadership.

Hewitt and Flett (2002) hypothesized that perfectionists were at risk of various forms of psychological distress because perfectionism is associated with a host of stress mechanisms and processes. That is, perfectionism is associated with stress reactivity, stress perpetuation, and stress generation. Regarding stress reactivity, Hewitt and Flett (2002) suggested that perfectionists are highly reactive to stress, in part because it violates their need for control. As alluded to earlier, general support has been found for a diathesis-stress model that is based on the notion that perfectionism is a diathesis factor that interacts with the experience of stressful life events to produce elevated levels of psychological distress. A higher degree of stress reactivity may come, in part, from the tendency to personalize negative events. Fry (1995) observed that perfectionists view stressful life events as more ego involving, thereby increasing their perception of the stressfulness of events. Fry compared women executives who had high or low levels of perfectionism and found that highly perfectionistic women executives rated their events as higher in 'primary centrality' (i.e. the perception that a stressful event has significant personal consequences).

Stress perpetuation can occur in a variety of ways, most of which involve deficient responses to stressful situations. One way that this can occur is by persisting at a task long after it is time to give up. Feather (1989) described the tendency for some people to refuse to quit at something even though it was highly adaptive to do so. Perfectionists have often been described as people with a dogged determination that can approach the point of being self-defeating.

Stress perpetuation for the perfectionistic leader can come in the form of an aversive reaction when presented with an opportunity to implement meaningful change. Leadership often involves the strategic need for change (see Hartley, 2000). Several attributes of perfectionists suggest that if they are in a leadership role, they will find it difficult to acknowledge the need for change as well as implement change. First, perfectionists tend to suffer from cognitive rigidity (see Ferrari and Mautz, 1997). Thus, once a position has been taken, giving it up may prove too threatening.

Second, to the extent that the perfectionist is characterized by perfectionistic self-presentation, they may be unwilling to lead in a new direction because this may require admitting that mistakes were make, and it is too aversive to publicly admit to shortcomings and errors in judgement. These are characteristics that are just the opposite of the failure tolerant leader (Farson and Keyes, 2002).

Third, change that comes with the prospect of some uncertainty may threaten the perfectionist's need for control and predictability. Some data indicate that perfectionists are low in their stated ability to tolerate ambiguity. A study by Wittenberg and Norcross (2001) found that all three perfectionism dimensions on the MPS (Hewitt and Flett, 1991) were associated with low tolerance for ambiguity in a sample of private practice psychologists. This same study found that socially prescribed perfectionism was associated negatively with job enjoyment.

The link with stress generation is perhaps one of the most debilitating aspects of perfectionism. It has been suggested that effective leaders are willing to handle difficult situations (Conway, 2000), but creating difficult situations is another matter entirely! Stress generation involves the notion that rather than simply being reactive to stressors once they occur, some people take an active role in creating or generating stress for themselves. Stress generation can occur in a variety of ways. One way to generate stress is to pursue unrealistic standards. The workaholic strivings and relentless drive of extreme perfectionists could be interpreted as a reflection of the stress inducing choices made by perfectionists because they are unable or unwilling to lower their goals. The perfectionist can also create stress and interpersonal conflict by criticizing and humiliating others who do not meet perfectionistic expectations.

Once stress is experienced, the perfectionist is at risk because perfectionists often have maladaptive coping styles and problem-solving deficits (Hewitt and Flett, 2002). The situation is not entirely bleak because there are some data linking self-oriented and other-oriented perfectionism with higher learned resourcefulness (Flett et al., 1991). This could be interpreted as evidence of leadership potential because learned resourcefulness is a planful, task-oriented style that is generally regarded as a proactive, adaptive orientation. Unfortunately, however, this greater learned resourcefulness does not seem to translate into greater hardiness among perfectionists. The hardiness construct was identified originally by Kobasa (1979), and it involves a sense of commitment, control, and challenge, all of which are components that would make for effective leadership. Indeed, several studies suggest that people high in hardiness, relative to those with low hardiness, respond to stressful and threatening situations with relatively higher performance (for a review, see Maddi et al., 2002). At present, research has not directly examined perfectionism and hardiness per se. However, Hull, Van Treuren, and Virnelli (1987) examined hardiness and components of self-punitiveness (i.e. high standards, self-criticism, and overgeneralization) and they found no evidence of a link between endorsing perfectionistic standards and greater hardiness. Instead, one element of selfpunitiveness found commonly among perfectionists (i.e. overgeneralization of negative outcomes to reflect the entire self) was actually associated with low hardiness.

Perfectionism and burnout

In light of these proposed associations between perfectionism and stress, it follows that perfectionism should be prone to job stress and job burnout. Indeed, Fry (1995) reported that female executives with high levels of perfectionism also had significantly elevated scores on the modified Maslach Burnout Inventory ($r = 0.48$). This research was limited by the fact that the Multidimensional Perfectionism Scale was treated as a unidimensional measure, but it did provide initial evidence of a link between perfectionism and job burnout.

Subsequent research on the dimensions of perfectionism and job stress and job burnout found that socially prescribed perfectionism is linked with burnout. For instance, a study conducted with teachers found that socially prescribed perfectionism was associated with both the frequency and intensity of job stress (Flett, Hewitt, and Hallett, 1995). Socially prescribed perfectionism was also linked with low job satisfaction. Another investigation that examined perfectionism at home and at work with a modified version of the Multidimensional Perfectionism Scale (Hewitt and Flett, 1991) found that socially prescribed perfectionism at work was associated with job burnout in the form of emotional exhaustion and cynicism (Mitchelson and Burns, 1998). We can infer from these findings that other-oriented perfectionists who impose perfectionistic demands on others are going to breed burnout and cynicism among their fellow employees or team members. Exposure to the pressure to be perfect can take quite a toll.

SUMMARY AND DIRECTIONS FOR FUTURE RESEARCH

In summary, our analysis of perfectionism and leadership was based on the important distinction between adaptive conscientiousness versus the maladaptive hyperconscientiousness that seems to be synonymous with extreme perfectionism. Perfectionism was described as a complex multidimensional construct with various features that should detract from effective leadership (e.g. overconcern with mistakes, doubts about actions, and other-oriented perfectionism). Although people high in other-oriented perfectionism see themselves as good leaders, they have a hostile and rigid interpersonal style that would detract from effective leadership. Other attributes of perfectionists that would undermine their leadership aspirations include a fear of failure, a contingent sense of self-worth, and a stress-generating and stress-enhancing workaholic style that contributes to burnout and health problems.

We noted at the outset of this chapter that there is a paucity of research on perfectionism and leadership. Accordingly, there are many issues that need to be explored in future research. One key issue is whether the association between perfectionism and leadership holds across various situational contexts. It is possible that perfectionism in one setting (e.g. an industrial organization) may be more deleterious than perfectionism in another setting (e.g. the military). A related situational component here is the personality characteristics of followers; various followers may respond quite differently to perfectionists in leadership roles depending on their own personality structure.

We also know very little about how people perceive perfectionists who aspire to be leaders. To what extent is perfectionism acknowledged and admired versus seen as a detriment? And how does this vary according to the different dimensions of perfectionism?

Another goal for future research should be the identification of factors that mediate or moderate the association between perfectionism and leadership. One factor that should be examined here is the actual skill level of the aspiring leader. To what extent are the problems associated with perfectionism compensated for by exceptional intelligence, creativity, and insight? Actual levels of ability must be taken into account given the successes of notorious perfectionists such as Steve Jobs and Martha Stewart.

Another key issue involves the incremental validity of perfectionism measures in predicting leadership outcomes. That is, to what extent can perfectionism predict over and above other predictors such as the traits assessed by the five-factor model? How does perfectionism compare in terms of the relative ability to predict outcomes?

Clearly, there is much work that needs to be done. In retrospect, it is surprising that perfectionism has not been investigated in a systematic way, given that the importance of setting appropriate goals and establishing high standards is widely acknowledged as vital in performance settings. But what happens when we have people in leadership roles who set standards and goals that are simply too high? Hopefully, future research will address these important questions.

REFERENCES

Adler, A. (1956) The neurotic disposition. In H. L. Ansbacher and R. R. Ansbacher (eds) *The individual psychology of Alfred Adler*. New York: Harper, pp. 239–62.

Bass, B. M. (1985) *Leadership and performance beyond expectations*. New York: Free Press.

Besser, A., Flett, G. L., and Hewitt, P. L. (2004) Perfectionism, cognition, and affect in response to performance success vs. failure. *Journal of Rational-Emotive and Cognitive-Behavior Therapy*, 22: 297–304.

Bono, J. E. and Judge, T. A. (2004) Personality and transformational and transactional leadership: A meta-analysis. *Journal of Applied Psychology*, 89: 901–10.

Burke, R. J. (1999) Workaholism in organizations: Measurement validation and replication. *International Journal of Stress Management*, 6: 45–55.

Burns, D. (1980, November) The perfectionist's script for self-defeat. *Psychology Today*, 34–51.

Burns, D. and Beck, A. T. (1978) Cognitive behavior modification of mood disorders. In J. P. Foreyt and D. P. Rathjen (eds) *Cognitive behavior therapy: Research and application*. New York: Plenum, pp. 109–39.

Burns, J. M. (1978) *Leadership*. New York: Harper & Row.

Conroy, D. E. (2001) Progress in the development of a multidimensional measure of fear of failure: The Performance Failure Appraisal Inventory. *Anxiety, Stress, and Coping*, 14: 431–52.

Conway, J. M. (2000) Managerial performance development constructs and personality correlates. *Human Performance*, 13: 23–46.

Covington, M. V. (2000) Goal theory, motivation, and school achievement: An integrative review. *Annual Review of Psychology*, 51: 171–200.

Covington, M. V. and Mueller, K. J. (2001) Intrinsic versus extrinsic motivation: An approach/avoidance reformulation. *Educational Psychology Review*, 13: 157–76.

Crocker, J., Luhtanen, R. K., Cooper, M. L., and Bouvrette, S. (2003) Contingencies of self-worth in college students: Theory and measurement. *Journal of Personality and Social Psychology*, 85: 894–908.

DiBartolo, P. M., Frost, R. O., Chang, P., LaSota, M., and Grills, A. E. (2004) Shedding light on the relationship between personal standards and psychopathology: The case for contingent self-worth. *Journal of Rational-Emotive and Cognitive-Behavior Therapy*, 22: 237–50.

Emmons, R. A. (1984) Factor analysis and construct validation of the narcissistic personality inventory. *Journal of Personality Assessment*, 48: 291–300.

Emmons, R. A. (1987) Narcissism: Theory and measurement. *Journal of Personality and Social Psychology*, 52: 11–17.

Enns, M. W., Cox, B. J., Sareen, J., and Freeman, P. (2001) Adaptive and maladaptive perfectionism in medical students: A longitudinal investigation. *Medical Education,* 35: 1–9.

Farson, R. and Keyes, R. (2002) The failure-tolerant leader. *Harvard Business Review*, 80: 64–71.

Feather, N. T. (1989) Trying and giving up: Persistence and lack of persistence in failure situations. In R. C. Curtis (ed.) *Self-defeating behaviors: Experimental research, clinical impressions, and practical implications*. New York: Plenum, pp. 67–95.

Ferrari, J. R. and Mautz, W. T. (1997) Predicting perfectionism: Applying tests of rigidity. *Journal of Clinical Psychology*, 53: 1–6.

Flett, G. L. and Hewitt, P. L. (2002) Perfectionism and maladjustment: Theoretical, definitional, and treatment issues. In G. L. Flett and P. L. Hewitt (eds) *Perfectionism: Theory, research, and treatment*. Washington, DC: American Psychological Association Press, pp. 5–31.

Flett, G. L., Besser, A., and Hewitt, P. L. (2005) Perfectionism, ego defense styles, and depression: A comparison of self-reports versus informant ratings. *Journal of Personality*, 73: 1355–96.

Flett, G. L., Hewitt, P. L., and Hallett, J. (1995) Perfectionism and job stress in teachers. *Canadian Journal of School Psychology*, 11: 32–42.

Flett, G. L., Hewitt, P. L., and Martin, T. R. (1995) Dimensions of perfectionism and procrastination. In J. R. Ferrari, J. L. Johnson, and W. G. McCown (eds) *Procrastination and task avoidance: Theory, research, and treatment*. New York: Plenum, pp. 113–36.

Flett, G. L., Strongolos, C., and Hewitt, P. L. (2005) *Perfectionism, workaholism, and work addiction: The downside of self-oriented perfectionism*. Manuscript in preparation.

Flett, G. L., Besser, A., Davis, R. A., and Hewitt, P. L. (2003) Dimensions of perfectionism, unconditional self-acceptance, and depression. *Journal of Rational-Emotive and Cognitive-Behavior Therapy*, 21: 119–38.

Flett, G. L., Hewitt, P. L., Blankstein, K. R., and Mosher, S. W. (1991) Perfectionism, self-actualization, and personal adjustment. *Journal of Social Behavior and Personality*, 6: 147–60.

Flett, G. L., Hewitt, P. L., Blankstein, K. R., and Mosher, S. W. (1995) Perfectionism, life events, and depressive symptoms: A test of a diathesis-stress model. *Current Psychology*, 14: 112–37.

Flett, G. L., Hewitt, P. L., Garshowitz, M., and Martin, T. R. (1997) Personality, negative social interactions, and depressive symptoms. *Canadian Journal of Behavioural Sciences*, 29: 28–37.

Flynn, C. A., Hewitt, P. L., Broughton, R., and Flett, G. L. (1998, August) *Mapping perfectionism dimensions onto the interpersonal circumplex*. Paper presented at the annual meeting of the American Psychological Association, San Francisco, CA.

Ford, J. K. and Oswald, F. L. (2003) Understanding the dynamic learner: Linking personality traits, learning situations, and individual behavior. In M. R. Barrick and A. M. Ryan (eds) *Personality and work: Reconsidering the role of personality in organizations*. San Francisco, CA: Jossey-Bass/Wiley, pp. 229–61.

Frost, R. O., Marten, P.A., Lahart, C. and Rosenblate, R. (1990) The dimensions of perfectionism. *Cognitive Therapy and Research*, 14: 449–68.

Frost, R. O., Heimberg, R. G., Holt, C. S., Mattia, J. I., and Neubauer, A. L. (1993) A comparison of two measures of perfectionism. *Personality and Individual Differences*, 14: 119–26.

Frost, R. O., Trepanier, K. L., Brown, E. J., Heimberg, R. G., Juster, H. R., Makris, G. S., and Leung, A. W. (1997) Self-monitoring of mistakes among subjects high and low in perfectionistic concern over mistakes. *Cognitive Therapy and Research*, 21: 209–22.

Fry, P. S. (1995) Perfectionism, humor, and optimism as moderators of health outcomes and determinants of coping styles of women executives. *Genetic, Social, and General Psychology Monographs*, 121: 211–45.

Garner, D. M., Olmstead, M. P., and Polivy, J. (1983) Development and validation of a multidimensional eating disorder inventory for anorexia nervosa and bulimia. *International Journal of Eating Disorders*, 2: 15–34.

Habke, A. M. and Flynn, C. A. (2002) Interpersonal aspects of trait perfectionism. In G. L. Flett and P. L. Hewitt (eds) *Perfectionism: Theory, research, and treatment*. Washington, DC: American Psychological Association Press, pp. 151–80.

Hallsten, L., Josephson, M., and Torgen, M. (2005) *Performance-based self-esteem: A driving force in burnout processes and its assessment*. Arbetslivsinstitutet: National Institute for Working Life.

Hamachek, D. E. (1978) Psychodynamics of normal and neurotic perfectionism. *Psychology*, 15: 27–33.

Hartley, J. F. (2000) Leading and managing the uncertainty of strategic change. In P. Flood, T. Droomgoole, S. Carroll, and L. Gorman (eds) *Managing strategic implementation*. Oxford: Blackwell, pp. 109–22.

Hewitt, P. L. and Flett, G. L. (1990) Perfectionism and depression: A multidimensional analysis. *Journal of Social Behavior and Personality*, 5: 423–38.

Hewitt, P. L. and Flett, G. L. (1991) Perfectionism in the self and social contexts: Conceptualization, assessment, and association with psychopathology. *Journal of Personality and Social Psychology*, 60: 456–70.

Hewitt, P. L. and Flett, G. L. (1993) Dimensions of perfectionism, daily stress, and depression: A test of the specific vulnerability hypothesis. *Journal of Abnormal Psychology*, 102: 58–65.

Hewitt, P. L. and Flett, G. L. (2002) Perfectionism and stress in psychopathology. In G. L. Flett and P. L. Hewitt (eds) *Perfectionism: Theory, research, and treatment*. Washington, DC: American Psychological Association Press, pp. 255–84.

Hewitt, P. L. and Flett, G. L. (2004) *The Multidimensional Perfectionism Scale: Manual*. Toronto, ON: Multi-Health Systems, Inc.

Hewitt, P. L., Flett, G. L., and Ediger, E. (1996) Perfectionism and depression: Longitudinal assessment of a specific vulnerability hypothesis. *Journal of Abnormal Psychology*, 105: 276–80.

Hewitt, P. L., Flett, G. L., Turnbull-Donovan, W. and Mikail, S. (1991) The multidimensional perfectionism scale: Reliability, validity, and psychometric properties in psychiatric samples. *Psychological Assessment: A Journal of Consulting and Clinical Psychology*, 3: 464–68.

Hewitt, P. L., Flett, G. L, Sherry, S. B., Habke, M., Parkin, M., Lam, R.W., McMurtry, B., Ediger, E., Fairlie, P., and Stein, M. (2003) The interpersonal expression of perfection: Perfectionistic self-presentation and psychological distress. *Journal of Personality and Social Psychology*, 84: 1303–25.

Hill, R. W., McIntire, K., and Bacharach, V. (1997) Perfectionism and the Big Five. *Journal of Social Behavior and Personality*, 12: 257–70.

Hill, R. W., Zrull, M. C., and Turlington, S. (1997) Perfectionism and interpersonal problems. *Journal of Personality Assessment*, 69: 81–103.

Hill, R. W., Huelsman, T. J., Furr, R. M., Kibler, J., Vicente, B. B. and Kennedy, C. (2004) A new measure of perfectionism: The Perfectionism Inventory (PI). *Journal of Personality Assessment*, 82: 80–91.

Hobden, K. and Pliner, P. (1995) Self-handicapping and dimensions of perfectionism: Self-presentation vs. self-protection. *Journal of Research in Personality*, 29: 461–74.

Hogan, J. and Ones, D. S. (1997) Conscientiousness and integrity at work. In R. Hogan, J. Johnson, and S. Briggs (eds) *Handbook of personality psychology*. New York: Academic Press, pp. 849–70.

Hull, J. G., Van Treuren, R. R., and Virnelli, S. (1987) Hardiness and health: A critique and alternative approach. *Journal of Personality and Social Psychology*, 53: 518–30.

Jones, A. and Crandell, R. (1986) Validation of a short index of self-actualization. *Personality and Social Psychology Bulletin*, 12: 63–73.

Judge, T. A., Bono, J. E., Ilies, R., and Gerhart, M. W. (2002) Personality and leadership: A qualitative and quantitative review. *Journal of Applied Psychology*, 87: 765–80.

Kobasa, S. C. (1979) Stressful life events, personality, and health: An inquiry into hardiness. *Journal of Personality and Social Psychology*, 37: 1–11.

Krantz, S. E. and Rude, S. (1984) Depressive attributions: Selection of different causes or assignment of dimensional meanings? *Journal of Personality and Social Psychology*, 47: 193–203.

Lee, K. and Ashton, M. C. (2004) Psychometric properties of the HEXACO Personality Inventory. *Multivariate Behavioral Research*, 39: 329–58.

Maddi, S. R., Khoshaba, D. M., Persico, M., Lu, J., Harvey, R., and Bleecker, F. (2002) The personality construct of hardiness II: Relationships with comprehensive tests of personality and psychopathology. *Journal of Research in Personality*, 36: 72–85.

Mann, R. D. (1959) A review of the relationships between personality and performance in small groups. *Psychological Bulletin*, 56: 241–70.

Martin, T. R., Flett, G. L., Hewitt, P. L., Krames, L., and Szantos, G. (1996) Personality correlates of depression and health symptoms: A test of a self-regulation model. *Journal of Research in Personality*, 31: 264–77.

Mitchelson, J. K. and Burns, L. R. (1998) Career mothers and perfectionism: Stress at work and at home. *Personality and Individual Differences*, 25: 477–85.

Missildine, W. H. (1963) Perfectionism – If you must strive to 'do better.' In W. H. Missildine (ed.) *Your inner child of the past*. New York: Pocket Books, pp. 75–90.

Mor, S., Day, H. I., Flett, G. L., and Hewitt, P. L. (1995) Perfectionism, control, and components of performance anxiety in professional performers. *Cognitive Therapy and Research,* 19: 207–25.

O'Connor, D. B. and O'Connor, R. C. (2004) Perceived changes in food intake in response to stress: The role of conscientiousness. *Stress and Health*, 20: 279–91.

Onwuegbuzie, A. J. (2000) Academic procrastinators and perfectionistic tendencies among graduate students. *Journal of Social Behavior and Personality,* 15: 103–9.

Pacht, A. R. (1984) Reflections on perfection. *American Psychologist*, 39: 386–90.

Porter, G. (2001) Workaholic tendencies and the high potential for stress among co-workers. *International Journal of Stress Management*, 8: 147–64.

Robinson, B. E. (1999) The Work Addiction Risk Test: Development of a tentative measure of workaholism. *Perceptual and Motor Skills*, 88: 199–210.

Robinson, B. E. (2000) *Chained to the desk: A guidebook for workaholics, their partners and children, and the clinicians who treat them*. New York: New York University Press.

Rose, R., Fogg, L., Helmreich, R., and McFadden, T. (1994) Psychological predictors of astronaut effectiveness. *Aviation, Space, and Environmental Medicine*, 65: 910–15.

Rude, S. S. (1989) Dimensions of self-control in a sample of depressed women. *Cognitive Therapy and Research*, 13: 363–75.

Slade, P. D. and Owens, R. G. (1998) A dual process model of perfectionism based on reinforcement theory. *Behavior Modification*, 22: 372–90.

Spangler, W. D., House, R. J., and Palrecha, R. (2004) Personality and leadership. In B. Schneider and D. B. Smith (eds) *Personality and organizations*. Mahwah, NJ: Erlbaum, pp. 251–90.

Spence, J. T. and Robbins, A. S. (1992) Workaholism: Definition, measurement, and preliminary results. *Journal of Personality Assessment*, 58: 160–78.

Stogdill, R. M. (1948) Personal factors associated with leadership: A survey of the literature. *Journal of Psychology*, 25: 35–71.

Sturman, T. S. (2000) The motivational foundations and behavioral expressions of three narcissistic styles. *Social Behavior and Personality*, 28: 393–407.

Watson, P. J., Varnell, S. P. and Morris, R. J. (1999–2000) Self-reported narcissism and perfectionism: An ego-psychological perspective and the continuum hypothesis. *Imagination, Cognition, and Personality*, 19: 59–69.

Wittenberg, K. J. and Norcross, J. C. (2001) Practitioner perfectionism: Relationship to ambiguity tolerance and work satisfaction. *Journal of Clinical Psychology*, 57: 1543–50.

Chapter 14

Workaholism types, satisfaction, and well-being

It's not how hard you work but why and how you work hard*

Ronald J. Burke

Leadership roles in organizations of all sizes are demanding and time consuming (Brett and Stroh, 2003; Kotter, 1999). There is some evidence that managers in industrialized countries are working more hours now than previously (Greenhouse, 2001; Schor, 1991). I have met managers who told me they work 80 to 100 hours per week. Working long hours may in fact be a prerequisite for achieving senior leadership positions (Jacobs and Gerson, 1998; Wallace, 1997).

Porter (2004) considers the questions of how and why people work, considering work, the work ethic, and work excess. How much work is too much? Can one make a distinction between a healthy work ethic and working to excess? One can work to have things (fanned by consumerism), to not be left behind (Reich, 2000), to confirm self-worth, to use to latest technology (tools), and to provide for children. The work ethic is based on viewing hard work as virtuous. But this doesn't address the question of when hard work becomes a problem. What determines too much work? It seems that the norm for amount of work has risen in the past decade. The reasons likely include economic recessions, organizational downsizings and restructurings, and levels of insecurity of those with jobs making it easier for them to choose to work harder.

Although the terms workaholic and work addict encompass all the problems that addiction brings (Oates, 1971), most academics believe that work is healthy, desirable, and protective of many illnesses. In support of this view, research has shown that holding multiple roles instead of a single role (e.g. homemaker) generally leads to favourable well-being outcomes among women (Barnett and Marshall, 1992).

* Preparation of this chapter was supported in part by the Schulich School of Business, York University. I thank Janet T. Spence for making her workaholism measure available to me. Several colleagues participated in the design and conduct of these projects: Zena Burgess, Fay Oberklaid, Astrid Richardsen, Stig Matthiesen, Lisa Fiksenbaum and Graeme MacDermid.

Workaholism and long working hours have positive connotations such as dedication, commitment, and organizational citizenship behaviour and negative connotations such as ill health and damaged family relationships. Number of hours worked per week, while obviously an element of workaholism, does not capture one's degree of work involvement, a psychological state or attitude. Hours worked per week is a behavioural manifestation of workaholism.

Many senior level executives identify themselves, sometimes sheepishly and with embarrassment, as workaholics and organization members often use the term workaholic to describe some of their colleagues. This chapter considers the literature on workaholism in organizations and the implications of this review for the exercise of leadership and the well-being of leaders. Workaholism has traditionally had negative connotations (Killinger, 1991). Are workaholic leaders sad and tragic figures doomed to unsatisfactory relationships and ill health? Is working long hours inevitably linked with distress?

Workaholism has received relatively little research attention to date (McMillan, O'Driscoll and Burke, 2003). As a consequence, data from non-managerial samples will be included with an indication of the particular samples involved, to expand our understanding of it. Application of these findings to leadership roles must be considered tentative until borne out by additional research.

Although the popular press has paid considerable attention to workaholism (Fassel, 1990; Garfield, 1987; Kiechel, 1989a, 1989b; Killinger, 1991; Klaft and Kleiner, 1988; Machlowitz, 1980; Waddell, 1993), very little research has been undertaken to further our understanding of it (McMillan *et al.*, 2001). Most writing has been anecdotal and clinical (Fassel, 1990; Killinger, 1991; Oates, 1971). Basic questions of definition have not been addressed, and measurement concerns have been avoided (Scott, Moore, and Miceli, 1997).

It should come as no surprise then that opinions, observations, and conclusions about workaholism are both varied and conflicting (McMillan *et al.*, 2002). Some writers view workaholism positively from an organizational perspective. Machlowitz (1980) conducted a qualitative interview study of 100 workaholics and found them to be very satisfied and productive. Others view workaholism negatively (Killinger 1991; Oates 1971). These writers equate workaholism with other addictions and depict workaholics as unhappy, obsessive, tragic figures who are not performing their jobs well and are creating difficulties for their co-workers (Porter 1996). The former would advocate the encouragement of workaholism; the latter would discourage it.

DEFINITIONS OF WORKAHOLISM

Oates (1971), generally acknowledged as the first person to use the word workaholic, defined it as 'a person whose need for work has become so excessive that it creates noticeable disturbance or interference with his bodily health, personal happiness, and interpersonal relationships, and with his smooth social functioning'.

Killinger (1991) defines a workaholic as 'a person who gradually becomes emotionally crippled and addicted to control and power in a compulsive drive to gain approval and success' Robinson (1998) defines workaholism 'as a progressive, potentially fatal disorder, characterized by self-imposed demands, compulsive overworking, inability to regulate work to the exclusion of most other life activities'. Porter (1996) defines workaholism as 'an excessive involvement with work evidenced by neglect in other areas of life and based on internal motives of behaviour maintenance rather than requirements of the job or organization'. Most writers use the terms excessive work, workaholism, and work addiction interchangeably.

Scott, Moore, and Miceli (1997) used a three-step process to develop what they term 'a reasonable definition' of the construct. They first collected characteristics attributed to workaholics in the practical and clinical literature. They then looked for conceptual similarities among these characteristics. They also differentiated the workaholic concept from similar constructs (e.g. job involvement) to reduce redundancy. They identified three elements in workaholic behaviour patterns using this process: discretionary time spent in work activities, thinking about work when not working, and working beyond organizational requirements.

Spence and Robbins (1992) define the workaholic as a person who 'is highly work involved, feels compelled or driven to work because of inner pressures, and is low in enjoyment at work'. Most writers view workaholism as a stable individual characteristic (Scott, Moore, and Miceli, 1997; Spence and Robbins 1992). Most definitions of workaholism portray it in negative terms.

MEASURES OF WORKAHOLISM

Two measures of workaholism have received some research attention. Robinson and his colleagues developed the Work Addiction Risk Test (WART). The WART contains 25 items drawn from symptoms (characteristics) reported by writers on workaholism (Robinson, 1998). Respondents rate items on a four-point Likert scale (1 = Never true, 4 = Always true) according to how well each item describes their work habits (e.g. 'It's important that I see the concrete results of what I do'). Scores can range from 25 to 100. Robinson (1998) states that scores of 25 to 56 indicate that you are not work addicted; scores from 57 to 66, mildly work addicted; and scores from 67 to 100, highly work addicted. Scores above 65 fall greater than one standard deviation above the mean. The items on the WART, based on a review of available literature, were grouped into five categories: over-doing, self-worth, control-perfectionism, intimacy, and preoccupation-future reference.

Spence and Robbins (1992) report the development of their workaholism measure, providing both reliability and concurrent validity information. Based on their definition of workaholism, developed from a review of the literature, they propose three workaholism components: work involvement, feeling driven to the work and work enjoyment. They developed multi-item measures of these components, each having internal consistency reliabilities greater than 0.67. Data were collected in this study from 368 social workers holding academic appointments. Profile analysis resulted in the same six profiles for women and men three workaholic types and three non-workaholic types. These profiles were: Work Addicts (WAs) score high on work involvement, high on feeling driven to work and low on work enjoyment. Work Enthusiasts (WEs) score high on work involvement, low on feeling driven to work and high on work enjoyment. Enthusiastic Addicts (EAs) score high on all three workaholism components. Unengaged Workers (UWs) score low on all three workaholism components. Relaxed Workers (RWs) score low on feeling driven to work and work involvement and high on work enjoyment. Disenchanted Workers (DWs) score high on feeling driven to work and low on work involvement and work enjoyment. Other work involving different samples and conducted in different countries has produced the same profiles (Elder and Spence, unpublished manuscript; Kanai, Wakabayashi and Fling, 1996; Buelens and Poelmans, 2004; Robbins, 1993).

TYPES OF WORKAHOLICS

Some researchers have proposed the existence of different types of workaholic behaviour patterns, each having potentially different antecedents and associations with job performance, work, and life outcomes (Naughton, 1987; Scott, Moore, and Miceli, 1997; Spence and Robbins, 1992). Naughton (1987) presents a typology of workaholism based on the dimensions of career commitment and obsession-compulsion. Job-involved workaholics (high work commitment, low obsession-compulsion) are hypothesized to perform well in demanding jobs, be highly job satisfied with low interest in non-work activities. Compulsive workaholics (high work commitment, high obsession-compulsion) are hypothesized to be potentially poor performers (staff problems resulting from impatience and ritualized work habits). Non-workaholics (low work commitment and obsession-compulsion) spend more time in other than work commitments. Compulsive non-workaholics (low work commitment, high obsession-compulsion) compulsively spend time in non-work activities.

Scott, Moore, and Miceli (1997) suggest three types of workaholic behaviour patterns: compulsive-dependent, perfectionist, and achievement-oriented. They hypothesize that compulsive-dependent workaholism will be positively related to job performance and job and life satisfaction. Perfectionist workaholism will be positively related to levels of stress, physical and psychological problems, hostile interpersonal relationships, low job satisfaction and performance, and voluntary turnover and absenteeism. Finally, achievement-oriented workaholism will be positively related to physical and psychological health, job and life satisfaction, job performance, low voluntary turnover, and pro-social behaviours.

Spence and Robbins (1992) propose three workaholic patterns based on their workaholic triad notion: Work Addicts, Work Enthusiasts, and Enthusiastic Addicts. The workaholic triad consists of three concepts: work involvement, feeling driven to work, and work enjoyment. These researchers then offer a number of hypotheses as to how these three workaholic patterns might differ from each other. Thus, for example, Work Addicts would be more perfectionistic, would experience greater stress and report more physical health symptoms. Oates (1971) identified five types of workaholics: dyed-in-the-wool workaholics, converted workaholics, situational workaholics, pseudo workaholics, and escapists posing as workaholics. Fassel (1990) described four types of workaholics: compulsive workers, binge workers, closet workers, and work anorexics. Robinson (1998) distinguished four types of workaholics: relentless workaholics, bulimic workaholics, attention deficit workaholics, and savouring workaholics. The existence of different types of workaholic patterns might help reconcile conflicting observations and conclusions cited above. However, the three workaholism types proposed by Spence and Robbins (1992) are the only ones that have received much research attention.

RESEARCH FINDINGS

The following sections of the chapter will review research findings that compare the personal demographics, job behaviours, work outcomes, extra-work-outcomes, and psychological health of the three types of workaholics proposed by Spence and Robbins (1992).

Personal demographic and work situational characteristics

A critical question involves potential differences between the three workaholism types on both personal demographic and work situation characteristics including hours worked per week. If the workaholism types were found to differ on these (e.g. organizational level, marital status, hours worked per week), these differences would account for any differences found on work and health outcomes.

A number of studies (Bonebright, Clay, and Ankenmann, 2000; Burke, 1999a; Burke, Burgess and Oberklaid, 2002; Spence and Robbins, 1992) have reported essentially no differences between the three workaholism types on a variety of personal and work situation characteristics. The workaholism types work the same number of hours and extra hours per week; the workaholism types working significantly more hours per week and more extra hours per week than the non-workaholism types.

Work behaviours

There has been considerable speculation regarding the work behaviours likely to be exhibited by workaholics. This list includes hours worked per week, extra hours worked per week, job involvement, job stress, non-delegation of job responsibilities to others, high (or low) levels of job performances, high levels of interpersonal conflict and of lack of trust. There is empirical research that examines some of these hypothesized relationships.

Burke (1999a) considered these relationships in a large sample of Canadian MBA graduates. Comparisons of the three workaholism types on a number of behavioural manifestations provided considerable support for the hypothesized relationships. First, there were no differences between WAs, Eas, and WEs on hours worked per week or extra hours worked per week; workaholism types working significantly more hours and extra hours per week than did the three non-workaholism types. Second, EAs devoted more time to their jobs in a psychological sense than did both WEs and WAs. Third, WAs reported greater job stress than did EAs, both reporting greater job stress than did WEs. Fourth, both EAs and WEs reported greater job involvement than did WAs. Fifth, WAs had greater inability and unwillingness to delegate than both WEs and EAs. Sixth, EAs were more perfectionistic than were WEs.

Spence and Robbins (1992) found that WAs reported higher levels of job stress, perfectionism, and unwillingness to delegate job duties to others than did WEs. Kanai, Wakabayashi, and Fling (1996), using the Spence and Robbins measures, reported that WAs and EAs scored higher than WEs on measures of job stress, perfectionism, non-delegation, and time committed to job.

In summary, WAs reported higher levels of work stress, more perfectionism and greater unwillingness or difficulty in delegating than one or both of the other workaholism types.

Antecedents of workaholism

Three potential antecedents of workaholism have received some conceptual and research attention. Two of these, family of origin and personal beliefs and fears, are the result of socialization practices within families and society at large. The third, organizational support for work–personal life imbalance, represents organizational values and priorities.

Family of origin

Robinson (1998) has written about work addiction as a symptom of a diseased family system. Work addiction, similarly to other addictive behaviours, is intergenerational and passed on to future generations through family processes and dynamics. In this view, work addiction is seen as a learned addictive response to a dysfunctional family of origin system. Pietropinto (1986) suggests that children of workaholics learn that parental love is contingent on their (the children's) high performance. Family of origin measures have not yet been used in studies employing the Spence and Robbins typology.

Personal beliefs and fears

Burke (1999b) examined the relationship of personal beliefs and fears and workaholism. Beliefs and fears are a reflection of values, thoughts, and interpersonal styles. Three measures of beliefs and fears developed by Lee, Jamieson, and Early (1996) were used: 'Striving against others', 'No moral principles', and 'Prove yourself'. Burke compared the three workaholism types on these measures of beliefs and fears. Was there a relationship between cognitions managers and professionals hold about their broader environment and types of workaholism? Analyses provided evidence of such a relationship. First, all three beliefs and fears were significantly and positively correlated with measures of feeling driven to work and negatively with work enjoyment. Second, comparisons of workaholism types showed significant type effects on all three measures of beliefs and fears as well as on their composite.

More specifically, WAs scored significantly higher than WEs and EAs on measures of striving against others and no moral principles, as well as on the composite measure. In addition, WAs scored higher on the need to prove self than did WEs. Workaholism thus emerges as work behaviours in response to feelings of low self-worth and insecurity. This is best reflected in managers' feelings of being driven to work. Paradoxically these beliefs and fears were also found to be associated with lower levels of work enjoyment.

Burke, Richardsen, and Martinussen (2004) found, in a study of 171 Norwegian owners and senior managers of construction companies, that WAs scored higher than WEs on Impatience–Irritation; EAs scored higher than WEs on Achievement Striving both being dimensions of Type A behaviour. Impatience–Irritation has been shown to be predictive of psychological distress.

Organizational values

Burke (1999c) compared perceptions of organization culture values supporting work-personal life imbalance across the three workaholism types. Organizational values encouraging work–family imbalance were measured by scales developed by Kofodimos (1993). WAs reported higher imbalance values than both WEs and EAs. Thus WAs see their workplaces as less supportive of work–personal life balance than the two other workaholism types.

Work outcomes

The relationship between workaholism and indicators of job and career satisfaction and success is difficult to specify. It is likely that different types of workaholics will report varying work and career satisfactions (Scott, Moore, and Miceli, 1997).

Burke (1999d) compared levels of work and career satisfaction and success among the workaholism profiles observed by Spence and Robbins (1992). Four work outcomes, all significantly intercorrelated, were used. Intent to Quit was measured by two items (e.g. 'Are you currently looking for a different job in a different organization?'). This scale had been used previously by Burke (1991). Work Satisfaction was measured by a seven-item scale developed by Kofodimos (1993). An item was 'I feel challenged by my work'. Career Satisfaction was measured by a five-item scale developed by Greenhaus, Parasuraman, and Wormley (1990). One item was 'I am satisfied with the success I have achieved in my career'. Future Career Prospects was measured by a three-item scale developed by Greenhaus, Parasuraman, and Wormley (1990). An item was 'I expect to advance in my career to senior levels of management'.

WAs scored lower than WEs and EAs on Job Satisfaction, Career Satisfaction, and Future Career Prospects, and higher than WEs on Intent to Quit. It should be noted that all three workaholic profiles (WAs, EWs, WEs) worked the same number of hours per week and had the same job and organizational tenure.

Workaholism types and flow at work

Csikszentmihalyi (1990) uses the term optimal experience to refer to times when individuals feel in control of their actions and masters of their own destinies. Optimal experiences commonly result from hard work and meeting challenges head on. Csikszentmihalyi believes that since so much time is invested and spent in working, the experience of flow at work is likely to have significant effects on one's quality of life (Csikszentmihalyi, 1997). Flow also plays a major role in how people respond to stress. Csikszentmihalyi reports data showing that women and men experience more flow at work than in leisure (Csikszentmihalyi, 2003). He also reports that managers and supervisors were more often in flow at work (64 per cent) than were clerical workers (51 per cent) and blue-collar workers (49 per cent). Apathy was reported at work more often by blue-collar workers than managers (23 versus 11 per cent), and in leisure more often by managers than by blue-collar workers (61 versus 46 per cent). Certain activities are more conducive to flow as they make optimal experience easier to achieved (e.g. learning skills, goals, and new solutions (Czikszentmihaly, 2003). Organizational leaders are likely to experience flow.

Psychological well-being

There is considerable consensus in the workaholism literature on the association of workaholism and poorer psychological and physical well-being. In fact, some definitions of workaholism incorporate aspects of diminished health as central elements. It is not surprising that this relationship has received research attention.

Burke (1999e) compared the three workaholism types identified by Spence and Robbins (1992) on three indicators of psychological and physical well-being in a sample of 530 employed women and men MBA graduates. Psychosomatic symptoms were measured by 19 items developed by Quinn and Shepard (1974). Respondents indicated how often they experienced each physical condition (e.g. 'headaches') in the past year. Lifestyle behaviours were measured by five items developed by Kofodimos (1993). One item was 'I participate in a regular exercise program'. Emotional well-being was measured by six items developed by Kofodimos (1993). An item was 'I actively seek to understand and improve my emotional well-being'.

Once again, the comparisons of the workaholism types on the three measures of psychological and physical well-being provided considerable support for the hypothesized relationships. WAs had more psychosomatic symptoms than both WEs and EAs and poorer physical and emotional well-being than did WEs.

In a study of 171 Norwegian construction company owners and senior managers, Burke, Richardsen, and Martinussen (2004) found that WAs reported higher levels of emotional exhaustion than both WEs and EAs; the three workaholism types were similar on levels of cynicism and personal efficacy.

Would the workaholism types differ in the experience of flow? In a study of 211 Norwegian journalists, Burke and Matthiesen (2004) found that journalists scoring higher on work enjoyment and lower on feeling driven to work because of internal needs indicated higher levels of flow or optimal experience at work. In this same study, Burke and Matthiesen found that WEs and EAs indicated higher levels of flow than did WAs.

Extra-work satisfactions and family functioning

A number of writers have hypothesized that workaholism is likely to impact negatively on family functioning (Killinger, 1991; Porter 1996; Robinson, 1999, 2001). Empirical examinations of this hypothesis are unfortunately few. Robinson and Post (1997) report data from a sample of 107 self-identified workaholics (members of

Workaholics Anonymous chapters in North America) who completed the WART and a family assessment instrument. Three levels of WART scores indicating various levels of workaholism were compared. High scores differed from low and medium scores on six of the seven family assessment scales indicating lower (poorer) family functioning in all cases.

Robinson (1998) also reviews the literature on children of workaholics. Robinson and Kelley (1998) asked 211 young adults (college students) to think back to their childhoods and rate the workaholism of their parents on the WART. Participants also completed measures of depression, anxiety, self-concept, and locus of control. College students who perceived their parents as workaholics scored higher on depression and external locus of control. Children of workaholic fathers scored higher on anxiety than did children of non-workaholic fathers. Interestingly mothers' workaholism had no effect on these outcomes. Robinson attributes the distress of children of workaholic fathers to the presence of a diseased family system more evidence that work addiction contributes to family dysfunction (Pietropinto 1986).

Burke (1999f) considered the relationship of the three workaholism types iden- tified by Spence and Robbins (1992) and extra-work satisfactions. Three aspects of life or extra-work satisfaction were included using measures developed by Kofodimos (1993). These were: Family Satisfaction, Relationship Satisfaction, Relationship Satisfaction, and Community Satisfaction. The comparisons of the workaholism types on the three measures of life or extra-work satisfactions provided moderate support for the hypothesized relationships. WAs reported less satisfaction on all three extra-work satisfaction measures than did WEs and less satisfaction on one (Family) than did EAs.

Evaluating workaholism components

The workaholism measures used in two or more research studies (i.e. Robinson, 1998; Spence and Robbins, 1992) all contain components or factors. Do each of these factors have similar and independent relationships with particular outcomes? Or might they have opposite relationships with some outcomes and no relation- ship with others?

Burke (1999g) considered the question of whether the workaholism triad components had different consequences. An examination of the relationships among specific workaholism components and the various types of job behaviours and outcome variables revealed an interesting, and complex, pattern of findings. First, work enjoyment and feeling driven to work were significantly related to all seven job behaviour validation measures, while work involvement was significantly related to three of the seven. Respondents scoring higher on the workaholism components also scored higher on job behaviours reflecting workaholism, with one exception: difficulty in delegating. In this instance, respondents scoring higher on work involvement and feeling driven to work and lower on work enjoyment reported greater difficulty in delegating. Second, joy in work was the only workaholism component related to work outcomes. Respondents reporting greater work enjoyment also reported more job satisfaction, more optimistic future career prospects, and more career satisfaction to date. Third, both work enjoyment and feeling driven to work were related to indicators of psychological well-being but in opposite directions. Respondents reporting greater work enjoyment and lesser feelings of being driven to work reported greater community satisfaction.

Although work enjoyment and feeling driven to work had consistent and similar effects on job behaviours reflecting workaholism, these two workaholism components had different effects on work outcomes and psychological well-being. One, work enjoyment, was associated with positive outcomes; the other, feeling driven to work, was associated with negative outcomes. Finally, none of the workaholism components showed consistent relationships with measures of extra-work satisfactions.

Addressing workaholism

There is a large speculative literature suggesting ways to reduce levels of workaholism. One part of this work focuses on individual and family therapy (Killinger, 1991; Robinson, 1998); a second part emphasizes organizational and managerial interventions.

Individual counselling

Workaholics Anonymous chapters have sprung up in some North American cities. These groups, patterned after Alcoholics Anonymous self-help groups, endorse the 12-step approach common to the treatment of a variety of addictions. Killinger (1991) and Robinson (1998) include chapters outlining actions an individual might pursue to reduce levels of workaholism; Seybold and Salomone (1994) offer suggestions on counselling approaches.

Family therapy

Robinson and his colleagues, consistent with their clinical and consulting perspective, focus on treatment, both individual and family. This is not surprising given the central role they give to both family of origin and current family functioning in the development maintenance and intergenerational transmission of workaholism. The treatment recommendations Robinson (1998) offers are similar to those offered to alcoholic families.

Thus, denial is common among workaholics and their family members. Family members are reluctant to complain. Workaholics define their behaviour and symptoms in a favourable light (Killinger, 1991; Porter, 1996). Parental expectations of children, often unrealistic, must be addressed. Family structures need to be identified. How do family members collude with the workaholic parent? Family members need help in expressing their negative feelings to the workaholic. Families need to learn to set boundaries around the amount they work together and talk about work. Family members can set goals to improve family dynamics (e.g. communication, roles, expression of feelings).

Workplace interventions

How can employers help workaholics and workaholics help themselves? Schaef and Fassel (1988) offer the following ideas. Employers should pay attention to the performance and work habits of employees and be alert to warning signs of workaholism. They should ensure that employees take vacation time away from work. Finally, job insecurity, work overload, limited career opportunities, and lack of control can make employees feel compelled to work longer. If these factors exist, employers should try to minimize their impact on the atmosphere within the organization.

Haas (1991) also highlights the role that managers can play in assisting their workaholic employees to change. Workaholic employees should be referred to an employee assistance programme or a recovery programme to start treatment processes. Managers should help prioritize projects for employees as long-term and short-term assignments. Workaholics must be encouraged and helped to delegate their work. At the end of each day, the manager should meet with the employee to discuss what has been accomplished during that day and to plan (down to short intervals) for the following day. The employee should be given specific times to take breaks and to leave work. It may also be possible to reduce the negative effects of workaholism, particularly well-being and health consequences, through stress-management training.

The development of workplace values that promote new, more balanced priorities and healthier lifestyles will support those workaholism types that want to change their behaviours.

IMPLICATIONS

Organizational leaders work long hours putting in more hours than managers and professionals working at lower organizational levels in many cases (Fisher, 1992; Hochschild, 1997; Maume and Bellas, 2001; Worthy, 1987). There is also some evidence that working extreme hours can harm psychological and physical health, productivity, and family and social relationships (Cartwright, 2000; Sparks, *et al.*, 1997; Worrell and Cooper, 1999).

This chapter compared the job behaviours, work and non-work outcomes, psychological well-being, and personal values among three types of workaholics, all of whom work equally long hours. A generally consistent pattern of findings emerged. WAs reported job behaviours likely to be associated with reduced contribution (job delegating) in comparison with WEs and EAs. WAs also indicated lower levels of psychological health than the two other types. And WAs indicated less non-work satisfactions.

Why would three types of managers working the same hours per week at the same organizational levels, having the same family structures, the same job and organizational tenure, and earning the same incomes indicate such different work and life experiences?

The findings shed some light on this. First, WAs had values and beliefs indicative of greater needs to prove themselves, greater insecurity (lower self-esteem), and a less supportive and trusting environment, in general. Second, WAs described their organizational values as less supportive of work–personal life balance. Third, they scored higher on feeling driven to work because of needs, probably related to their beliefs and values. Fourth, they worked in ways that created higher levels of work stress for themselves perfectionistic, non-delegating. Thus, it was not a question of how hard they worked but why (their motivations) and how (their behaviours) they worked hard that mattered.

CONTRASTING MOTIVES FOR LONG HOURS AT WORK

Porter (2001) distinguishes two motivations for long hours at work. A person can work long hours because of joy in the work. This is a constructive, highly committed achievement-oriented style of workaholism. This expenditure of time results in achievement. A person can also put in long hours in a compulsive, perfectionistic fashion, driven to achieve perfectionistic standards. Such individuals react to criticism with hostility and resentment, experience frustration from failing to meet superhuman standards, and express anger and competition with colleagues in the workplace.

WAs are addicted to the process of work; outcomes are important only as they supply external rewards for temporarily enhancing self-esteem. WAs strive for increasing accomplishments to achieve self-worth. WAs are given to rigid thinking and perfectionism. They have difficulty delegating, which limits the development of others around them – WAs are likely not effective team contributors. They are striving to be in control, in control of their work activities and other people around them. As a consequence they increased the chances of ill health, poor relationships and diminished leadership contribution – theirs and others around them.

There is an old saying that 'hard work never killed anybody'. Our research bears this out. Hard work that provides feelings of accomplishment and joy undertaken for noble not selfish motives is likely to enrich a leader's life.

285

REFERENCES

Barnett, R. C. and Marshall, N. L. (1992) Worker and mother roles, spillover effects, and psychological distress. *Women and Health*, 19: 13–41.

Bonebright, C. A., Clay, D. L., and Ankenmann, R. D. (2000) The relationship of work-aholism with work-life conflict, life satisfaction, and purpose in life. *Journal of Counseling Psychology*, 47: 469–77.

Brett, J. M. and Stroh, L. K. (2003) Working 61 plus hours a week: Why do managers do it? *Journal of Applied Psychology*, 88: 67–78.

Buelens, M. and Poelmans, S. A. Y. (2004) Enriching the Spence and Robbins typology of workaholism: demographic, motivational and organizational correlates. *Journal of Organizational Change Management*, 17: 446–58.

Burke, R. J. (1991) Early work and career experiences of female and male managers: reasons for optimism? *Canadian Journal of Administrative Sciences,* 8: 224–30.

Burke, R. J. (1999a) Workaholism in organizations: measurement validation and repli-cation, *International Journal of Stress Management,* 6: 45–55.

Burke, R. J. (1999b) Workaholism in organizations: the role of personal beliefs and fears, *Anxiety, Stress and Coping*, 14: 1–12.

Burke, R. J. (1999c) Workaholism in organizations: the role of organizational values. *Personnel Review*, 30: 637–45.

Burke, R. J. (1999d) Are workaholics job satisfied and successful in their careers? *Career Development International,* 26: 149–58.

Burke, R. J. (1999e) Workaholism in organizations: psychological and physical well-being consequences, *Stress Medicine*, 16: 11–16.

Burke, R. J. (1999f) Workaholism and extra-work satisfactions. *International Journal of Organizational Analysis*, 7: 352–64.

Burke, R. J. (1999g) Its not how hard you work but how you work hard: evaluating workaholism components, *International Journal of Stress Management*, 6: 225–39.

Burke, R. J. and Matthiesen, S. (2004) Workaholism among Norwegian journalists: Antecedents and consequences. *Stress and Health*, 20: 301–8

Burke, R. J., Burgess, Z., and Oberklaid, F. (2002) Workaholism, job and career satis-faction among Australian psychologists. *International Journal of Management Literature*, 2: 93–103.

Burke, R. J., Richardsen, A. M., and Martinussen, M. (2004) Workaholism among Norwegian senior managers: New research directions. *International Journal of Management*, 21: 415–26.

Cartwright, S. (2000) Taking the pulse of executive health in the UK. *Academy of Management Executive*, 14: 16–23.

Csikszentmihalyi, M. (1990) *Flow: The psychology of optimal experience*. New York: HarperCollins.

Csikszentmihalyi, M. (1997) *Finding flow: The psychology of engagement with everyday life*. New York: Basic Books.

Csikszentmihalyi, M. (2003) *Good business*. New York: Viking.

Elder, E. D. and Spence, J. T. Workaholism in the business world: Work addiction versus work-enthusiasm in MBAs. Unpublished manuscript. Austin, TX: Department of Psychology, University of Texas.

Fassel, D. (1990) *Working ourselves to death: The high costs of workaholism, the rewards of recovery*. San Francisco, CA: HarperCollins.

Fisher, A. B. (1992) Welcome to the age of overwork. *Fortune*, 126 (30 November): 64–71.

Garfield, C. A. (1987) *Peak performers: The new heroes of American business*. New York: William Morrow.

Greenhaus, J. H., Parasuraman, S., and Wormley, W. (1990) Organizational experiences and career success of black and white managers. *Academy of Management Journal*, 33: 64–86.

Greenhouse, S. (2001) Report shows Americans have more 'Labor Days'. *New York Times*, 1 September, p. A6.

Haas, R. (1991) Strategies to cope with a cultural phenomenon – workaholism. *Business and Health*, 36: 4.

Hochschild, A. (1997) *The time bind*. New York: Henry Holt.

Jacobs, J. A. and Gerson, K. (1998) Who are the overworked Americans? *Review of Social Economy*, 56: 442–59.

Kanai, A. Wakabayashi, M., and Fling, S. (1996) Workaholism among employees in Japanese corporations: An examination based on the Japanese version of the workaholism scales. *Japanese Psychological Research*, 38: 192–203.

Kiechel, W. (1989a) The workaholic generation, *Fortune*, 10 April, 50–62

Kiechel, W. (1989b) Workaholics anonymous. *Fortune*, 14 August, 117–18.

Killinger, B. (1991) *Workaholics: The respectable addicts*. New York: Simon & Schuster.

Klaft, R. P. and Kleiner, B. H. (1988) Understanding workaholics. *Business*, 33: 37–40.

Kofodimos, J. (1993) *Balancing Act*. San Francisco, CA: Jossey-Bass.

Kotter, J. (1999) *What leaders really do*. Boston, MA: Harvard Business School Press.

Lee, C., Jamieson, L. F., and Earley, P. C. (1996) Beliefs and fears and Type A behavior: implications for academic performance and psychiatric health disorder symptoms. *Journal of Organizational Behavior*, 17: 151–78.

Machlowitz, M. (1980) *Workaholics: Living with them, working with them*. Reading, MA: Addison-Wesley.

Maume, D. J. and Bellas, M. L. (2001) The overworked American or the time bind? *American Behavioral Scientists*, 44: 1137–56.

McMillan, L. H. W., Brady, E. C., O'Driscoll, M. P., and Marsh, N. V. (2002) A multi-faceted validation study of Spence and Robbins' (1992) Workaholism battery. *Journal of Occupational and Organizational Psychology*, 75: 357–68.

McMillan, L. W. H., O'Driscoll, M. P., Marsh, N. V., and Brady, E. C. (2001) Understanding workaholism: Data synthesis, theoretical critique, and future design strategies. *International Journal of Stress Management,* 8: 69–92.

McMillan, L. H. W., O'Driscoll, M. P., and Burke, R. J. (2003) Workaholism in organizations: A review of theory, research and future directions. In C. L. Cooper and I. T. Robertson (eds) *International Review of Industrial and Organizational Psychology.* New York: Wiley, pp. 167–90.

Naughton, T. J. (1987) A conceptual view of workaholism and implications for career counseling and research. *The Career Development Quarterly,* 14: 180–7.

Oates, W. (1971) *Confessions of a workaholic: The facts about work addiction.* New York: World.

Pietropinto, A. (1986) The workaholic spouse, *Medical Aspects of Human Sexuality,* 20: 89–96.

Porter, G. (1996) Organizational impact of workaholism: Suggestions for researching the negative outcomes of excessive work. *Journal of Occupational Health Psychology,* 1: 70–84.

Porter, G. (2001) Workaholics as high-performance employees: The intersection of workplace and family relationship problems. In B. E. Robinson and N. Chase (eds). *High-performing families: Causes, consequences, and clinical solutions,* pp. 43–69.

Porter, G. (2004) Work, work ethic and work excess. *Journal of Organizational Change Management,* 17: 424–39.

Quinn, R. P. and Shepard, L. J. (1974) *The 1972–73 Quality of Employment Survey,* Ann Arbor, MI: Institute of Social Research, University of Michigan.

Reich, R. B. (2000) *The future of success.* New York: Knopf.

Robbins, A. S. (1993) Patterns of workaholism in developmental psychologists. Unpublished manuscript. Austin, TX: Department of Psychology, University of Texas.

Robinson, B. E. (1998) *Chained to the desk: a guidebook for workaholics, their partners and children and the clinicians who treat them,* New York: New York University Press.

Robinson, B. E. (1999) Spouses of workaholics: clinical implications for psychotherapy. *Psychotherapy,* 35: 260–8.

Robinson, B. E. (2001) Workaholism and family functioning: A profile of familial relationships, psychological outcomes and research considerations. *Contemporary Family Therapy,* 23: 123–35.

Robinson, B. E. and Kelley, L. (1998) Adult children of workaholics: self-concept, anxiety, depression, and locus of control, *American Journal of Family Therapy,* 26: 35–50.

Robinson, B. E. and Post, P. (1997) Risk of work addiction to family functioning, *Psychological Reports,* 81: 91–5.

Schaef, A. W. and Fassel, D. (1988) *The addictive organization.* San Francisco, CA: Harper Row.

Schor, J. B. (1991) *The overworked American,* New York: Basic Books.

Scott, K. S., Moore, K. S., and Miceli, M. P. (1997) An exploration of the meaning and consequences of workaholism. *Human Relations,* 50: 287–314.

Seybold, K. C. and Salomone, P. R. (1994) Understanding workaholism: A view of causes and counseling approaches, *Journal of Counseling and Development,* 73: 4–9.

Sparks, K., Cooper, C., Fried, Y., and Shirom, A. (1997) The effects of hours of work on health: A meta-analytic review. *Journal of Occupational and Organizational Psychology,* 70: 391–409.

Spence, J. T. and Robbins, A. S. (1992) Workaholism: Definition, measurement, and preliminary results. *Journal of Personality Assessment,* 58: 160–78.

Taris, T. W., Schaufeli, W. B., and Verhoeven, L. C. (2005) Workaholism in the Netherlands: Measurement and implications for job strain and work-nonwork conflict. *Applied Psychology: An International Review*, 54: 37–60.

Waddell, J. R. (1993) The grindstone. *Supervision,* 26: 11–13.

Wallace, J. E. (1997) It's about time: A study of hours worked and work spillover among low firm lawyers. *Journal of Vocational Behavior*, 50: 227–48.

Worrell, L. and Cooper, C. L. (1999) *Quality of work life survey*. London: Institute of Management.

Worthy, F. S. (1987) You're probably working too hard. *Fortune*, 27 (April): 133–9.

Part V

Developing leaders and leadership

Chapter 15

Lopsidedness in leaders

Strategies for assessing it and correcting it

Robert Kaplan

Frank Farr brought a strong strategic bent to his job as division president.[1] Beyond having an excellent understanding of the marketplace, which he continually refreshed, he had a gift for 'seeing over the next hill' and developing a vision of where the organization should go. He also had a gift for communicating his vision vividly and charismatically.

As much as his visionary sense served the company well, the imbalance in Frank Farr's leadership was predictable. He was relatively weak on the operational side. For one thing, he was externally oriented rather than internally oriented. For another, preferring to fly at relatively high altitudes, he didn't go in for all that operational detail. This helped to account for his tendency to be overly ambitious strategically: he just didn't fully take into account what was actually involved in making the strategic moves. He wasn't 'grounded in the realities of implementation', as one co-worker put it.

It wasn't that he ignored operations. Anything but. He conducted quarterly operations reviews. He expected his line managers to deliver on their commitments and he was none too happy if they didn't. But his staff could tell where his true interests lay; they could detect his attitude toward what he privately referred to as the 'drudgery' of running the business. His relative inattention to the operational side seemed to account for the fact that neither of the two businesses he was responsible for made plans the previous two years.

That Frank Farr was overbalanced on the strategic-and-operational dichotomy, too concerned with the long term and not oriented enough to the short term was not unusual. Nothing unusual in the fact that he was lopsided: everywhere we look we find managers who lack balance: too task oriented and not people oriented enough (or the reverse); too tough and not responsive enough to people's needs (or the reverse). Another variant: the work–life balance of many managers is out of whack.

The idea of the two-sidedness of life and leadership has been around for a long time. About 650 BC, Pythagoras assembled a much-studied table of opposites.[2] The contemporary field of leadership has seen many two-sided models: Blake and Mouton's 'managerial grid', with its two axes, concern for production and concern for people; Douglas McGregor's Theory X and Theory Y; Robert Quinn's competing managerial values, results and relationships, stability and change; to name just a few.[3]

Where our two-sided model of leadership differs is that it makes room for the idea that a manager could be lopsided – placing too much weight on one side and too little weight on the other side. Unless your conception makes room for over-doing it, it can't identify lopsidedness. What is remarkable isn't just that lopsid-edness doesn't receive conceptual attention. It is that standard assessment tools don't assess for it. How could that be? How can we rectify the situation?

WHAT IT TAKES TO IDENTIFY LOPSIDEDNESS

To pick up lopsidedness, our models of leadership need to be two-sided, since that's what lopsidedness is. From our firm's research and its extensive experience consulting to senior managers on leadership, we have concluded that there are two basic balances to be struck: first, strategic and operational leadership; second, forceful and enabling leadership. If there are others as basic to leadership as these two, we haven't found them.

There is nothing revolutionary about defining leadership requirements in terms of dichotomies like this.[4] Somehow the competency models that have come to dominate the practice of leadership assessment consist of lists of single dimensions.

To identify lopsidedness, or its productive counterpart, versatility, a two-sided model is necessary but not sufficient. We must have a way to determine if a given leader is doing too little, too much or the right amount on each dimension. If it is the ubiquitous 360-degree feedback survey, it could employ a rating scale that allows us to make this determination. The problem is that most feedback surveys are not designed to let the respondent identify behaviours that are overdone.

In managers, not to mention humans, you can find instances every day of going too far. A manager noted for being quick – quickly assessing a situation, quickly deciding – has a tendency to make hasty decisions. A manager who uses a highly disciplined follow-up system has a tendency to micromanage. As the Center for Creative Leadership's research on derailment showed, the strengths that propel managers up the ladder can become liabilities.[5] In light of how painfully common-place overdoing it is, it is a striking oversight that standard assessment tools aren't designed to capture it like they get at underdoing it.[6]

Consider one of the two most common rating scales, what is known as a frequency scale. In other words, to what extent does the manager in question perform various behaviours like plan for the future, delegate, offer praise, and so on. Since this less-to-more scale does not provide a clear line between 'very often' and 'too often', it, in effect, assumes that more is better. The other rating scale in common use is the evaluation scale, which has raters indicate how competent or effective the manager is on each behaviour. The drawback of this scale is it leaves it unclear whether a low score indicates the manager does too little or too much of the desired quality.

What is needed is a rating scale that respects the reality of sub-par performance as either deficiency or excess. Following is one way to do that.

−3	−2	−1	0	+1	+2	+3
Much too little	Too little	A little too little	The right amount	A little too much	Too much	Much too much

We know from 10 years of experience using this scale or a next-generation version of it in our 360-degree survey, the Leadership Versatility Index, that it picks up both deficiency and excess.[7]

The rating scale is founded on a principle that goes all the way the back to Aristotle, who postulated that being good at something or simply good or virtuous entails doing a right amount of that something, and not doing too little or too much of it.[8] Note that, with Aristotle and with theorists of leadership whose position it is that the situation determines what behaviour will work best, we understand the right amount as being not fixed but relative to what's needed. While top executives much of the time need to operate at 50,000 or 100,000 feet, on selected critical issues the right amount of their involvement is heavy.[9]

Because the Leadership Versatility Index is equipped to identify overdoing, it is able to capture lopsidedness. Of ten co-workers who rated one executive, eight indicated that he was too task-oriented and all ten that he was not people-oriented enough. Of ten co-workers rating another executive, seven indicated that she was too focused on her own unit's success and nine that she was not enough of a team player.

In addition to referring to these individual examples, extreme cases chosen to make the point, let's examine our firm's sample of senior managers in the aggregate. Using an early version of the Leadership Versatility Index we constructed two statistically sound five-item scales, one to measure forceful leadership and the other, enabling leadership. If it is true that as a body managers tend to be lopsided on forceful and enabling leadership, then would we not expect the two scales to correlate inversely? In an inverse relationship, the more forceful managers are, the less enabling; and the more enabling they are, the less forceful. In fact, that is what we found, a correlation of −0.56. Using a revised version of the instrument we found a slightly stronger correlation of −0.64.[10] Thus, many managers do not move freely between forceful and enabling leadership. The reason is typically that they are biased in favour of one mode and against its complement. What is striking is that the many studies done on this basic distinction, by whatever name, have turned up not a negative correlation but either a negligible or, most often, a positive correlation.[11] Why? We suspect the reason is that research to date has not directly measured overdoing.

THE FLIP SIDE OF LOPSIDEDNESS, VERSATILITY

In pursuing the idea of versatility, we are walking a path blazed over three decades ago by 'contingency theorists' who worked the idea that different approaches work better in different situations.[12] The Situational Leadership Theory of Paul Hersey and Ken Blanchard, for example, is predicated on the principle of handling subordinates differently according to their level of ability and motivation. During the same period Victor Vroom put forward his decision-making tree that helps managers determine how much to involve others in a decision according to the importance of decision quality, acceptance, speed, and so on.

Many a manager has gone through training on how to use these kinds of 'it depends' models yet struggled with applying the prescribed behaviour back in the ebb and flow of the workplace. Could the reason be deeper than behaviour? This is a point we will take up later.

In our view it is useful to define versatility, the healthy alternative to lopsidedness, in terms of a pair of opposing virtues. Table 15.1 contains a partial list of forceful virtues and of enabling virtues, in the middle columns. In the end columns are the virtues taken to an extreme. Table 15.2 contains a comparable set of lists for strategic and operational leadership.

Because virtues like these are opposites, managers can experience them as in tension with each other, even as contradictory or incompatible. That describes the challenge of achieving versatility: managers must do what humans, even very smart ones, can find it so hard to do, hold two ideas in their heads at the same time. Human beings are susceptible to polarizing. We see it in the we/they dynamic that springs up between departments, or even countries. In lopsided leaders the polarizing takes place inside their heads.

To be versatile on forceful and enabling leadership, then, is to possess good ability on both sides of the duality despite the tendency for managers to have a bias in favour of one and against the other. Likewise for strategic and operational leadership.

Versatility matters. Our research has found a close association between versatility, as measured by our leadership questionnaire, and overall effectiveness.[13] In three samples of senior managers we have studied, we found substantial

Table 15.1 Forceful and enabling leadership – virtues and vices

Forceful leadership		Enabling leadership	
Virtues	Taken to an extreme	Virtues	Taken to an extreme
Takes charge – in control of his/her unit	Dominant to the point of eclipsing subordinate	Empowers subordinates to run their own units; able to let go	Empowers to a fault; gives people too much rope
Lets people know clearly and with feeling where he/she stands on issues. Declares himself/herself	Other people don't speak out, aren't heard	Interested in where other people stand on issues, receptive to their ideas	People don't know where they stand
Makes tough calls – including those that have an adverse effect on people	Insensitive, callous	Compassionate; responsive to people's needs and feelings	Overly accommodating; nice to people at the expense of the work
Holds people strictly accountable	Rigid, demoralizing	Understanding when people are not able to deliver	Tender-hearted; lets people off the hook

Table 15.2 Strategic and operational leadership – virtues and vices

Strategic leadership		Operational leadership	
Virtues	Taken to an extreme	Virtues	Taken to an extreme
Focused on setting long-term strategy	Too much looking down the road	Focused on getting short-term results	Tunnel vision; myopic
Thinks broadly – pays attention to the big picture	Hopelessly conceptual; lost in the clouds	Detail-oriented, gets into the specifics of how things actually work	Bogged down in details
Expansive – aggressive about growing the business	Too ambitious; at risk of strategic overreach	Respects the limits on the organization's capacity to grow	Conservative; too respectful of limits

correlations between ratings of versatility and effectiveness.[14] Versatile managers are consistently regarded as the most effective leaders in their organizations. In the cases where we have readministered the Leadership Versatility Index and the measure of effectiveness in our consulting practice, we have found that a higher rating of effectiveness is associated with greater versatility. And in one case where, under extreme stress, the executive became even more lopsided, his effectiveness rating went down.

There is another pattern in which managers underdo both sides of an opposition — for example, on 'Forces issues' and 'Fosters harmony'. Managers who exhibit this 'disengaged' pattern, which is reminiscent of laissez-faire leadership, get the lowest ratings of effectiveness, even lower than lopsided managers.

Note that versatility on an opposition is not moderation. Quite different from camping out in the middle, versatility is the capacity to range freely from one side to the other and can consist of very immoderate behaviour when extreme circumstances require it. Parents who yell when their child is in danger or seriously out of line and not responding to reason are using self-assertion to the right degree.

CORRECTING LOPSIDED LEADERSHIP

A focus on lopsidedness opens a pathway to change that action-oriented managers might otherwise overlook – change from the inside out. Finding a manager's behaviour to be off, too much of one thing and too little of the opposite thing, we naturally wonder: What throws the behaviour off? Why does a particular general manager go overboard on operational detail and at the same time give short shrift to strategy? What do we find when we draw back from his lopsided behaviour? In this general manager's case, he wrongly believed that if he didn't 'know everything' about the business, people would think the less of him; and, truth be known, he skimped on strategic work not just because of the sucking action of his excessive orientation to detail but also because he harboured a fear of not being smart enough. This is where using not just a two-sided leadership model but also a yardstick with too much and too little on it proves to be useful: it captures lopsidedness and that in turn raises a practical question: What are the drivers?

In the face of a pair of leadership virtues, managers often choose one over the other, and may not realize they are making a choice. The reason: they fall prey to the human tendency to be one-sided.

Let's take the case of an executive, a composite of men and women we've consulted to, who excels at treating people well. Lydia Milde is an executive who listens exceptionally well and creates an atmosphere where people feel comfortable speaking up in meetings. She empowers her staff and supports them when they need help. She is soft-spoken and non-threatening. And she believes strongly in this way of leading. She identifies with it powerfully. If one wall in her conference room represents this respectful, supportive approach, then she in effect faces that wall and embraces what it represents.

The hitch is that she has turned her back on the wall behind her; she has an aversion to it. That wall represents power and self-assertion. And because she turned away from it, it became her blind side.

Lydia has married herself to the be-good-to-people side and has divorced herself from the assertive, enforcing side. It is easy to understand why she feels that way about the type of leadership she disclaims: she keys on its excesses – like throwing one's weight around – and overlooks its virtues.

When a leader's behaviour is off, we find that often what throws it off are distorted beliefs or sensitivities or both. This is not always true: sometimes the culprit is something as simple as a skill deficiency or lack of knowledge. Even then, however, a belief or feeling may have steered the manager away from picking up the knowledge or skill.

In the case of distorted beliefs, even generally clear-thinking, objective, rational managers can have screwy ideas about certain parts of the managerial job. They often have an unrealistic sense of what is expected of them, wildly overblown ideas about their capability or painfully self-diminishing estimates of their skill in one or another area. They also have exaggerated expectations about the consequences of not being so intense or they have twisted beliefs about the horrible things that might happen if they engage in what for them is taboo behaviour. Sustaining these beliefs further, they are quite capable of rationalizing the counterproductive extremes to which they go as well as their persistent tendencies to neglect certain parts of their job. The fix is to straighten out the warped portions of their mental maps.

In addition to distorted beliefs, a substratum of sensitivities lies beneath off-kilter leadership.[15] Managers worry needlessly, and the solution is if not to overcome the fear to at least recognize it and contain it. Much of it is fear of being inadequate, in a task sense or in a relationship sense. No one likes to be incompetent and humans of all ages and all walks of life are famous for avoiding activities we think we're not good at; in effect, underdoing it, which becomes a self-fulfilling prophecy. Humans are equally capable, when threatened with the prospect of not doing something well, of doubling their efforts and thereby overdoing it.

In order to grow, lopsided managers must contend with the fear of what they would become if they move toward the neglected side. What do overly forceful managers worry about? That they will become weak. What do overly enabling managers, contemplating a move in the forceful direction, worry about? That they will become SOBs. Each class of manager, looking over the fence, sees not the virtues of the other side but the worst excesses, and they recoil. The more lopsided the manager, the more polarized the mind-set and the stiffer the emotional challenge.

The first step in correcting our own lopsidedness is to know that it is there, for it is the nature of lopsidedness that we may see the posture we take as good when it's not. Because all of this seems so self-evident in our head, we rarely put it to a reality test. As a result, many a manager doesn't recognize the biases that distort how he or she thinks about leadership and how he or she leads. We found this in our data: self-ratings of versatility bore no relationship to self-ratings of overall effectiveness.[16] Most of these managers seemed to have the idea that their preferred style is what works best.

Rather than tend to regard their behaviour as off-target, many managers to look upon it as the right and proper response to the task at hand. Because they place a high value on those things they overdo, they have a difficult time seeing how they could do too much of that thing. Because they place a low value on the things they underdo, they have trouble seeing how they could be neglecting that thing. It is no wonder that performance problems don't get corrected easily.

Even more striking in our research was the finding that self-ratings were barely related to co-worker ratings – on versatility, effectiveness, or on the link between the two. Yet superior, peer, and subordinate ratings showed substantial convergence with each other. It seems that everyone sees lopsidedness and its link to ineffectiveness except for the person in question. It could be that being married to one side, along with writing off the other, leads managers to perceive their one-sided behaviour as correct. This amounts to a failure to recognize two-sidedness.

Making up a deficiency

Filling a gap in their repertoire is not simply a matter of learning a new skill or getting better at it; it is also getting over a bad attitude about that skill. Managers are poor prospects to learn something if they do not see the value of it. To reverse an instance of underdoing, then, often means contending with a misconception, a bias, a prejudicial attitude, or inhibition.

The easiest internal change to make is simply to recognize what the job, usually a new and different job, requires. Upon moving up to an executive job, a manager we worked with said: 'Oh, I didn't realize that at this level my job is not so much to make decisions as to manage the process by which decisions get made.' It took work to make the adjustment in his or her behaviour but at the idea level it was no trouble at all to correct this misconception of what his new job entailed.[17]

Often, however, the mental adjustment is more complicated than that. Beyond not knowing, biases enter in. As we saw in the opening case, some executives neglect the operational part of the job because, in effect, they see it as beneath them. They think of it as being consumed with 'details' and as taking them away from a higher calling. They will never do justice to this part of their job unless they overcome their bias.

It can also be difficult to put aside a way of operating that is rooted in a pattern of adaptation adopted at a much younger age. Take those individuals who, because of whatever childhood circumstances, learned to fend for themselves and who, unthinkingly, project that need, or the lack of it, onto their staff. It takes some growing on their part to acknowledge the validity of their staff's needs for support.

We have seen executives avoid technical functions like IT or RandD out of, it emerged, a fear of inadequacy. To do justice to this responsibility, they must loosen the grip of this fear. Also, we have seen staff executives, saddled by their growing-up families with compunctions about self-promotion or egotism, have the hardest time asserting themselves or otherwise putting themselves forward. Said one staff executive, 'I grew up in a family with a strong ethic against boastfulness, and I find it distasteful when people put themselves forward.' Therefore to fill the role, staff executives like this one must not only work at modifying their behaviour but must also keep these childhood commandments in check.

In correcting lopsidedness it is not enough to bring up the weak side; we must also tamp down the excessively strong side.

Modulating strengths taken too far

The key to modulating a strength taken too far is to learn to use it more selectively, and often the key to making that adjustment is to do a little inner work. A fair portion of overdoing it springs from out-of-this-world expectations about what it means to work hard or to do well. Driven people lack objectivity about what is reasonable to expect of themselves, and others. The remedy is obvious, but learning that good enough is generally good enough is not like picking up facts in a textbook. And perfectionism can prove resistant to change.

One level of inner work on overused strengths is to stop placing an excessively high value on that capability. Frank Farr, the executive in the opening case, for example, would need to depart from his view that the true work of senior leadership was positioning the business for the future. Similarly, Lydia Milde, the executive who placed a supremely high value on being good to people, would have to modify that view to make room for greater tough-mindedness.

At deeper level the work consists of facing one's fears. Underneath distorted beliefs or exaggerated values often lies unacknowledged needs or fears. We have, for example, encountered executives with a towering sense of responsibility who lived in fear of not being responsible enough, and inadvertently deprived senior people working for them of the opportunity to assume full responsibility themselves.[18]

In general, to rectify leadership behaviour that tilts to one or the other on major oppositions like strategic–operational leadership or forceful–enabling leadership, we need to come to grips with our inner leanings.

CONCLUSION

Whether our concern is with our own development or the development of others, it is important to recognize that leadership is two-sided and to appreciate which basic balances that need to be struck. And once we get the conception of leadership right, assessment technology must follow suit. Leaders need to be assessed for that pervasive malady, imbalance, and, to accomplish that, assessment tools need to be redesigned so they can detect excess and not just deficiency. What is lopsidedness but excess on one side of an opposition and deficiency on the other? Then when leaders turn from feedback to corrective action, that effort needs to include not just the outer, behavioural work of development but also the inner work. In particular, that inner work needs to follow the logic and psycho-logic of imbalance/lopsidedness, which is the polarized mind-set that always underlies imbalance. For leaders to strike better balances on the crucial oppositions, they must outgrow the black-and-white thinking that threw their leadership out of whack.

NOTES

1   All examples in this chapter are based on one or more of our executive clients. Names and certain facts of circumstance have been changed for obvious reasons.

2   Pythagoras, see Fideler (1987).

3   See Blake and Mouton (1964); McGregor (1960); and Quinn (1988).

4   For a comprehensive review of the many variations on this theme, see Bass (1990).

5   See McCall and Lombardo (1983); and Lombardo and McCauley (1988).

6   The idea that overused strengths can become weaknesses is not entirely absent from the field of leadership assessment. It is, however, rarely reflected in the design of standard tools. When the idea is taken into account, it tends to be treated as an afterthought rather than integral to the design of the measure. For instance, there are instruments that render prescriptions for development by comparing ratings of 'how often' the manager in question does a particular thing to an 'ideal amount' that is estimated from a statistical formula. And there are a few instruments that have respondents rate how often the manager does a number of specific behaviors. Then at the end, they ask for global prescriptions on the handful of dimensions those behaviors comprise: do more, less, or the same. See examples in Leslie and Fleenor (1998).

7   The original research data reported here can be found in Kaplan and Kaiser (2003), and Kaiser and Kaplan (2002).

8   Aristotle, *The Nicomachean Ethics* (1975).

9   Another advantage of the type of scale we have designed is that it allows for the fact that what is too much of something like taking charge in one organization or in a particular job is likely different from what is too much in another organization or job. We let the rater decide how much is too much or too little. Despite this 'eye-of-the-beholder' subjectivity, we have found a great deal of agreement between

raters within the same source as well as across superior, peer, and subordinate sources. See Kaplan and Kaiser (2003).

10   In Kaplan and Kaiser (2003), and Kaiser and Kaplan (2002).

11   Bass (1990) summed up the results from several reviews that examined the correlation between these two sides of leadership across hundreds of primary studies and noted that it is troubling that they are so often positively related and rather strongly so (Ch. 24).

12   'Contingency theory' was a popular movement in the study of leadership that began in the 1960s. These theories argued that what was the most effective leader behavior depended on circumstantial factors. See Hersey and Blanchard (1977), and Vroom and Yetton 1973).

13   We use a statistical formula derived from Pythagorean geometry to create a versatility index, a percentage that represents how close an individual's ratings are to 'the right amount' on both sides of a duality. See Kaplan and Kaiser (2003).

14   The correlation between effectiveness and versatility on the forceful-enabling duality was +.53 in Kaplan and Kaiser (2003), and +.81 in Kaiser and Kaplan (2002). In an unpublished study of ratings from 265 co-workers, the correlations with effectiveness were +.59 for forceful-enabling versatility and +.61 for strategic-operational versatility.

15   See Kaplan and Kaise (in press).

16   Kaplan and Kaiser (2003).

17   The changes in perspective and values that are required in making upward transitions have been described most recently by Charan, Drotter, and Noel (2001).

18   R. E. Kaplan (2002).

REFERENCES

Aristotle (1975) *The Nicomachean Ethics,* translated by H. Rackham. Cambridge, MA: Harvard University Press.

Bass, B. M. (1990) *Bass and Stogdill's handbook of leadership: Theory, research, and managerial applications,* 3rd edn. New York: Free Press, pp. 415–543.

Blake, R. R. and Mouton, J. S. (1964) *The managerial grid.* San Francisco, CA: Gulf.

Charan, R., Drotter, S. and Noel, J. (2001) *The leadership pipeline.* San Francisco, CA: Jossey-Bass.

Fideler, D. (ed.) (1987) *The Pythagorean sourcebook and library,* translated by K. S. Guthrie, Grand Rapids, MI: Phanes Press.

Hersey, P. and Blanchard, K. H. (1977) *Management of Organizational Behavior.* Englewood Cliffs, NJ: Prentice Hall.

Kaiser, R. B. and Kaplan, R. E. (2002) *Leadership versatility index: User's guide.* Greensboro, NC: Kaplan DeVries.

Kaplan, R. E. (2002) Know your strengths. *Harvard Business Review* 80 (March): 20–1.

Kaplan, R. E. and Kaiser R. B. (2003) Rethinking a classic distinction in leadership: Implications for the assessment and development of executives. *Consulting Psychology Journal: Research and Practice*, 55(1): 15–26.

Kaplan, R. E. and Kaiser, R. B. (in press) The turbulence within: How sensitivities throw off performance in executives. In R. J. Burke and C. L. Cooper (eds) *Leading in turbulent times*. Oxford: Blackwell.

Leslie, J. B. and Fleenor, J. W. (1998) *Feedback to managers: A review and comparison of multi-rater instruments for management development*. Greensboro, NC: Center for Creative Leadership.

Lombardo, M. M. and McCauley, C. *The dynamics of management derailment*. Greensboro, NC: Center for Creative Leadership.

McCall, W. M. and Lombardo, M. M. (1983) *Off the track: Why and how successful executives get derailed*. Greensboro, NC: Center for Creative Leadership.

McGregor, D. (1960) *The human side of enterprise*. New York: McGraw-Hill.

Quinn, R. E. (1988) *Beyond rational management*. San Francisco, CA: Jossey-Bass.

Vroom, V. H. and Yetton, P. W. (1973) *Leadership and decision-making*. New York: Wiley.

Chapter 16

360-degree feedback and leadership development

Ioannis Nikolaou, Maria Vakola, and Ivan T. Robertson

At the beginning of the new millennium organizations are faced more than ever with an unprecedented demand for competent leadership. The constant change they have to cope with, irrespective of their size, nature, and geographical area of activity, requires on behalf of their management and especially their top management, strong leadership skills. It calls for individuals exhibiting not only the appropriate dispositional traits, but also demonstrating a series of relevant skills, abilities, perceptions, and attitudes. Collins and Holton (2004) state that increased strategic vision is now a prerequisite of leaders' profile as a result of the almost continuous restructuring activities, demographic changes in the workforce, and technological changes in a complex and fast-paced environment. Multinational companies face the constant need to develop the ability to compete in the global market, something that is contingent upon their ability to change and adapt resources strategically. Global organizations are also faced with dual reporting structures, proliferation of communication channels, overlapping responsibilities, and barriers of distance, language, time, and culture. All these conditions require efficient changes, immediate reaction and effective interaction from people who combine visions, insight and reality perception. There is a need for something more than managers used to be. There is a strong request for leaders.

Effective leadership has been identified as a central goal. Many organizations are concerned about the leadership inadequacies of their employees and are committed to education and training to develop managers' skills, perspectives, and competencies. As a result, budgets for leadership development programmes are expected to grow even further at the beginning of the new millennium. Such development programmes typically focus on improving leadership skills, awareness, and behaviours. As companies become aware of the shortage of talented managers and the importance of developing strong future successors to widen perspectives to compete in a global market, a wide range of leadership development programmes have been commissioned and delivered.

One major mistake is the organization's perception that leadership development interventions will result indisputably in improved leadership skills. This appears to be taken for granted by many corporations, professional management associations, and consultancy companies. Research indicates that organizations are spending little time evaluating the effectiveness of their interventions and, more specifically, evaluating whether those programmes improve organizational performance (Collins and Holton, 2004; Day, 2000). Similarly, organizations appear to believe that improving knowledge and skills of individual employees automatically enhances the organization's effectiveness. What is commonly evaluated is the improved inter-personal skills and work performance of individual managers. Measurement of organizational effectiveness is somewhat more difficult, because it often involves analysis at multiple levels of the organization, such as the effectiveness of an organization in achieving outcomes as defined by its strategic goals, or an increase of a return on investments.

LEADERSHIP DEVELOPMENT

Managers have always wondered, even from their earliest career stages, what it takes to become a leader. Is it their own individual/personality characteristics? Is it a genetically predisposed ability to act as a leader or is it situation specific as contingency theories of leadership imply? Van Velsor and McCauley (2004) suggest that without doubt, leadership effectiveness is rooted in genetics but also in early childhood and adult experience. If that's the case, then it would be simply a matter of a successful recruitment and selection procedure to attract, select, and maintain competent leaders. However, practical experience has shown that people can effectively enhance their strengths and improve their weaknesses, if they want to, while organizations have adopted strategies to assist their employees by providing them with learning – and other – opportunities to accelerate into effective leadership. London and Maurer (2004) identified three major trends in designing leadership development programmes. These are the need to integrate organizational and individual development in alignment with learning theories; secondly, the need to assess, guide and support leadership competencies; and, finally, leaders' need for self-assessment and behavioural change.

In the last 20 years we have witnessed a proliferation of leadership development programmes in organizations (Hernez-Broome and Hughes, 2004). Although traditional classroom-type training remains the most widely used method, it is now complemented by a number of different strategies (McCauley and van Velsor, 2004). A full range of leadership development experiences includes mentoring, formal coaching, hardships, job assignments, feedback-intensive systems, on-the-job experiences, developmental relationships, leader–follower relationships, networking, action learning, and formal training (Day, 2000; McCauley and van Velsor, 2004).

Day (2000), in a significant review of the most widely used leadership development techniques, made the distinction between leader and leadership development, following the parallelization of management and leadership development. Management development primarily includes management education and training and the acquisition of specific knowledge, skills, and abilities to enhance task performance in managerial positions, whereas leadership development expands the collective ability of organizational members to engage successfully in leadership roles. According to van Velsor and McCauley (2004) leader development refers to the expansion of an individual's ability to be effective in leadership roles and processes, and should more closely linked to 'personal development'. Therefore, leader development is only an aspect of the broader concept of leadership development, which is the expansion of the organization's capacity to endorse the most important leadership tasks needed for organization-wide work, such as guiding, directing, and aligning. Day (2000) refers to this distinction as the 'conceptual context' in leadership research and practice. The focus of this chapter is on leader development and more specifically on one of the most contemporary methods of leader development, namely 360-degree feedback.

360-DEGREE FEEDBACK

The assessment of work performance is one of the most significant and difficult issues faced by organizations throughout the world. Large companies especially have invested heavily in introducing improved techniques and methods of assessment since organizational performance is related to its employees' level of performance and this is especially the case for managerial and top management positions. One of the most significant developments in the field of employee performance and development is the introduction and use of 360-degree (or multisource, multi-rater) feedback. Seifert, Yukl, and McDonald (2003) define multisource feedback as a programme where the manager receives information about how she is perceived by various groups of people with whom she interacts regularly. Fletcher and Baldry (1999) describe the multisource, multi-rater assessment systems as entailing a process whereby a targeted manager is rated on various behavioural dimensions or competencies by one or more bosses, peers, subordinates, and – sometimes – customers.

More recently, the 360-degree feedback has become more widely accepted as a managerial tool for leadership development, in hopes of improving workplace attitudes and organizational performance. In spite of its complex and multidimensional characteristics, organizations are increasingly implementing 360-degree feedback. As has been proved from research and practice, there are both benefits and potential problems associated with 360-degree feedback, especially if used as an evaluation system rather than just as a personal development technique. Before discussing the contribution of 360-degree feedback to leadership development, it is essential to identify the major advantages and disadvantages that relate to this methodology.

One of the major advantages is that 360-degree feedback provides ratees with information on how they are perceived by others. Combined with self-evaluation results, it can lead to intrinsic changes in managers' perceptions and behaviour. 360-degree programmes provide the richest information about the ratee compared to any other assessment technique. It is an open procedure for the participants but with confidential results and feedback for the ratee. Confidentiality and openness force both the participants and the organization to examine the results carefully and make suggestions for improvement on aspects that probably could never be identified as significant. Furthermore, observations can be obtained from different groups with special insights. Almost everybody related to the individual can participate in the assessment process, enhancing in the organization a positive feeling for future organization-wide implementations, as 360-degree feedback may become an ongoing process.

On the other hand, there are a number of disadvantages related to 360-degree feedback. Some opponents argue that showing up managers' weaknesses, and putting pressure on them to change, cannot be an effective way to increase their performance. As a result, rather than openness, appraisal systems can often create defensiveness and low morale. Furthermore, 360-degree feedback provides an overwhelming amount of information, making it difficult for ratees to understand and analyse effectively. Another criticism of the process is that guidance – usually from an external facilitator – is needed not only during the implementation but also for the feedback evaluation and development as well. Further, if the organization has not foreseen training and/or coaching, the effectiveness of the 360-degree programme will not reach the desired level. Moreover, differences between self-ratings and others' ratings could cause confusion and negative feelings, and end up creating personal conflicts, especially when the confidentially of the process is breached. Finally, the question of the assessors' ability to rate employees' performance for developmental purposes only with the aid of a 360-degree programme, without being biased, either positively or negatively, by the official performance appraisal process remains largely unanswered.

MAIN ISSUES IN 360-DEGREE FEEDBACK AND LEADERSHIP DEVELOPMENT

Although any organization member whose job interacts with other people can participate in multisource feedback, 360-degree feedback is typically provided to managers, hence its relationship with leadership development. However, 360-degree process could be implemented for a variety of corporate roles. In order for a 360-degree feedback to be successful, especially in leadership development, some main points and considerations should be clearly defined.

The context

The introduction and implementation of a multisource feedback should take place in a compatible environment. The requirements for that compatibility should already be in place. Otherwise, the organization should first apply the necessary conditions and then implement the 360-degree feedback procedure. Individuals should be aware about their involvement in the procedure, and a trustful relationship should be developed among managers and employees. They should be aware of all the important instructions about the procedure and have a clear understanding of the criteria. This is vital for the acceptance of the procedure by all parties involved.

Performance is enhanced, apart from the trust, with the use of training as well. Especially in the case of the initial implementation of the 360-degree feedback, leaders and individuals of all levels should be trained for the clarity of the criteria, the rating of individuals and the interpretation of the results, the reaction to the feedback and the steps involved in the follow-up and development stages.

Another issue that needs to be resolved in relation to 360-degree feedback is the objective it aims to satisfy. Is it going to be purely developmental in nature or is it going to serve as an administrative and evaluative tool as well? In the latter, the results of the feedback are used from the organization in order to facilitate HR-related decisions, such as hiring, promoting, and rewarding, whereas in the former the exclusive objective of the programme is to further develop the targeted individual. Pollack and Pollack (1996) have claimed that when the purpose of the 360-degree is evaluative, rather than developmental, it is hard for the programme to succeed. The parties involved tend to inflate their evaluations when they know that the results will be used for decision-making in the organization. The anonymity of the procedure may assist the emergence of negative feelings on behalf of the participants and an 'opportunity for revenge'. However, when the owner of the results is the targeted individual and not the organization (Chappelow, 2004) he has the sole responsibility not only to choose who to share his/her results and report with but also to take the appropriate actions for personal development.

Assessment and criteria

The first step in the implementation of a multisource feedback programme for leadership development is the assessment stage. Here, information is sought by individuals who are linked to the individual, such as colleagues, supervisors, clients, etc. However, the most important member of the 360-degree process is the individual herself, and this is especially so for leader development. Although the practical applications of multisource feedback may vary (e.g. performance appraisal, assignment selection, facilitation of organizational change) (Tornow, 1993a), it is widely acknowledged and accepted that the single most important use of it is the developmental aspect and more specifically the opportunity it provides to enhance self-awareness and prompt behaviour change of the targeted participants (Waldman, Atwater, and Antonioni, 1998).

This information is usually gathered through company-specific questionnaires or off-the-self surveys, completed by raters anonymously. Following the completion of the questionnaires is the analysis and reporting of the results, which may occur either in-company or by an external consultancy. Criteria should be carefully developed, defined, and selected. As with any assessment procedure, the criteria chosen should capture and identify those behaviours and characteristics that are associated with effective performance, as defined by organizational goals. Simply knowing and understanding the criteria by which one will be evaluated can help increase job performance. The criteria communicate performance expectations to the person evaluated, the supervisor, and others who are asked to rate an individual's performance. Thus role expectations are clarified for the parties involved.

Raters' selection

Multisource feedback by definition involves multiple raters. The typical 360-degree feedback paradigm involves collection of information from the whole range of people involved with the targeted individual. Tornow (1993a), in the introductory article of a special issue of *Human Resource Management* on 360-degree feedback (Tornow, 1993b), refers to 'significant others' as the individuals who typically provide feedback to the target individual, such as co-workers, subordinates, supervisors, as well as customers. Chappelow (2004) mentions that in some cases even family members may be included in the process. There are two main points about the raters: how they are chosen and if they will keep their anonymity. In 360-degree feedback raters may be chosen from the full web of working relationships associated with the ratee. Vertical relationships include superiors and subordinates. Lateral relationships include peers within the work group or even outside the organization, such as customers. The question of who chooses the raters is also an important one. The incumbent may be in the best position to identify those who have sufficient knowledge of herself to provide a useful and accurate appraisal. Supervisors on the other hand may feel the need to select raters in order to provide a balanced review and to minimize the possibility of ratees selecting their raters solely on the basis of the expectation of a positive evaluation.

When 360-degree feedback is implemented, individuals rate their own performance as well. While many problems have been associated with the results of this procedure, many organizations are in favour of doing this. The main reason for this is to construct a complete picture of every individual's performance. Considerable attention has been given to studying agreement between self and other ratings, because there seems to be a positive relationship between agreement and effective managerial performance (Van Velsor, Taylor, and Leslie, 1993; Yammarino and Atwater, 1993). The tendency to rate oneself higher, lower, or in agreement with other constituencies has been shown to be influenced by demographic and personality characteristics (Brutus, Fleenor, and London, 1998).

Finally, there is the question of raters' anonymity. In order to ensure confidentiality, the grouped results of the different sources must be aggregated. Therefore, when there is a very small group of people from a particular group (e.g. subordinates or clients) it might be worth excluding them from the process, in order to ensure confidentiality. If anonymity is not assured, some raters may not be willing to be frank, both because of reluctance to provide what they consider to be negative feedback, and also because of fear of retribution.

Feedback

The subsequent and most important step of the procedure is the feedback session. Managers often receive informal feedback during their daily activities and interaction with the 'significant others'. They 'read' the messages sent by colleagues, subordinates, and/or customers. However, because of the hectic pace at which most of them function, they rarely have the opportunity to reflect upon themselves and most importantly to systematically 'compare' their own perception of themselves with that of others. This is the opportunity provided by multisource feedback and it is especially applicable in and useful for leadership development. Kluger and DeNisi (1996) defined feedback as 'actions taken by an external agent to provide information regarding some aspect(s) of one's task performance' (p. 235). The results of their meta-analysis on feedback interventions found that on average, feedback is positively related to positive job outcomes. Formal feedback is an essential part of any multisource feedback programme. It provides the opportunity of reflecting on the breadth of information gathered at the previous stage. However, in order to be effective and objective it is essential to maintain a formalized structure and a neutral character (Chappelow, 2004), while at the same time remaining primarily developmental in nature. Chappelow (2004) also suggests that the feedback session should be carried out by a facilitator who has experience with the particular instrument.

To provide the greatest possible return from the process, training in both giving and receiving feedback can be given to all involved. In giving feedback it is important that individuals understand how to provide it in a non-threatening way that focuses on the behaviour and not the person. Those receiving feedback can be trained in receiving feedback non-defensively so that they may be open to learning more about how their behaviour is perceived by others. The maximum benefit may be attained by focusing on how the individual employee can use the feedback to improve performance. Feedback that is judgemental, punitive, or threatening will raise defensiveness, block progress, and may well activate psychological processes that lead to dysfunctional behaviour. It will also serve to act as a deterrant to future 360-degree attempts. Feedback is needed to set development goals. Supervisors and raters will share the data together and will define ways to satisfy the desired outcomes.

Follow-up or development

Probably the most significant part of the 360-degree feedback is the response to the question 'what happens next?' Feedback is more effective when it is accompanied by goal-setting activities (DeNisi and Kluger, 2000). The participant, often with the assistance and guidance of a 'personal coach' or facilitator, establishes and agrees on a development plan aiming to improve her performance in the future, focusing not only on her weaknesses but also on further developing her strengths. The development plan is based on the mutual understanding between the two parties, i.e. the organization and the participant, that the former will provide the necessary resources to the latter to facilitate his personal improvement. Also, on behalf of the participant, that she understands and accepts the issues involved in the development plan and, more importantly, that she wants to be involved in a self-development procedure. In a similar vein, McCauley (2001) distinguished three major components of leadership development: (a) developmental experiences (i.e. opportunities to learn), (b) the ability to learn (a mix of motivational, personal orientation, and skills), and (c) organizational support for development, including a variety of contextual factors, such as coaching, feedback, and rewards for development.

Chappelow (2004, p. 66) summarizes the following points in assisting employees to receive the maximum impact of the 360-degree feedback session:

- establishing a systematic and safe learning environment by maintaining confidentiality of the data;
- giving participants access to a trained facilitator for clarification of the data and assistance in putting together a personal development plan;
- following a top-down approach where the first involved in the process will be the top management of the company;
- allowing the participant and the immediate supervisor to meet in advance in order to discuss the objectives of the 360-degree process;
- offering organizational support for the methods and tools that are know to contribute to effective leadership development;
- exploring with the participant ways to establish ongoing feedback after the formal 360-degree process is over; and
- identifying with the organization ways to follow up and adjust, when necessary, the development plan.

EFFECTIVENESS DEPENDS ON A VARIETY OF FACTORS

The ultimate criterion of 'success' for the use of 360-degree feedback for leadership development depends on the results of the organization's performance. Among particular individuals success is defined differently depending on the constituent group one is trying to satisfy. Raters, for example, would consider a 360-degree process successful if ratees appeared to accept the feedback and change their behaviours, if their working relationships with ratees are improved, if they provide objective evaluation and honest feedback, and if the overall feedback climate is improved. Similarly, each of the principal constituencies (ratees, top management, clients, and the organization itself) has its own definition of the factors that contribute to successful implementation of the process.

However there are some elements that are able to improve and create an appropriate basis for the successful implementation of the 360-degree feedback for both the organization and the individuals, and counteract any potential deficiencies.

Top management commitment

As is the case in most organization-wide interventions, the participants should feel that the top management acknowledges the importance of this attempt, providing the appropriate support and necessary resources. This is especially the case for the use of 360-degree feedback for leadership development because of the significant requirements it entails both at the initial stages of its implementation (e.g. confidentiality and trust culture) and at the follow-up of the programme (e.g. the provision of the necessary development opportunities). Further, leadership development involves the notion of succession planning for most organizations. When the leaders-to-be are involved in an intensive appraisal and development process, such as a 360-degree programme, their expectations and ambitions are raised. The top management of the company should actively demonstrate their desire to utilize successfully the results of the programme by incorporating them in fast-track succession planning processes for leadership positions within the organization. As a result, the motivation of the participants and their commitment to the process will increase.

Customization

A 360-degree programme is almost never the same as another 360-degree programme. Every company has a different culture, and there is a need to customize some or all the parts of the assessment and appraisal procedure, especially if an off-the-shelf method or measure is used. This need may occur because of the differences among industries, individual differences, particular democratic characteristics, cultural differentiations, and, in most cases, due to the use of different core competencies. These differences will be reflected in the criteria that will be used in the assessment process. Customization should match 360-degree appraisal with the internal environment and the organization's culture in order to give the desired improvement in the organization's performance.

Pilot test

Managers tend to be impressed by an innovative idea and want immediate action. A pilot implementation of the 360-degree programme may last a year or longer, something that makes it look unattractive for most organizations, considering the resources that need to be applied. However, the benefits of a pilot study can be immense. In organizations with traditional structures, the inversion of the organizational pyramid that accompanies 360-degree feedback can be threatening and problematic. Pilot studies can identify the potential threats and problems.

A pilot test can be used in a few departments before full-scale implementation throughout the organization. Many problems could be identified and fixed following its implementation and before its official roll-out. For example, employees' and managers' resistance and fear are potential problems that can be countered with briefing sessions or further training for all employees in the targeted departments.

Coaching

The effectiveness of 360-degree feedback has been combined with coaching focused on enhanced self-awareness and behaviour management and can result in improved individual – manager and employee – satisfaction, commitment, and, indirectly, the firm's performance (Smither et al., 2003). Feedback coaching helps managers evaluate the great amount of information they receive from 360-degree feedback (Antonioni, 1996) in order to reconcile and develop strategic goals. These goals focus on reducing the rating discrepancies between themselves and others and enhancing self-awareness.

It is therefore suggested that 360-degree feedback should be accompanied by systematic coaching. It is common for organizations to hire external coaches when their aim is the individual's leadership development (Ting and Hart, 2004). Regular one-to-one meetings are held between the coach and the coachee. These meetings cover issues arising from the feedback process, as well as other organizational problems and pressures. Wherever possible, the coaches are guided and assisted to the development and follow-up of their action plans by the coach and regularly review them and update during the coaching process.

Climate of trust and security between managers and employees

Trust is an essential part of the contextual factors the organization should take into account when implementing 360-degree feedback for leadership development. The participants, both the raters and the ratees, should feel comfortable in responding to the survey and the targeted individuals should feel comfortable and secure in their positions when receiving feedback from the survey. Both the feedback and the follow-up stages of the 360-degree programme will provide the maximum benefit to the targeted individual if she trusts her organization to carry out this procedure in order to develop her skills and her potential in the company. However, in cases where the relationships between the participating parties are not appropriate, the assessment process will not work successfully and will most likely create rather than resolve problems.

Confidentiality

Confidentiality is probably the single most significant key for successful results. The 360-degree programme needs to be implemented on a basis of honesty and confidentiality. It prescribes that the company will require the highest levels of honesty from individuals, demonstrating the willingness to address the emerged issues, and simultaneously providing the best means for confidential execution of the various stages of the appraisal and development process.

Accountability

Another significant factor influencing the effectiveness of 360-degree feedback as a leadership development technique is the accountability of those involved. London, Smither, and Adsit (1997) suggest that the accountability of all major groups involved is very important: the raters (to provide honest feedback), the ratees (to use the feedback), and the organization (to support the process). They also claim that the components of the 360-degree programme include sources of accountability (e.g. the boss and organizational policies), the objective (i.e. the behaviour or outcomes for which the actor is accountable), forces used by the sources to affect the actor's feelings of accountability (such as reinforcement for performance improvement), and mechanisms for activating these forces and holding someone accountable.

IMPACT OF 360-DEGREE FEEDBACK ON DEVELOPMENT

The increased use of 360-degree feedback implies that it is related to improved performance. A number of studies have investigated the impact of multisource feedback interventions on changes in self-awareness and behaviour for ratees. The results are not conclusive and a major reason is the extensive use of cross-sectional samples and correlational research designs, which do not allow for the examination of a cause–effect relationship between feedback and recipient performance and development. This is especially important, but even more difficult, when researching in leadership development. This is probably one of the main reasons why there is very limited research published in scientific journals exploring the links between 360-degree feedback and leadership development.

Earlier studies have generally shown modest improvements in ratings provided by other sources following feedback (Atwater, Waldman, and Brett, 2002). That is, self-ratings become more similar to others' ratings after feedback, emphasizing the positive consequences of feedback. Atwater, Roush, and Fischthal (1995) in a study using students from the US Naval Academy investigated changes in self-ratings following feedback and they found that people who rated themselves higher relative to how other people rated them lowered their self-ratings following feedback, while under-raters raised their self-ratings. In a similar vein were the results of Hazucha, Hezlett, and Schneider (1993) and Waldman and Atwater (2001). Atwater and Brett (2005) investigated the factors influencing the leaders' reactions to 360-degree feedback and the subsequent developmental activities and changes in leader behaviour. Personality was not related with reactions to feedback and the latter was not related to follow-up activities but was related to the degree of change in ratings over time. Leaders who overrated themselves relative to their raters' ratings were more motivated than underraters, and this was especially true for overraters with high self–other agreement, as opposed to underraters or leaders who overrated themselves but where there was low self–other agreement. The results of this study replicate previous findings which suggest that increased self-awareness, as defined by high self–other agreement is related to increased follow-up and developmental action by the managers. However, the results of London, Larson, and Thisted (1999) were not so positive. They explored the relationship between feedback-seeking and self-development in a large Danish organization, which is quite interesting since the vast majority of 360-degree studies have been carried out in the US. Contrary to predictions, perceptions of feedback and empowerment were not related to self-development. The results also showed that managers who were rated higher in job performance perceived more positive reinforcement, non-threatening feedback, and empowerment. Positive reinforcement was more important than the other feedback factors in predicting performance. Unfortunately, the results did not support the idea that a supportive environment enhances self-development.

CONCLUSIONS

The use of 360-degree feedback for leadership development is nowadays considered a very effective tool in organizations. Subject to a set of requirements, as described in the previous sections, it may provide organizations with very useful information about the potential of their future leaders. The 'objectivity' of the information provided to participants by various sources, if supported by the necessary resources and further leadership development programmes, such as coaching or on-the-job experiences rather than traditional in-class training, may assist managers' development dramatically.

Top management should note, however, that 360-degree feedback can only be useful if it is an essential part of a development culture within an organization. A development culture requires much more than simply the existence of a valid and reliable 360-degree tool. It requires enhanced trust between management and employees, and accountability as discussed earlier, but also a climate of trust, transparency, and meritocracy. As a result, organizations have to be patient with the implementation of such a programme. Unfortunately, because of the constant change they have to cope with, organizations often hope that the results of such a programme, which is usually quite expensive, will have an immediate impact on organizational performance, or can be treated as a stand-alone process. This is probably the most common mistake organizations make when attempting to implement a 360-degree feedback process.

Both future leaders and organizations as a whole can benefit the most from 360-degree programmes for leadership development, despite the controversial research findings on the effectiveness of such programmes in personal development, if they correctly apply the requirements discussed earlier in this chapter and at the same time avoid the common pitfalls of these programmes.

REFERENCES

Antonioni, D. (1996) Designing an effective 360-degree appraisal feedback process. *Organizational Dynamics,* 25(2): 24–38.

Atwater, L. E. and Brett, J. F. (2005) Antecedents and consequences of reactions to developmental feedback. *Journal of Vocational Behaviour,* 66: 532–48.

Atwater, L. E., Roush, P., and Fischthal, A. (1995) The influence of upward feedback on self- and follower ratings of leadership. *Personnel Psychology,* 48(1): 35–59.

Atwater, L. E., Waldman, D., and Brett, J. F. (2002) Understanding and optimizing multi-source feedback. *Human Resource Management,* 41(2): 193–208.

Brutus, S., Fleenor, J., and London, M. (1998) Does 360-degree feedback work in different industries? A between-industry comparison of the reliability and validity of multi-source performance ratings. *Journal of Management Development,* 17(3): 177–90.

Chappelow, C. T. (2004) 360-degree feedback. In C. D. McCauley and E. van Velsor (eds) *The Center for Creative Leadership handbook of leadership development.* San Francisco, CA: Jossey-Bass, pp. 58–84.

Collins, D. B. and Holton, E. F. (2004) The effectiveness of managerial leadership development programs: a meta-analysis of studies from 1982 to 2001. *Human Resource Development Quarterly,* 15(2): 217–48.

Day, D. V. (2000) Leadership development: A review in context. *Leadership Quarterly,* 11(4): 581–613.

DeNisi, A. S. and Kluger, A. N. (2000) Feedback effectiveness: Can 360-degree appraisals be improved? *Academy of Management Executive,* 14(1): 129–39.

Fletcher, C. and Baldry, C. (1999) Multi-source feedback systems: A research perspective. In C. L. Cooper and I. T. Robertson (eds) *International review of industrial and organizational psychology,* Vol. 14. Chichester: Wiley, pp. 149–94.

Hazucha, J. F., Hezlett, S. A., and Schneider, R. J. (1993) The impact of 360-degree feedback on management skills development. *Human Resource Management,* 32(2–3): 325–52.

Hernez-Broome, G. and Hughes, R. L. (2004) Leadership development: Past, present, and future. *Human Resource Planning,* 24–32.

Kluger, A. N. and DeNisi, A. S. (1996) The effects of feedback interventions on performance: A historical review, a meta-analysis, and a preliminary feedback intervention. *Psychological Bulletin,* 119: 254–84.

London, M. and Maurer, T. J. (2004) Leadership development. In J. Antonakis, A. T. Cianciolo, and R. J. Sternberg (eds) *The nature of leadership.* London: Sage, pp. 222–45.

London, M., Larson, H. H., and Thisted, L. N. (1999) Relationships between feedback and self-development. *Group Organization Management,* 24(1): 5–27.

London, M., Smither, J. W., and Adsit, D. J. (1997) Accountability: The Achilles' heel of multisource feedback. *Group and Organization Management,* 22(2): 162–84.

McCauley, C. (2001) Leader training and development. In S. J. Zaccaro and R. J. Klimoski (eds) *The nature of organizational leadership.* San Francisco, CA: Jossey-Bass, pp. 347–83.

McCauley, C. D. and van Velsor, E. (eds) (2004) *The Center for Creative Leadership handbook of leadership development.* San Francisco, CA: Jossey-Bass.

Pollack, D. M. and Pollack, L. J. (1996) Using 360 degree feedback in performance appraisal. *Public Personnel Management,* 25(4): 507–28.

Seifert, C. F., Yukl, G., and McDonald, R. A. (2003) Effects of multisource feedback and a feedback facilitator on the influence behaviour of managers towards subordinates. *Journal of Applied Psychology,* 88(3): 561–9.

Smither, J. W., London, M., Flaut, R., Vargas, Y., and Kucine, I. (2003) Can working with an executive coach improve multisource feedback ratings over time? A quasi-experimental field study. *Personnel Psychology,* 56: 23–44.

Ting, S. and Hart, E. W. (2004) Formal coaching. In C. D. McCauley and E. van Velsor (eds) *The Center for Creative Leadership handbook of leadership development.* San Francisco, CA: Jossey-Bass, pp. 116–50.

Tornow, W. W. (1993a) Introduction to special issue on 360-degree feedback. *Human Resource Management,* 32(2–3): 211–20.

Tornow, W. W. (1993b) Special issue on 360-degree feedback. *Human Resource Management,* 32(2–3).

Van Velsor, E. and McCauley, C. D. (2004) Our view of leadership development. In C. D. McCauley and E. van Velsor (eds) *The Center for Creative Leadership handbook of leadership development.* San Francisco, CA: Jossey-Bass, pp. 1–22.

Van Velsor, E., Taylor, S., and Leslie, J. B. (1993) An examination of the relationships among self-perception accuracy, self-awareness, gender, and leader effectiveness. *Human Resource Management,* 32(2–3), 249–64.

Waldman, D. A. and Atwater, L. E. (2001) Attitudinal and behavioral outcomes of an upward feedback process. *Group Organization Management,* 26(2): 189–205.

Waldman, D. A., Atwater, L. E., and Antonioni, D. (1998) Has 360 degree feedback gone amok? *Academy of Management Executive,* 12(2): 86–94.

Yammarino, F. J. and Atwater, L. E. (1993) Understanding self-perception accuracy: Implications for human resource management. *Human Resource Management,* 32(2–3): 231–48.

Chapter 17

Developing women leaders

Marian N. Ruderman

Over 25 years ago Federated Technologies made a concerted effort to hire more women into the managerial and professional ranks. Defining the problem as not enough women in the pipeline, they recruited at the top business schools all over the world. Federated offered attractive salaries and the potential for an exciting career. They figured they could increase the number of women in leadership roles by simply getting women into the organization and then following traditional strategies of leadership development. Twenty-five years into this approach, they still emphasize recruiting, making a big show of the number of women hired each year to the press. The only problem is that they can't seem to keep the outstanding women they hire over the long term. Now that women have been in Federated long enough to make their mark, women are still scarce in the upper reaches of the hierarchy. Many women decide to leave and those that stay seem to get stuck in middle-management positions. What has gone wrong?

Federated's situation is not unusual. Women have made great strides in entering the managerial ranks in many countries of the world. In the US, women hold 50.5 per cent of the managerial jobs (US Census Bureau, 2004) but only 15.7 per cent of corporate officer positions (Catalyst, 2002). In the UK women hold 7.2 per cent of the directorships in FTSE companies (Singh and Vinnicombe, 2004). In Japan, women hold only 9 per cent of key leadership positions (Yuasa, 2005). The problem is that although companies are successful at attracting women leaders, they can't seem to keep them. Why is it so hard for women to achieve top leadership positions in big companies? Why can't companies effectively include women in the executive ranks?

Many explanations have been advanced to explain this worldwide phenomenon. One theory gaining prominence in the media is that women are deciding to opt out of the corporate world in order to concentrate on family (Belkin, 2003); they are leaving because it is just too hard to sustain both a career and a family life. Another view focuses on the prejudice and discrimination women face in corporate settings as a force expelling them (Eagly, 2003). Or, there is the often-mentioned explanation that women simply don't have the necessary line experience to advance. Finally, there remains the view that women just aren't up to the demands of the executive world – they aren't willing to work hard (Tischler, 2004) or don't really want to exercise power (Mero and Sellers, 2003).

This chapter suggests an alternative view: the problem is that organizations are failing in their efforts to develop women leaders because they ignore women's expectations with regard to learning, growth, and development. Despite all the change in recent years, organizations are still built on the assumption that top leaders are men with traditional career plans and patterns. As women have entered leadership roles, organizations have changed their climate and culture to some extent, but not enough to really encourage the retention and development of large numbers of women into top leadership roles. It is time to reflect on the leadership development expectations of women and for organizations to take these into account. The world has changed and leadership development techniques need to address the expectations and experiences of both men and women.

This chapter discusses five basic expectations women have about their development. We believe that organizations with climates that support these needs will be more able to effectively retain and thereby include women managers in their uppermost ranks. First this chapter will consider these five needs: authenticity, connection, agency, wholeness, and self-clarity. With this as a backdrop, it will then discuss techniques of leadership development (feedback-intensive training, experiential learning, and developmental relationships), and finally the chapter will turn to initiatives an organization will need to consider in order to develop a more inclusive culture that develops women leaders in addition to men.

It is critical that organizations reconsider how their environment attracts and develops women. Companies all over the world are recognizing the business imperative to have the most talented staff. This can only happen if our organizations engage and encourage managers of both genders. An important step in capitalizing on the talents of women is to build a company climate that recognizes and respects issues of importance to women.

WOMEN'S LEADERSHIP JOURNEY

Women experience the leadership journey differently than men and have distinctive expectations regarding their development. Mainiero and Sullivan (2005) examined the different ways the careers of men and women unfold. They found that men as a group are more likely to have linear career paths, following the traditional wisdom of working continuously in a series of progressively more complex jobs in a single industry. In contrast, women have less predictable careers. Their careers are marked by interruptions, employment gaps, and a tendency to build a career crafted out of a combination of available opportunities, personal passions, and the needs of others close to them. Hewlett and Luce (2005) describe women's careers as having off-ramps and on-ramps as women travel on the road to organizational advancement taking time off to address other aspects of life. Ruderman and Ohlott (2002) suggest that conventional career wisdom based on the experience of married white men does not readily apply to women. They argue that the leadership journey for women is indeed distinctive; one that is characterized by five themes underlying the many career and life choices confronting high-achieving women.

Based on an intensive study of the lives of 61 female high-achievers in the organizational world, Ruderman and Ohlott (2002) identified the following developmental expectations of women:

- *authenticity* – the desire to have a healthy alignment between inner values and beliefs and outer behaviours;
- *connection* – the need to be close to other human beings; to feel attached to others and needed;
- *control of one's own destiny* – this refers to agency, the drive to act on our own behalf in order to influence the environment around us;
- *wholeness* – the desire to integrate the personal and professional life goals;
- *self-clarity* – the drive to understand your own motives, strengths, weaknesses, and behaviours within the context of your environment.

These themes provide a basis for understanding the career and life decisions of high-achieving women. Although these themes will be examined uniquely, they are intertwined and build on one another.

The women who participated in the study all held managerial positions in large corporations, non-profit organizations, or the government. They were motivated to further their own leadership development and participated in a five-day leadership development programme conducted by the Center for Creative Leadership. The research study followed their progress on their developmental goals for a year after having participated in the programme. They were interviewed at three points in time about their development as a leader and choices emerging in their personal and professional lives. In addition, the women completed a battery of psychological tests and performance measurements as part of their participation in the feedback-intensive leadership development programme. The five themes are based on an analysis of this data.

Authenticity has to do with the desire to have a healthy alignment between inner values and beliefs and outer behaviours. Someone who is authentic has a good understanding of her own priorities, values, and emotions. She knows what is important to her and is aware of the choices and trade-offs she is making.

Authenticity is more of a state or a condition rather than a personality character-istic. It is not something you keep once you achieve it. It is something you must constantly maintain. Women who are authentic design their lives and careers to suit their highest priorities. Their decisions stem from their own, rather than their organization's standard of success.

There are two main ways in which high-achieving women tend to struggle with authenticity. Authenticity can become an issue when there are organizational changes. A woman may notice her feelings about authenticity changing as her job evolves. For example, a reorganization or new strategic initiative may alter her feelings of fit with the organization. Authenticity may also be an issue when a woman (or man) is asked to fit into a leadership environment that may feel unnat-ural or forced. For example, women with participative leadership styles may feel that they are inauthentic when asked to operate in a control and command type of organization. The women in the Ruderman and Ohlott study wanted to make a mark on their organizations but wanted to do it in their own way with a style that felt true.

Making connections has to do with the fundamental need to be close to other human beings, to feel attached and needed. Relationships are a source of pleasure and meaning in our lives. Traditionally, women have defined their identity though their relationships with others – wife, mother, daughter, friend, and sister. In the modern world, women still value these identities and the question is how to act on them when the world of work can be such a demanding taskmaster driving out time for connections and relationships. Over many years, psychologists have docu-mented the importance of this sense of connection to other people to the well-being of women (Gilligan, 1982; Jordan *et al.*, 1991; Miller and Stiver, 1997). Relationships provide women leaders with support, enhanced well-being, and facilitation of learning and growth.

According to Ruderman and Ohlott (2002), high-achieving women experience two problems of connection. The first is that many women would like to feel that they have more of a reference group. Because women are still so rare at elite levels of leadership, high-achieving women still struggle with being the odd one out. Many high–achieving women feel that they have no community at work. They have few female peers and don't feel entirely accepted by the men. The other way (dis)connection is experienced is through a lack of one-to-one intimacy. Many women want closer, more intimate relationships with another individual be it a significant other, very close friend, or family members. The time demands of tradi-tional organizations can drive out opportunities for developing and strengthening relationships.

The *desire to control one's own destiny* is one of the strongest drives of high-achieving women. This fundamental need, first described by psychologist David Bakan (1966), is what motivates us to act on our own behalf, to excel, make things happen, and influence the environment. Bakan called this desire agency and saw it in opposition to the drive of communion (similar to connection discussed earlier, the drive to have relationships with others).

Traditional psychological models see the qualities typically associated with agency associated with masculinity and the qualities typically associated with connection with femininity. This mind-set gives women a lot of latitude to act with regard to connection but much less latitude to develop control over one's own destiny. This bias puts women in organizations in a difficult place. Essentially when they act in a forceful way, they can be 'damned if they do' and 'damned if they don't'. Society has such strong expectations that they give women very little latitude for behaving in ways contrary to stereotypical expectations (Eagly, 2003; Ridgeway, 2001). Morrison, White, and Van Velsor (1987) have referred to this quandary as the 'narrow band'. Women have a very limited range of behaviours they can use to be effectively agentic. A challenge for women in organizational leadership positions is to find the right amount of agency and to act in a way that is both forceful and acceptable to the organizational environment at large. Acting agentically can be a dilemma on a good day with no particular problems because of the extreme societal expectations associated with gender; however, it can be an extremely difficult challenge when the organizational situation is unusually problematic requiring significant change. During reorganizations, downsizing, and business downturns when change is expected, women can face even greater obstacles in trying to act agentically.

Specialists in the development of women stress that for women to be effectively agentic they must also recognize the importance of relationships and in particular the importance of interdependence in relationships where people facilitate growth and learning in each other. Miller and Stiver (1997) argue that strong actions must be viewed in the context of the relationships and connections in which they are embedded. According to this view, effectiveness rests on the combination of agency and connection. Eagly (2003) suggests that when women do not temper agentic behaviours with adequate displays of more stereotypic nurturing feminine behaviour, they tend to incur a backlash.

The fourth expectation of high achieving women is that they will be able to *achieve wholeness*. The desire to integrate personal and professional life goals is a driving force in the behaviour of many women leaders. The 24/7 demands of the business world often make this hard for women to achieve. Mainiero and Sullivan (2005) go as far as to offer a new model called 'kaleidoscope careers' to explain the impact of this drive on careers. According to this model, career decisions are a natural outgrowth of decisions to blend work and non-work lives. Women in effect build their career in the context of relationships with others. Family and personal goals act as a context influencing key career decisions. A kaleidoscope is used as a metaphor because as one part moves so do the other pieces, reflecting the way women integrate work and non-work factors in career decisions.

In the Center for Creative Leadership study, wholeness played a central theme. Many of the women complained of feeling lopsided as a consequence of being a workaholic. They had major difficulties feeling whole. They emphasized the work-related aspects of their life so much that they had little time for personal interests. Typically, they would experience a disappointment at work such as a missed promotion and then wonder what else was left in life besides career. They were driven to modify things so that they didn't have to sacrifice hobbies, friends, families, and exercise.

A second type of struggle identified had to do with the inherent conflicts between work and personal life. Many women were intent on doing it all – raising children, taking care of elderly relatives, and pursuing a demanding career. Personal and work demands would compete such that the women felt worn out, torn, and conflicted, worrying that something was wrong with them. The reality was that the world they lived in didn't make it easy for them to fashion the life they wanted.

Although wholeness is difficult to achieve, it is not impossible. It also is critically important. Wholeness and related concepts such as commitment to multiple roles have been related to well-being (Ruderman *et al.*, 2002). People with a whole life feel better about themselves because a multiplicity of roles provides resources such as additional sources of support and opportunities for success in multiple arenas. Multiple roles offer a variety of sources of esteem that can be really helpful when trouble strikes in one aspect of life.

In addition to well-being, commitment to both personal and work related roles is also related to enhanced performance. Ruderman *et al.* (2002) identified an association between commitment to multiple life roles and performance in managerial jobs. Regardless of the level of commitment to the managerial role, the stronger a manager's commitment to roles outside work, the better the manager was rated in her job. It is important to note that the manager's own boss, peers, and direct reports made the ratings of job performance. This isn't proof that multiple roles caused enhanced job performance but it is evidence of a link. According to role accumulation theorists (Marks, 1977; Sieber, 1974), learning from one role can be accumulated and incorporated into another. In other words, learning from one domain of life such as raising a family can be incorporated into another domain of life such as managing. Family and personal roles develop women in important ways. They learn how to support others, how to solve problems, how to gain perspective. These lessons bear on work-related roles as well and show an organizational benefit to having employees who are driven to feel whole, integrated, and complete.

Self-Clarity is the final developmental expectation of high-achieving women. Self-clarity has to do with the desire to understand your own motives, strengths, and weaknesses in the context of the environment. It is knowing who you are and how you fit into the world around you – how forces in your organization and society at large affect the way others see you. A strong sense of self-clarity enables high-achieving women to navigate effectively through life.

Self-clarity acts as a facilitator for growth in the other four themes. It allows for the recognition of values necessary for an authentic life, it enables agentic behaviour, improves the ability to connect with other, and allows for choices that create a feeling of wholeness. Self-clarity helps people figure out what they want and how these desires fit in with the opportunities in the surrounding environment. Without self-clarity, people are in danger of accepting situations that don't support their growth and needs.

Different levels of self-clarity create different types of problems. For women who have low levels of self-clarity, one of the most noticeable problems is that they run into obstacles stemming from their own weaknesses or limitations without seeing the problem or making any attempt to address it. These women tend to blame the organization for all problems.

Women with higher levels of self-clarity struggled with other issues. One of these was understanding the gendered nature of organizations. A number of women yearned to better understand how the organization viewed women in general and how this impacted their career in particular. There was a drive to better understand gender dynamics as a way of better understanding their own situation. Women seeking self-clarity reported that they did not get the feedback they desired that would allow them to better understand how they were viewed in the organization. Women tended to be excluded from many sources of informal feedback, making it difficult for them to view themselves more objectively. This is important to understand because there is a tendency to question women's leadership skills because leadership ability is more stereotypically associated with men (Eagly, 2003). This creates a feedback conundrum in understanding what is effective and what stems from gender stereotyping. Another dilemma was learning how to avoid over-personalizing tense business situations. The women worked to learn how to see themselves in perspective so that they could better separate out the actions required by their managerial role from their identity as a human being. This was particularly important when a manager had to deal with some of the harsher realities of managerial life such slashing staff or budgets.

ADDRESSING THE LEADERSHIP DEVELOPMENT EXPECTATIONS OF HIGH-ACHIEVING WOMEN

Specifically, there are a number of leadership development techniques that can be used to help promote the development of women in these areas. This chapter highlights three types of leadership development techniques: feedback-intensive training programmes, experiential learning, and developmental relationships.

Feedback-intensive training programmes

A feedback-intensive programme is built on the premise that development means helping a manager to see patterns in her behaviour and understanding the attitudes, values, and preferences that result in those patterns. It also involves understanding personal goals and assessment with regard to how effectively the individual is reaching those goals (Guthrie and Kelly-Radford, 1998). Such programmes are powerful because intense feedback is delivered in the context of a supportive environment amidst an understanding of frameworks for leadership. According to Guthrie and Kelly-Radford (1998), these programmes are associated with the further development of knowledge about leadership, self-awareness, changes in perspective, goal attainment, and behavioural change.

These programmes come in many varieties and flavours. Different versions of these programmes are more or less suitable for the development of women leaders. For many years, now women have had the option of attending *women-only training programmes*. These programmes are offered by colleges, universities, and training organizations such as Simmons College, Center for Creative Leadership, Cranfield (in the UK), Insead (France), and IMD (Switzerland). These programmes focus on issues of leadership in a setting that encourages additional content having to do with identity issues and complexities in the workplace. Although many types of training programmes can address developmental expectations of women, women-only programmes tend to be particularly well-suited for these purposes.

For example, the programmes often help with the issue of self-clarity. According to Ohlott (2002) and Koonce (2004), women attending these programmes report a validating experience. Through the sharing that takes place, they learn that what they are experiencing and feeling is similar for other women. They are not alone on their leadership journeys. This feeling of normalization can be wonderful.

At the Center for Creative Leadership programme, participants get feedback on a series of personality inventories, value assessments, and performance evaluations. This feedback is intended to encourage greater self-awareness and to help participants develop their awareness of strengths and weaknesses. The various instruments and experiences provide the participant with an in-depth look at how their leadership behaviours come across to others. In a women-only programme, this feedback is often normed against the experiences of other women. These norms can indeed provide validation that women have different experiences in organizations than men do.

The delivery of feedback in a women-only programme helps managers figure out what aspects of their individual feedback are unique to them and what aspects are functions of being in a non-dominant position in an organization. This happens through discussion of feedback, presentation of normative data for their group, and peer feedback from other managers in the programme. With negative performance feedback, women typically have to go through the extra step of figuring out what is valid in the feedback and what may be filtered through prejudicial lenses. Women-only training programmes help with this process because facilitators are attuned to the problem and incorporate material to address this. One technique used by the Center is that of peer feedback in which participants learn how to give situationally based feedback to each other and proceed to do it. This is helpful because participants can use this experience to figure out what in their feedback from home represents 'honest' feedback and what may represent 'sexism'. More often than not, participants are impressed by how closely their peer feedback matches their feedback from work. Women inclined to deny feedback on the grounds it may be from someone who doesn't want to see women advance often have to rethink the validity of this assertion. Feedback intensive programmes can be particularly important for the development of self-clarity because many women don't have access to quality informal feedback in organizations. These programmes emphasize how to give feedback, how to receive feedback, how to evaluate it, and how to learn from it.

Single identity programmes are also extremely helpful for women to acknowledge questions about their own authenticity. The programme at the Center for Creative Leadership contains considerable content helping women understand their key values or motivators. This heightened sense of priorities helps women to articulate questions about the alignment of their inner values and outer behaviours. It provides a language women can use to explore concerns about key choices.

Whether or not a training programme is feedback intensive, women-only training programmes are known for their safe, supportive environment. They allow a place for women to practise new skills or 'let their guard down' in a safe, supportive environment. Women don't have to worry about being seen as either too masculine or too feminine in these groups. These programmes tend to be seen as very supportive because many high-level women managers do not have a reference group in their own organization to be part of. They allow for risk-taking in an environment of trust (Koonce, 2004). The comfort-with-your-own-kind factor that senior white male managers tend to have kicks in for these women. Women have been known to develop professional connections in these programmes that last long beyond the event. Many engaging in these types of programmes later decide to join professional women's networks so they can maintain that sense of having a reference group. They address the female leader's expectations about connection by providing content about how to network and the experience of networking with a group of women. They also provide a group of role models and reference points that can be especially helpful for women in fields where women are scarce.

Another feature of these programmes is that they can contain content designed specifically with women in mind. In the case of the programme at the Center for Creative Leadership, content specific to women is threaded throughout the programme. Articles based on the lives and managerial experiences of women are referenced. Data about women leaders is freely mentioned in the programme, as are examples of top women leaders. Case studies feature women executives as the main players. Another feature of the programme that reflects some of this tailoring is the practice of holistic goal setting. Responding to the desire of women to address wholeness as an issue, this type of goal setting places career goals in the context of the whole life. Most training programmes end with some type of goal setting for actions for the future. The difference here is that career goals viewed in relation to other personal and family goals. Health-related, family-oriented, volunteer oriented, and other personal goals are considered in the same venue as work-related goals. This form of goal setting recognizes that women tend to develop their careers on their own terms blending work with personal concerns (Mainiero and Sullivan, 2005).

Much of the content in women-only programmes (as well as in mixed-group programmes) is intended to help participants develop effective levels of agency. In the Center for Creative Leadership's programme, influencing skills and political behaviours are emphasized in the curriculum. Women are videotaped in an influencing situation and then get feedback as to how they came across. They are also given tools and techniques for using relationships wisely in the pursuit of key goals.

Despite their many benefits, these programmes also have their disadvantages making them quite controversial. Among these is the possibility that because these programmes highlight perceived differences, they may prove detrimental to women in the long run. Programmes designed only for women can inadvertently foster prejudices in men or the view that women are somehow deficient. According to Ohlott (2002), one way for single-identity programmes to address these concerns is by emphasizing that these programmes are as rigorous as mixed-gender programmes and contain similar content.

There is also the problem that these programmes do not mirror the 'real world'. Proponents of this view believe that training environments should replicate the complexity of the real world, in this case organizations dominated by men. The argument is that skills learned in a women-only programme may not be generalizable to the real world.

So, which is better? The question of whether to attend a women-only programme or a mixed-group programme is one only the manager involved can answer. Both venues can be helpful ways to foster learning and support for development. Women managers need to decide, if they would prefer this exploration in a traditional way or if they prefer it in a way that emphasizes the gender. Women-only programmes have an advantage when it comes to understanding the aspects of self-clarity that have to do with being in a gendered environment but it is also quite possible for this issue to come out in a mixed-gender programme. The important point is that feedback-intensive training programmes can be a way for women to get feedback necessary for helping them address issues of self-clarity, authenticity, wholeness, connection, and agency.

329

Experiential learning

Learning from experience is one of the most important approaches to leadership development (McCall, Lombardo, and Morrison, 1988). This really refers to the old adage that people 'learn best from doing'. Traditionally, in the context of leadership development, experiential learning is thought of in terms of assignment-based learning. However, in light of the developmental expectations of women for wholeness and the kaleidoscope model of careers, it is also critical to consider learning from life.

Assignment-based learning builds on the finding that many executives, both male and female, consider job experiences the primary form of development (McCall, Lombardo, and Morrison, 1998; Morrison, White and Van Velsor, 1987; Ohlott, 2004). Challenging job assignments are experiences that push people to do something new or differently. A developmental job pushes a manager to out of her comfort zone and requires her to think and act differently. Challenging assignments teach many lessons: (1) handling relationships, (2) setting and implementing agendas, (3) basic values, (4) personal insights, and (5) executive temperament (McCall, Lombardo, and Morrison, 1998). These lessons are particularly helpful for the development of agency, authenticity, and self-clarity.

Without formal interventions in organizations, women and men report differences with regard to exposure to developmental assignments. In particular, women tend to report a lesser variety of challenging job assignments than men (Van Velsor and Hughes-James, 1990). Women report having fewer opportunities to have rich developmental assignments than do men. Compared to men at the same level of management, women experience their jobs as less critical and less visible to the organization (Ohlott, Ruderman and McCauley, 1994). Moreover, women report that in addition to the elements of a job that require new or different thinking, they also experience contextual challenges such as prejudice and differential treatment (Douglas, 2003; Morrison, White, and Van Velsor, 1987). In other words, they have to handle possible discrimination on top of the job challenges. This can make it extra difficult to learn from a challenging assignment. It is critical that women get the same exposure to challenging assignments as men if they are to hold the same jobs. However, it is important that these challenges don't come with the extra baggage associated with discrimination, prejudice, and harassment. Challenging assignments work best as a developmental tool in environments that encourage the advancement of both women and men.

Learning from life is another way in which women leaders develop. Work is not the only pertinent source of leadership development experience. The personal sphere of life is an incredibly rich venue for experiential learning (Ruderman and Ohlott, 2002; Ruderman et al., 2002). Women leaders report many occasions in which they transferred learning from the personal realm of life to the managerial arena. Recognizing the importance of this channel for learning helps to address

330

expectations regarding wholeness. In response to a question about the contributions of personal lives to their managerial performance, women in the Center for Creative Leadership study spoke about four ways in which lessons learned through personal life experiences enhanced managerial performance. These include: relational skills, multi-tasking skills, using personal background to understand constituents, and leadership practice.

Personal roles were a venue in which women reported that they learned how to understand motivate, and respect others. Parenting was often mentioned as a great opportunity to learn about others. In-law experiences were developmental as well. Specifically, the women in the Center for Creative Leadership study learned patience, respect for individual differences, motivation techniques, how to develop others, influence skills, acceptance of failure, empathy, and how to give feedback from personal life relationships. The women leaders reported that these experiences helped them to better lead their staffs.

Planning and prioritizing multiple tasks at home also proved to be fertile ground for the acquisition of managerial skills. Women leaders explained that dealing with a house, a job, having a spouse, volunteering, caring for elderly parents, and dealing with childcare issues promotes efficiency, focus, and organization. Many executives said they were adept at juggling multiple responsibilities at work because they did it all the time at home.

Personal interests and background also enter in the work performance picture. Women in sales and marketing positions in particular used their consumer experiences as fodder for decisions. For example, being the only person in a meeting who has actually worn pantyhose gives a hosiery executive added knowledge about the product.

Finally, personal leadership experiences also are relevant to leadership development at work. Volunteer positions provide an important way to practise leadership responsibilities. Leadership roles in community, educational, and religious organizations provide a way of learning skills such as how to set a vision, get commitment to the vision, and keep people motivated.

In addition to providing opportunities for learning, personal life experiences are venues for gaining psychological strength. Experiences outside of work can provide perspective; they emphasize sources of self-esteem from non-work roles. They can also provide plain old-fashioned psychological support and encouragement. Friends, parents, spouses, siblings, and community partners can all be drawn upon as sources of social support.

An implication of this beneficial relationship between the personal and public spheres of life is that 'learning from life' should be recognized as a valuable source of leadership development opportunities. All too often, organizations overlook the value of non-work activities in the leadership arena. Ignoring non-work roles as a learning opportunity demeans these experiences. Given the importance of wholeness to women, it is important that the value of these non-work learning opportunities be addressed. Learning from life can be incorporated in training programmes through the insertion of thoughtful questions about these developmental opportunities. Personal life roles should be considered as a means of learning job-related competencies; being aware of leadership opportunities provided by off-the-job experiences is a first step. Development planning activities should contain activities that encourage review of all sources of development and allow time for learning from personal life venues. This is mentioned here in the context of women leaders, but the advice is relevant to men as well. Research on fatherhood, demonstrates the power of this experience in teaching adult males relational skills. As the desire for wholeness grows among leaders, recognizing the power of off-the-job learning is especially significant.

Developmental relationships

Developmental relationships refer to alliances that shape learning and development. Ask leaders to reflect on their key learning experiences, and about a third will discuss learning from relationships (e.g. Douglas, 2003; McCall, Lombardo and Morrison, 1988; Morrison, White, and Van Velsor, 1992). Developmental relationships are particularly important for women because they can help women overcome key career barriers (Ragins, 1997a, 1997b) and provide additional sources of support and power. Three types of developmental relationships are highlighted here: coaching relationships, mentoring, and network relationships.

Coaching as a formal developmental activity has increased in popularity in recent years. Formal one-to-one coaching is:

> a practice in which the coach and coachee collaborate to assess and understand the coachee and his or her developmental task, to challenge current constraints while exploring new possibilities, and to ensure accountability and support for reaching goals and sustaining development.
>
> (Ting and Hart, 2004, p. 116)

In a formal coaching relationship, the coach and coachee have an explicit agreement to work together to understand and commit to the goals of the coachee. Typically coaches are professionals with training in creating behaviour change, although it is possible for a coach to come from a different background.

Ting and Hart (2004) offer a helpful framework for understanding the coaching process. They point out that coaching occurs in the context of a relationship characterized by rapport, collaboration, and commitment. Within the bounds of this relationship, the coach provides assessment of the individual to help her attain greater self-awareness, challenges the executive to learn and grow, and supports the coachee in her growth. Finally, the coach works with the executive to achieve results and holds her accountable.

332

For coaching to be most effective it is important that the coach understand the coachee environment. For women leaders, this means that the coach whether it be male or female have a solid understanding of what it is like to be a female leader in that particular organization. In other words, the coach needs to pay attention to the role of gender in that particular organizational environment. Without this knowledge, a coach is handicapped in helping the client figure out reasonable goals and courses of action.

Although coaching women is not all that different from coaching men, there are several nuances to take into account in using coaching as a leadership development technique for women. The relationship, use of assessment, challenge, and support, and results may unfold differently for women than for men. In particular there are several aspects of the coaching relationship to be mindful of.

Research on women suggests that coaching may be a particularly appropriate methodology of leadership development for women leaders. Relationships are often a catalyst for growth for women. Relational theory (Gilligan, 1982; Miller, 1986) argues that the central mode of growth for girls and women is through connection with others. In other words, women develop most effectively in the context of safe and authentic relationships. This stands in contrast to masculine theories of development that assume that growth occurs through separation and individual effort. Men's development is characterized by increasing autonomy. According to relational theory (Miller and Stivers, 1997), healthy relationships characterized by mutual empathy and empowerment foster development in women. This suggests that coaching may be especially well suited for the development of women leaders, particularly those who are seeking greater connection.

A second issue to be mindful of in employing coaching as a leadership development technique is that sexual tension may enter in the relationship when the coach is male and the coachee is female. There is little if anything on this in the literature. However, anecdotal information suggests that both coaches and coachees are mindful of this. One male coach mentioned that he is mindful of this and is careful to avoid the possibility of the relationship having sexual overtones. For example he is very clear in the contracting phase to be as specific about the coaching relationship as possible. He is also very aware of his own body language and never sits between the coachee and the door. Finally, he does not meet with female coachees in restaurants, hotel rooms, or anywhere ambiguity about the relationship could surface. There is little actual research as to whether it makes any difference if a male or female coaches a woman. Anecdotal conversations with coaches suggest that the key thing is having a good relationship with the coachee and not the coach's gender. It remains a very open question as to whether gender of the coach makes a difference to female coachees.

Coaching can be extremely useful in addressing the expectations of executive women to develop as whole human beings. The ability to be able to discuss key decisions with someone who knows what questions to ask is especially valuable.

Coachees can help frame the issues around values and priorities that are essential to the development of wholeness.

Further, coaching is an ideal method of helping adults develop self-clarity. Built on a foundation of trust and mutual regard, a good coaching relationship can work to help an executive see herself more objectively. It can also help in better understanding the dynamics of the organization that are in play.

Nonetheless, it is important to note that research on coaching is relatively scarce. There is no strong evidence of the relative value (or lack thereof) of coaching for women. Anecdotal reports suggest that it can be an extremely valuable developmental tool.

Mentoring is another approach for encouraging learning and development. Mentoring encompasses both personal aspects of support such as friendship and career aspects such as sponsorship (Kram, 1988). In contrast to coaching, which involves a relationship between a manager and an expert with professional training in behaviour change, mentoring relationships typically occur between a junior and senior manager. Mentoring relationships can occur naturally or can be formally set up by an organization. Formal mentoring programmes are usually created with the expectation that the relationships will provide career and personal development supports for managers with high potential. They are often discussed in the context of developing women leaders because informal mentoring relationships are frequently unavailable to women leaders. Formal mentoring programmes are seen as a way of equalizing the playing field.

Mentoring can help women in a variety of ways. Most importantly, these relationships can develop a sense of connection. This can be especially important for women who are feeling isolated in organizations. They can also be helpful in addressing issues of agency by providing women with an opportunity to learn about political behaviours in the context of her own organization. Information about the organizational context can also contribute to helping the female manager develop a stronger sense of the organization and how she fits in which contributes to a sense of self-clarity.

Despite their power as a developmental technique, mentoring programmes come with cautions and potential drawbacks. One issue, regardless of the gender of the participant, has to do with the senior managers acting as mentors in a formal programme. Not all managers have the interpersonal skills or wisdom to mentor effectively. Furthermore, negative experiences are quite possible due to favouritism, manipulation by the mentor, or neglect.

When gender is taken into account, the creation of a formal mentoring relationship becomes particularly tricky. Discomfort working closely with someone from the opposite sex can be felt by both men and women. Research on mentoring suggests that cross-gender developmental relationships do have some complicated dynamics and there is the worry that such relationships may be misconstrued as romantic (Clawson and Kram, 1984). Also male–female pairings can be given extra attention in the organization. Mentoring relationships between two women are not without hazards either. Due to the constraints on women's advancement in organizations, women may be seen as less valuable mentors.

Networking, a third type of developmental alliance, is becoming increasingly popular. According to Morrison (1992), networks offer a variety of benefits: support for mangers who share similar challenges, information channels, opportunities for feedback, social capital, and a means of increasing organizational savvy. In the Center for Creative Leadership study, women used networks to enhance their feelings of connection and to improve their self-clarity. They joined networks organized by region, industry, organization, or profession. They enhanced feelings of connection because they helped women to be part of another community, one that provided a sense of belonging and attachment. Networks helped to enhance organizational savvy by helping women to better understand their organizational environments and to discern how they were operating within the context of those environments. The chance to chat about one's organization helped women to see events more objectively and to better understand how their own experiences fit into a larger context.

PUTTING IT ALL TOGETHER

The various techniques associated with single-identity training, experiential learning, and developmental relationships can go a long way to developing a high potential individual. However, by themselves, these techniques are insufficient for addressing the issue of creating a leadership cadre inclusive of women. The organizational environment must nurture the growth of women as well. Consider the following agricultural analogy. Even the best seeds will yield a poor crop if the ground is not fertilized and the plant is not watered. It is the same with leadership development. Seeds, or in this case managers who have benefited from the above developmental techniques, will not flourish if they are in a hostile environment without the nutrients and conditions needed for growth. It is not enough to provide good training for women leaders, expose them to developmental opportunities, and to strengthen their developmental relationships. The organizational climate must be supportive as well.

Organizations can do a lot to help women develop into authentic, whole, agentic, connected, self-understanding leaders. Organizations that do so should profit from having the best in the workforce leadership positions, not simply the best of the men. It is outside the purview of this chapter to go into the literature on organizational change in detail, but global suggestions can be made.

Focusing on the key aspects of each of the five developmental themes, this means organizations should create environments that:

1 *Allow women to act authentically*. One of the key needs of women executives is to be in an environment in which their everyday behaviours mirror their values. They want environments that allow them to act in a way that feels genuine and honest. One way to do this is to encourage organizational cultures that jointly optimize both organizational effectiveness and personal development. In these sorts of climates, individuals can develop in ways consistent with their true talents and goals. Kofodimos (1993) calls this a 'climate for self-realization'. Such a climate recognizes that all people don't have the same needs or goals but can still make valuable organizational contributions. There are several human resource practices that support such a climate. These include having multiple career paths, for example career ladders that value both management expertise and technical skills. Another human resource practice is to create career paths that allow people who have left the workforce to opt back so as to better recognize the career patterns of women today (Mainiero and Sullivan, 2005). Organizations would be able to advance more women if provisions were made for career interruptions (Hewlett and Luce, 2005). Currently, many women who opt out of organizations want to do so only temporarily and the lack of 'on-ramps' to corporate careers makes re-entry nearly impossible (Hewlett and Luce, 2005). A second practice is linking personal goals with career planning. Most organizations have annual performance appraisals but they don't take personal goals into account. Systems that do are likely to foster motivation and self-realization. This is a type of organizational career planning that would allow for holistic goals encompassing career in relationship to the rest of life.

2 *Authorize women to act powerfully*. Too often organizational environments limit the tools women can use to excel. Women are not allowed to show influence and control the way a man can. It is frustrating to stay in an environment that won't allow you to act powerfully and/or reward you for doing so. Although acts of blatant harassment or discrimination may be a thing of the past, organizations must still deal with the more subtle kind of discrimination in which women are questioned more than men and not given the same types of chances. Addressing these types of issues requires the commitment of the most senior managers. They must demonstrate visibly that subtle discrimination is unacceptable. Most organizations in the US have policies against sexism and discrimination in its various forms, but a problem is that these policies are not always used. Most of the women interviewed in the Center for Creative Leadership study had reported some type of subtle experience with discrimination.

Perhaps the biggest factor hindering the development of agency is discriminatory reward systems. According to the US Department of Labor, in the year 2000, women in managerial positions were paid only 68 per cent of the salary their male counterparts received. This sends a strong message that women just aren't as valuable to organizations as men. Addressing gender inequities in salaries and benefits would go a long way to demonstrating that women have the same power to act in organizations as men. Without appropriate recognition, women are undermined in efforts to act powerfully. Paying women the same rates as men would show they have equal status.

3   *Encourage women to make connections with others*. Many women told us of the isolation they continue to experience and their longing to create more meaningful connections both at work and at home. In response to this, organizations might emphasize the use of networking groups, mentors, and coaches. Organizations can strengthen women's feelings of connection by creating, developing, and recognizing networks. Participation in such groups gives women opportunities to interface with upper management and gain visibility.

Another point is that organizations need to recognize people who do connective work. Organizations tend to expect and reward individual accomplishments even though managers operate in teams. Team-based organizations can require advanced relational skills. Yet this kind of skill is often not fully recognized or rewarded in organizations (Fletcher, 1999). Addressing the importance of these skills legitimizes the expectation for connection.

4   *Foster feelings of wholeness*. It is not surprising that women told us that their organizations encouraged the prioritization of work over other roles in life and that they felt lopsided and torn in response. There are a variety of tools for work and life integration that organizations can use to foster wholeness. These include flexible work plans, job sharing, telework, plans for non-linear careers, sabbaticals, etc. Many organizations have implemented these programmes that allow for greater work life integration. However, the implementation of these programmes leaves something to be desired. Many managers, both male and female, are hesitant to use these programmes because they fear taking advantage of such offerings will penalize their career advancement and it is unclear how they contribute to organizational efficiency.

Fletcher and Bailyn (2005) argue that wholeness needs to be addressed through the better design of work. They argue that work needs to be reconceptualized in a way that couples equity and effectiveness. According to this perspective changes need to go beyond HR practices designed for a family-friendly organization to create an environment recognizes that the fundamental linkages between work and personal lives. Equity is conceptualized as the belief that every employee has some form of a private life that needs attention and that should be considered in the design of work. Work practices that involve planning, information flow, and project scheduling are more substantive ways to create a climate for wholeness than simply adding work–life integration policies to an organization without making fundamental changes in assumptions and structures.

5   *Enable women to gain self-understanding*. One key to greater self-understanding is getting honest feedback. Organizations seem to have trouble providing women

with the informal feedback so necessary for growth as a leader. One of the most important ways to help women (and men) develop self-clarity is through a feedback-rich environment that emphasizes constructive and accurate feedback. Organizations often pay attention to the mechanics of performance feedback (e.g. when it is delivered) rather than the process of feedback. To enhance self-clarity, the feedback must be accepted and delivered in a safe environment. Top management can play a key role in creating a climate that values the delivery of quality feedback. Senior executives should model that they take their own feedback seriously. Feedback skills can be taught but it is insufficient to simply teach high potential women. These skills must be developed widely in the organization so the benefits are as broad as possible. Strong feedback skills will help develop all high potentials regardless of gender.

Women also have few opportunities to come together with other women to discuss the workplace and figure out how they fit in that context. Self-clarity involves this type of understanding as well. As discussed in terms of connection, network, coaching, and mentoring programmes help women to make sense of their environment. Also, senior managers can aid self-clarity by discussing as much contextual information as possible. For anyone to succeed in a managerial position, it is helpful to know what the big picture strategic and contextual issues are and how one's own work fits into that larger picture.

Other considerations

Organizations are at a critical point with regard to the advancement of women into the uppermost leadership positions. Progress advancing women can continue to be made or women can simply stagnate where they are in middle management. Individuals, development experts, and organizations can take steps to foster the development of women. The themes of authenticity, connection, self-determination, wholeness, and clarity can help guide those steps. Senior leaders can be held accountable for establishing climates that are more supportive of the developmental expectations of women.

However, the ultimate progress of women in business organizations is also very much a function of larger society. Societal factors such as laws, policy traditions, customs, power relationships, and values go a long way to explaining the ultimate progress of women in a particular society (Ridgeway, 2001). Governments can challenge perceptions of the appropriate role of women in society. They can push society to a more androgynous view of leadership roles. To usher in a new era of women in leadership positions, it is important that individuals, organizations, and governments work in concert to address the development of women leaders. This is the work of the coming years. For our organizations to truly leverage the talents of women in leadership roles, it is imperative that individuals, organizations, and societies work together to achieve this goal.

REFERENCES

Bakan, D. (1966) *The duality of human existence*. Boston, MA: Beacon Press.

Belkin, L. (2003) Q: Why don't more women choose to get to the top? A: They choose not to. *New York Times Magazine*, 26: 42–7, 58, 85.

Catalyst (2002) *Catalyst census of women corporate officers and top earners of the Fortune 500*. New York: Catalyst.

Clawson, J. G. and Kram, K. E. (1984) Managing cross-gender mentoring. *Business Horizons*, 27: 22–32.

Douglas, C. A. (2003) *Key events and lessons for managers in a diverse workforce: A report on research and findings*. Greensboro, NC: Center for Creative Leadership.

Eagley, A. H. (2003) Few women at the top: How role incongruity produces prejudice and the glass ceiling. In D. van Knippenberg and M. Hogg (eds) *Leadership and power: Identity processes in groups and organisations*. London: Sage, pp. 79–83.

Fletcher, J. K. (1999) *Disappearing acts: Gender, power, and relational practice at work*. Cambridge, MA: MIT Press.

Fletcher, J. and Bailyn, L. (2005) The equity imperative: Redesigning work for work-family integration. In E. Kossek and S. Lambert (eds) *Work and life integration: Organisational, cultural, and individual perspectives*. Mahwah, NJ: Lawrence Erlbaum Associates, pp. 171–89.

Gilligan, C. (1982) *In a different voice: Psychological theory and women's development*. Cambridge, MA: Harvard University Press.

Guthrie, V. A. and Kelly-Radford, L. (1998) Feedback-intensive programmes, in C. McCauley, R. Moxley, and E. Van Velsor (eds) *The Center for Creative Leadership handbook of leadership development*. San Francisco, CA: Jossey-Bass, pp. 66–105.

Hewlett, S. A. and Luce, C. B. (2005) Off-ramps and on-ramps: Keeping talented women on the road to success. *Harvard Business Review*, March, 43–54.

Jordan, J., Kaplan, A. G., Miller, J. B., Stiver, I. P., and Surrey, J. L. (1991) *Women's growth in connection: Writings from the Stone Center*. New York: Guilford Press.

Kofodimos, J. (1993) *Balancing act: How managers can integrate successful careers and fulfilling personal lives*. San Francisco, CA: Jossey-Bass.

Koonce, R. (2004) Women-only executive development. *T+D*, 58: 78–85.

Kram, K. E. (1988) Mentoring in the workplace. In D. T. Hall and Associates (eds) *Career Development in Organisations*. San Francisco, CA: Sage, pp. 160–201.

Maineiro, L. A. and Sullivan, S. E. (2005) Kaleidoscope careers: An alternate explanation for the 'opt-out' revolution. *Academy of Management Executive*, 19: 106–23.

Marks, S. R. (1977) Multiple roles and role strain: Some notes on human energy, time and commitment. *American Sociological Review*, 42: 921–36.

McCall, M. W. Jr, Lombardo, M. M. and Morrison, A. M. (1988) *The lessons of experience: How successful executives develop on the job*. Lexington, MA: Lexington Books.

Mero, J. and Sellers, P. (2003) Power: Do women really want it? *Fortune*, 148: 80–8.

Miller, J. B. (1986) *Toward a new psychology of women*. Boston, MA: Beacon Press.

Miller, J. B. and Stiver, I. P. (1997) *The healing connection: How women form relationships in therapy and in life*. Boston, MA: Beacon Press.

Morrison, A. M. (1992) *The new leaders: Guidelines on leadership diversity in America*. San Francisco, CA: Jossey-Bass.

Morrison, A. M., White, R. P. and Van Velsor, E. (1987) *Breaking the glass ceiling: Can women reach the top of America's largest corporations?* Boston, MA: Addison-Wesley.

Morrison, A. M., White, R. P. and Van Velsor, E. (1992) *Breaking the glass ceiling: Can women reach the top of America's largest corporations?* Updated edition, New York: Perseus Books.

Ohlott, P. J. (2002) Myths versus realities: Single-identity development. *T+D*, November, 1–4.

Ohlott, P. J. (2004) Job assignments. In C. McCauley and E. Van Velsor (eds) *The Center for Creative Leadership handbook of leadership development*, 2nd edn. San Francisco, CA: Jossey-Bass, pp. 151–82.

Ohlott, P. J. Ruderman, M. N. and McCauley, C. D. (1994) Gender differences in managers' developmental job experiences. *Academy of Management Journal*, 37: 46–67.

Ragins, B. R. (1997a) Antecedents of diversified mentoring relationships. *Journal of Vocational Behavior*, 51: 90–109.

Ragins, B. R. (1997b) Diversified mentoring relationships in organisations: A power perspective. *Academy of Management Review*, 22: 482–521.

Ridgeway, C. L. (2001) Gender, status, and leadership. *Journal of Social Issues*, 57: 637–55.

Ruderman, M. N. and Ohlott, P. J. (2002) *Standing at the crossroads: Next steps for high-achieving women*. San Francisco, CA: Jossey-Bass.

Ruderman, M. N., Ohlott, P. J., Panzer, K., and King, S. N. (2002) Benefits of multiple roles for managerial women. *Academy of Management Journal*, 45: 369–86.

Sieber, S. D. (1974) Toward a theory of role accumulation. *American Sociological Review*, 39: 567–78.

Singh, V. and Vinnicombe, S. (2004) Why so few women directors in top UK boardrooms? Evidence and theoretical explanations. *Corporate Governance*, 12: 479–88.

Ting, S. and Hart, W. (2004) Formal coaching. In C. McCauley and E. Van Velsor (eds) *The Center for Creative Leadership handbook of leadership development*, 2nd edn. San Francisco, CA: Jossey-Bass, pp. 116–50.

Tischler, L. (2004) Where are the women. *Fast Company*, February, 52–60.

US Census Bureau (2004) *Statistical Abstract of the United States 2004–2005*, 124th edn. Washington, DC.

Van Velsor, E. and Hughes-James, M. W. (1990) *Gender differences in the development of managers: How women managers learn from experience*. Greensboro, NC: Center for Creative Leadership.

Yuasa, M. (2005) Japanese women in management: Getting closer to 'realities' in Japan. *Asia Pacific Business Review*, 11: 195–211.

Index

Pages containing relevant figures and tables are indicated in *italic* type.